54027001151701

Department of Health

CW01466900

MEDICINAL PRODUCT LIABILITY AND REGULATION

The piecemeal developments in product liability reform in Europe have their origins in the tragic association of phocomelia in children with thalidomide in 1962. In many ways these events have continued to generate pressure for reform of product liability, especially for the victims of drug-induced injury. This monograph attempts to address the major problems that typify claims for drug-induced injury, as well as highlighting the complex interrelationship between liability exposure and drug regulation.

While medicinal products are subject to strict liability under the product liability directive, the claimant may have considerable difficulty in establishing that the relevant product is defective and that it caused the damage. It may also be necessary to overcome the development risk defence where this is pleaded. The monograph addresses these problems on a comparative jurisprudential basis, and seeks to determine whether medicinal products should be treated as a special case in the field of product liability.

It examines the role of epidemiological evidence in assessing causation in product liability cases concerning medicinal products in the light of recent developments in the UK Supreme Court, the United States, Canada, Australia and France. In particular, it addresses the difficulties in reconciling the standards of proof in law and science, including the theory that causation can be proved on the balance of probabilities by reference to the doubling of risk of injury. An important case study compares and contrasts the approaches of the UK and the US to the measles, mumps, rubella litigation.

The book also examines the question of whether compliance with regulatory standards should protect pharmaceutical manufacturers from product liability suits. It seeks to support a *via media* whereby the victims of drug-induced injury can receive justice, while at the same time encouraging drug safety and innovation in drug development.

Medicinal Product Liability and Regulation

Richard Goldberg

·HART·
PUBLISHING
OXFORD AND PORTLAND, OREGON
2013

Published in the United Kingdom by Hart Publishing Ltd
16C Worcester Place, Oxford, OX1 2JW
Telephone: +44 (0)1865 517530
Fax: +44 (0)1865 510710
E-mail: mail@hartpub.co.uk
Website: http://www.hartpub.co.uk

Published in North America (US and Canada)
by Hart Publishing
c/o International Specialized Book Services
920 NE 58th Avenue, Suite 300
Portland, OR 97213-3786
USA
Tel: +1 503 287 3093 or toll-free: (1) 800 944 6190
Fax: +1 503 280 8832
E-mail: orders@isbs.com
Website: http://www.isbs.com

British Library Cataloguing in Publication Data
Data Available

ISBN: 978-1-84113-251-8

Typeset by Compuscript Ltd, Shannon
Printed and bound in Great Britain by
TJ International Ltd, Padstow, Cornwall

FSC
www.fsc.org

MIX
Paper from
responsible sources
FSC® C013056

Preface

In the twenty-first century, a multitude of new drugs continues to emerge. As new technologies such as genomics become more significant in drug discovery, fresh drug safety problems arise. Medicinal products, more than any other type of product, continue to exemplify the problem of scientific uncertainty. At the same time as these developments, the reputation of the pharmaceutical industry is in decline, due to worldwide concerns over the promotion of drugs for unapproved uses and the failure to report adverse effects to the regulator. Since the debacle of the MMR litigation, there have been increasing problems over the scope of funding of multi-party actions concerning medicinal products, and the abolition of legal aid for personal injury litigation in England and Wales is likely to make these problems worse. In the meantime, the substantive law surrounding product liability and medicinal products remains relatively underdeveloped in the European Union, whilst in the United States the topic continues to generate extensive litigation and academic commentary. With these problems in mind, I felt that it was timely to write an academic monograph on Medicinal Product Liability and Regulation.

In writing this book, I have continued to benefit greatly from the scholarship and assistance of others. I am especially grateful to Professor David Owen of the University of South Carolina, for his scholarly contributions in the field, together with those of Professor Michael Green of Wake Forest University School of Law, Professor Joseph Sanders of the University of Houston Law Center, Professor Mark Geistfeld of New York University School of Law, Professor CJ Miller of the University of Birmingham, Professor Simon Whittaker of the University of Oxford, Professor Christopher Newdick of the University of Reading, Professor Mark Mildred of Nottingham Trent University, Professor Richard Wright of Chicago-Kent College of Law, Professor Harvey Teff of Durham University, Professor Geraint Howells of the University of Manchester, Professor Jane Stapleton of the University of Texas School of Law and Professor Jean-Sébastien Borghetti, Professor à l'université Panthéon-Assas (Paris II). I have also received very helpful assistance from my colleague, Dr Duncan Fairgrieve, Director of the Product Liability Forum of the British Institute of International and Comparative Law. In statistical matters, I have been helpfully assisted by Professor Philip Dawid of the University of Cambridge, Professor David Madigan of Columbia University New York, and Professor David Goldberg of the University of Glasgow. There continue to be real difficulties in keeping abreast of the case law of other jurisdictions of the EU. In seeking to do so, I have been assisted by the regular issues of the *International Product Liability Review*, published by the City firm, Hogan Lovells, and more generally by Rod Freedman, Cécile Derycke and Agnès Roman-Amat of that firm. I am most grateful to the Carnegie Trust for the Universities of Scotland for awarding me a Research Grant to help meet the costs of some of the research undertaken whilst I was a Visiting Scholar in the Faculty of Law, McGill University in March–April 2011.

I owe an immense debt to my wife, Maureen, for her patience, tolerance and whole hearted support during the last 20 years. She continues to sacrifice much and put up with rooms littered with law reports and periodicals. In addition, I am most grateful for the assistance I have received from the production team at Hart Publishing; in particular, I wish to thank Richard Hart, Rachel Turner, Melanie Hamill and Tom Adams for their continued patience and support. The book is dedicated to my late father, Professor Sir Abraham Goldberg, who encouraged me to pursue this fascinating field of law.

I have endeavoured to state the law as at 1 January 2013, but it has been possible to add some additional references to more recent material.

Richard Goldberg
Durham Law School
April 2013

Contents

Table of Cases

Australia

Austria

Canada

European Court of Justice

Alphabetical

Numerical

France

Germany

Ireland

Italy

Netherlands

New Zealand

Spain

United Kingdom

United States of America

Table of Statutes

Australia

European Union

Directives

Regulations

France

Germany

Spain

Sweden

United Kingdom

Statutory Instruments

United States of America

Introduction

The piecemeal developments in product liability reform in Europe have their origins in the tragic association of phocomelia in children with thalidomide in 1962. In many ways these events have continued to generate pressure for reform of product liability, especially for the victims of drug-induced injury. This monograph attempts to address the major problems that typify claims for drug-induced injury, as well as highlighting the complex interrelationship between liability exposure and drug regulation.

While medicinal products are subject to strict liability under the Product Liability Directive, the claimant may have considerable difficulty in establishing that the relevant product is defective and that it caused the damage. It may also be necessary to overcome the 'development risk' defence where this is pleaded. The monograph addresses these problems on a comparative jurisprudential basis, and seeks to determine whether medicinal products should be treated as a special case in the field of product liability.

Chapter one attempts to place medicinal product liability in its historical, legal and social context. It examines the genesis of product liability reform, as well as the various arguments that have been made in favour of treating pharmaceuticals as a special case. A brief discussion is made of the current law under the Product Liability Directive and the Consumer Protection Act 1987, which treats liability for medicinal products in the same way as liability for any other product. This can be contrasted with § 6 of the *Restatement Third, Torts: Products Liability*, which establishes special liability rules for prescription drugs and medical devices in the US, and with specific pharmaceutical liability regimes present in Germany and some Nordic countries. It discusses the important role of legal aid in funding product liability litigation involving medicinal products and the impact of its withdrawal in England and Wales. A brief survey of vaccine damage is provided, together with an analysis of current European pharmaceutical product liability regimes in operation.

Arguably the single most difficult part of the Product Liability Directive and Part I of the Consumer Protection Act 1987 is the core definition of a defect. Nowhere is the challenge of determining whether a product is defective more complex than in the context of medicinal products. Chapter two seeks to provide an overview of the problem of defective medicinal products in the US and UK: the following two chapters focus on two specific types of defect which have given rise to the greatest challenges in this field, namely design defects and warning defects. The US is used as a comparator due to its wealth of jurisprudence in the prescription drug liability field, and also the fact that prescription drugs are now treated as a distinct category of product under the *Restatement Third, Torts: Products Liability*.

Medicinal products may be defective if they are unsafe for their intended or contemplated purpose because of a basic design deficiency. Chapter three examines the US experience of dealing with design defects and pharmaceutical products, including an analysis of comment *k* of § 402A the *Restatement, Second, Torts* and the so-called net benefit test of § 6(c) of the *Restatement Third, Torts: Products Liability* for prescription drugs. In the light of this US experience, it attempts to comprehend the true nature of a medicinal product design defect under the Product Liability Directive and to devise a coherent and workable approach for determining whether a medicinal product's design is defective.

The category of warnings about risks and instructions for use is the most significant factor relevant to determining the expectation of safety with medicinal products. Chapter four explores the thorny issue of warning and instruction defects in the context of medicinal products. In the absence of a developed body of case law on warnings and instructions in the United Kingdom, it is useful to refer first to the position as it has developed in the United States, before examining the position of warnings and instructions in the context of medicinal products under the Product Liability Directive. It will be seen that, notwithstanding the significance of warnings and instructions and medicinal products, the position under the Directive is a much more uncertain one than in the United States.

Proof of causation in toxic tort litigation is an inherently difficult problem, which regularly requires time-consuming analysis of complex scientific evidence. The difficulties in proving both general causation (whether the product was capable of causing the damage alleged) and specific causation (whether the product did so in the individual case) are magnified in the context of medicinal products. With a multitude of new kinds of drugs emerging as a harvest of the scientific and technological revolutions of both the twentieth and early twenty-first centuries, the cases have become even more complex, demanding much from lawyers and scientific experts on both sides and from the judges themselves. Epidemiological evidence is regularly presented to courts in determining proof of causation in medicinal product liability litigation. Building on the foundations of the author's previous monograph, which supported the use of epidemiological evidence in dealing with problems of proof of causation in alleged cases of adverse drug reactions, Chapter five revisits this perennial problem of the role of epidemiological evidence in assessing causation in product liability cases in a twenty-first-century context, examining the recent cases involving the role of epidemiological evidence in assessing causation in product liability cases in the UK, US, Australia and in Canada. In essence, it seeks to determine the extent to which the courts in the highlighted cases have been pragmatic and fair in their interpretation and utilisation of epidemiological evidence from the perspective of both consumers and pharmaceutical manufacturers.

Over the last 15 years, stories surrounding the challenging condition of autism have never been far from the headlines. Many parents who have autistic children continue to search for a possible cause. When, in 1998, Andrew Wakefield and his colleagues hypothesised that there could be an association between MMR and autism, several though not all parents of autistic children became partially or totally convinced that this was the answer. As a consequence, many parents in the UK took to seeking legal advice as to whether they could proceed in a legal action against the manufacturers of the vaccine. In the US, these proceedings were brought against the Secretary for Health and Human Services under the National Childhood Vaccine Compensation Program. Chapter six seeks to assess the significance of the rise and fall of this litigation in the US and UK. The importance of the 1998 Wakefield study to the fuelling of such litigation is explained, as well as the reasons for its collapse pre-trial in the UK. It then examines the value of the relevant scientific evidence exposed in six test cases of the Omnibus Autism Proceeding (OAP) under the National Childhood Vaccine Injury Act of 1986 (NVIA), decided in February 2009 and March 2010.

The position in the United States is contrasted with the much more liberal approach to causation established in France by the Cour de cassation for medicinal product liability cases in the context of injury allegedly caused by the Hepatitis B vaccine, through the use of presumptions of causation. Finally, a discussion of the outcome of the General Medical Council Hearing on Dr Wakefield and his two co-authors to the 1998 study is provided. The chapter concludes with some lessons to be learned from this litigation, both in the UK and in France in the light of its liberal approach.

In highlighting the complex interrelationship between liability exposure and drug regulation, Chapter seven seeks to address the question as to whether compliance with regulatory standards should protect pharmaceutical manufacturers from product liability suits. It examines the current position surrounding compliance with common practice, regulatory and statutory standards of the pharmaceutical industry from the perspectives of both negligence and strict liability, as well as the currently available defence to strict liability that a defect is attributable to mandatory statutory or Community requirements. In the United States, by far the most significant attempt to eliminate product liability claims involving drugs has been through the doctrine of federal preemption, which is predicated on a similar basis to a defence of compliance with regulatory standards, namely that since the US Food and Drug Administration determines the safety and efficacy of drugs and their labelling, and is equipped with the power to act if new information emerges over time, a lay jury should be prevented from second-guessing the expert decisions of the FDA by stating that a drug is defective or its accompanying warning inadequate. In this context, the chapter examines recent developments in *Wyeth v Levine*, in which the Supreme Court has ruled that FDA labelling approvals do not preempt State laws and shield companies from State product liability claims. In the light of the rationales behind this decision, particularly the Court's emphasis on the role of State law as a complement to the FDA's mission of consumer protection, and the increasing importance of pharmacovigilance and post-marketing surveillance in both Europe and the US respectively, the chapter concludes with a discussion of the advantages and disadvantages of introducing a regulatory compliance defence for medicinal products under the Product Liability Directive.

One of the most controversial elements of the Product Liability Directive and the Consumer Protection Act 1987, particularly in respect of medicinal products, has been the so-called 'development risk' defence. Chapter eight examines the interpretation, scope and the impact of the defence in the context of medicinal products, including the meaning and implications of discoverability of defects, scientific and technical knowledge and the problem of known but undetectable defects.

It is hoped that this book makes a contribution to the resolution of the legal problems in this complex and controversial area of tort law. In a wider compass, it aims to contribute to an appreciation of the significance of these problems, which bestride both the legal and medical disciplines.

1

Medicinal Product Liability in Context

I. INTRODUCTION

This chapter attempts to place medicinal product liability in its medical, legal and social context. It examines the genesis of product liability reform, which has its origins in the thalidomide disaster of 1959–62, as well as the various arguments that have been made in favour of treating pharmaceuticals as a special case. A brief discussion is made of the current law under the Product Liability Directive and the Consumer Protection Act 1987, which treats liability for medicinal products in the same way as liability for any other product. This can be contrasted with § 6 of the *Restatement Third, Torts: Products Liability*, which establishes special liability rules in the United States for prescription drugs and medical devices, and with specific pharmaceutical liability regimes present in Germany and Nordic countries. It discusses the important role of legal aid in funding product liability litigation involving medicinal products and the impact of its withdrawal in England and Wales. A brief survey of vaccine damage is provided, together with an analysis of European pharmaceutical product liability regimes currently in operation.

II. HISTORICAL BACKGROUND: A SPECIAL CASE? THE UNIQUE CHARACTERISTICS OF MEDICINAL PRODUCTS

The piecemeal developments in product liability reform, culminating in the introduction of strict liability within Europe, have their origins in the tragic events of 1959–62 surrounding the drug thalidomide.[1] Indeed, it has been observed that in many ways these events continue to fuel the pressure for reform of product liability, especially for the victims of alleged medicinal product-induced injury.[2] The inability of victims to establish negligence in the thalidomide case in England,[3] and an appreciation of the inadequate

---

[1] See R Goldberg, *Causation and Risk in the Law of Torts: Scientific Evidence and Medicinal Product Liability* (Oxford, Hart Publishing, 1999) 17; see generally H Sjöström and R Nilsson, *Thalidomide and the Power of Drug Companies* (Harmondsworth, Penguin, 1972).

[2] See Miller, *Product Liability and Safety Encyclopaedia* (London, LexisNexis Butterworths, 2013) Div III, para 113.

[3] *S v Distillers (Biochemicals) Ltd* [1970] 1 WLR 114; but cf the criminal proceedings brought against nine persons at Chemie Grünenthal, the initial developers of thalidomide. While the trial was eventually suspended, the German court made a declaration that a causal connection had been established between thalidomide and nerve damage and also thalidomide and malformation in the human foetus: Sjöström and Nilsson (above n 1) 207–70. On 14 January 2010, the UK government finally expressed 'their sincere regret and deep sympathy for the

regulatory machinery in place in 1962, both in the United Kingdom and in Europe more generally, led to the enactment of the Medicines Act 1968, and to Council Directive 65/65/ EEC of 26 January 1965 on the approximation of provisions laid down by law, regulation or administrative action relating to proprietary medicinal products.[4]

While the thalidomide disaster was arguably the strongest impetus behind the establishment of the Pearson Commission, the Commission recognised that there were a number of particular difficulties faced by pharmaceutical manufacturers if strict liability were applied to medicinal products which are available only on prescription. Though recognising that these difficulties would be aggravated by the imposition of strict liability, they concluded that there was no justification for the special treatment of drugs.[5] The English and Scottish Law Commissions' Report similarly noted three main arguments in favour of treating pharmaceuticals as a special case, namely that (i) if drugs were completely safe they would not work and hence a general standard of safety was inappropriate; (ii) many drugs were available only on prescription, and the suitability of the particular drug for the particular patient was monitored not by the producer but by the practitioner; and (iii) strict liability might inhibit research into new products.[6] However, the Law Commissions provided a rejoinder to each in turn. In respect of the first argument, this was answered by reference to the establishment of a standard of reasonable safety as the test for determining whether the medicinal product was defective for the purposes of imposing strict liability.[7] Secondly, the Law Commissions stated that the fact that many drugs were available only on prescription was immaterial, not least since pharmaceutical products may be defective by virtue of contamination or some other error in production.[8] Finally, in responding to the argument that strict liability may inhibit pharmaceutical research, the Law Commissions concluded that market forces provide a strong impetus to the development of new products, which would not be significantly inhibited by the imposition of strict liability.[9] Justifying the treatment of medicinal products as a special case has therefore been problematic.

injury and suffering endured by all those affected' and announced a £20 million, three-year pilot scheme to help the needs of thalidomide sufferers: The Minister of State, Department of Health (Mr Mike O'Brien), *Hansard*, HC Deb 14 January 2010, vol 503, col 859. A new 10-year grant in the region of £80 million was announced on 20 December 2012, which came into force in April 2013: The Minister of State, Department of Health (Norman Lamb), *Hansard*, HC Deb 20 December 2012, col 1008.

[4] [1965] OJ L369/65; [1965–6] OJ Spec Ed 20. The term 'medicinal product' is used in this book in conformity with the definition in Article 1(2) of Directive 2001/83/EC Medicinal Products Directive [2001] OJ L311/67 as amended by Dir 2004/27/EC [2004] OJ L136/34. It is defined as a substance or combination of substances (a) presented as having properties for the treatment or prevention of disease in human beings or (b) which may be used in or administered to human beings either with the purpose of restoring, correcting or modifying physiological functions by exerting a pharmacological, immunological or metabolic action or for making a medical diagnosis: Medicines Act 1968, s 130(1). The book also uses the term prescription-only medicines (POMs) to refer to medicinal products which may be supplied only in accordance with the prescription of an 'appropriate practitioner': Medicines Act 1968, ss 58, 58A. This in effect is equivalent to the use of the term 'prescription drug' in US law: see 21 USC §§ 333(b), 353(b) (2006).

[5] *Report of the Royal Commission on Civil Liability and Compensation for Personal Injury* (the Pearson Commission Report) (Cmnd 7054-1, 1978) paras 1273–75.

[6] *Liability for Defective Products* (Law Com No 82, Scot Law Com No 45) (Cmnd 6831, 1977) para 56.

[7] Ibid para 57.

[8] Ibid para 58.

[9] Ibid para 59. While the Scottish Law Commission agreed with its English counterpart that strict liability for injuries caused by defective pharmaceuticals should rest on those who produced them, it considered that there might be a case for the application of special legislative provisions to producers of certain pharmaceuticals, particularly prescription medicines. In addition, the Scottish Law Commission was concerned with the fear that it might be virtually impossible to obtain insurance against 'catastrophic' risks: ibid paras 62, 65.

Nevertheless, there are still further arguments for treating medicinal products as a special case. These include: the difficulty of obtaining insurance cover; the screening role of the Commission on Human Medicines (CHM) in recommending the approval of applications for marketing authorisations;[10] the danger that adverse effects of drugs may become apparent only after several years, and may occur not only in the patient but in her offspring, as in the case of diethylstilbestrol (DES); and the fact that some adverse effects are often hard to distinguish from the adverse progression or the recrudescence of the underlying condition for which the product was given, coupled with the fact that such effects may result from biological idiosyncrasies, interaction with other medicines or foods, or overdosage.[11] In addition, such problems may be accentuated where a person has taken several different drugs for separate conditions or, in the light of the increasing generic prescription of medicinal products, a series of similar drugs from different manufacturers for one condition.[12] In the US, commentators have noted several reasons why drugs are different. In particular, emphasis has been placed on the fact that: (1) drugs are heavily regulated by the Federal Food, Drug, and Cosmetic Act; (2) drugs have high social utility; (3) learned intermediaries assist patients in determining which drugs are appropriate; and (4) drugs that are unreasonably dangerous for some consumers may be beneficial to another class of consumers.[13]

III. POSITION UNDER THE PRODUCT LIABILITY DIRECTIVE AND THE CONSUMER PROTECTION ACT 1987

Medicinal products are subject to strict liability under the Product Liability Directive[14] (the Directive) and Part I of the Consumer Protection Act 1987 (the 1987 Act), including all finished products and any component parts or raw material.[15] Given the thalidomide disaster's

---

[10] This body came into being on 30 October 2005 as a consequence of the merger of the Medicines Commission, established under the Medicines Act 1968, s 2, and the Committee on the Safety of Medicines, established under the Medicines (Committee on Safety of Medicines) Order 1970, SI 1970/1257; see, further, L Mulcahy, 'Civil Law Liability' in P Feldschreiber, *The Law and Regulation of Medicines* (Oxford, Oxford University Press, 2008) para 8.112.

[11] DHSS, Product Liability: Special Features of the Medical Sector, Medicines Division Consultation Paper (DHSS, 1979) para 5; CJ Miller, *Product Liability and Safety Encyclopaedia* (above, n 2) Div III, para 113; I Dodds-Smith, M Spencer and J Bore, 'Product Liability for Medicinal Products' in MJ Powers, NH Harris and A Barton (eds), *Clinical Negligence*, 4th edn (London, Tottel Publishing, 2008) para 24.3; H Teff, 'Products Liability in the Pharmaceutical Industry at Common Law' (1974) 20 *McGill Law Journal* 102, 105 and 'Products Liability' in A Grubb, J Lang and J McHale (eds), *Principles of Medical Law*, 3rd edn (Oxford, Oxford University Press, 2010) para 18.04.

[12] See *Mann and Close v Wellcome Foundation* (20 January 1989, QBD, unreported), in which two plaintiffs claimed damages for their profound deafness and consequential loss alleged to have been caused by the administration of a particular neomycin spray to severe burns sustained by them when they were very young children. Counsel for the plaintiffs ultimately conceded that there was insufficient evidence that the defendant's subsidiary (Calmic Ltd) had supplied the particular sprays used in each case: this led to a collapse of the case against the manufacturer.

[13] MD Green, 'Prescription Drugs, Alternative Designs and the Restatement (Third): Preliminary Reflections' (1999) 30 *Seton Hall Law Review* 207, 215–22.

[14] Dir 85/374/EEC on the approximation of the laws, regulations and administrative provisions of the Member States concerning liability for defective products: [1985] OJ L210/29.

[15] See Art 2 of the Directive and the definition of 'product' in s 1(2) of the 1987 Act. This is reaffirmed by the fact that 'goods' include 'substances', which are in turn defined as 'any natural or artificial substance'. Lord Denning opined that the fear of new drugs development being inhibited, particularly in regard to AIDS, supported the limitation of strict liability for pharmaceuticals through the 'development risk' defence: *Hansard*, HL Deb (series 5) vol 483, cols 825–26 (20 January, 1987).

impetus behind the reform of product liability, and the fact that drugs are commonly associated with injury, it would have been remarkable if medicinal products had been exempted from the Directive.[16] It is possible that until the amendment of the Consumer Protection Act 1987 with effect from 4 December 2000,[17] 'natural' products might have benefited from the exclusion of agricultural produce[18] which had not undergone an industrial process.[19] If so, the exclusion will continue to apply to products supplied before that date. In any event, thereafter the 1987 Act will cover any natural product (such as a herbal or blood product) which, even if not strictly 'manufactured', still has 'essential characteristics' attributable to an industrial or other process.[20]

In the UK, and in the majority of countries in the EU, the current law therefore treats liability for medicinal products in the same way as liability for any other product. This can be contrasted with § 6 of the *Restatement Third, Torts: Products Liability*, which establishes special liability rules in the US for prescription drugs and medical devices, and with specific pharmaceutical liability regimes present in Germany and Nordic countries.[21] As will be seen later, although medicinal products are subject to strict liability under the 1987 Act, the claimant may have considerable difficulties in establishing that the relevant product is defective[22] and that it caused the damage;[23] and it may also be necessary to overcome the so-called 'development risk' defence where this is pleaded.[24] By far the majority of claims against pharmaceutical manufacturers, (eg Opren,[25] pertussis vaccine,[26] benzodiazepines,[27] Measles Mumps Rubella Vaccines[28] and third generation oral contraceptives[29]) have been initially funded by the Legal Aid Board in England and Wales (which became the Legal Services Commission).[30] This body was responsible for providing legal aid for Multi-Party

[16] A Clark, 'The Consumer Protection Act 1987' (1987) 50 *Modern Law Review* 614, 615.

[17] See the Consumer Protection Act 1987 (Product Liability) (Modification) Order 2000, SI 2000/2771.

[18] As then defined in s 1(2) to mean 'any produce of the soil, of stock-farming or of fisheries'. *Quaere* whether many medicinal products would fall within this definition? See also J Finch and P Ranson (eds), *Product Liability in Europe: What the New EEC Directive Will Mean for Pharmaceutical Companies* (PCP Publication, 1986) 26.

[19] See s 2(4) of the unamended version of the Act, discussed in CJ Miller and RS Goldberg, *Product Liability*, 2nd edn (Oxford, Oxford University Press, 2004) paras 9.06–9.07 and 9.12–9.18.

[20] See the definition of 'producer' in s 1(2)(c), discussed in Miller and Goldberg (above, n 19) paras 8.11–8.15; also I Dodds-Smith, M Spencer and J Bore, 'Product Liability for Medicinal Products' in MJ Powers, NH Harris and A Barton (eds), *Clinical Negligence*, 4th edn (London, Tottel Publishing, 2008) para 24.48.

[21] See below.

[22] See below chapters 2, 3, and 4 of this volume.

[23] See generally, R Goldberg, *Causation and Risk in the Law of Torts: Scientific Evidence and Medicinal Product Liability* (above, n 1), and below, chapters 5 and 6 of this volume.

[24] See below, chapter 8 of this volume; and, further, R Goldberg, *Causation and Risk in the Law of Torts: Scientific Evidence and Medicinal Product Liability* (above, n 1) ch 8 and 'The Development Risk Defence and the European Court of Justice; Increased Injury Costs and the Supplementary Protection Certificate' in R Goldberg and J Lonbay (eds), *Pharmaceutical Medicine, Biotechnology and European Law* (Cambridge, Cambridge University Press, 2000) 185.

[25] *Davis v Eli Lilly* [1987] 3 All ER 94.

[26] *Loveday v Renton* [1990] 1 Med LR 117.

[27] *AB and others v John Wyeth & Brother Ltd and Others (No 2)* [1994] 5 Med LR 149; *AB and others v John Wyeth & Brother Ltd; AB and Others v Roche Products Ltd* (LEXIS 13 December 1996).

[28] *Sayers v Smithkline Beecham Plc, Smith Kline & French Laboratories Ltd, Merck & Co Inc and Sanofi Pasteur MSD Ltd* [2007] EWHC 1346 (QB).

[29] *XYZ v Schering Health Care Ltd* [2002] EWHC 1420, (2002) 70 BMLR 88 (QB).

[30] Access to Justice Act 1999, s 1(1), repealed by the Legal Aid, Sentencing and Punishment of Offenders Act 2012, s 38, Sch 5(1) para 51(a) (April 1, 2013 subject to saving and transitional provisions as specified in SI 2013/534, regs 6–13). The Legal Services Commission was abolished by the Legal Aid, Sentencing and Punishment of Offenders Act 2012, s 38. An Executive Agency within the Ministry of Justice (the Legal Aid Agency) has been created within the Ministry of Justice to administer legal aid.

Actions, providing the individuals satisfied a financial means test and that the case met a legal merits test, which required cases to have a reasonable prospect of success, and for the cost of the action to be reasonable, compared to the potential damages.[31] The legal merits test was set at '50–60', although a case with Sufficient Wider Public Interest' could be brought if the merits were judged to be only 'borderline'.

Principally as a result of the complexity of the litigation, and the need for expert scientific and legal opinion to overcome the substantive hurdles, it has been noted that in the absence of legal aid, claims against pharmaceutical companies are 'prohibitively expensive'.[32] Even with legal aid coverage, not one claim has resulted in damages being awarded by a court against a pharmaceutical company. It will, however, be seen that the substantive aspects of medicinal product liability were explored in detail in the successful claim concerning blood products in *A v National Blood Authority*,[33] though both the reasoning and the outcome of that case is controversial.[34] Since the collapse of the MMR Litigation,[35] in the few product liability cases which the Legal Services Commission was prepared to fund (Vigabratrin, Seroxat,[36] and the Fetal Anti-Convulsant Litigation[37]), the funding became considerably more limited in scope.[38] Six years in preparation and three weeks before the Fetal Anti-Convulsant Litigation case was due to come to trial in November 2010, the Legal Services Commission withdrew legal aid.[39] In respect of claims against Merck concerning the cardiovascular problems linked to Vioxx, while claims were brought in Australia[40] and the US, legal aid was refused in England and Wales[41] (though not Scotland,[42] where public

---

[31] The Legal Services Commission (LSC) Funding Code set out the criteria according to which cases could be funded, in accordance with the Access to Justice Act, s.8 (Repealed by Legal Aid, Sentencing and Punishment of Offenders Act 2012, Sch 5(1) para 51(a)). The criteria were laid down in Part 1 of the Code. The criteria for Multi-Party Actions (MPAs) are described in the *Legal Services Commission Manual*, vol 3, Part C, ch 15. See also the *LSC Manual*, vol 3, Part C, ch 4, Merits, Costs and Damages. From 1 April 2013, civil legal services provided in relation to personal injury or death are exempted from legal aid: Legal Aid, Sentencing and Punishment of Offenders Act 2012, Sch 1(2) para 1. Personal injury claims against pharmaceutical companies will no longer be eligible for legal aid.

[32] E Jackson, *Law and the Regulation of Medicines* (Oxford, Hart Publishing, 2012) 119.

[33] [2001] 3 All ER 289.

[34] See chapters 2, 3, 4 and 8 of this volume.

[35] See chapter 6 of this volume.

[36] Seroxat Group Litigation Order No 68 29.10.08. Over 500 claimants joined the Group Litigation Order (GLO) against GlaxoSmithKline UK, alleging to have suffered withdrawal symptoms when reducing, discontinuing or attempting to discontinue use of the antidepressant Seroxat. Legal Aid for the claims was withdrawn in England: D Body, 'Product Liability Claims Under the Consumer Protection Act 1987: Some Practical Problems' [2012] *Journal of Personal Injury Law* 79, 81, fn 8.

[37] *Multiple Claimants v Sanofi Synthelabo Ltd* [2007] EWHC 1860 (QB); (2007) 98 BMLR 192; *Claimants Registered to the GLO v Sanofi Synthelabo Ltd* [2009] EWHC 95 (QB) (application by claimants to adduce expert evidence of a forensic accountant concerning the worldwide value of sales of Epilim and its profitability, together with evidence of the pricing structures in place which governed sales to the NHS, rejected).

[38] D Body, 'Product Liability Claims Under the Consumer Protection Act 1987: Some Practical Problems' [2012] *Journal of Personal Injury Law* 79, 81.

[39] See J Meikle, 'Legal Aid Withdrawal Means Epilim Case Likely to be Dropped', *The Guardian*, 8 November 2010; J Robins, 'The Epilim Compensation Case Joins a Dismal Roll Call', *The Guardian*, 1 February 2011: www.guardian.co.uk/law/2011/feb/01/epilim-compensation-case-roll-call, accessed 15 April 2013.

[40] See chapters 2, 4, 5, 7 and 8, of this volume.

[41] An attempt to bring a product liability claim in New Jersey on behalf of 98 plaintiffs residing in England and Wales was rejected by the Supreme Court of New Jersey on *forum non conveniens* grounds. The UK was held to provide an adequate alternative forum for products liability litigation in terms of both substantive and procedural law: *In re Vioxx Litigation* 928 A 2d 935, 937, 944 (NJ Sup AD 2007).

[42] See *Cooper v Merck Sharp & Dohme Ltd* [2012] CSOH 48 (motion seeking discharge of diet of proof refused). 196 other actions (ie non legally aided) were raised in March 2010 in the Court of Session in respect of

funding was granted to a pursuer who alleged that Vioxx caused him to suffer a stroke). It has been argued that one of the reasons why claims have remained rare is that the notion of a defective medicinal product and the assessment of the appropriate level of consumer expectation have remained vague and uncertain.[43] This central problem will be explored in this book.

In the face of a reduction of 23 per cent in its overall budget, in November 2010 the Ministry of Justice proposed 'fundamental reform' of the legal aid scheme.[44] It considered that legal aid funding was not justified for clinical negligence cases, since there was a viable form of alternative, in the form of Conditional Fee Agreements (CFAs), (of which 'no win, no fee' agreements are the most common), which were likely to be more readily available in these cases than in other claims. The government therefore proposed to exclude civil legal aid from all clinical negligence cases.[45] While recognising that there were likely to be cases such as obstetrics, with high disbursement costs, which were currently funded by legal aid, but for which clients might find it hard to secure funding under a CFA, they did not consider that this represented a sufficiently high proportion of cases to justify retaining clinical negligence within the scope of legal aid.[46] On 21 June 2011, the Secretary of State for Justice confirmed this position in his introduction of the Legal Aid, Sentencing and Punishment of Offenders Bill,[47] stating that with 80 per cent of clinical negligence cases being undertaken on a no win no fee basis, and only 20 per cent using legal aid, a no win, no fee basis of funding was 'probably the better way forward'.[48] Accordingly, from 1 April 2013, in England and Wales, civil legal services provided in relation to personal injury or death are exempted from legal aid.[49] Personal injury claims against pharmaceutical companies will no longer be eligible for legal aid in England and Wales, although they will continue to be eligible in Scotland.[50] Conditional Fee Agreements (CFAs), of which 'no win, no fee' agreements are the most common, will be available. In the light of the costs involved in such litigation, and the fact that not one claim has resulted in damages being awarded by a court against a pharmaceutical company, it has been suggested that 'few lawyers would be prepared to enter into a "no win, no fee" arrangement in relation to this sort of litigation'.[51] However,

---

pursuers who claimed to have suffered strokes, heart attacks or sudden cardiac death as a result of taking the drug. Four actions have also been raised against another drug manufacturer, the Pfizer Group, in respect of Celebrex: *Hamilton and Others v Merck Sharp & Dohme Ltd* [2012] CSOH 144, [5].

[43] D Body, 'Product Liability Claims Under the Consumer Protection Act 1987: Some Practical Problems' [2012] *Journal of Personal Injury Law* 79.

[44] Ministry of Justice, Proposals for the Reform of Legal Aid in England and Wales, CP12/10 (Cm 7967, 2010), pp 3, 5.

[45] Ibid para 4.166.

[46] Ibid para 4.167.

[47] The Lord Chancellor and Secretary of State for Justice (Mr Kenneth Clarke), *Hansard*, HC Deb, 21 June 2011, col 166.

[48] Ibid col 174. But cf the Government's own admission that clinical negligence cases against the NHS are funded approximately 50:50 between legal aid and CFAs (the latter in the form of no win, no fee agreements): see. *Ministry of Justice, Proposals for Reform of Civil Litigation Funding and Costs in England and Wales* (November 2010) Cm 794, 2.9, 70-75, paras 220–237.

[49] Legal Aid, Sentencing and Punishment of Offenders Act 2012, Sch 1(2) para 1. This does not extend to Scotland: s 152(1).

[50] Ibid s 152(1).

[51] E Jackson, *Law and the Regulation of Medicines* (Oxford, Hart Publishing, 2012) 119; see, further, R Goldberg, 'Medical Malpractice and Compensation in the UK' (2012) 87 *Chicago-Kent Law Review* 101, 130–31. The President of the Law Society of England and Wales has claimed that withdrawal of legal aid funding in England and Wales will 'leave pharmaceutical companies beyond the reach of the law': 'Legal aid cuts "deprive

a case against GlaxoSmithKline is being brought on a 'no win, no fee' basis in respect of claims for compensation for death or harm in the form of heart failure and heart attacks allegedly caused by the diabetes drug Avandia.[52]

IV. VACCINE DAMAGE

In its extensive and illuminating examination of the question of compensation for vaccine damage,[53] the Pearson Commission differentiated between vaccines and other medicinal products on the premise that vaccine damage merits special treatment by virtue of the difference in the social implications between vaccines and other drugs. The Commission considered that since vaccination is recommended by the Government or a local authority, the Government or local authority should be strictly liable in tort for serious and lasting damage suffered by anyone, whether adult or child, as a consequence of vaccination recommended in the community's interest.[54]

On the recommendations of the Pearson Commission, the Vaccine Damage Payments Act 1979 was enacted 'to provide a single tax-free payment'[55] for vaccine-damaged persons for death or severe disablement[56] proved, on a balance of probabilities, to have been caused[57] by vaccination against diphtheria, tetanus, whooping cough, poliomyelitis, measles, rubella, tuberculosis, smallpox, and any other disease specified by the Secretary of State by statutory instrument.[58] Over the years, several additional diseases have been specified, viz mumps, the haemophilus influenza type b infection (Hib), meningococcal Group C (meningitis C), pneumococcal infection and the human papillomavirus (HPV). The Vaccine Damage Payments (Specified Disease) Order 2009 added influenza carried by the pandemic influenza (H1N1) 2009 virus (swine flu) to this list of specified diseases.[59] As in the case of the other listed diseases, the Secretary of State must be satisfied that a person was severely disabled as a result of vaccine damage.[60] However, the 2009 Order modified the conditions of entitlement in section 2(1)(b) of the 1979 Act, so that it was not a condition in respect of influenza caused by the H1N1 virus 2009 that the vaccinated person was under 18 at the time the vaccination was administered or that there was an outbreak of the disease within the UK or Isle of man at that time. Accordingly, the Order extended the 1979 Act to those vaccinated against the H1N1 virus at a time when they were 18 years or older.

drug claimants of day in court"', *BBC News*, 18 January 2011, www.bbc.co.uk/news/health-12212234, accessed 15 March 2013.

[52] S Boseley, 'Families Battle with GSK Over Danger Drug', *The Guardian*, 30 January 2013, p 1.

[53] See the Pearson Commission Report (above, n 5) ch 25.

[54] See the Pearson Commission Report (above, n 5) ch 25, para 1408.

[55] *Hansard*, HC Deb (series 6) vol 352, col 719, Mr Alistair Darling (27 June 2000). According to the then Secretary of State for Social Security, Mr Alistair Darling, the scheme is not regarded as a compensation scheme: *Hansard*, ibid col 726.

[56] Vaccine Damage Payments Act 1979, s 1(1).

[57] Ibid s 3(5); see R Goldberg, *Causation and Risk in the Law of Torts: Scientific Evidence and Medicinal Product Liability* (above, n 1) 170–78.

[58] Vaccine Damage Payments Act 1979, s 1(2).

[59] The Vaccine Damage Payments (Specified Disease) Order 2009 No 2516, art 2, revoked by the Vaccine Damage Payments (Specified Disease) (Revocation and Savings) Order 2010/1988, art 3. The Order continues to apply to any person who received the vaccination before 1 September 2010: ibid art 4.

[60] Section 1(1).

It should be noted that the Act applies to protect an unborn child whose mother has been so vaccinated.[61] If a causal link is established and disablement suffered is 60 per cent or more[62] a lump sum of £120,000 is awarded.[63] Of particular relevance to causation is section 4(1) of the 1979 Act, which provides for review of the question as to whether the vaccination caused the disablement by reference to a First Tier tribunal. In deciding an appeal, the Tribunal shall consider all the circumstances of the case (including any not obtaining at the time when the decision appealed against was made).[64] The failure rates are high. In January 2010, in response to a request from Dr Duncan Fairgrieve of the British Institute of International and Comparative Law, the Vaccine Damage Payments Unit revealed that since 1979, there had been 5,581 claims, 930 of those resulting in awards. There were 3,768 medical rejections stating that 'causation due to vaccination has not been accepted', and 120 where 'causation is accepted but disablement due to vaccination is less than 60%'.[65] The remaining rejections are for a variety of reasons.[66] The scheme is without prejudice to the ability to pursue the alternative course of claiming compensation against the manufacturer of the vaccine. However, this course is fraught with difficulty, as several high-profile cases have shown.[67]

On a comparative note, the United States National Vaccine Injury Compensation Program was enacted as part of the National Childhood Vaccine Injury Act 1986. The programme establishes a no-fault compensation system for adverse reactions to vaccines for immunising children in the United States. The injured party must have been administered a vaccine listed in a vaccine injury table and have suffered an injury covered by the Act and occurring within a specified time listed in the table.[68] If a petitioner demonstrates a compensatable injury within this time, causation is presumed.[69]

---

[61] Section 1(3).

[62] Section 1(4). The original 80% requirement for severe disablement was substituted by 60% by the Regulatory Reform (Vaccine Damage Payments Act 1979) Order 2002/1592, art 2 (16 June 2002).

[63] The Vaccine Damage Payments Act 1979 Statutory Sum Order 2007, SI 2007/1931.

[64] An example of a successful appeal to the tribunal was a decision in 2010, where a majority found on a balance of probabilities that Robert Fletcher's brain damage was caused by the MMR vaccine injection, given when he was 13 months old. He suffered a seizure 10 days after the vaccination and went on to be epileptic and severely mentally retarded. The tribunal concluded that it was this temporal association between the vaccine and the seizure that showed on a balance of probabilities that the vaccine triggered the epilepsy. The tribunal ordered the Department of Health to pay £91,500 in compensation: see S-K Templeton, 'Mother wins MMR payout after 18 years', *The Sunday Times*, 29 August 2010, www.thesundaytimes.co.uk/sto/news/uk_news/Health/article381972. ece, accessed 15 April 2013; and further, M Brazier and E Cave, *Medicine, Patients and the Law*, 5th edn (London, Penguin Books, 2011) 302–3, fn148.

[65] Personal communication from Dr Duncan Fairgrieve, British Institute of International and Comparative Law, 6 January 2010. See, further, R Goldberg, *Causation and Risk in the Law of Torts: Scientific Evidence and Medicinal Product Liability* (Oxford, Hart Publishing, 1999) 174–75 (analysis of tribunal results 1989–93).

[66] Ibid. These include: child under two years of age, over 21 when vaccinated, disease not included in the Act, claim received out of time, child not vaccinated in the UK, etc.

[67] Notably such cases as *Loveday v Renton* [1990] 1 Med LR 117, *The Times*, 31 March 1988 (damage allegedly caused by pertussis (or whooping cough) vaccine) and the recent measles, mumps, and rubella (MMR) vaccine litigation. See, further, chapter 6 of this volume.

[68] 42 USC § 300aa-11(c)(1)(C)(i).

[69] HR Rep No 908; 99th Cong 2d Sess 6, 15; R Goldberg, *Causation and Risk in the Law of Torts: Scientific Evidence and Medicinal Product Liability* (Oxford, Hart Publishing, 1999) 163–70; W Mariner, 'The National Vaccine Injury Compensation Program in the United States: a preliminary overview' in S Shulman and L Lasagna (eds), *Trends in Product Liability Law and No-Fault Compensation for Drug-Induced Injuries* (Boston, MA, The Tufts Center for the Study of Drug Development, 1990). For further discussion in the context of the MMR litigation and the Omnibus Autism Proceeding (OAP), see chapter 6 of this volume.

V. EUROPEAN PHARMACEUTICAL PRODUCT LIABILITY REGIMES

A. The United Kingdom

The unique problems of the pharmaceutical industry led the Royal College of Physicians and the Association of the British Pharmaceutical Industry (ABPI) to submit proposals for alternative compensation schemes when giving evidence to the Pearson Commission.[70] The ABPI proposed that in cases of death and major injuries the injured party should merely be required to prove an accident and the amount of his loss. The state would then pay compensation to the injured party for such loss, without any reduction for contributory negligence, and be subrogated to the rights of the injured party and recover from any manufacturer who was at fault, but allowing for a reduction in respect of any contributory negligence.[71] However, while recognising that the difficulties faced by pharmaceutical manufacturers would be aggravated by the imposition of strict liability, the Pearson Commission concluded that there was no justification for the special treatment of drugs.[72] Similarly, the Law Commissions concluded that strict liability for injuries caused by defective pharmaceuticals should be imposed on their producers. While they did not oppose the idea of a central compensation fund for those injured by pharmaceuticals, this was considered to be beyond their remit and a question for the Pearson Commission to consider.[73]

B. Germany

As the centre of the Contergan (thalidomide) disaster, and seen as the strongest European pharmaceutical industry, West Germany made stringent efforts to overhaul its drug regulatory system and to introduce a strict liability compensation regime in its Medicines Act 1976 (*Arzneimittelgesetz* 1976) (AMG).[74]

Prior to its recent amendment, § 84 of the AMG imposed liability on a drug manufacturer when the pharmaceutical produced such injurious effects as are unjustifiable in the light of medical knowledge and found its source in the development or manufacture of the drug,[75] or where physical damage resulted from labelling, instructions for use or instructions to professionals which did not correspond to medical knowledge.[76] The German

---

[70] Miller, *Product Liability and Safety Encyclopaedia* (above, n 2) Div III, para 115.

[71] Memorandum of Evidence to the Royal Commission on Civil Liability and Compensation for Personal Injury (October 1974) paras 1, 4 and 8.

[72] Pearson Commission Report (above, n 5) para 1275.

[73] Law Coms Rep (above, n 6) para 61. While the Scottish Law Commission agreed with its English counterpart that strict liability for injuries caused by defective pharmaceuticals should rest on those who produced them, it considered that there might be a case for the application of special legislative provisions to producers of certain pharmaceuticals, particularly prescription medicines. In addition, the Scottish Law Commission was concerned with the fear that it might be virtually impossible to obtain insurance against 'catastrophic' risks: ibid paras 62, 65.

[74] AMG 1976; J Fleming, 'Drug Injury Compensation Plans' (1982) 30 *American Journal of Comparative Law* 297–98; W Van Gerven, J Lever and P Larouche, *Ius Commune Casebooks for the Common Law of Europe: Tort Law* (Oxford, Hart Publishing, 2000) 655; Howells, *Comparative Product Liability* (Aldershot, Dartmouth, 1993) 136, 138–41.

[75] § 84(1) AMG 1976.

[76] § 84(2) AMG 1976.

Product Liability Act provisions do not apply to pharmaceutical products, which are specifically covered by the § 84 of the AMG.[77]

There have been some important procedural modifications to the German pharmaceutical compensation system through a second Act of Parliament to change the rules relating to damages.[78] The Act reverses the burden of proof of causation in § 84 of the AMG, requiring the manufacturer to show that the source of the injurious effect did not originate in the drug's development or manufacture. Secondly, it introduces a presumption of causation where the claimant can show that the pharmaceutical product in question was capable of causing the particular damage. The manufacturer may rebut the presumption by showing that the harm was caused by other factors. However, a qualifying provision to the presumption that the injury was caused by the impugned medicinal product has also been inserted. Whereas the general rule is that the administration of other drugs may not be invoked to challenge causation, an exception to this rule applies where there are medicinal products of different manufacturers involved and where the manufacturers of the other products which may have caused the damage cannot be held liable for reasons other than causation, notably because the adverse effects are acceptable when the benefit–risk ratio is taken into consideration. Damages for pain and suffering are also introduced for such claims, and the maximum amounts recoverable have been raised.[79] Since 2 August 2000, a specific State Compensation Act has existed for hepatitis C virus (HCV)-infected patients, who were infected in the former German Democratic Republic in 1978 and 1979 as a result of compulsory post-partum administration of anti-D-immunoglobulins.[80]

---

[77] This appears to be consistent with Art 13 of the Product Liability Directive, which states that the Directive is without prejudice to special liability systems existing at the moment the Directive was notified (ie enacted). It has been said that this did not mean that Member States could exclude the Directive's application where such 'special liability systems' exist. Thus it must not be assumed that § 84 AMG constitutes the German implementation of the Directive in respect of pharmaceutical products: Van Gerven and others, *Ius Commune Casebooks for the Common Law of Europe: Tort Law* (above, n 74) 654, fn 577. It remains unclear whether the German implementation of the Directive in respect of pharmaceutical products is correct. However, in proceedings brought by the European Commission against France and Greece over their alleged failure to implement the Directive properly (Case C-52/00 *Commission v France* [2002] ECR I-3827; Case C-154/00 *Commission v Greece* [2002] ECR I-3879) and in the separate case covering similar issues on the reference from Spain (Case C-183/00 *González Sanchez v Medicina Asturiana SA* [2002] ECR I-3901) Geelhoed AG suggested that Art 13 aimed to protect special pharmaceutical regimes, as mentioned in the 13th recital to the Directive (such as exists in Germany) and did not aim to protect a regime like the Spanish Consumer Protection Act 1984, which covered all consumer goods: for criticism, see G Howells, 'Product Liability—A Maximal Harmonisation Directive' (December 2001) Lovells' *European Product Liability Review*, Issue 5, 10, 12.

[78] Drucksache 14/8780, Deutscher Bundestag–14-Wahlperiode, 16 April 2002. It has been argued, however, that Art 13 does not permit these new causation rules, since the ECJ's emphasis on maximum harmonisation within its scope (see Case C-183/00 *Gonzalez Sanchez v Medicinia Asturiana SA* [2002] ECR I-3901, para 24; Case C-52/00 *Commission v France* [2002] ECR I-3827, para 24 Case C-154/00 *Commission v Greece* [2002] ECR I-3879, para 20; and Case C-402/03 *Skov v Bilka* [2006] ECR I-199, paras 22, 23, 44) suggests a reading which would not allow the German legislator to change the co-existing product liability system in a meaningful way: S Lenze, 'German Product Liability Law: Between European Directives, American Restatements and Common Sense in D Fairgrieve (ed), *Product Liability in Comparative Perspective* (Cambridge, Cambridge University Press, 2005) 121.

[79] P Gruenes, 'Ministry of Justice Proposes Pro-consumer Amendments Concerning Damages and the Burden of Proof' (September 2001) Lovells' *European Product Liability Review*, Issue 4, 12–13; I Brock, 'German Parliament Passes the Second Act to Change the Rules Relating to Damages' (June 2002) Lovells' *European Product Liability Review*, Issue 7, 17, 17–18.

[80] Act on assistance for patients infected with the hepatitis-C-virus by anti-D-immunoglobulins (*Gesetz über die Hilfe für durch Anti-D-Immunprophylaxe mit dem Hepatitis-C-Virus infizierte Personen* (*Anti-D-Hilfegesetz*, 'Anti-DHG') BGB1 I 2000, no 38, pp 1270 ff: enacted with retrospective effect, 1 January 2000); I Brock, 'State Compensation for HCV Infections in the Federal Republic of Germany', (December 2000) Lovells' *European Product Liability Review*, Issue 1, 16, 16–17.

C. Sweden, Finland and Norway

A Swedish pharmaceutical insurance scheme has existed since 1 January 1988. It is based on a public undertaking made by every pharmaceutical manufacturer and importer in favour of persons injured by their product.[81] The scheme provides no-fault compensation if it is reasonable to accept that an injury has occurred as a result of using a pharmaceutical product.[82] Thus the basic principle is that compensation is determined by causation, as opposed to fault or defectiveness.[83] The standard of proof of causation is one of 'preponderant probability'[84] and a 'statistical causal relationship' or chronological connection is accepted.[85] Whereas basic losses are met by a social security scheme, further loss is dealt with by the pharmaceutical scheme.[86] There is no development risk defence, and so compensation may be paid even if an adverse reaction was unforeseeable due to the limitations of medical and scientific knowledge at the time.[87]

The principal advantages of the Swedish scheme are the cooperation amongst those running it and its flexibility. On the other hand, it has been argued that it is uncertain how the system would operate throughout the European Union without Sweden's generous social security system, social homogeneity and responsible state, pharmaceutical and insurance industries.[88]

A voluntary drug insurance scheme was established in Finland on 1 July 1984. While not replacing a right to bring an action in the courts, those injured by drugs are given an opportunity to bring their claim under an insurance policy held by a cooperative society, the members of which are manufacturers and importers of pharmaceuticals.[89] The scheme is modelled on the Swedish version, but with some distinguishing features. Damages recoverable are more generous under the Finnish scheme, but the administrators of the scheme are stricter on causation than their Swedish counterparts.[90] Norway has a similar scheme to Finland, but it is operated on a statutory basis.[91]

VI. REFORM

So far as potential changes in the law are concerned, in their response to the European Commission Green Paper on liability for defective products,[92] the European Federation

---

[81] Undertaking to disperse indemnity for drug-related injuries, 1 January 1988 (Swedish Pharmaceutical Insurance Scheme).

[82] Undertaking to disperse indemnity for drug-related injuries, § 3.

[83] C Oldertz, 'Security Insurance, Patient Insurance, and Pharmaceutical Insurance in Sweden' (1986) 34 *American Journal of Comparative Law* 635, 650.

[84] Undertaking to disperse indemnity for drug-related injuries, § 3.

[85] Oldertz (above n 82) 648–9.

[86] Undertaking to disperse indemnity for drug-related injuries, § 8.8; Fleming (above n 73) 303.

[87] D Brahams, 'The Swedish Medical Insurance Schemes. The Way Ahead for the United Kingdom?' (1988) 575 *Lancet* 1, 43.

[88] See G Howells, *Comparative Product Liability* (Aldershot, Dartmouth, 1993) 165; C Hodges, 'Nordic Compensation Schemes for Drug Injuries' (2006) 29 *Journal of Consumer Policy* 143, 173; Miller and Goldberg (above, n 19) para 9.50.

[89] G Howells, *Comparative Product Liability* (Aldershot, Dartmouth, 1993) 167.

[90] Ibid 168.

[91] Ibid.

[92] COM(1999)396 final.

of Pharmaceutical Industries and Associations (EFPIA)[93] warned against changes in the law or legal environment in Europe which would favour consumers. The EFPIA argued that any such change in the balance between the interests of consumer protection and the encouragement of industrial innovation could result in a potential increase in costs and risks and the threatening of the availability of useful and innovatory products.[94] In the light of government controls on pharmaceutical pricing and reimbursement of medicines, they state that pricing constraints are such that resulting costs could not be recovered through future price increases.[95] Moreover, they have argued that any change which seeks to increase consumer protection would not do so in practice, given the high standards of European pharmaceutical regulation.[96] In the study on the economic impact for industry, insurance, consumers and society as a whole of the removal of the development risk defence,[97] which was undertaken and reported on by the Fondazione Rosselli in 2004,[98] it was considered that steps should be taken to harmonise the approach to the application of the defence in Member States. It envisaged the creation of a mixed public-private compensation fund at EU level to guarantee EU citizens adequate protection from product development risks. It was suggested that the option of having different industry-specific schemes should be evaluated.[99] The study made reference to several national compensation schemes, including special compensation schemes for damage caused by infected blood, medicinal products and vaccines, as well as foodstuffs and chemicals.[100]

However, the suggestion of a mixed public-private compensation fund at EU level appears unworkable for two main reasons. First, the special schemes have been established in respect of either specific products or specific injuries and would appear to be at odds with a general compensation scheme funded by compulsory contributions by industry.[101] Secondly, the establishment of centralised compensation funds would appear to have major economic disadvantages.[102] In particular, it has been argued that two basic obstacles or preconditions would need to be overcome to make a compensation scheme within other Member States or across the Community viable, viz the presence of other sources of compensation to cover a significant proportion of the payments, and the absence of a right of recourse between the sources of compensation.[103]

It may be said that, although there are considerable difficulties in applying strict liability to medicinal products, politically it would be singularly difficult to create an exception for pharmaceuticals, unless it were in the form of a centrally-funded or insurance-based no-fault scheme such as exists in Germany or Sweden.[104] Moreover, it is uncertain how such a

---

[93] Response to Product Liability Green Paper by European Federation of Pharmaceutical Industries and Associations (EFPIA, 1999).

[94] Ibid para 11.1.

[95] Ibid para 5.5.

[96] Ibid paras 6.2, 11.

[97] See chapter 8 of this volume.

[98] Analysis of the Economic Impact of the Development Risk Clause as provided by Directive 85/374/EEC on Liability for Defective Products (Fondazione Rosselli, 2004).

[99] Ibid.

[100] Ibid 85–86, 91–100.

[101] R Freeman, 'The Future of the Development Risk Defence in EU Strict Liability Laws Hits the Spotlight' (2004) 15 *European Product Liability Review* 31, 32–33.

[102] C Hodges, 'Nordic Compensation Schemes for Drug Injuries' (2006) 29 *Journal of Consumer Policy* 143, 173.

[103] Ibid.

[104] See Miller and Goldberg (above, n 19) paras 9.48–9.52.

system would operate throughout the European Union without a generous social security system such as exists in Sweden.[105] Accordingly, the remainder of this book presupposes that medicinal products remain within the strict product liability regime, but that they merit distinct treatment within that regime, as occurs in the United States.

VII. CONCLUSION

The piecemeal developments in product liability reform, culminating in the introduction of strict liability within Europe, have their origins in the thalidomide disaster, and in many ways thalidomide continues to fuel the pressure for reform of product liability, especially for the victims of alleged medicinal product-induced injury.

While the various Commissions that have examined this area of law have argued against treating drugs as a special case, it seems that there are strong arguments in favour of doing so. In the US, commentators have noted several reasons why drugs are different. In particular, emphasis has been placed on the fact that: (1) drugs are heavily regulated by the Federal Food, Drug, and Cosmetic Act; (2) drugs have high social utility; (3) learned intermediaries assist patients in determining which drugs are appropriate; and (4) drugs that are unreasonably dangerous for some consumers may be beneficial to another class of consumers. It is submitted that it is important to appreciate these reasons when examining whether EU countries should move from treating liability for medicinal products in the same way as liability for any other product, to the US approach of establishing special liability rules for prescription drugs, or to specific pharmaceutical liability regimes, such as are present in Germany and in some Nordic countries.

By far the majority of claims against pharmaceutical manufacturers have been initially funded by the Legal Aid Board in England and Wales. Now that personal injury claims against pharmaceutical companies will no longer be eligible for legal aid in England and Wales, and in the light of the costs involved in such litigation, and the fact that not one claim has resulted in damages being awarded by a court against a pharmaceutical company,

---

[105] See G Howells, *Comparative Product Liability* (Aldershot, Dartmouth, 1993) 165; C Hodges, 'Nordic Compensation Schemes for Drug Injuries' (2006) 29 *Journal of Consumer Policy* 143, 173; Miller and Goldberg (above, n 19) para 9.50. In August 2009, the Scottish Government announced the creation of a short-life working group, the No-Fault Compensation Review Group, chaired by Professor Sheila McLean. The Group's remit was to consider the potential benefits for patients in Scotland of no-fault compensation, and whether such a scheme could be introduced alongside the existing clinical negligence arrangements, taking into account: (1) the cost implications; (2) the consequences for health care staff, and the quality and safety of care; (3) the wider implications for the system of justice and personal injury liability; and (4) the evidence on how no-fault compensation has operated in other countries: see SAM McLean, *No Fault Compensation Review Group, Report and Recommendations: Vol 1*(Scottish Govt, 2011), para 1.4, available at: www.scotland.gov.uk/Topics/Health/NHS-Scotland/No-faultCompensation/NFCGReport. The group explored several well-established no-fault schemes in other jurisdictions, in particular the New Zealand and Swedish models: ibid para 7.6. The Group reported in February 2011, and recommended that consideration should be given to the establishment of a no-fault compensation scheme for medical injury, along the lines of the Swedish model: ibid para 7.11, Recommendation 1. This is a separate scheme from the Swedish pharmaceutical insurance scheme. The McLean report recommended that the no-fault scheme should cover all medical treatment injuries that occur in Scotland. Such injuries could be caused by, for instance, the treatment itself, failure to treat, as well as faulty equipment, in which case there would be third party liability: ibid Recommendation 3. No mention was explicitly made of the position surrounding the administration of medicinal products in hospitals or by general practitioners, though seemingly this could fall within the ambit of a medical treatment injury. For further discussion of the report, see R Goldberg, 'Medical Malpractice and Compensation in the UK' (2012) 87 *Chicago-Kent Law Review* 131, 140–42.

it seems unlikely that solicitors will be keen to enter into 'no win, no fee' arrangements in the near future, unless the probability of success in the particular case is high. Nonetheless, a case against GlaxoSmithKline is being brought on a 'no win, no fee' basis in respect of claims for compensation for death or harm in the form of heart failure and heart attacks allegedly caused by the diabetes drug Avandia, and its progress is awaited by lawyers and academics with interest.

Although there are considerable difficulties in applying strict liability to medicinal products, and the failure rates under the UK Vaccine Damage Payment Scheme are high, politically it would be singularly difficult to create an exception for pharmaceuticals, unless it were in the form of a centrally-funded or insurance-based no-fault scheme such as exists in Germany or Sweden. Moreover, it is uncertain how such a system would operate throughout the European Union without a generous social security system such as exists in Sweden. In the current political climate, there would appear to be little impetus for a no-fault scheme for drug-induced injury. Accordingly, the remainder of this book presupposes that medicinal products continue to exist within the strict product liability regime, but that they merit distinct treatment within that regime, as occurs in the United States.

2

Defective Medicinal Products in the US and UK: An Overview

I. INTRODUCTION

Arguably the single most difficult part of the Product Liability Directive and Part I of the Consumer Protection Act 1987 is the core definition of a defect. Nowhere is the challenge of determining whether a product is defective more complex than in the context of medicinal products. This chapter seeks to provide an overview of the problem of defective medicinal products in the US and UK: the following two chapters focus on two specific types of defect which have given rise to the greatest challenges in this field, namely design defects and warning defects. The US is used as a comparator due to its wealth of jurisprudence in the prescription drug liability field, and also the fact that prescription drugs are now treated as a distinct category of product under the *Restatement, Third, Torts: Products Liability*.

II. DEFECTIVE MEDICINAL PRODUCTS IN THE US

In the United States, much of the case law has been influenced by the *Restatement, Second, Torts* § 402A. Section 402A does not distinguish between prescription and other products and hence liability is imposed where the product is 'in a defective condition unreasonably dangerous to the user or consumer' even where 'the seller has exercised all possible care in the preparation and sale of his product'. However, unlike the position under *Restatement, Second, Torts* § 402A, special liability rules for prescription drugs and medical devices are now established in § 6 of the *Restatement, Third, Torts: Products Liability*.

The crucial issue, which is the single most ignored one in pharmaceutical liability, is 'identifying the legal standard for defectively designed drugs'.[1] While there has been much comment on whether Comment *k* abolishes negligent design defect liability as well as strict liability design claims, the real question is 'what do we mean by a design defect of a drug, whether based on strict liability or negligence?'[2] The position in respect of both design defects and 'failure to warn' defects in the context of prescription drugs is examined in detail in chapters three and four below.

---

[1] MD Green, 'Prescription Drugs, Alternative Designs and the Restatement (Third): Preliminary Reflections' (1999) 30 *Seton Hall Law Review* 207, 217.

[2] Ibid.

III. DEFECTIVE MEDICINAL PRODUCTS IN THE UK

A. Definition of Defect

The heart of the Directive lies in its definition of a defective product in Article 6(1). This provides:

> A product is defective when it does not provide the safety which a person is entitled to expect, taking all circumstances into account, including:
>
> (a) the presentation of the product;
> (b) the use to which it could be reasonably be expected that the product would be put;
> (c) the time when the product was put into circulation.

The Directive then adds that 'a product shall not be considered defective for the sole reason that a better product is subsequently put into circulation' (Article 6(2)).

Section 3 of the Consumer Protection Act 1987, which implements Article 6 of the Product Liability Directive, provides the following definition of defect:

> (1) … there is a defect in a product … if the safety of the product is not such as persons generally are entitled to expect; and for those purposes 'safety', in relation to a product, shall include safety with respect to products comprised in that product and safety in the context of risks of damage to property, as well as in the context of risks of death or personal injury.
>
> (2) In determining for the purposes of subsection (1) above what persons generally are entitled to expect in relation to a product all the circumstances shall be taken into account, including—
>
> > (a) the manner in which, and purposes for which, the product has been marketed, its get-up, the use of any mark in relation to the product and any instructions for, or warnings with respect to, doing or refraining from doing anything with or in relation to the product;
> > (b) what might reasonably be expected to be done with or in relation to the product; and
> > (c) the time when the product was supplied by its producer to another;
>
> and nothing in this section shall require a defect to be inferred from the fact alone that the safety of a product which is supplied after that time is greater than the safety of the product in question.

Applying the Act's definition in the context of medicinal products, a medicinal product is defective if it does not provide the safety that persons generally are entitled to expect (section 3(1)), taking all circumstances into account (section 3(2)). Such circumstances include: (a) the manner in which and purposes for which the medicinal product has been marketed, its 'get-up', and the use of warnings and instructions; (b) what might reasonably be expected to be done with or in relation to the medicinal product; and (c) the time when the medicinal product was supplied by its producer to another.

Conceivably the single most difficult part of the Product Liability Directive and Part I of the 1987 Act—the core definition of a defect—has been widely held to contain substantial overtones of a negligence standard. This is clearly true (and perhaps inevitably so) where the concern is with alleged defects of design or inadequate warnings which may be seen as requiring a balancing of the risks and benefits involved in supplying certain types of products.[3]

---

[3] CJ Miller and RS Goldberg, *Product Liability*, 2nd edn (Oxford, Oxford University Press, 2004) paras 10.13, 10.19.

That the Product Liability Directive imposes fault-based liability on manufacturers for the design and presentation of their products follows from the link between the Articles provided by the common notion of 'defect' in Articles 1, 4, 6 and 7, and by the references to time in Articles 6 and 7.[4] In the commissioned Report on Product Liability in the European Union, the possibility was discussed of defining the defect concept in the Directive more precisely so as to clarify the issues that remain controversial. However, it was also observed that it might be more helpful not to adopt this course, not least because this could fetter the ability of judges to address such matters on a case-by-case basis. The Report stated that it might be expected that a body of case law will emerge that will provide a guide to the interpretation of this concept, and that the concept may come to be clarified in due course by the European Court of Justice.[5] As shall be seen, there is little doubt that the definition of defect is greatly challenged by the complexity of medicinal products and the paucity of case law on the topic has done little to help matters.

B. Consumer Expectations and Risk–Utility

The essence of the definition of defect is a lack of safety. In basing liability on a failure to meet the level of safety which a person is entitled to expect, the wording of Article 6 of the Directive reflects the 'consumer expectations' terminology associated with § 402A of the *Restatement, Second, Torts* (1965). In particular, the test appears to be derived from comments *g* and *i* of § 402A's standard of a 'defective condition unreasonably dangerous to the user or consumer or to his property'. Prima facie, consumer expectations may appear a suitable test in that it focuses on the condition of a product, as opposed to a manufacturer's conduct, and recognises the evolution of strict tort liability from the law of warranty.[6]

However, the key problem with a medicinal product design defect claim under consumer expectations is that it does not provide anything to consumers beyond that which is already provided by an adequate warning obligation. Its practical effect in the US has been 'to insulate design liability of a manufacturer as long as it has provided an adequate warning'.[7] As long ago as 1979, the Department of Health had been acutely aware of the problems of applying a consumer expectations test to medicinal products, observing that:[8]

> [M]edicines … are different from most other products in that their purpose is to modify the physiological processes of the body, which are themselves variable, and therefore medicinal products by their nature all carry a risk of side effects. In the case of the more potent medicines, it is well recognized that this risk has to be weighed against the anticipated benefits of treatment. But even simple over-the-counter remedies for minor ailments may produce side effects in a small minority of people because of such factors as biological idiosyncrasies, interaction with other medicines or food, or overdosage. The consumer cannot therefore reasonably expect *absolute* safety and it becomes very much a question of the *degree* of safety which he is entitled to expect. This must clearly vary from medicine to medicine and, indeed, from patient to patient.

---

[4] J Stapleton, 'Liability for Drugs in the US and EU: Rhetoric and Reality' (2007) 26 *Review of Litigation* 991, 1006.

[5] J Meltzer, R Freeman, and S Thomson, *Product Liability in the European Union: A Report for the European Commission*, MARKT/2001/11/D (Lovells, 2003) 2.2(b), 49.

[6] Miller and Goldberg (above, n 3) paras 10.21–10.22.

[7] MD Green (above, n 1) (1999) 30 *Seton Hall Law Review* 207, 218, fn 39.

[8] DHSS, *Product Liability: Special Features of the Medical Sector*, Medicines Division Consultation Paper (DHSS, 1979) para 5.

Commentators have stressed the weight to be attached to the word 'entitled' to expect[9] or have suggested that judges in the United Kingdom 'will test the reasonableness of consumer expectation'.[10] There would appear to have been elements of this approach in *Richardson v LRC Products Ltd*[11] where Ian Kennedy J explained that, although the user's expectation was that a condom would not fail, the defendants had not claimed that a condom would never fail and no one supposed that any method of contraception would be 100 per cent effective.[12] Nonetheless, having examined the expectations of consumers (albeit not in terms of the possibility of a higher level of legitimate expectation) he added, in a language analogous to a risk–utility analysis, that evidence showed that the condom in question had failed inexplicably under standards higher than the British ones applicable in the case. It is submitted that this suggests that in assessing consumer expectations, risk–utility factors will also need to be taken into consideration, supporting a dual or combined consumer expectations-risk–benefit approach, or even an eclectic approach.[13] In the context of medicinal products, this utility or benefit is an *anticipated* benefit of treatment, since there can be no guarantee of cure, symptom relief, or disease prevention in any case.[14] In utilising such approaches, it should be noted that the standard of defectiveness should be regarded as the *minimum* standard of what is an acceptable level of safety.[15] By contrast, in the hepatitis C litigation, *A v National Blood Authority*,[16] Burton J rejected the application of a minimum standard approach to the facts of the case and concluded that the hepatitis C-infected blood products were defective since 'the public at large was entitled to expect that the blood transfused to them would be free from infection'.[17]

C. Expectations of 'Persons Generally'

The reference in section 3(1) of the 1987 Act to what persons generally are entitled to expect is fraught with difficulty.[18] There is much to be said for the view that, in the context of medicinal products, 'there is a certain artificiality in trying to determine what "persons

[9] J Stapleton, 'Restatement (Third) of Torts: Products Liability, an Anglo-Australian Perspective' (2000) 39 *Washburn Law Journal* 363, 377; Dr Clark submits that focusing on what the consumer is *entitled* to expect supports the protection of consumer expectations, and that complex or technological products (which would include medicinal products) 'give rise to the same expectations of entitlement': AM Clark, *Product Liability* (London, Sweet & Maxwell, 1989) 37.

[10] G Howells in Howells (ed), *The Law of Product Liability*, 2nd edn (London, LexisNexis Butterworths, 2007) para 4.151.

[11] [2000] Lloyd's Rep Med 280.

[12] Ibid 285.

[13] R Goldberg, 'Paying for Bad Blood: Strict Product Liability after *A v National Blood Authority*' (2002) 10 *Medical Law Review* 105, 129.

[14] I Dodds-Smith, M Spencer and J Bore, 'Product Liability for Medicinal Products' in MJ Powers, NH Harris and A Barton (eds), *Clinical Negligence*, 4th edn (London, Tottel Publishing, 2008) para 24.59.

[15] J Stapleton, *Product Liability* (London, Butterworths, 1994) 259. Stapleton's approach was followed in *Worsley v Tambrands Ltd* [2000] *PIQR* P95, P103.

[16] *A v National Blood Authority* [2001] 3 All ER 289.

[17] Ibid [80].

[18] Miller and Goldberg (above, n 3) para 10.45, referring to the views of Michael Howard QC, the Minister responsible for piloting the Consumer Protection Bill through the House of Commons, who stated that: '[t]he intention here is that this reference should be regarded as a reference to general expectations; not general persons but general expectations': HC, Official Report, Standing Committee D, col 26 (5 May 1987).

generally are entitled to expect".[19] The matter was considered by Burton J in *A v National Blood Authority*,[20] where there was considerable common ground between the parties as to the nature of the test to be applied, viz the legitimate expectations of persons generally. As Burton J explained:[21]

> The question to be resolved is the safety or the degree or level of safety or safeness which persons generally are entitled to expect. The test is not that of an absolute level of safety, nor an absolute liability for any injury caused by the harmful characteristic … In the assessment of that question the expectation is that of persons generally, or the public at large … The safety is not what is actually expected by the public at large, but what they are *entitled* to expect … The common ground is that the question is what the legitimate expectation is of persons generally, ie what is legitimately to be expected, arrived at objectively. 'Legitimate expectation', rather than 'entitled expectation', appeared to all of us to be a more happy formulation (and is analogous to the formulation in other languages in which the directive is published) … The court decides what the public is entitled to expect: Dr Harald Bartl in *Produkthaftung nach neuem EG-Recht* (1989) described the judge (as translated from the German) as 'an informed representative of the public at large' … Such objectively assessed legitimate expectation may accord with actual expectation; but it may be *more* than the public actually expects, thus imposing a higher standard of safety, or it may be *less* than the public actually expects. Alternatively the public may have no *actual* expectation—e.g. in relation to a new product—the word coined in argument for such an imaginary product was a 'scrid'.

Applying this test of the *legitimate expectations of persons generally*, Burton J concluded that the blood products were defective since 'the public at large was entitled to expect that the blood transfused to them would be free from infection'.[22] This was not least because of the paucity of warnings or material publicity of the risks involved. The absence of a public awareness of a risk was also relevant to the determination of the issue of defectiveness in *Scholten v Foundation Sanquin of Blood Supply*,[23] a decision of the County Court of Amsterdam. In that case Scholten underwent heart surgery in an Amsterdam hospital, during which he received an HIV-infected blood transfusion from a donor. The donor had only just contracted the virus, so that his infection could not be detected during this 'window period' between the donor acquiring the infection and the formation of HIV antibodies. Scholten argued that the blood was defective within the definition of Article 6, and that, when determining whether the blood product was as safe as persons were entitled to expect, it was the expectation of the general public that was relevant. The Court held that

---

[19] H Teff, 'Products Liability' in A Grubb, J Lang and J McHale (eds), *Principles of Medical Law*, 3rd edn (Oxford, Oxford University Press, 2010) para 18.60; cf the more useful sixth recital to the preamble of the Product Liability Directive, referring to the 'safety which the public at large is entitled to expect': Dir 85/374/EEC. Accordingly, the expectations of the individual consumer are not significant except to the extent that they are a reflection of more general public expectations. See the 'public at large' interpretation in the Australian Trade Practices Act 1974 (Cth), s 75AC (now s 9 of Sch 2 of the Competition and Consumer Act 2010 (Cth)), (which provides a similar definition to s 3(1) of the 1987 Act) by the Full Federal Court of Australia in *Glendale Products Pty Ltd v Australian Competition and Consumer Commission* (1998) 90 FCR 40, 47, approved by the Federal Court of Australia in *Morris v Alcon Laboratories (Australia) Pty Ltd* [2003] FCA 151 (6 March 2003) (support for an inferential evidentiary foundation in establishing defectiveness).

[20] *A v National Blood Authority* [2001] 3 All ER 289.

[21] Ibid [31].

[22] Ibid [80]; applied in *B (A Child) v McDonald's Restaurants Ltd* [2002] EWHC (QB) 490, [77].

[23] *Scholten v Foundation Sanquin of Blood Supply* H 98.0896 (3 February 1999, unreported). For further discussion, see CC Van Dam, 'Dutch Case Law on the EU Product Liability Directive' in D Fairgrieve (ed), *Product Liability in Comparative Perspective* (Cambridge, Cambridge University Press, 2005) 128–30. See also below, chapter 8 of this volume for discussion in the context of the development risk defence.

the blood product was defective because the general public expected that blood products in the Netherlands had been 100 per cent HIV free for some time. It stated:[24]

> The fact that there is a small chance that HIV could be transmitted via a blood transfusion, which the foundation estimates at 1 in a million, is in the opinion of the court, not general knowledge. It cannot therefore be said that the public does not or cannot be expected to have this expectation. The fact that the foundation acted in accordance with the relevant guidance and that the use of an HIV-1 RNA test at the time could not have detected the HIV virus does not have any bearing on this.

However, the test presents difficulties when applied to medicinal products which pose a danger to certain sections of the public only, such as children or those who are likely to suffer an allergic reaction.[25] In appropriate cases, this should be taken into account in the drug's design or in accompanying warnings.[26] The term 'legitimate expectation' was not used in *Piper v JRI (Manufacturing) Ltd.*[27] After a hip replacement operation, that involved the implantation of a prosthesis, the prosthesis sheared in two. Rejecting the claimant's action under the Consumer Protection Act 1987, the Court of Appeal held that the prosthesis was not defective at the time it was supplied to the hospital. The statutory defence under section 4(1)(d) that 'the defect did not exist at the relevant time' was therefore established.[28] Thomas LJ made no reference to the term 'legitimate expectation', preferring to place his emphasis on what persons generally were entitled to expect. In the context of prosthesis, a person:[29]

> was plainly entitled to expect a prosthesis to be so designed and manufactured as to withstand the procedures and forces ordinarily used on implantation. If it was not so designed and manufactured, then it would be defective at the time it was supplied to the hospital.

D. Circumstances Taken into Account in Assessing Defectiveness

(i) Introduction

In determining what persons generally are entitled to expect in relation to a product, the 1987 Act requires that 'all the circumstances shall be taken into account'.[30] Section 3(2) of the 1987 Act provides a non-exhaustive[31] list of circumstances which are to be taken into account. These include: (a) the manner in which and purposes for which the medicinal

---

[24] The translation is taken from the judgment in *A v National Blood Authority* [2001] 3 All ER 289, [44].

[25] Miller, *Product Liability and Safety Encyclopaedia*, Div III, para 255. For further discussion of allergies, see Miller and Goldberg (above, n 3) paras 4.102–4.103, 12.58–12.64 and 16.27–16.31.

[26] Ibid.

[27] *Piper v JRI (Manufacturing) Ltd.* [2006] EWCA Civ, 1344.

[28] Ibid [30].

[29] Ibid [34].

[30] Section 3(2); Dir 85/374/EEC, Art 6(1).

[31] The Federal Court of Australia has emphasised the inclusive and non-exhaustive nature of the circumstances listed in s 75AC(2)(a)–(f) of the Trade Practices Act 1974 (now s 9(2) of Sch 2 of the Competition and Consumer Act 2010 (Cth)), (the equivalent to the circumstances listed in s 3(2)(a)–(c) of the 1987 Act), and that the absence of evidence supporting any of the circumstances listed would not be fatal to making out a cause of action for defective goods under s 75AC(1): *Morris v Alcon Laboratories (Australia) Pty Ltd* [2003] FCA 151, paras 16–17.

product has been marketed, its 'get-up', and the use of warnings and instructions: (b) what might reasonably be expected to be done with or in relation to the medicinal product; and (c) the time when the medicinal product was supplied by its producer to another. These can be classified into three categories, which correspond with the paragraphs of section 3(2) of the Act and Article 6(1) of the Directive, concerning (a) marketing, presentation, instructions, and warnings; (b) reasonably expected use; and (c) the time of supply of the product by the product to another.

(ii) Marketing, Presentation, Instructions, and Warnings

This category is the most significant factor relevant to determining the expectation of safety with medicinal products.[32] While the Directive merely refers to the 'presentation of the product',[33] the Act provides a more detailed elaboration of this factor, which includes:

> the manner in which, and purposes for which, the product has been marketed, its get-up, the use of any mark in relation to the product and any instruction for, or warnings with respect to, doing or refraining from doing anything with or in relation to the product.

This suggests that it is quite acceptable to qualify the consumer's expectations of safety surrounding a medicinal product by contra-indications, warnings and precautions, whether issued to an intermediary (such as a prescribing GP) or the user direct.[34] The expression 'the manner in which, and purposes for which, the product has been marketed' indicates that the relevant circumstances include statements and claims made in relation to the product in general advertising and promotional material. It is critical to refrain from overselling a medicinal product's safety. The over-promotion of medicinal products by so-called 'detail men' in the United States, and also in the United Kingdom and Europe more generally, has continued to be a source of concern since it may reduce the effect of written warnings in the drug's product information.[35] The relevance of marketing is consistent with a consumer expectations standard of defectiveness. Accordingly, such safety expectations are heightened if a medicinal product is marketed as being safe for children or the elderly.[36] Titles VIII and VIIIa of Directive 2001/83 govern the advertising of medicinal products and the provision of information about medicinal products to the public and health professionals,[37] and both the Medicines and Health Care Products Regulatory Agency (MHRA) and the Association of the British Pharmaceutical Industry (ABPI), through the independent Prescription

---

[32] I Dodds-Smith, M Spencer and J Bore, 'Product Liability for Medicinal Products' in MJ Powers, NH Harris and A Barton (eds), *Clinical Negligence*, 4th edn (London, Tottel Publishing, 2008) para 24.56.

[33] Dir 85/374/EEC, Art 6(1)(a).

[34] I Dodds-Smith, M Spencer and J Bore, 'Product Liability for Medicinal Products' in MJ Powers, NH Harris and A Barton (eds), *Clinical Negligence*, 4th edn (London, Tottel Publishing, 2008) para 24.58; CJS Hodges, *Product Liability: European Laws and Practice* (London, Sweet & Maxwell, 1993) para 2-014.

[35] See, eg, *Incollingo v Ewing* 282 A 2d 206 (Pa 1971).

[36] G Howells in Howells (ed), *The Law of Product Liability*, 2nd edn (London, LexisNexis Butterworths, 2007) para 4.162.

[37] Dir 2001/83/EC on the Community Code Relating to Medicinal Products for Human Use [2001] OJ L311/67, as amended by Dir 2004/27/EC [2004] OJ L136/34, Arts 86–100. In the UK, see now Human Medicines Regulations 2012, SI 2012/1916, Part 14.

Medicines Code of Practice Authority exercise increasing vigilance to ensure that the safety and efficacy of medicinal products is not over-promoted.[38]

The purposes for which the product is marketed will play a role in determining whether a product is defective. In view of the uncontroverted evidence showing that the drug caused malformations in unborn foetuses, thalidomide would be considered defective if marketed as a pregnancy drug.[39] However, thalidomide received an FDA authorisation in 1998 for non-pregnancy uses in the treatment of leprosy and in 2008 the EMEA granted approval for it to be used for the treatment of multiple myeloma;[40] it has also been used in the treatment of AIDS,[41] and is used in the United Kingdom on a named patient basis.[42] It is suggested that thalidomide would not appear to be defective if it was marketed solely for these safe purposes.

(iii) Reasonably Expected Use

In determining the expectations of safety, section 3(2)(b) provides that the relevant circumstances include 'what might reasonably be expected to be done with or in relation to the product'. The issue will be whether the use to which the product was in fact put when it caused the damage was a reasonably expected one, based on an objective test of reasonableness.[43] The provision acknowledges that while most (if not all) products are capable of causing harm if used in an unreasonable way, if they do so, this does not imply that they have failed to achieve the required level of safety.[44] In a case from the Netherlands, a District Court rejected a claim that an OB 'comfort mini' tampon was defective because it was possible to insert it into the urethra, as a young girl had done. The Court held that the way in which the tampon had been used could not reasonably have been expected by the producer, not least because Johnson & Johnson had sold a considerable number of such tampons, but had never received a report or a complaint of a similar kind.[45]

---

[38] *R v Roussel LaboratoriesLtd, sub nom R v Good* (1989) 88 Cr App R 140; See generally, *Code of Practice for the Pharmaceutical Industry: Second 2012 Edition* (Association of the British Pharmaceutical Industry, 2012), available at: www.pmcpa.org.uk/thecode/Documents/Code%20of%20Practice%202012.pdf (covering the promotion of medicines for prescribing to health professionals and setting out standards for the provision of information about prescription only medicines to the public and patients); I Dodds-Smith, M Spencer and J Bore, 'Product Liability for Medicinal Products' in MJ Powers, NH Harris and A Barton (eds), *Clinical Negligence*, 4th edn (London, Tottel Publishing, 2008) 24.104.

[39] H Sjöström and R Nilsson, *Thalidomide and the Power of Drug Companies* (Harmondsworth, Penguin, 1972) 156–59.

[40] See 'Lenalidomide and thalidomide for multiple myeloma', MHRA, Drug Safety Update, Vol 2, Issue 1, August 2008, available at: www.mhra.gov.uk/Safetyinformation/DrugSafetyUpdate; N Hawkes, 'Fifty years on, thalidomide is back. Now they say it's a good thing', *The Times*, 22 April 2008.

[41] Stapleton, *Product Liability* (above, n 15) 234; M Schulz, Review, 'Dark Remedies: The Impact of Thalidomide and its Revival as a Vital Medicine' (2001) 322 *British Medical Journal* 1608.

[42] RJ Powell, Editorial, 'New Rules for Thalidomide' (1996) 313 *British Medical Journal* 377–78.

[43] Hodges, *Product Liability: European Laws and Practice* (above, n 34) para 2-014.

[44] Miller and Goldberg (above, n 3) para 10.60.

[45] District Court Zwolle dd 24 April 2002, (noted in L Mattheussens, 'District Court of Zwolle Considers Questions of Defect and Adequacy of Warnings', (December 2002) Lovell's *European Product Liability Review*, Issue 9, 43, 44).

(iv) Time of Supply of Product by Producer to Another

Both section 3(2)(c) of the Consumer Protection Act 1987 and Article 6(1)(c) and 6(2) of the Directive acknowledge that the level of safety which has to be assessed in determining what persons generally are entitled to expect is the one which was considered appropriate at the time when the product was supplied[46] by its producer to another. It is not the standard which might have been achieved at the time the damage was suffered. The point is reinforced in the closing words of section 3(2), reflecting those of Article 6(2), whereby 'nothing in this section shall require a defect to be inferred from the fact alone that the safety of a product which is supplied after that time is greater than the safety of the product in question'. Determining whether a medicinal product is defective must therefore be judged by reference to the circumstances prevailing at the date of supply, notwithstanding whether subsequent advances in science have allowed others to license and supply a product with an improved safety profile for the same indication. However, once the improved medicinal product is available, it will be harder to justify the continued supply of the older generation products: it many nevertheless be possible to claim advantages of such products for specific groups of patients.[47]

The adoption of this approach goes some way towards assimilating the principles to be applied in strict liability and in negligence, but has been subject to criticism. For instance, Professor Stapleton has observed that the approach involves the need to reconstruct the state of the art at a point often considerably in the past and act on information which is usually complex and costly to gather, and often more within the knowledge of the defendant than the plaintiff.[48] This would seem particularly true in the context of medicinal products, where adverse effects many manifest themselves many years after clinical trials have been conducted. Nonetheless, to have adopted a different approach would have provided little incentive to improve safety standards over the years,[49] at least during the period in which the 10-year period for potential liability under the Act was still running.[50]

(v) Apparently Irrelevant Circumstances

Although the list of circumstances specified in section 3(2) of the 1987 Act is non-exhaustive, the relevance or otherwise of other suggested circumstances was one of the principal issues addressed in *A v National Blood Authority*.[51] The background to the case,

---

[46] For the definition of supply see s 46(1) of the 1987 Act.

[47] I Dodds-Smith, M Spencer and J Bore, 'Product Liability for Medicinal Products' in MJ Powers, NH Harris and A Barton (eds), *Clinical Negligence*, 4th edn (London, Tottel Publishing, 2008) para 24.54.

[48] J Stapleton, 'Products Liability Reform—Real or Illusory?' (1986) 6 *Oxford Journal of Legal Studies* 392, 412–13; also J Stapleton, *Product Liability* (above, n 15) (London, Butterworths, 1994) 244–47. Suppose also that, with the advance of time, additional beneficial effects of a medicinal product supplied in 2005 are discovered only in 2013 when the damage is suffered and the claim made. It would be strange indeed if the manufacturer were unable to lead evidence of these beneficial effects in any risk–utility analysis: Miller and Goldberg, *Product Liability* (above, n 3) para 10.64, fn 190.

[49] Miller and Goldberg (above, n 3) para 10.64.

[50] See Limitation Act 1980, s 11A(3), which was added by Sch 1 to the 1987 Act. Note that in some cases the legitimate expectations of standards of safety will not change over the years: *Abouzaid v Mothercare (UK) Ltd* [2000] All ER (D) 2436; *The Times*, 20 February 2001, Pill LJ, [25]; see further, Miller and Goldberg (above, n 3) para 10.65.

[51] [2001] 3 All ER 289. The other main issue was the scope and application of the development risk defence: see below, chapter 8 of this volume.

which involved some 114 claimants, was both complex and tragic. The claimants had been infected with hepatitis C through blood transfusions or blood products from 1 March 1988, usually in the course of undergoing surgery. The source of the infection was not contamination by an outside agent but was, rather, within the donor's blood. The National Blood Authority was legally responsible for the obligations arising from its supply. It was a central feature of the case that during the period of infection the risk was known to the medical profession in general terms, but impossible to avoid either because the hepatitis C virus itself had not been discovered or identified or, at a later stage and until April 1991, because it was undetectable through a screening test in any individual case. Liability under the Product Liability Directive and hence the 1987 Act was, in principle, strict and not dependent on negligence but the issue was whether it extended to a case of this kind.

Although there was much common ground between counsel for the opposing sides as to the way in which the test was to be formulated and applied, there were also important differences. According to the claimants, with the elimination of the need to prove negligence, questions of avoidability and of what the defendants could and should have done differently did not arise. Neither was it relevant to inquire whether there were any steps or precautions reasonably available or whether any such steps were impracticable or economically unreasonable.[52] The defendants responded by submitting that, whereas the conduct of the individual producer was irrelevant, it remained relevant to identify and specify the safety precautions that the public could or would reasonably expect from a producer of such products. So, the submission went, in as much as avoiding the risk was at the time impossible and unattainable, avoidability *was* a circumstance to be taken into account, as the public did not and/or was not entitled to expect 100 per cent clean blood. The most they could legitimately expect was that all legitimately expectable (reasonably available) precautions—or in this case tests—had been taken or carried out.[53]

After a detailed examination of the issues, which included both citation of academic literature and consideration of the limited assistance to be gained from the case law of other jurisdictions, Burton J concluded, in the context of discussing what he termed 'non-standard' products,[54] that the following circumstances were *not* relevant and so could not be taken into account:[55]

(i) avoidability of the harmful characteristic—i.e. impossibility or unavoidability in relation to precautionary measures; (ii) the impracticality, cost or difficulty of taking such measures; and (iii) the benefit to society or utility of the product (except in the context of whether—with *full information* and *proper knowledge*—the public does and ought to accept the risk).

He added, in the context of discussing 'standard products', that there was no room in the basket of relevant circumstances for consideration of '(i) what the producer could have done differently; and (ii) whether the producer could or could not have done the same as the others did'.[56] On the facts of the case there was no evidence to suggest that the patients

---

[52] [2001] 3 All ER 289, para 32.
[53] Ibid.
[54] See further, text to nn 94–97 below.
[55] [2001] 3 All ER 289, para 68. While avoidability of the risk of harm through scalding was not a relevant circumstance for the purposes of s 3 of the 1987 Act in *B v McDonald's Restaurants Ltd* [2002] EWHC (QB) 490, paras 73, 77–78, elements of a risk–utility analysis clearly formed at least part of the basis for the conclusion that the product (a hot drink) was not defective.
[56] Ibid para 71.

knew that there was a risk that blood was, or was likely to be, infected with hepatitis C and the conclusion was that the blood products were defective.[57]

There is no doubt that the conclusion on this issue is controversial.[58] As the author has previously noted, there is an element of irony about the rejection of risk–utility for hepatitis C, in respect of such community-used natural resources, since

> the circumstances in which the expectation is not 100% are going to be situations where the public are aware that a risk-benefit assessment has been made to put the product on the market, e.g. the AIDS drug AZT.[59]

The writer submits that the public expectation in these circumstances 'is shaped by risk-benefit assessment'.[60] Accordingly, Professor Whittaker is surely correct to opine that avoidability 'is properly *relevant* to the assessment of a product's defect whether or not it is known to people generally, but it will not *conclude* it'.[61] As he explains, such an approach is not inconsistent with the Directive's assertion that it imposes liability without fault, even if it is evocative of the cost–benefit analysis in the English law of negligence.[62] Moreover, in the context of blood, avoidably unsafe products have been a defined category identified with whole blood and blood products for several years in the US, and indeed much of this policy was incorporated there in State blood shield statutes, exempting blood banks and hospitals from strict liability.[63] It is conceded that Burton J does not deny the relevance or possibility of a risk–utility analysis even in the case of 'non-standard' products, since he postulates that it operates, but only where the public has 'full information and proper knowledge' of the benefits to society of the product and then accepts and ought to accept,

---

[57] Ibid para 55.

[58] For comment, see eg R Goldberg, 'Paying for Bad Blood: Strict Liability after *A v National Blood Authority*' (2002) 10 *Medical Law Review* 165; J Stapleton, 'Bugs in Anglo-American Product Liability' (2002) 53 *South Carolina Law Review* 1225, 1249–54; S Whittaker, *Liability for Products: English Law, French Law, and European Harmonisation* (Oxford, Oxford University Press, 2005) 489–92; G Howells and M Mildred, 'Infected Blood: Defect and Discoverability, A First Exposition of the EC Product Liability Directive' (2002) 65 *Modern Law Review* 95; C Hodges, 'Compensating Patients' (2001) 117 *Law Quarterly Review* 528.

[59] R Goldberg, 'Paying for Bad Blood: Strict Liability after *A v National Blood Authority*' (2002) 10 *Medical Law Review* 165, 183.

[60] Ibid. This is consistent with Stoppa's 'dual approach' in respect of complex design defect cases: A Stoppa, 'The concept of defectiveness in the Consumer Protection Act 1987: A critical analysis' (1992) 12 *Legal Studies* 210, 217.

[61] S Whittaker, *Liability for Products: English Law, French Law, and European Harmonisation* (Oxford, Oxford University Press, 2005) 501. Both Fairgrieve and Howells concede that Burton J 'may even have gone too far in his concern to avoid slipping back into a negligence-type analysis by totally excluding factors such as avoidability from the list of relevant circumstances and rejecting any scope for the application of the risk:utility analysis': D Fairgrieve and G Howells, 'Rethinking Product Liability: A Missing Element in the European Commission's Third Review of the European Product Liability Directive' (2007) 70 *Modern Law Review* 962, 968.

[62] Ibid. In his view, if the European Court of Justice treated the issue as one of interpretation, it should not feel obligated by the references in the Directive's preamble to 'liability without fault' to restrict the range of circumstances adumbrated in art 6 in order to exclude avoidability: ibid 493. That there is an absence of analysis of avoidability of a harmful characteristic as a legal issue in French cases assessing defectiveness is explained by Whittaker, as being due to treatment of this question by the juges du fond as a matter of fact rather than law.

[63] See further, R Goldberg, 'Paying for Bad Blood: Strict Liability after *A v National Blood Authority*' (2002) 10 *Medical Law Review* 165, 183, 191–95. Professor Teff notes that some of the unease about Burton J's refusal to countenance a risk-utility approach stemmed from the policy issues raised and that the case 'highlights the predicament of a public body, under a legal duty to provide a vital commodity, but unable to spread its losses': H Teff, 'Products Liability' in A Grubb, J Lang and J McHale (eds), *Principles of Medical Law*, 3rd edn (Oxford, Oxford University Press, 2010) para 18.78.

the risk.[64] However, this is a high hurdle to overcome since in such matters the public at large may well have no such information and knowledge.[65] Indeed, while increasing consumer information may be a positive objective in the blood context, 'it is not at all clear that informing the public of the risk is helpful or actually enhances the consumer's choice'.[66]

It is also entirely possible that with such community-used natural resources as blood a previously uninformed and representative cross-section of the public would agree, after the event and having acquired such knowledge, that a low, but inevitable, risk was consistent with the standard of safety which was legitimately to be expected, albeit that this would not be so in the case of an equivalent risk of exploding bottles or car tyres. It may be objected that basing conclusions on legitimate public expectations as to safety where there is no pre-existing knowledge of the dangers associated with a product would be unsatisfactory. However, the overall conclusion of Burton J would have been more compelling if he had given some explanation as to why the knowledge of the medical profession treating the patients was not in point. As to this he said no more than that:

> Doctors and surgeons knew, but did not tell their patients unless asked, and were very rarely asked. It was certainly, in my judgment, not known and accepted by society that there was such a risk, which was thus not 'sozialadäquat' (socially acceptable).[67]

He later added:

> There were no warnings and no material publicity, certainly none officially initiated by or for the benefit of the defendants, and the knowledge of the medical profession, not materially or at all shared with the consumer, is of no relevance.[68]

There are clear comparisons to be drawn here with the learned intermediary rule which operates against the background of a general expectation that doctors and others will explain the nature and extent of risks involved in any given course of action.[69] In general, it is right to confine the rule to this type of case. Yet with infected blood there is an element of unreality in (it seems) requiring the knowledge of the medical profession to be typically shared with consumers before it becomes relevant. The patient may well be unconscious and, in any event, in life-threatening circumstances the choice between running a very small risk of infection and a highly probable death is hardly a meaningful one. It may be that in this respect blood is in a category of its own and that the position would be different where other products such as semen used in artificial insemination[70] and vaccines are concerned.[71] The test is, of course, what persons generally are *entitled* to expect and in the case of blood it can be argued that the entitlement should not be contingent on the danger having been widely publicised in advance. Nor would it be logical to distinguish between

---

[64] [2001] 3 All ER 289, para 68.

[65] Indeed, as in other areas, perceptions may be based almost entirely on impressions formed from reading incomplete or simply inaccurate accounts in the Press—or reliance on 'junk science' as Sedley LJ described the evidence against immunisation advanced in *B (A child)* [2003] EWCA Civ 1148, para 36.

[66] S Whittaker, *Liability for Products: English Law, French Law, and European Harmonisation* (Oxford, Oxford University Press, 2005) 490–91.

[67] [2001] 3 All ER 289, para 55.

[68] Ibid para 80.

[69] For discussion of the learned intermediary doctrine, see chapter 4 of this volume.

[70] As in *Kobe ter Neuzen v Korn* (1995) 127 DLR (4th) 577. See below, chapter 8 of this volume.

[71] Miller and Goldberg (above, n 3) para 10.88.

the conscious patient who is warned and an unconscious accident victim for whom no warning is possible.

It has been argued that blood products are different from medicinal products, and that the finding that people who receive blood transfusions are entitled to expect they will be free from infection 'is not a good precedent for establishing that people who take drugs are entitled to expect that they will never cause adverse reactions'.[72] While the present writer would consider that blood and medicinal products are in fact similar, at least in terms of their complexity, and that a pure unadulterated consumer expectations test, shorn of risk–utility does little to help determine defectiveness with both types of product, there is no doubt that *A v National Blood Authority* is an unhelpful precedent to follow in the context of medicinal products. Significantly, although the Full Federal Court of Australia in *Merck Sharp & Dohme (Australia) Pty Limited v Peterson*[73] upheld the decision of the trial judge that the anti-inflammatory drug Vioxx had a defect[74] in that in some people, by some unknown mechanism, it increased the risk of myocardial infarction (MI) and the supplier provided no information, advice or warning as to this effect, they nevertheless stressed that the trial judge did not find that persons generally are entitled to expect that all drugs will be free of side-effects.[75]

That there is an absence of analysis of avoidability of a harmful characteristic as a legal issue in French cases assessing defectiveness is explained by Whittaker as being due to treatment of this question by the juges du fond as a matter of fact rather than law.[76] The juges du fond have a large discretion, and the assessment of defect is 'based often on a single, uncontrovertible expert opinion, very limited documentary information as to historical facts and an opaque judicial decision all but unchallengeable before the Cour de cassation'.[77] Nonetheless, a risk–utility approach to defectiveness has been mooted by

---

[72] E Jackson, *Law and the Regulation of Medicines* (Oxford, Hart Publishing, 2012) 118.

[73] *Merck Sharp & Dohme (Australia) Pty Ltd v Peterson* [2011] FCAFC 128, leave to appeal refused, [2012] HCATrans 105.

[74] Section 75AD of Part VA of the Trade Practices Act 1974 (Cth) (now s 138 of Schedule 2 of the Competition and Consumer Act 2010 (Cth)) gives individuals the right to be compensated by a manufacturer for loss suffered by the individual as a result of injury caused by the defective goods. Part VA introduced strict liability based on the Product Liability Directive. Section 75AC of the Trade Practices Act (now s 9 of Schedule 2 of the Competition and Consumer Act 2010 (Cth)) similarly defines goods (its equivalent to a product) as being defective 'if their safety is not such as persons generally are entitled to expect'. The trial judge (Jessop J) had held that 'the safety of Vioxx was less than what persons generally were entitled to expect because, as a matter of composition, the consumption of Vioxx had the potential to increase the risk of suffering a myocardial infarction, in circumstances which included the absence of any relevant information or warning communicated to the applicant's doctor': [2010] FCA 180, (2010) 184 FCR 1, [924].

[75] *Merck Sharp & Dohme (Australia) Pty Limited v Peterson* [2011] FCAFC 128; [196]; [2010] FCA 180, (2010) 184 FCR 1, [917]. The Explanatory Memorandum to the Trade Practices Amendment Bill 1992, para 21 provides that there are known *unavoidable* side effects associated with certain pharmaceuticals and vaccines. Since such products are known to confer substantial benefits which flow to the wider community, '[t]he small statistical chance of injury associated with them does not of itself mean that they are "defective"': [2011] FCAFC 128, [191]. The trial judge had held that '[p]ersons generally are entitled to expect that, to the extent that a drug is known or believed to have side-effects, or to carry the potential for side-effects (particularly of a serious nature), practitioners will, in whatever terms, and by whatever means are appropriate, be furnished by the drug supplier with information or warnings sufficient to permit a balanced, cautious and informed judgment to be made': (2010) 184 FCR 1, [917].

[76] Ibid 492.

[77] Ibid 484.

some French courts in the context of medicinal products.[78] However, the French Cour de cassation[79] has overruled the use of a general risk–utility analysis in the determination of defectiveness in the context of the hepatitis B vaccination litigation. The Court of Appeal of Versailles[80] had ruled that the temporal proximity between the hepatitis B vaccination and the appearance of the demyelinating disease, in the absence of any other known cause for the disease, allowed a presumption that the vaccine had caused the claimant's injury. Nonetheless, the appellate court rejected the claim against the vaccine producer, by determining, utilising a risk–benefit analysis, that the vaccine was not defective.[81] The decision on defectiveness was subsequently overturned by the Cour de cassation, which held that the Court of Appeal should have checked if the elements, on the basis of which causation had been presumed, did not also allow a presumption that the vaccine was defective. The Cour de cassation suggests that defectiveness could be assessed on a case-by-case basis, independently from a 'general' risk–benefit analysis, taking into account the specific considerations of the product. In so doing, the Court has failed to provide a meaningful explanation of what the defectiveness of a vaccine means, and how it should be substantively defined.[82] The Third Commission Report on the Application of the Directive noted that the appropriateness of a court undertaking a risk–benefit analysis when assessing what a person is entitled to expect, and the extent to which the actual conduct of a producer is relevant 'have yet to be finally resolved by the courts in any Member State'.[83] It is to be hoped that the Cour de cassation's failure to articulate the position meaningfully will not be the last word on this matter, but the case clearly adds to the uncertainty over the issue. If the approach of the trial judge in *Merck Sharp & Dohme (Australia) Pty Limited v Peterson*[84] that he 'could not hold ... that persons generally are entitled to expect that all drugs will be free of side effects' was followed in the courts of Member States, there might be some currency in Professor Howells' support for an 'abstract approach to defectiveness', taking into account factors other than the product's condition, including general perceptions of safety legitimately expected.[85] However, the experience in France and in *A v National Blood*

---

[78] This risk–benefit approach had been adopted in two previous decisions involving medicinal products, viz Isomeride (Versailles, 17 March 2006, n° 04/08435; Paris, 19 June 2009, n° 06/13741) and in 3 cases involving the vaccine against hepatitis B (Versailles, 16 March 2007, n° 05/09525; 29 March 2007, n° 06/00496; 5 November 2007, n° 06/106435).

[79] Cass civ 1, 26 September 2012, n° 11-17.738.

[80] Cour d'appel de Versailles, 10 February 2011.

[81] This risk–benefit approach had been adopted in two previous decisions involving medicinal products, viz Isomeride (Versailles, 17 March 2006, n° 04/08435; Paris, 19 June 2009, n° 06/13741) and in 3 cases involving the vaccine against hepatitis B (Versailles, 16 March 2007, n° 05/09525; 29 March 2007, n° 06/00496; 5 November 2007, n° 06/106435).

[82] J-S Borghetti, 'Qu'est-ce qu'un vaccin défectueux?', *Recueil Dalloz* 2012, 2853. This approach of examining all elements at hand, when considering the product's defectiveness and the existence of a causal link has been upheld by the Cour de cassation: Cass civ 1, 29 May 2013, n° 12-20.9033. See ch 3, 6.

[83] Third Commission Report of 31 January 2001 on the Application of Directive 85/374 on liability for defective products, COM(2006) 496 final, 10.

[84] [2010] FCA 180, (2010) 184 FCR 1, [917].

[85] G Howells, 'Defect in English Law—Lessons for the Harmonisation of European Product Liability Litigation' in D Fairgrieve (ed), *Product Liability in Comparative Perspective* (Cambridge, Cambridge University Press 2005) 141, 152. Howells concedes that avoidability should be considered in determining defectiveness under his abstract approach, but only as one of a range of factors: ibid 143. cf Professor Newdick, who submits that there are three issues crucial to the question of defectiveness and medicinal products, viz the requirement of balancing the benefits with the risks of taking medicines; the relevance of warnings and instructions that can render drugs safer; and the significance of regulatory approval by the licensing authority: C Newdick, 'Special Problems of Compensating

Authority suggests that there is a danger if these courts were to adopt this approach that they would resort to 'near equation of *actual* and *legitimate* expectations'[86] in the context of medicinal products and blood products.

E. The Defect Taxonomy

(i) The Traditional Taxonomy

The definitions of defect in Article 6 of the Directive and section 3 of the Act do not distinguish explicitly between manufacturing or production defects and defects in a product's design or through a failure to warn.[87] By contrast, the American *Third Restatement* on Products Liability has abandoned the doctrinal labels of strict liability and negligence and established separate functional definitions of liability for the traditional three types of defect taxonomy, namely a manufacturing defect,[88] a design defect,[89] and a warning defect.[90] Notwithstanding the absence of such functional definitions in the Directive and the Act, it has been said that the traditional distinction between manufacturing defects, design defects, and failure to warn defects is 'probably how the courts would tackle the problem in practice'.[91] As will be seen, the traditional form of classification is arguably the one most suited to medicinal products.

(ii) The Alternative Taxonomy: Burton J's Standard/Non-standard Product Dichotomy[92]

In line with the traditional taxonomy of product defects, the claimants in *A v National Blood Authority* submitted that the infected blood was a manufacturing defect and that the blood products were thus 'rogue products' or 'lemons', whereas the defendants submitted that if the infected blood were a defect, it was a design defect.[93] However, Burton J concluded, that no assistance could be gained from the 'boxing' or categorisation of defects in

---

Those Damaged by Medicinal Products' in SAM McLean (ed), *Compensation for Damage: An International Perspective* (Aldershot, Dartmouth, 1993) 8. For further discussion of risk–benefits, warnings and instructions and the impact of regulatory approval on defectiveness, see chapters 3, 4, and 7 of this volume respectively.

[86] H Teff, 'Products Liability' in A Grubb, J Lang and J McHale (eds), *Principles of Medical Law*, 3rd edn (Oxford, Oxford University Press, 2010) para 18.77.

[87] Similarly, section 75AC of the Australian Trade Practices Act 1974 (Cth) also does not distinguish between these categories of defects. However, the Explanatory Memorandum to the Trade Practices Amendment Bill 1992, para 15 makes this distinction by utilising the traditional categories of design defects, which relate 'to matters such as the form, structure and composition of the goods', manufacturing defects, relating 'to matters such as the process of construction and assembly' and instructional defects, ie 'those caused by incorrect or inadequate warnings and instructions'. The Memorandum explains that all these categories of defect are deemed to fall within the meaning ascribed to a defect in s 75AC.

[88] *Restatement, Third, Torts: Products Liability* § 2(a).

[89] Ibid § 2(b).

[90] Ibid § 2(c).

[91] A Stoppa, 'The Concept of Defect in the Consumer Protection Act 1987: a Critical Analysis' (1992) 12 *Legal Studies* 210, 211.

[92] This section builds on the author's commentary in R Goldberg, 'Paying for Bad Blood: Strict Product Liability after *A v National Blood Authority*' (2002) 10 *Medical Law Review* 165, 179–87.

[93] *A v National Blood Authority* [2001] 3 All ER 289, [36], [39].

this way.[94] Instead, he preferred the distinction between a 'standard' and a 'non-standard' product which he drew as follows:[95]

> [A] *standard* product is one which is and performs as the producer intends. A *non-standard* product is one which is different, obviously because it is deficient or inferior in terms of safety, from the standard product: and where it is the harmful characteristic or characteristics present in the non-standard product, but not in the standard product, which has or have caused the material injury or damage.

On the basis of this taxonomy, the claimants submitted that the infected bags of blood were non-standard products. The defendants disagreed, and submitted that they were standard products since 'all blood, derived as it is from a natural raw material, albeit then processed, is inherently risky'.[96] Describing the latter approach as 'very philosophical', Burton J concluded that the infected bags of blood were 'non-standard' products[97] and went on to develop his own steps for consideration of Article 6 of the Directive, which were related to his standard/non-standard product bifurcation.

The first step was to identify the harmful characteristic which caused the injury.[98] Since it was clear that the hepatitis C virus in the whole blood was the harmful characteristic which caused the patients to contract hepatitis, there was no difficulty. But it seems that one would have to ascertain the factual causal link between defect and damage before the first step could be satisfied. Burton J is thus identifying the primacy of causation before any investigation of defect can take place. This could result in a vigorous contest of the causation issue at a preliminary stage and could also involve a requirement that the claimant prove the respect in which the product is alleged to be defective with a relatively high level of specificity.

Burton J then stated that to establish whether there was a defect within the meaning of Article 6, 'the next step will be to conclude whether the product is standard or non-standard'.[99] He adopts this taxonomy, notwithstanding the absence of such an approach in European Community or American law. In the absence of admission by the producer, he said that this would be done 'by comparing the offending product with other products of the same type or series produced by that producer'.[100] If the respect in which the offending product differs from the series includes the harmful characteristic, then it is a non-standard

---

[94] Ibid para 39.

[95] Ibid para 36.

[96] Ibid para 37.

[97] Ibid para 65. Cf GW Conk, 'The True Test: Alternative Safer Designs for Drugs and Medical Devices in a Patent-Constrained Market' 49 *UCLA Law Review* 737, 772–3 (2002) who submits in an analogous context involving haemophiliacs that such cases involve design and not manufacturing defects since: 'Every batch of the concentrated blood proteins was made without departure from its intended design.' This was, in effect, a reiteration of a his view in GW Conk, 'Is There a Design Defect in the Restatement (Third) of Torts: Products Liability?' (2000) 109 *Yale Law Journal* 1087, 1098–1101, 1111–14, 1117. But see, JA Henderson Jr and AD Twerski, 'Drug Designs *Are* Different' (2001) 111 *Yale Law Journal* 151, 160–61 (cases were not design defects but strict liability manufacturing defects, though § 2(b) *Restatement, Third, Torts: Products Liability* applied to the design of the defendant's *method of production* rather than the products themselves) and L Noah, 'This is Your Products Liability Restatement on Drugs' (2009) 74 *Brooklyn Law Review* 839, 916, fn 332 (citing *Restatement, Third, Torts: Products Liability* § 19 cmt *c* (1998): in the absence of blood shield statutes, cases involve product contamination and would lead to 'an imposition of strict product liability for manufacturing defects').

[98] [2001] 3 All ER 289, [67]. Dir 85/374/EEC, Art 4, provides that: 'The injured person shall be required to prove the damage, the defect and the causal relationship between the defect and the damage'.

[99] [2001] 3 All ER 289, [67].

[100] Ibid.

product. Conversely, if the offending product does not so differ, or if the respect in which it differs does not include the harmful characteristic, but all the other products, albeit different, share the harmful characteristic, then it is to be treated as a standard product.[101] Thus, for example, in the case of thalidomide, the harmful characteristic would appear to be the drug structure itself, and since the drug as a whole shared the harmful characteristic, it would appear to be a standard product. On the other hand, hepatitis C-infected blood is to be treated as a non-standard product since the harmful characteristic was not present in all bags of blood.

There are several points to be made about this attempt to shift away from the type of defect (manufacturing, design, or a failure to warn) to the type of product (standard or non-standard). Although Burton J was at pains to avoid the traditional 'boxing' or categorisation of defects, it is difficult to see how his own classification differs from it, other than in terminology. Thus 'non-standard' products are substituted for manufacturing defects, 'standard products' are associated with design defects, 'non-standard' products appear to be essentially the same as products which have manufacturing defects and 'standard products' are those with inherent design flaws. It is perhaps the case that he was reluctant to describe as a manufacturing defect a situation where the defect was not *positively created* by a manufacturing process, but involved, rather, a *failure to eliminate an infection* in a 'natural' product.[102] Nonetheless, it is arguable that the expression 'manufacturing defect' would normally be regarded as a suitable shorthand for describing both situations.[103] It is also possible that the suggested terminology was adopted in an attempt to avoid the terminology of § 2 of the *Third Restatement*, with its avowed emphasis on a risk–benefit approach, and its rejection of the consumer expectation approach of § 402A of the *Second Restatement*, in assessing defectiveness.[104] Unfortunately, no guidance is to be gained from the *Third Restatement* in respect of blood or blood products, other than the fact that they are expressly excluded from the rules of the *Restatement* under § 19(c). In any event, it seems clear that, at least in respect of *non-standard* products, Burton J was seeking to minimise the extent to which a risk–benefit analysis could enter into the assessment of defectiveness. Thus he rejects[105] the view of Lord Griffiths et al that, although English judges would not overtly adopt a risk–benefit approach, they would 'as an educated response to the facts of a particular case undertake a balancing exercise of an analogous kind'.[106] In Sir Michael's judgment the adoption of risk-utility would, it seems, be a permissible exercise only in the context of deciding 'whether—with full information and proper knowledge—the public does and ought to accept the risk'.[107] It is only with such information and knowledge that legitimate public expectations would be shaped by a risk–benefit assessment.

---

[101]   Ibid.

[102]   The distinction is seen as important by Prof Stapleton in her instructive discussion of pre-manufacture generic infection cases: see 'Bugs in Anglo-American Products Liability' (2002) 53 *South Carolina Law Review* 1225, esp 1232–34.

[103]   Miller and Goldberg (above, n 3) para 10.95. For criticism of the distinction between standard and non-standard products as problematic, see S Whittaker, *Liability for Products: English Law, French Law, and European Harmonisation* (Oxford, Oxford University Press, 2005) 491.

[104]   For further detail on the *Third Restatement*, see J Stapleton, 'Restatement (Third) of Torts: Products Liability, an Anglo-Australian Perspective' (2000) 39 *Washburn Law Journal* 363, 376.

[105]   [2001] 3 All ER 289, [69].

[106]   Rt Hon The Lord Griffiths, P de Val, RJ Dormer, 'Developments in English Product Liability Law: A comparison with the American System' (1988) 62 *Tulane Law Review* 353, 382.

[107]   [2001] 3 All ER 289, [68].

In addressing his approach to 'standard' products and the assessment of defectiveness, Burton J said:[108]

> If a standard product is unsafe, it is likely to be so as a result of alleged error in design, or at any rate as a result of an allegedly flawed system. The harmful characteristic must be identified, if necessary with the assistance of experts. The question of presentation/time/circumstances of supply/social acceptability etc will arise as above. The sole question will be safety for the foreseeable use. If there are any comparable products on the market, then it will obviously be relevant to compare the offending product with those other products, so as to identify, compare and contrast the relevant features. There will obviously need to be a full understanding of how the product works—particularly if it is a new product, such as a scrid,[109] so as to assess its safety for such use. Price is obviously a significant factor in legitimate expectation, and may well be material in the comparative process. But again it seems to me there is no room in the basket: for: (i) what the producer could have done differently; and (ii) whether the producer could or could not have done the same as the others did.

The above passage is of significance for several reasons. It links the concept of a 'standard' product to alleged errors in design and acknowledges the obvious need to compare the product with 'comparable products on the market', thus pointing to a reasonable alternative design approach to design defects, as in § 2(b) of the *Third Restatement*.[110] However, in the *Restatement*, and probably more generally in the United States, the 'reasonable alternative design' approach is accorded primacy and at the *expense* of a consumer expectations-based approach.[111] Price is also regarded as an important factor in legitimate expectation and may be material in the comparative process.[112] However, there is, in Burton J's judgment, no room for consideration of (i) what the producer could have done differently, and (ii) whether the producer could or could not have done the same thing as the others did.

An important question emerging from the above is what is envisaged as being *excluded* from consideration. Clearly, it cannot be a comparison with the relevant safety features of comparable products. Indeed, these are expressly included, as is price. Nor, in the case of

---

[108] Ibid [71].

[109] The word 'scrid' was coined to describe a new product of which the public had no actual expectation: ibid [31].

[110] Section 2(b) provides that: [A product] 'is defective in design when the foreseeable risks of harm posed by the product could have been reduced or avoided by the adoption of a reasonable alternative design by the seller or other distributor, or a predecessor in the commercial chain of distribution, and the omission of the alternative design renders the product not reasonably safe'.

[111] See J Stapleton, 'Restatement (Third) of Torts: Products Liability, an Anglo-Australian Perspective' (2000) 39 *Washburn Law Journal* 363, 376. The adoption of the 'reasonable alternative design standard' in 'classic design defect cases' reflects the consensus view, and consumer expectation is regarded as an inappropriate standard for defectiveness in such cases: JA Henderson Jr and AD Twerksi, 'Achieving Consensus on Defective Product Design' (1998) 83 *Cornell Law Review* 867, 872, 879, 901, 920. Classic design defect cases are 'the majority of design cases that do not involve product malfunctions, violations of safety regulations or egregiously dangerous products': JA Henderson Jr and AD Twerski, 'What Europe, Japan and other Countries can learn from the new American Restatement of Products Liability' (1999) 34 *Texas International Law Journal* 1, 17. Professor Stapleton, however, regards the classic design defect category as a residuary one, which has been over-emphasised by its primacy in § 2(c): Stapleton (above) (2000) 39 *Washburn Law Journal* 363, 386.

[112] Cf the conclusion that the sales and pricing structure of the drug in issue (Epilin) and profit made from it could not 'sensibly inform the question' whether the product was defective at the time of supply: *Claimants Registered in the GLO v Sanofi-Synthelabo Ltd* [2009] EWHC 95 (QB), [16 i], Burnett J. Accordingly, an application by the claimants to adduce expert evidence of a forensic accountant concerning the worldwide value of sales of Epilim and its profitability since it first went onto the market, together with evidence of the pricing structures in place which governed sales to the NHS, was rejected: ibid [28].

standard products, is there *expressly* any exclusion of a risk–utility analysis as an element shaping legitimate consumer expectations.[113] However, his assessment of the travaux pré-paratoires to the Directive, which he claimed had rejected risk–utility analysis,[114] suggests that, in his view, risk–utility may have no role to play in the context of design defects either.[115] What is clearly excluded is a comparison with what might have been done differently in a respect which would otherwise have been relevant in the discovery of the condition which gave rise to the danger. This was, of course, the very issue in the hepatitis C litigation itself and it was seen by Burton J as being the province of the very narrow development risk defence afforded by Article 7(e) of the Directive and section 4(1)(e) of the 1987 Act.[116]

A problem with Burton J's approach to 'standard' products and the assessment of defectiveness is that it is doubtful whether a reasonable alternative design method could be of assistance in respect of medicinal products or whole blood products. As Professor Michael Green has noted: 'Unlike durable goods, drugs cannot be designed in an alternative fashion, at least not in the light of current technological capabilities'.[117] In a similar style, Professor David Owen submits that a drug's design 'normally' cannot be changed to improve its safety.[118] As we shall see, the *Restatement, Third, Torts: Products Liability* avoids the reasonable alternative design test of § 2(b) and adopts a so-called net benefit test for pharmaceuticals and medical devices in § 6(c).[119] Nevertheless, it is arguable that there are some exceptions to the rule that drugs are not amenable to design modification to build in more safety, viz where the danger in some drugs may be reduced by altering prescribed dosage, omitting active ingredients in combination drugs, or changing inert ingredients used in a drug.[120] The use of bioengineering to design drugs to improve their benefit–risk ratio is a further possible

---

[113] This is mentioned only as an item (number (iii)) under the heading '*Non-standard products*', but it does not appear under the heading '*Standard products*': see respectively, [2001] 3 All ER 289, [68] and [71].

[114] Ibid [35], [43].

[115] See I Dodds-Smith, M Spencer and J Bore, 'Product Liability for Medicinal Products' in MJ Powers, NH Harris and A Barton (eds), *Clinical Negligence*, 4th edn (London, Tottel Publishing, 2008) para 24.59.

[116] For discussion of the development risk defence, see chapter 8 of this volume.

[117] MD Green, 'Statutory Compliance and Tort Liability: Examining the Strongest Case' (1997) 30 *University of Michigan Journal of Law Reform* 461, 471; MD Green, 'Prescription Drugs, Alternative Designs and the Restatement (Third): Preliminary Reflections' (1999) 30 *Seton Hall Law Review* 207, 208–11.

[118] DG Owen, 'Dangers in Prescription Drugs: Filling a Private Law Gap in the Healthcare Debate' (2010) 42 *Conneticut Law Review* 733, 739.

[119] Section 6(c) provides: 'A prescription drug or medical device is not reasonably safe due to defective design if the foreseeable risks of harm posed by the drug or medical device are sufficiently great in relation to its foreseeable therapeutic benefits that reasonable health-care providers, knowing of such foreseeable risks and therapeutic benefits, would not prescribe the drug or medical device for any class of patients'. See further, chapter 3 of this volume.

[120] MD Green, (1997) 30 *University Michigan Journal Law Reform* 461, 474; see further, MD Green, (1999) 30 *Seton Hall Law Review* 207, 210–12. Since combination drugs contain multiple active ingredients they can be designed differently by removing or adding active ingredients. Green gives an example of Fiorinal, a prescription drug for headaches, which originally contained a barbiturate, aspirin, caffeine, and phenacetin (an analgesic). In 1981, the phenacetin was removed from the market because of safety concerns. Fiorinal, was redesigned without the phenacetin component. The second exception is that of recommended dose. Experience with a drug, eg an oral contraceptive, may reveal that the same therapeutic benefits could be obtained with a lower dose, and that reducing the dose decreases the risk of adverse effects: see *Brochu v Ortho Pharmaceutical Corp* 642 F 2d 652 (1981), where absence of reference in a package insert to finding a 'positive correlation ... between the dose of oestrogen and the risk of ... cerebral thrombosis' was held to be a ground for upholding a jury finding that the manufacturer's warnings were factually inaccurate and that the pill was defective and unreasonably dangerous: ibid 655, 658–59.

exception.[121] However, there appears to be no reasonable alternative to whole blood.[122] So-called recombinant anti-haemophilic globulin (AHG) for the treatment of haemophiliacs is no substitute. Moreover, there remains no effective method of inactivating the hepatitis C virus or AIDS virus in whole blood or non-plasma products, eg red blood cells, white blood cells and platelets, despite the fact that physical heat or chemical detergents can inactivate the virus in plasma products.[123] It is, therefore, difficult to see how Burton J's standard/non-standard product dichotomy adds to any clarity in establishing a taxonomy of defects in medicinal products.

IV. CONCLUSION

Arguably the single most difficult part of the Product Liability Directive and Part I of the 1987 Act, the core definition of a defect, has been widely held to contain substantial overtones of a negligence standard. Nowhere is the challenge of determining whether a product is defective more complex than in the context of medicinal products. We have seen that the definition of defect in Article 6 of the Product Liability Directive and section 3 of the Consumer Protection Act 1987 is greatly challenged by the complexity of medicinal products, and the paucity of case law on the topic has done little to help matters. Indeed, when some cases have been decided on defective products and blood or medicinal products, they have failed to understand the special problems created by such products. In *A v National Blood Authority*, it is respectfully submitted that Burton J's choice of a consumer expectation approach and a rejection of a risk–utility analysis and avoidability of a harmful characteristic in determining whether hepatitis C blood was defective, was an overly intuitive response to the problem. The decision of the Cour de cassation[124] to overrule the use of a general risk–utility analysis in the determination of defectiveness in the context of the hepatitis B vaccination litigation and to assess defectiveness on a case-by-case basis is problematic, since the Court failed to provide a meaningful explanation of what the defectiveness of a vaccine means, and how it should be substantively defined.

Since we have seen it is difficult to see how Burton J's standard/non-standard product dichotomy adds any clarity in establishing a taxonomy of defects in medicinal products,[125] the following chapters will examine the application of the defectiveness standard in the context of the traditional defect taxonomy of manufacturing or production defects, design defects and defects arising through a failure to warn. The principle focus will be on design defects and failure to warn, since these are where the main controversies concerning defective medicinal products lie. It will also be instructive to turn to the extensive experience of design defects and warning defects in the context of prescription drugs in the United States. It is to this, in the context of design defects, that we now turn.

---

[121] MD Green, (1999) 30 *Seton Hall Law Review* 207, 210–12.

[122] Any biotechnologically produced blood products, such as recombinant AHG (anti-haemophilic globulin) only concern plasma products.

[123] See GW Conk, 'Is there a Design Defect in the Restatement (Third) of Torts: Products Liability?' (2000) 109 *Yale Law Review* 1087, 1109, citing Institute of Medicine, *HIV and the Blood Supply: An Analysis of Crisis Decisionmaking* (National Academy Press, 1995) 5, 81.

[124] Cass civ 1, 26 September 2012, n° 11-17.738.

[125] While the basic principles of legitimate expectation in *A* were applied in *B (A Child) v MacDonald's* [2002] EWHC 490, QBD, no reference was made to the standard/non-standard product dichotomy.

3

Design Defects and Medicinal Products

I. INTRODUCTION

Medicinal products may be defective if they are unsafe for their intended or contemplated purpose because of a basic design deficiency. Design defects are the most problematic category of defects in medicinal products since the concept of safety is harder to apply to such products, where safety is a relative concept.[1] While in the United States the issue of design defect liability for prescription products seems secondary,[2] virtually all of the important product liability litigation in the United Kingdom concerning medicinal products relates to design defects.[3]

This chapter examines the US experience of dealing with design defects and pharmaceutical products, including an analysis of comment *k* of § 402A of the *Restatement, Second, Torts* and the so-called net benefit test of § 6(c) of the *Restatement, Third, Torts: Products Liability* for prescription drugs. In the light of this US experience, it attempts to comprehend the true nature of a medicinal product design defect under the Product Liability Directive and to devise a coherent and workable approach for determining whether a medicinal product's design is defective. It will be submitted that some form of analysis of the benefits and disadvantages associated with a medicinal product (or risk–utility) cannot realistically be avoided in this context.

---

[1] I Dodds-Smith, M Spencer and J Bore, 'Product Liability for Medicinal Products' in MJ Powers, NH Harris and A Barton (eds), *Clinical Negligence*, 4th edn (London, Tottel Publishing, 2008) para 24.78.

[2] As Professor Owen has noted, the issue of drug design defectiveness is 'a troublesome but largely phantom issue in modern drug litigation': DG Owen, 'Dangers in Prescription Drugs: Filling a Private Law Gap in the Healthcare Debate' (2010) 42 *Conneticut Law Review* 733, 750; and see, also, Mike Green, who states that 'the liability game is with the warnings candle, not with design': MD Green, 'Prescription Drugs, Alternative Designs and the Restatement (Third): Preliminary Reflections' (1999) 30 *Seton Hall Law Review* 207, 209.

[3] I Dodds-Smith, M Spencer and J Bore, 'Product Liability for Medicinal Products' in MJ Powers, NH Harris and A Barton (eds), *Clinical Negligence*, 4th edn (London, Tottel Publishing, 2008) para 24.81 and fn 6 (citing the MMR/MR litigation, the third generation oral contraceptive litigation and the foetal anti-convulsant litigation).

II. DESIGN DEFECTS AND PHARMACEUTICAL PRODUCTS: THE US EXPERIENCE

A. Comment *K*

(i) General

In the absence of a developed body of case law in the United Kingdom, it is again useful to refer to the position as it has developed in the United States, where much of the case law on design defects and prescription drugs has been influenced by the *Restatement, Second, Torts* § 402A. Section 402A does not distinguish between prescription and other products and hence liability is imposed where the product is 'in a defective condition unreasonably dangerous to the user or consumer' even where 'the seller has exercised all possible care in the preparation and sale of his product'.[4]

It has been widely recognised that there are inherent difficulties in applying strict tort liability to prescription drugs. For instance, strict liability—through defendants' fear of large adverse monetary judgments—might result in reduction in innovation and hence the availability of pharmaceuticals, and it has been suggested that the additional expense of insuring against such liability 'could place the cost of medication beyond the reach of those who need it most'.[5] Similarly, in *Kearl v Lederle Laboratories*,[6] which involved an oral polio vaccine, the appellate court, in reversing the trial court's approval of a standard of strict liability for design defects, observed that the application of such a strict liability standard could cause delay in the marketing of pharmaceutical products and could deter their research, manufacturing and marketing.[7] The Court added that while strict liability was 'socially beneficial in the vast majority of products cases', 'it might not be appropriate with regard to some special products that are extremely beneficial to society and yet pose an inherent and substantial risk that is unavoidable at the time of distribution'.[8]

The much cited comment *k* of § 402A specifically addresses such concerns. In acknowledging that many pharmaceutical products, including prescription products, 'are quite incapable of being made safe for their intended and ordinary use', the comment establishes that both the marketing and the use of such products are fully justified, notwithstanding the unavoidable high degree of risk which they involve. Such a product, comment *k* explains, 'properly prepared, and accompanied by proper directions and warnings, is not defective nor is it unreasonably dangerous'.[9] Comment *k* adds that this is also true of

---

[4] See § 402A(1) and (2)(a) and, in general, DG Owen, *Products Liability Law*, 2nd edn (St Paul, MN, 2008) § 5.3.

[5] *Brown v Superior Court (Abbott Laboratories)* 751 P 2d 470, 479 (1988) (Cal Sup Ct.).

[6] *Kearl v Lederle Laboratories* 218 Cal Rptr 453 (Cal App, 1985).

[7] Ibid 458–59.

[8] Ibid 459.

[9] The full text of Comment *k* provides:

'*k*. Unavoidably Unsafe Products. There are some products which, in the present state of human knowledge, are quite incapable of being made safe for their intended and ordinary use. These are especially common in the field of drugs. An outstanding example is the vaccine for the Pasteur treatment of rabies, which not uncommonly leads to very serious and damaging consequences when it is injected. Since the disease itself invariably leads to a dreadful death, both the marketing and the use of the vaccine are fully justified, notwithstanding the unavoidable high degree of risk which they involve. Such a product, properly prepared, and accompanied by proper directions and warning, is not defective, nor is it *unreasonably* dangerous. The same

many new or experimental drugs as to which, because of lack of time and opportunity for sufficient medical experience, there can be no assurance of safety ... but such experience as there is justifies the marketing and use of the drug notwithstanding a medically recognizable risk.[10]

The rationale behind comment *k* is therefore to 'strike a balance between a manufacturer's responsibility and the encouragement of research and development of new products'.[11] Most American courts (30 States and the District of Columbia) have accepted that comment *k* correctly exempts prescription drugs from strict liability, providing that they are properly prepared and accompanied by adequate directions and warnings.[12] Conversely, this means that a prescription product with inadequate packaging, labelling, warnings, or instructions will not fall within the protection of comment *k* and so will constitute a defective and unreasonably dangerous product.[13] The application of comment *k* to prescription pharmaceuticals is exemplified in the Ohio Supreme Court's decision of *White v Wyeth Laboratories Inc*,[14] where the manufacturer of diphtheria, tetanus, pertussis (DTP) wholecell vaccine was held not to be strictly liable for a child's encephalopathy and mental retardation, the Court holding that DTP was an unavoidably unsafe product. Whether such a product qualified as 'unavoidably unsafe' under comment *k* was a determination to be made on a case-by-case basis.[15] At the time that the DTP was administered to the child, the manufacturer could not have legally marketed an alternative pertussis vaccine that was equally effective but with less risk.[16] In addition, the Court held that the evidence overwhelmingly demonstrated that the warnings of side-effects and adverse reactions were adequate.[17]

(ii) The Extent of Comment K's Application: Unavoidably Unsafe Drugs or All Prescription Drugs?

There is considerable disagreement over the extent of comment *k*'s application. A lack of consensus subsists in whether comment *k* applies to all prescription drugs or whether such an application is confined to a preliminary determination (by court or jury) of the drug in issue as 'unavoidably unsafe'. In *Feldman v Lederle Laboratories*,[18] the Supreme Court of

---

is true of many other drugs, vaccines, and the like, many of which for this very reason cannot legally be sold except to physicians, or under the prescription of a physician. It is also true in particular of many new or experimental drugs as to which, because of lack of time and opportunity for sufficient medical experience, there can be no assurance of safety, or perhaps even of purity of ingredients, but such experience as there is justifies the marketing and use of the drug notwithstanding a medically recognizable risk. The seller of such products, again with the qualification that they are properly prepared and marketed, and proper warning is given, where the situation calls for it, is not to be held to strict liability for unfortunate consequences attending their use, merely because he has undertaken to supply the public with an apparently useful and desirable product, attended with a known but apparently reasonable risk'.

[10] Ibid.
[11] F Woodside, *Drug Product Liability* (NJ, Mathew Bender, 2010), vol 2, ch 14, § 14.06[4][b], 14-192.5.
[12] DG Owen (above, n 2) (2010) 42 *Conneticut Law Review* 733, 744 (citing LR Frumer, MI Friedman, CS Sklaren, *Products Liability* (NJ, Mathew Bender, 2011) § 8.07[3]).
[13] DG Owen, *Products Liability Law*, 2nd edn (St Paul, MN, Thomson/West, 2008) § 8.10; *Madden & Owen on Products Liability*, § 22:2.
[14] *White v Wyeth Laboratories Inc* 533 NE 2d 748 (1988).
[15] Ibid 752.
[16] Ibid.
[17] Ibid 755.
[18] *Feldman v Lederle Laboratories* 479 A 2d 374 (NJ 1984).

New Jersey ruled that whether a drug qualified for the protection of comment *k* by being unavoidably unsafe should be determined on a case-by-case basis.[19] The *Feldman* approach was developed in *Kearl v Lederle Laboratories*,[20] where a California intermediate appellate court set forth a risk–benefit analysis—to be carried out at a 'mini trial' before a judge—as a prerequisite to determining whether comment *k* exempted the drug from strict liability.[21] In the landmark case of *Brown v Superior Court (Abbott Laboratories)*,[22] the California Supreme Court rejected the requirement of *Kearl* that comment *k* should only be applied if the manufacturer could convince a judge that the drug was 'unavoidably dangerous',[23] on the grounds that such a requirement would substantially impair the public interest in the development and marketing of new drugs. Without the protection of comment *k*, a manufacturer's incentive to develop a superior product would be diminished since it could be held strictly liable for harmful side-effects if a trial court later decided that another product which was on the market would have achieved the same result.[24] The Court concluded that comment *k* presumptively applied to all prescription pharmaceuticals,[25] thus obviating the need for a case-by-case determination of whether the product qualified as 'unavoidably unsafe'.

However, while a few courts have followed *Brown* in applying the exemption to all prescription drugs,[26] such a presumption of blanket immunity has not been favoured by the majority,[27] which have adopted the *Feldman/Kearl* case-by-case approach on the grounds of a reluctance 'to surrender judicial oversight'[28] of a drug manufacturer's responsibility for design safety. For example, in *Freeman v Hoffman-La Roche Inc*,[29] a case involving a prescription acne medication, the Supreme Court of Nebraska concluded that comment *k* operated as an affirmative defence when the standard consumer expectation test of a defect had been established, and that it should be construed as exempting the prescription drug producer from strict liability 'when it is shown that (1) the product is properly manufactured and

---

[19] Ibid, 383.

[20] *Kearl v Lederle Laboratories* 218 Cal Rptr 453 (Cal App 1985).

[21] Ibid 463–64. The trial court would decide to exempt a product from strict liability only after first taking evidence outside the jury's presence as to: '(1) whether, when distributed, the product was intended to confer an exceptionally important benefit that made its availability highly desirable; (2) whether the then-existing risk posed by the product both was "substantial" and "unavoidable"; and (3) whether the interest in availability (again measured at the time of distribution) outweighs the interest in promoting enhanced accountability through strict liability design defect review': ibid 464.

[22] *Brown v Superior Court (Abbott Laboratories)* 751 P 2d 470 (Cal 1988).

[23] Ibid 482.

[24] Ibid 481–82.

[25] Ibid 482.

[26] See, eg, *Transue v Aesthetech* 341 F 3d 911, 916 (9th Cir 2003) (Washington Supreme Court would be likely to hold that all medical devices and products will be afforded comment *k* exemption); *McKee v Moore* 648 P 2d 21, 24 (Okla 1982); *Adams v Wyeth* No 3452, 2005 WL 1528656 (Pa Com Pl) at *3; *Grundberg v Upjohn Co* 813 P 2d 89, 95 (Utah 1991) (holding that 'all prescription drugs should be classified as unavoidably dangerous in design because of their unique nature and value, the elaborate regulatory system overseen by the FDA, the difficulty of relying on individual lawsuits as a forum in which to review a prescription drug's design, and the significant public policy considerations noted in *Brown*').

[27] See, eg, *Hill v Wyeth, Inc*, 2007 WL 674251 at *4; (ED Mo); *Bryant v Hoffman-La Roche, Inc* 585 SE 2d 723, 728 (Ga App 2003); *Bennett v Madakasira* 821 So 2d 794, 809 (Miss 2002); *Freeman v Hoffman-La Roche Inc* 618 NW 2d 827, 837, 840 (Neb 2000); *Glassman v Wyeth Labs, Inc* 606 NE 2d 338, 342 (Ill App Ct 1992); *West v Searle & Co* 806 SW 2d 608, 612 (Ark 1991); *Adams v GD Searle & Co* 576 So 2d 728, 733 (Fla App 2 Dist, 1991); *Savina v Sterling Drug, Inc* 795 P 2d 915, 924 (Kan 1990); *White v Wyeth Laboratories Inc* 533 NE 2d 748, 752 (Ohio 1988); *Castrignano v ER Squibb & Sons, Inc* 546 A 2d 775, 781 (RI 1988); *Toner v Lederele Laboratories* 732 P 2d 297, 308 (Idaho 1987).

[28] DG Owen (above, n 2) (2010) 42 *Connecticut Law Review* 733, 746.

[29] *Freeman v Hoffman-La Roche Inc* 618 NW 2d 827, 837, 840 (Neb 2000).

contains adequate warnings, (2) its benefits justify its risks, and (3) the product was at the time of manufacture and distribution incapable of being made more safe'.[30]

The majority of jurisdictions rely on comment k to apply what is effectively a negligence standard.[31] In particular, the important decision of the Californian Supreme Court in *Brown v Superior Court (Abbott Laboratories)*[32] suggests, in the context of a case involving the prescription drug diethylstilbestrol, the need to find fault on the part of the pharmaceutical producer before liability may be imposed. The Court concluded that

> comment k, by focusing on the blameworthiness of the manufacturer, sets forth a test which sounds in negligence, while imposition of liability for failure to warn without regard to the reason for such failure is consistent with strict liability since it asks only whether the product that caused injury contained a defect.[33]

It has been said that most commentators have concluded that the guidelines in § 402A, comment *k*, of the *Restatement* are unintelligible and that the cases which attempt to interpret that section are confusing.[34] Indeed, even if strict liability is permitted in prescription drug cases, the utility of strict liability for drug design defects is limited.[35] Since it is the doctor who acts as the consumer in such cases, the consumer expectations test provides no relief to patients suffering foreseeable drug injuries when the manufacturer has warned the doctor of the risk. If the drug contains foreseeable dangers that are not expected by physicians, persons injured by such drugs are protected by failure to warn claims, as opposed to design defect claims. Moreover, since virtually all American jurisdictions shield manufacturers from liability for unforeseen dangers, patients injured in such circumstances have no claim under any liability test or theory.[36]

B. Third Restatement

Unlike the position under *Restatement, Second, Torts* § 402A, special liability rules for prescription drugs and medical devices are established in § 6 of the *Restatement Third, Torts: Products Liability*.[37] In respect of claims involving alleged design defects in prescription drugs or medical devices, § 6(c) adopts a so-called net benefit test. It provides that:

> A prescription drug or medical device is not reasonably safe due to defective design if the foreseeable risks of harm posed by the drug or medical device are sufficiently great in relation to its

---

[30] Ibid 840. See also *Shanks v Upjohn Co* 835 P 2d 1189, 1195 (Ala 1992), requiring a prescription drug to perform as safely as an ordinary doctor would expect. The case, which involved the drug Xanax, had dramatic overtones as the patient had committed suicide soon after taking it. Note that *Freeman's* establishment of a prima facie case for drug design liability if the drug does not meet consumer expectations has been emphatically rejected by two of the erstwhile Reporters of *Restatement, Third, Torts: Products Liability*: J Henderson and AD Twerski, 'Drug Designs *Are* Different' (2001) 111 *Yale Law Journal* 151, 177.

[31] F Woodside, *Drug Product Liability* (NJ, Mathew Bender, 2010) vol 2, ch 14, §14.06[4][b], 14-192.6.

[32] 751 P 2d 470 (Cal 1988).

[33] Ibid 476, fn 4.

[34] J Henderson and AD Twerski, 'Drug Designs *Are* Different' (2001) 111 *Yale Law Journal* 151, 180.

[35] DG Owen, 'Dangers in Prescription Drugs: Filling a Private Law Gap in the Healthcare Debate' (2010) 42 *Connecticut Law Review* 733, 747.

[36] Ibid.

[37] See, generally, TM Schwartz, 'The Impact of the New Products Liability Restatement on Prescription Products' (1995) 50 *Food and Drug Law Journal* 399.

foreseeable therapeutic benefits that reasonable health care providers, knowing of such foreseeable risks and therapeutic benefits, would not prescribe the drug or medical device for any class of patients.

The test for liability is thus narrow: a drug is defectively designed if no reasonable health care provider with knowledge of all relevant facts would prescribe the drug for any class of patients.

Section 6 of the new *Restatement* has been subject to trenchant criticism by some commentators,[38] and the decision of the Supreme Court of Nebraska in *Freeman v Hoffman-La Roche Inc* has rejected adoption of § 6(c) as being too restrictive a rule, under which recovery would be nearly impossible.[39] However, others have defended it as reflecting the unanimous refusal of courts to review prescription drug designs in the light of confidence in a prescription drug market system which involves rigorous drug regulation, learned and informed health care providers, full and accurate warnings of risks and a substantial absence of third-party effects. The rule effectively embodies a presumption of non-defectiveness which is rebuttable by plaintiffs on narrow grounds. It also reflects the view that providing one or more classes of patient need a particular medicinal product it should not be removed from the market by judicial decree merely because other patients are put at risk by an inappropriate prescription of the drug.[40]

The reason for rejecting § 6(c) is the view that drug designs should be subject to a private law challenge on the basis of a normal risk–utility test (on proof of a safer alternative

---

[38] See TM Schwartz, 'Prescription Products and the Proposed Restatement (Third)' (1994) 61 *Tennessee Law Review* 1357, 1364, 1378–85, 1405, and 'The Impact of the New Products Liability Restatement on Prescription Products' (1995) 50 *Food and Drug Law Journal* 399, 407 (suggesting § 6(c) establishes a kind of 'super' negligence standard of liability which would in effect eliminate a cause of action for defectively designed drugs); RL Cupp Jr, 'Rethinking Conscious Design Liability for Prescription Drugs: the Restatement (Third) Standard v. A Negligence Approach' (1994) 63 *George Washington Law Review* 76, 110 (advocating a negligence standard as a middle step between strict liability and the Restatement's near immunity); FJ Vandall, 'Constructing a Roof Before the Foundation is Prepared: the Restatement (Third) of Torts: Products Liability, §2(b) Design Defect' (1997) 30 *University of Michigan Journal of Law Reform* 261, 270–71, 279 (advocating strict liability and describing distinction between mechanical products covered by § 2(b) and prescription drugs covered by § 6(c) as artificial and arbitrary); GW Conk, 'Is There a Design Defect in the Restatement (Third) of Torts: Products Liability?' (2000) 109 *Yale Law Journal* 1087, 1089, 1118–32 (arguing that under § 6(c) designers and manufacturers of drugs and medical devices would not be liable even if the products could have been rendered safer, rejecting the use of § 6(c) and supporting use of alternative safer design test in § 2(b) and its application to prescription drug designs); GW Conk, 'The True Test: Alternative Safer Designs for Drugs and Medical Devices in a Patent-Constrained Market' (2002) 49 *UCLA Law Review* 737, 788 (§ 6(c) fails to provide adequate guidance for courts and is patently inadequate for analysis of drug design defects).

[39] *Freeman v Hoffman-La Roche Inc* 618 NW 2d 827, 840 (2000) (CJ Miller and RS Goldberg, *Product Liability*, 2nd edn (Oxford, Oxford University Press, 2004) para 9.64). *Freeman* made several criticisms of § 6(c). In particular, the Nebraska Court stated that (i) § 6(c) did not accurately restate the law and instead sought to formulate a new law with no precedential support; (ii) the reasonable physician test had been criticised as artificial and difficult to apply; (iii) the test lacked flexibility and treated drugs of unequal utility equally; and (iv) it allowed a consumer's claim to be defeated merely by a statement from the defence's expert witness that the drug in issue had some benefit for a single class of people. The Court concluded that, even though the rule had been reformulated, any application of § 6(c) would provide the same blanket immunity from liability for design defects as did the application of comment *k*: ibid 839–40.

[40] JA Henderson Jr, 'Prescription Drug Design Liability Under the Proposed Restatement (Third) of Torts: A Reporter's Perspective' (1996) 48 *Rutgers Law Review* 471, 494–95; JA Henderson Jr and AD Twerski, 'Drug Designs *Are* Different' (2001) 111 *Yale Law Journal* 151, 153, 163, 167–68, 175–78, 180–81 (*Restatement* is correct in treating prescription drug designs differently from other product designs).

design)[41] or a macro-balance test (on proof that a drug caused patients as a whole more harm than good).[42] However, it is clear that neither a risk–utility approach nor a macro-balance approach works well in the majority of cases involving drugs. As has been previously noted, risk–utility on proof of a safer alternative design does not work with drugs because 'most drugs cannot be redesigned, since their hazards are inherent'.[43] In respect of a macro-balance test, while there is truth in the view that any prescription drug that causes more harm than good is 'defective' from a utilitarian perspective, particular classes of patients (eg lepers, or those suffering from multiple myeloma) merit therapy from drugs (such as thalidomide), even if doctors sometimes misuse these drugs on other classes of patients.[44] Moreover, as David Owen astutely puts it:

> [T]here is a devil residing in the process of distinguishing which drugs, on balance, have net value from those that produce net harm—and in the threat of repeated litigation over the ultimate social value of any type of drug that causes someone harm because it did not suit that patient.[45]

While the previous case law did not provide much direct support for the standard promulgated in § 6(c),[46] and § 6(c) is very narrow and incomplete in that it fails to identify important exceptions, it seems basically correct.[47] Indeed, it seems that the substantive objections to it 'do not withstand close scrutiny'.[48]

---

[41] Section 2(b) provides that: [A product] 'is defective in design when the foreseeable risks of harm posed by the product could have been reduced or avoided by the adoption of a reasonable alternative design by the seller or other distributor, or a predecessor in the commercial chain of distribution, and the omission of the alternative design renders the product not reasonably safe'. It has been convincingly argued by one commentator that the US courts are able to overcome any difficulties with § 6(c); adequately labelled prescription drugs leave questions of utility in the appropriate hands of physicians and patients, and not judges and jurors; and, in the light of the 'unpredictable variability in patient response', it is a non sequitur to argue that a reasonable alternative design (RAD) exists for a drug if a fully informed health care professional would chose it for some patients: L Noah, 'This is Your Products Liability Restatement on Drugs' (2009) 74 Brooklyn Law Review 839, 848.

[42] DG Owen, 'Toward a Proper Test for Design Defectiveness: "Micro Balancing" Costs and Benefits' (1997) 75 Texas Law Review 1661, 1670–77.

[43] DG Owen, above, n 2 (2010) 42 Conneticut Law Review 733, 739–40; MD Green, 'Statutory Compliance and Tort Liability: Examining the Strongest Case' (1997) 30 University of Michigan Journal of Law Reform 461, 471; MD Green, 'Prescription Drugs, Alternative Designs and the Restatement (Third): Preliminary Reflections' (1999) 30 Seton Hall Law Review 207, 208–11.

[44] DG Owen, above, n 2 (2010) 42 Conneticut Law Review 733, 750.

[45] Ibid.

[46] L Noah, 'This is Your Products Liability Restatement on Drugs' (2009) 74 Brooklyn Law Review 839, 848.

[47] DG Owen, above, n 2 (2010) 42 Conneticut Law Review 733, 750; MD Green, 'Prescription Drugs, Alternative Designs and the Restatement (Third): Preliminary Reflections' (1999) 30 Seton Hall Law Review 207, 208–11.

[48] L Noah, 'This is Your Products Liability Restatement on Drugs' (2009) 74 Brooklyn Law Review 839, 848. Cf the resurrection of a twin-test approach to design defect litigation, (similar to Barker v Lull Engineering Co 573 P 2d 443 (Cal 1978)), basing manufacturer's liability on either a product's failure to satisfy a risk–utility analysis or its failure to accord with the established safety expectations of consumers: DA Kysar, 'The Expectations of Consumers' (2003) 103 Columbia Law Review 1700, 1704–5. Kysar makes no attempt to engage his theory with prescription drugs. Indeed, when he expresses support for the role of lay risk perception in the light of social science investigation of human behaviour and decision making (ibid 1706), it is interesting to note the dangers of this approach in the September 2012 Report to the President on Propelling Innovation in Drug Discovery, Development and Innovation, which states that 'there is a public perception on the part of many that FDA approval signals near-certainty that a drug is safe and effective': Report to the President on Propelling Innovation in Drug Discovery, Development and Innovation (President's Council of Advisors on Science and Technology, 2012) 32 (citing a study of approximately 3,000 American adults, (LM Schwartz and S Woloshin, 'Communicating Uncertainties About Prescription Drugs to the Public (2011) 17 Archives of Internal Medicine 1463–68), which found that 39 per cent believed that the FDA only approves 'extremely effective' drugs, and that 25 per cent believed that the FDA only approves 'drugs without serious side effects').

III.   DESIGN DEFECTS AND PHARMACEUTICAL PRODUCTS UNDER
THE PRODUCT LIABILITY DIRECTIVE

A.   General

Medicinal products may be defective if they are unsafe for their intended or contemplated purpose because of a basic design deficiency. Design defects are the most problematic category of defects in medicinal products since the concept of safety is harder to apply to such products, where safety is a relative concept.[49] While in the US the issue of design defect liability for prescription products seems secondary,[50] virtually all of the important product liability litigation in the UK concerning medicinal products relates to design defects.[51]

Professor Stapleton has noted that the issue of liability for resulting injuries caused by design defects will be determinative of whether product liability reform is of real significance.[52] She also considers that while the concept of a defect superficially suggests a uniform approach to injuries from manufacturing defects and from design defects there is in reality an 'asymmetry of liability for design and manufacturing errors'.[53] The reason advanced is that whereas it is assumed that a manufacturing error will constitute a defect without account being taken of cost-benefit considerations, such considerations will be taken into account where the alleged defect is one of design. This is seen as resulting in substantial anomalies. For instance, she gives the example of a vaccine causing cataracts in a recipient. If the adverse reaction is attributable to a manufacturing error, no account will be taken of cost–benefit considerations, whereas if the adverse reaction is attributable to an uneliminable design danger, a cost–benefit approach can allow a producer to avoid liability.[54]

Notwithstanding the progression from negligence to strict liability in the European Union, the movement in the US over the last three decades has been in the opposite direction. This is especially so in the context of design defects, where the consumer expectation test has been widely criticised as an 'abject failure' as a test for defectiveness.[55]

B.   What is a Medicinal Product Design Defect?

It is important to understand the true nature of a medicinal product design defect. Helpful guidance is provided by Professor Stapleton who asserts that a design allegation of defect

---

[49]   I Dodds-Smith, M Spencer and J Bore, 'Product Liability for Medicinal Products' in MJ Powers, NH Harris and A Barton (eds), *Clinical Negligence*, 4th edn (London, Tottel Publishing, 2008) para 24.78.

[50]   As Professor Owen has noted, the issue of drug design defectiveness is 'a troublesome but largely phantom issue in modern drug litigation': DG Owen (above, n 2) (2010) 42 *Conneticut Law Review* 733, 750; and see, also, Mike Green, who states that 'the liability game is with the warnings candle, not with design': MD Green (above, n 2) (1999) 30 *Seton Hall Law Review* 207, 209.

[51]   I Dodds-Smith, M Spencer and J Bore, 'Product Liability for Medicinal Products' in MJ Powers, NH Harris and A Barton (eds), *Clinical Negligence*, 4th edn (London, Tottel Publishing, 2008) para 24.81 and n 6 (citing the MMR/MR litigation, the third generation oral contraceptive litigation and the foetal anti-convulsant litigation).

[52]   J Stapleton, 'Products Liability Reform—Real or Illusory' (1986) 6 *Oxford Journal of Legal Studies* 392, 399.

[53]   Ibid 404.

[54]   Ibid.

[55]   JA Henderson Jr and AD Twerski, 'What Europe, Japan and Other Countries Can Learn From the New American Restatement of Products Liability' (1999) 34 *Texas International Law Journal* 1, 4, 13.

in a medicinal product is necessarily a complaint about the 'chemical effects of the product and can be assessed independently of the state of the art and knowledge at the time of supply'.[56] This has an important consequence in that *undiscoverability* of the product hazard given the state of the art is no answer to a claim for design defects, since design defect claims are akin to claims of breaches of the warranty of merchantability.[57] Under a design allegation defect, the issue of the level of safety to which there is legal entitlement focuses 'not on the discoverability of that hazard given the state of the art at supply', but merely 'on the impact of the chemical formula as it is now known at trial to have been'.[58] That this is true seems highly likely in that if a medicinal product proves to be unsafe when used in the manner apparently intended or according to its normal instructions, it is likely to be found defective.[59] Nonetheless, this is not abundantly clear from the legislation since, as has been previously noted, the Directive fails to develop a suitable taxonomy for products, let alone medicinal products.

However, unlike warranty, the Directive provides a defence under Article 7(e), based on discoverability of the defect, viz the problem of discovering the detrimental effect of a product's design. In the case of medicinal products, this is the problem of discovering the detrimental effects of the chemical design. So where a medicinal product's design is judged to have failed to provide the level of safety to which we are legally entitled, the issue of liability will turn on the development risk defence in Article 7(e).[60]

C. The Approach for Determining Whether a Medicinal Product's Design is Defective: Consumer Expectations v Risk–Benefit; Cost–Benefit; Net Benefit

There is arguably doctrinal incoherence in Member States' laws in respect of establishing that medicinal products are defective in design within the definition in Article 6 of the Product Liability Directive. The issue has created controversy in the limited case law decided in this field. Medicinal products all carry a risk of adverse drug reactions, even if in only a minority of consumers. These consumers are not necessarily entitled to expect that the products will be risk free. Most commentators consider that while section 3 of the Consumer Production Act 1987 and Article 6 of the Directive adopt the language of expectation, a risk–utility or risk–benefit approach is accommodated within the framework of the Directive and the 1987 Act. Indeed, in the case of alleged defects of design, it is almost inevitable that the standards of safety which persons are entitled to expect will be contingent in part on a weighing of the risks and benefits associated with pharmaceutical products.

Notwithstanding the problems with a risk–utility approach, if the Directive is to have any meaning in the context of allegations of defective design of medicinal products, an

---

[56] J Stapleton, 'Liability for Drugs in the US and EU: Rhetoric and Reality' (2007) 26 *Review of Litigation* 991, 1019, 1030.

[57] Ibid 1019.

[58] Ibid 1020, 1030.

[59] I Dodds-Smith, M Spencer and J Bore, 'Product Liability for Medicinal Products' in MJ Powers, NH Harris and A Barton (eds), *Clinical Negligence*, 4th edn (London, Tottel Publishing, 2008) para 24.83.

[60] J Stapleton, above n 56 (2007) 26 *Review of Litigation* 991, 1019, 1020–21, 1030. For discussion of the development risk defence and medicinal products, see chapter 8 of this volume.

analysis of the benefits and disadvantages associated with a product (or risk–utility)is inescapable. An obvious contemporary example is in the case of litigation involving the MMR (mumps, measles and rubella) triple vaccine. Thus even if it were accepted that the vaccine was capable of having severe side-effects[61] this should not mean that it is automatically to be adjudged defective. The risks would have to be balanced against the serious risks involved in not immunising children, and in all probability a court would conclude that the benefits of vaccination outweigh the perceived risks. This is equally so whether the issue arises in the context of a dispute between parents as to whether a child should be vaccinated[62] or in product liability litigation. The relevance of such factors is predominant in the area of design defects.[63]

In Stapleton's view, the approach to undertake in determining a claim for defectively designed medicinal products is to utilise a cost–benefit approach, including consideration of the public interest in a particularly valuable medicinal product.[64] Sometimes a medicinal product's design will be determined to have provided the level of safety to which persons are entitled. For instance, Zidovudine (AZT) can be used for the prevention of maternal transmission of AIDS to children.[65] However, Stapleton suggests that the chemical formula of a morning sickness drug such as thalidomide does not provide the safety to which we are legally entitled, taking all circumstances into account, including the time when the product was put into circulation, if it massively deforms the unborn child.[66] But as has been previously noted, thalidomide is effective for non-pregnancy uses in the treatment of leprosy, multiple myeloma and AIDS.[67] In such circumstances, it might not be defective if it included a warning against use by pregnant women, and was prescribed in exceptional circumstances with limited distribution.[68] However, it has been previously noted that a risk–utility approach does not work well in the majority of cases involving drugs in the US.

The other possibility is to adopt a 'gestalt judgment of defectiveness' by comparing a drug's overall benefits and risks and declare a drug defective when its risks outweigh its overall therapeutic benefits.[69] However, this form of a macro-balance test has also been subject to criticism.[70] Owen concurs with the Third Restatement Reporters, Professors Henderson and Twerski, who have argued that such a macro-balancing approach 'would

---

[61] For discussion of the MMR Litigation, see chapter 6 of this volume.

[62] As in *Re B (A Child); sub nom In re Vaccination/MMR Litigation* [2003] EWCA Civ 1148 where the Court of Appeal strongly supported the decision of Sumner J holding in favour of the parent advocating immunisation.

[63] See, generally, Miller and Goldberg (above, n 39) paras 10.82, 11.19–11.31.

[64] J Stapleton, above n 56 (2007) 26 *Review of Litigation* 991, 1020 following the kind of balancing exercise as suggested by Lord Griffiths et al that, although English judges would not overtly adopt a risk-benefit approach, they would 'as an educated response to the facts of a particular case undertake a balancing exercise of an analogous kind': Rt Hon The Lord Griffiths, P de Val and RJ Dormer, 'Developments in English Product Liability Law: A comparison with the American System' (1988) 62 *Tulane Law Review* 353, 382. But note the disregard of cost under the net benefit approach of § 6(c) of the *Restatement Third, Torts: Products Liability*.

[65] EM Connor et al, 'Reduction of Maternal Infant Transmission of Human Immunodeficiency Virus Type 1 With Zidovudine Treatment' (1994) *New England Journal of Medicine* 1173 (showing that Zidovudine (AZT) reduces the risk of maternal infant HIV transmission by approximately two-thirds).

[66] J Stapleton, above n 56 (2007) 26 *Review of Litigation* 991, 1020.

[67] See 'Lenalidomide and thalidomide for multiple myeloma', MHRA, Drug Safety Update, vol 2, Issue 1, August 2008, available at: www.mhra.gov.uk/Safetyinformation/DrugSafetyUpdate; N Hawkes, 'Fifty years on, thalidomide is back. Now they say it's a good thing', The Times, 22 April 2008.

[68] Green considers that thalidomide would not be defective under § 6(c) and suggests that 8 out of 10 judges would rule that way as a matter of law. MD Green (above, n 2) (1999) 30 *Seton Hall Law Review* 207, 228.

[69] MD Green, above, n 2 (1999) 30 *Seton Hall Law Review* 207, 231.

[70] See above, pp 43–44.

require courts to deny classes of patients access to a particular drug that provides them unique benefits in order to protect other patients from the risks of misprescription by negligent physicians' and that such an approach 'is both unfair and inefficient'.[71] Yet an eclectic approach, which combines macro-balancing with consumer expectations and an examination of all circumstances, in terms of section 3(2)/Article 6(1), is probably the closest one will get to applying the Directive properly in the context of design defects and medicinal products.

D. Relevance of Risk–Benefit to Determining Design Defectiveness: The Member States' Jurisprudence

To what extent has the risk–benefit approach been adopted in the UK and in other Member States? To a major extent, the problem has been exacerbated by the paucity of case law available. Yet one case involving a design issue seems to point to inroads in this direction. In *Richardson v LRC Products Ltd*,[72] a female claimant brought an action for damages under the Consumer Protection Act 1987 for personal injuries suffered when a condom manufactured by the defendants failed and she became pregnant. Ian Kennedy J held that the condom was not defective. He explained that although the user's expectation was that the condom would not fail, taking into account the safety that persons generally were entitled to expect in all the circumstances, in terms of section 3, the defendants had never claimed that a condom would never fail and no-one had ever supposed in the circumstances that any method of contraception would be a 100 per cent effective. Having examined the expectations of the consumer, he added, in language analogous to risk–utility, that evidence showed that the condom had failed inexplicably under standards higher than the British ones applicable in the case. Thus the fact of the condom's fracture did not prove that it was defective in terms of section 3.[73]

In the context of design defects, the German Supreme Court held in 2009 that a cost–benefit analysis may be appropriate to determine whether a product is defective in design. It stated that the court should have regard inter alia to 'the costs of production, the marketability of the alternative design as well as a cost-benefit balance' and in this respect expressly referred to 'the risk utility test under US law'.[74] While the design defect in question was not in the context of medicinal products (the German Product Liability Act provisions do not apply to pharmaceutical products, which are specifically covered by a strict liability compensation regime in the Medicines Act 1976 (*Arzneimittelgesetz* 1976) (AMG)),[75] the case indicates that the notion of risk–benefit is relevant to liability for design defects. Moreover, while reaffirming that the producer's conduct 'is entirely unimportant' and that a defect is

---

[71] JA Henderson and AD Twerski, 'Drug Designs *Are* Different' (2001) 111 *Yale Law Journal* 151, 152–53.

[72] *Richardson v LRC Products Ltd* [2000] Lloyd's Rep Med 280.

[73] Ibid 285.

[74] BGH, 16 June 2009, VI ZR 107/08, 18.

[75] Miller and Goldberg (above, n 39) paras 9.48–9.50. See, further, S Lenze, 'German Product Liability law; between European Directives, American Restatements and common sense' in D Fairgrieve (ed), *Product Liability in Comparative Perspective* (Cambridge, Cambridge University Press 2005) 119–21.

an objective notion, referring to 'safety and to nothing else',[76] Professor Taschner, one of the principal architects of the Directive, has conceded that risk–utility may be *relevant* to determining the safety which the public at large legitimately expects.[77]

However, the French Cour de cassation[78] has taken what appears to be an unhelpful approach to the determination of defectiveness in the context of the hepatitis B vaccination litigation. The Court of Appeal of Versailles[79] had ruled that the temporal proximity between the hepatitis B vaccination and the appearance of the demyelinating disease, in the absence of any other known cause for the disease, generated a presumption that the vaccine had caused the claimant's injury. As will be seen in a later chapter,[80] this approach to causation, which has been accepted since 2008, is extremely controversial. Nonetheless, the appellate court rejected the claim against the vaccine producer, by determining, utilising a risk–benefit analysis, that the vaccine was not defective.[81] However, the decision on defectiveness was overturned by the Cour de cassation, which held that the Court of Appeal should have checked whether the elements, on the basis of which causation had been presumed, did not also allow for a presumption that the vaccine was defective. It therefore suggests that the elements that allow for a presumption of causation may also allow for a presumption of defectiveness. The Cour de cassation suggests that defectiveness could be assessed on a case-by-case basis, independently from a 'general' risk–benefit analysis, taking into account the specific considerations of the product. However, as Professor Borghetti has noted, the Court has failed to provide a meaningful explanation of what the defectiveness of a vaccine means, and how it should be substantively defined.[82] Moreover, if this means that hepatitis B vaccines may be considered defectively designed, notwithstanding their benefit to society as a whole, and that it has not been scientifically proven that they can cause demyelinating diseases, then the decision appears to be unjustified.[83]

It is submitted that some form of analysis of the benefits and disadvantages associated with a medicinal product (or risk–utility) is inevitable. However, it has to be said that an element of doubt may have been cast on the relevance of a risk–utility analysis by the decision of Burton J in the English hepatitis C litigation. In *A v National Blood Authority*,[84] Burton J held that risk–utility analysis was irrelevant[85] to determining the safety of what he termed 'non-standard products'—ie products which fail to perform as the producer intended due to a harmful characteristic or characteristics not present in the other

---

[76] HC Taschner, 'Product Liability: Basic Problems in a Comparative Law Perspective' in D Fairgrieve (ed), *Product Liability in Comparative Perspective* (Cambridge, Cambridge University Press 2005) 161.

[77] Ibid 159.

[78] Cass civ 1, 26 September 2012, n° 11-17.738.

[79] Cour d'appel de Versailles, 10 February 2011.

[80] See chapter 6 of this volume.

[81] This risk–benefit approach had been adopted in two previous decisions involving medicinal products, viz Isomeride (Versailles, 17 March 2006, n° 04/08435; Paris, 19 June 2009, n° 06/13741) and in 3 cases involving the vaccine against hepatitis B (Versailles, 16 March 2007, n° 05/09525; 29 March 2007, n° 06/00496; 5 November 2007, n° 06/106435).

[82] J-S Borghetti, 'Qu'est-ce qu'un vaccin défectueux?', *Recueil Dalloz* 2012 2853. This approach of examining all elements at hand, when considering the product's defectiveness and the existence of a causal link has been upheld by the Cour de cassation: Cass civ 1, 29 May 2013, n° 12-20.9033.

[83] See, further, J-S Borghetti, 'Litigation on Hepatitis B Vaccination and Demyelinating Diseases in France: Breaking Through Scientific Uncertainty?' (2012) (on file with author). I am grateful to Professor Jean-Sébastien Borghetti, Professor à l'université Panthéon-Assas (Paris II) for a copy of this paper.

[84] *A v National Blood Authority* [2001] 3 All ER 289.

[85] Ibid para 68.

products of the same type produced by that producer.[86] Nevertheless, he did not expressly exclude a risk–utility analysis[87] as an element shaping legitimate consumer expectations in the case of 'standard products', ie those products which perform as the producer intends but which share the harmful characteristic and have an error in design.[88] However, his assessment of the travaux préparatoires to the Directive, which he claimed had rejected risk–utility analysis,[89] suggests that, in his view, risk–utility may have no role to play in the context of design defects either.[90]

IV. REFORM: A NET BENEFIT APPROACH TO DRUG DESIGN DEFECTS OR COMBINED CONSUMER-EXPECTATIONS RISK–UTILITY

A. Net Benefit Approach to Drug Design Defects

In the light of the problems with consumer expectations and risk–utility, there is much to be said for the view that reformers should be looking towards the US approach in § 6(c) of the Restatement Third, which does not require proof of an alternative feasible design but permits a finding based on 'categorical liability', viz a determination of defectiveness based on the inherent risks that a product poses without proof of an alternative design.[91] Medicinal products would therefore have their own test for design defects, utilising a net-benefit approach in line with § 6(c). Essentially, this would require a removal of the determination of design defectiveness from Article 6(1)/section 3(2), and a radical change to Directive. It would also dramatically change the perspective from which determinations of defective drugs would be made, since it would shift the perspective from that of 'a person' (in Article 6(1) of the Directive) to that of 'reasonable health care providers' (in § 6(c) of the Restatement Third). The most persuasive argument in favour of a net-benefit approach is Owen's conclusion that

> there is a devil residing in the process of distinguishing which drugs, on balance, have net value from those that produce net harm-and in the threat of repeated litigation over the ultimate social value of any type of drug that causes someone harm because it did not suit that patient.[92]

While his argument attains greater significance in the context of the US tort system, which is dependent on the existence of juries, the process is equally as problematic for a single trier of fact alone. Yet the argument against a § 6(c)-type approach is the advantage of the *Feldman/Kearl* case-by-case approach to determining whether a prescription is unavoidably

---

[86] Ibid para 36.
[87] Risk–utility is mentioned only as an item (number (iii)) under the heading '*Non-standard products*', but it does not appear under the heading '*Standard products*': see, respectively, [2001] 3 All ER 289, paras 68 and 71.
[88] Ibid paras 36, 67. Thus, for example, in the case of thalidomide, the harmful characteristic would appear to be the drug structure itself, and since the drug as a whole shared the harmful characteristic, it would appear to be a standard product: in R Goldberg, 'Paying for Bad Blood: Strict Product Liability after *A v National Blood Authority*' (2002) 10 *Medical Law Review* 165, 181.
[89] Ibid paras 35, 43.
[90] See I Dodds-Smith, M Spencer and J Bore, 'Product Liability for Medicinal Products' in MJ Powers, NH Harris and A Barton (eds), *Clinical Negligence*, 4th edn (London, Tottel Publishing, 2008) para 24.59.
[91] MD Green (above, n 2) (1999) 30 *Seton Hall Law Review* 207, 218.
[92] DG Owen, (2010) 42 *Conneticut Law Review* 733, 750.

unsafe, namely the refusal 'to surrender judicial oversight'[93] of a drug manufacturer's responsibility for design safety.

As to whether the Member States of the EU would benefit from a § 6(c) approach is a difficult question. Much will depend on whether a suitably coherent body of case law will emerge over a period of time. The other significant point is that under the Directive, design defects are subject to the potential operation of the development risk defence, which is sufficiently pro-manufacturer as to insulate them from unforeseeable defects. Indeed, it could be argued that de facto there may be little difference between the combined effect of Article 6 and Article 7(e) in the context of design defects and that of § 6(c). Nonetheless, if this is true, this suggests that—at least for those Member States who accept the option of the development risk defence—the Directive is providing a circuitous route to avoiding liability for unforeseeable design defects in the context of medicinal products.

B. Combined Consumer-Expectations Risk–Utility

If a net-benefit approach to drug design defects is unlikely to be seen as reflecting a careful balance between the interests of the consumer and manufacturers of goods, then some form of analysis of the benefits and disadvantages associated with a medicinal product (or risk–utility) cannot realistically be avoided. At the very least, in view of the US experience of dealing with design defects for many years and the views of commentators, it will be submitted that it seems entirely appropriate for the Directive and the 1987 Act to be construed as being based, in complex cases concerning medicinal products, on a *combined* consumer-expectation risk–utility analysis. This is apparently consistent with the Directive and the Act, since 'all the circumstances' should be taken into account in determining what persons generally are entitled to expect. Thus it would seem that an eclectic approach, which combines macro-balancing with consumer expectations and an examination of all circumstances, in terms of section 3(2)/Article 6(1), is probably the closest to applying the Directive properly in the context of design defects and medicinal products. In exercising this eclectic approach, determinations of the MHRA on risk–benefit would clearly be relevant but not dispositive to the overall outcome.[94] The new changes to European pharmacovigilance legislation,[95] including the new extension of Risk Management Plans (RMPs) to all new medicinal product applications,[96] and the creation of a new scientific committee in the European Medicines Agency—the Pharmacovigilance Risk Assessment Committee

---

[93] Ibid 746.

[94] On the development of an appropriate quantitative assessment model for medicinal products, see F Mussen, S Salek and S Walker, *Benefit-Risk Appraisal of Medicines* (Sussex, John Wiley & Sons Ltd, 2009) 155–58, 184 (noting the importance of developing a framework for benefit–risk assessment, and supporting overall a qualitative or semi-qualitative framework); and, further, LD Phillips, B Fasolo, N Zafiropoulos and A Beyer, 'Is Quantitative Benefit-Risk Modelling of Drugs Desirable or Possible?' (2011) 8 *Drug Discovery Today: Technologies*, e3 (showing quantitative benefit–risk modelling can integrate scientific data with expert value judgments, thereby extending the capabilities of regulators, and encouraging the emergence of new insights about trade-offs).

[95] See generally: www.mhra.gov.uk/Howweregulate/Medicines/Pharmacovigilancelegislation/index.htm. The legislation has been transposed into UK law in the Human Medicines Regulations 2012, SI 2012/1916, Part II, and, further, chapter 7 of this volume.

[96] Directive 2001/83, Art 104(3)(d); 104a(2).

(PRAC)[97]—should help in the process of generating transparent and consistent information for this purpose. Conversely, it should also be recommended that information generated about risk–benefit from any litigation determining defectiveness of medicinal products will be used by the regulators to reassess their determinations on drug safety.[98]

V. CONCLUSION

There is arguably doctrinal incoherence in Member States' laws in respect of establishing that medicinal products are defective in design within the definition in Article 6 of the Product Liability Directive. The issue has created controversy in the limited case law decided in this field. Medicinal products all carry a risk of adverse drug reactions, even if in only a minority of consumers. These consumers are not necessarily entitled to expect that the products will be risk free. Most commentators consider that while section 3 of the Consumer Production Act 1987 and Article 6 of the Directive adopt the language of expectation, a risk–utility or risk–benefit approach is accommodated within the framework of the Directive and the 1987 Act. Indeed, in the case of alleged defects of design, it is almost inevitable that the standards of safety which persons are entitled to expect will be contingent in part on a weighing of the risks and benefits associated with pharmaceutical products.

It is submitted that some form of analysis of the benefits and disadvantages associated with a medicinal product (or risk–utility) is inevitable. However, it has to be said that an element of doubt may have been cast on the relevance of a risk–utility analysis by the decision of Burton J in the English hepatitis C litigation. Nonetheless, it has been noted that a risk–utility approach does not work well in the majority of cases involving drugs in the US. In the light of the problems with consumer expectations and risk–utility, there is much to be said for the view that reformers should be looking towards the US approach in § 6(c) of the Restatement, Third, which does not require proof of an alternative feasible design but permits a finding based on 'categorical liability', viz a determination of defectiveness based on the inherent risks that a product poses without proof of an alternative design.[99] Medicinal products would therefore have their own test for design defects, utilising a net-benefit approach in line with § 6(c). Essentially, this would require a removal of the determination of design defectiveness from Article 6(1)/section 3(2), and a radical change to Directive. Whether the Member States of the EU would benefit from a § 6(c) approach is a difficult question. Much will depend on whether a suitably coherent body of case law will emerge over a period of time. The other significant point is that under the Directive, design defects are subject to the potential operation of the development risk defence, which is sufficiently pro-manufacturer as to insulate them from unforeseeable defects. Indeed, it could be argued that de facto there may be little difference between the combined effect of Article 6 and Article 7(e) in the context of design defects and that of § 6(c). Nonetheless, if this is true, this suggests that—at least for those Member States who accept the option

---

[97] Regulation (EC) No 726/2004, Art 56(1)(aa).

[98] CT Struve, 'The FDA and the Tort System: Postmarketing Surveillance, Compensation and the Role of Litigation' (2005) 5 *Yale Journal of Health Policy & Ethics* 587, 593, 662–66, 658–59. Note that in the EU, both health professionals and patients are now able to report suspected ADRs: Directive 2001/83, Art 107(h).

[99] MD Green (above, n 2) (1999) 30 *Seton Hall Law Review* 207, 218.

of the development risk defence—the Directive is providing a circuitous way to avoiding liability for unforeseeable design defects in the context of medicinal products.

Even if a net-benefit approach to drug design defects is unlikely to be seen as reflecting a careful balance between the interests of the consumer and manufacturers of goods, some form of assessment of the benefits and disadvantages associated with a medicinal product (or risk–utility) is still inescapable. At the very least, in view of the US experience of dealing with design defects for many years and the views of commentators, it seems entirely appropriate for the Directive and the 1987 Act to be construed as being based in complex cases concerning medicinal products on a *combined* consumer expectation-risk–utility analysis.

4

Warning and Instruction Defects and Medicinal Products

I. INTRODUCTION

As has been noted in a previous chapter,[1] it is the category of warnings about risks and instructions for use[2] which is the most significant factor relevant to determining the expectation of safety with medicinal products. This chapter explores the thorny issue of warning and instruction defects in the context of medicinal products. In the absence of a developed body of case law on warnings and instructions in the United Kingdom, it is useful to refer first to the position as it has developed in the United States, before examining the position of warnings and instructions in the context of medicinal products under the Product Liability Directive. It will be seen that, notwithstanding the significance of warnings and instructions and medicinal products, the position under the Directive is a much more uncertain one than in the United States.

II. WARNING AND INSTRUCTION DEFECTS AND PHARMACEUTICAL PRODUCTS: THE US EXPERIENCE

A. Main Form of Liability

In the United States 'failure to warn' claims are said to be the most common form of litigation in product liability cases.[3] Indeed, as the Third Restatement has observed: 'Failure to instruct or warn is the major basis of liability for manufacturers of prescription drugs and medical devices'.[4]

---

[1] See chapter 2 of this volume, p 24.

[2] The function of a warning is to acquaint the user or a responsible third party with dangers associated with a medicinal product, whereas directions or instructions for use indicate how the most beneficial results are to be obtained from use of such a product: see further, CJ Miller and RS Goldberg, *Product Liability*, 2nd edn (Oxford, Oxford University Press, 2004) paras 12.02, 12.06 and 14.96–14.98.

[3] Restatement, Third, Torts: Products Liability, § 6 cmt *d.*

[4] See also Mike Green who has commented that, 'the liability game is with the warnings candle, not with design': MD Green, 'Prescription Drugs, Alternative Designs and the Restatement (Third): Preliminary Reflections' (1999) 30 *Seton Hall Law Review* 207, 209.

B. Use of Negligence Principles

In the United States, failure to provide adequate warnings in cases involving prescription drugs is actionable under principles of negligence, strict liability, or warranty or a combination of such actions.[5] A majority of American courts have concluded that failure to warn claims brought under negligence or strict liability are largely indistinguishable.[6]

However, in the prescription drug case of *Carlin v Superior Court*,[7] while conceding 'that the knowledge or knowability requirement for failure to warn infuses some negligence concepts into strict liability cases' and that 'in the failure to warn context, strict liability is to some extent a hybrid of traditional strict liability and negligence doctrine', the Californian Supreme Court continued to insist that failure to warn in strict liability 'differs markedly from failure to warn in the negligence context'.[8] It concluded that 'in strict liability, as opposed to negligence, the reasonableness of the defendant's failure to warn is immaterial' and presented two hypothetical scenarios to support its view:[9]

> Stated another way, a reasonably prudent manufacturer might reasonably decide that the risk of harm was such as not to require a warning as, for example, if the manufacturer's own testing showed a result contrary to that of others in the scientific community. Such a manufacturer might escape liability under negligence principles. In contrast, under strict liability principles the manufacturer has no such leeway; the manufacturer is liable if it failed to give warning of dangers that were known to the scientific community at the time it manufactured or distributed the product. Similarly, a manufacturer could not escape liability under strict liability principles merely because its failure to warn of a known or reasonably scientifically knowable risk conformed to an industry-wide practice of failing to provide warnings that constituted the standard of reasonable care.

Nevertheless, as erstwhile Reporters of the Products Liability Restatement, Professors Henderson and Twerski have reaffirmed that there is little, if any, substantial difference between the failure to warn approaches in negligence and strict liability.[10] Indeed, in response to the above two hypothetical scenarios presented by the Californian Supreme Court in *Carlin*, Henderson and Twerski provide forceful rejoinders in stating that:[11]

> These hypotheticals ... fall short of establishing any true distinction between California's strict liability approach to failure to warn and a typical negligence standard. A manufacturer cannot escape liability under negligence principles simply because its testing does not reveal the same dangers as that of the scientific community. The choice to ignore the findings of the scientific community would certainly raise a question for the trier of fact as to whether such a choice constituted negligence. In addition, a manufacturer may not avoid liability under a negligence regime by simply conforming to industry-wide standards of care. While such standards may be relevant to the issue

---

[5] *Larkin v Pfizer, Inc* 153 SW 3d 758, 761 (Ky 2004); See, further, F Woodside, *Drug Product Liability* (NJ, Mathew Bender, 2010), vol 2, ch 14, § 14.02[1][a].

[6] See, eg *Gourdine v Crews*, 955 A 2d 769, 782 (2008) (claims in negligence and strict liability are 'morphed together'); *Stupak v Hoffman-La Roche, Inc*, 2007 US Dist LEXIS 88800 at *7 (MD Fla Nov 29, 2007), aff'd 326 Fed Appx 553, 2009 US App LEXIS 12482 (11th Cir 2009) (unpublished) (no difference in standard of proof required between negligence failure to warn claim and strict liability failure to warn claim; both are assessed in an identical manner).

[7] *Carlin v Superior Court* 920 P 2d 1347 (Cal 1996).

[8] 920 P 2d 1347, 1351 (Cal 1996).

[9] Ibid.

[10] Reporters' Notes to Restatement, Third, Torts: Products Liability § 2, comment *m*, p 105.

[11] Ibid 106.

of negligence, it is an elementary principle of tort law that conformance with such standards will never completely insulate the manufacturer from liability under a negligence regime.

Courts have continued to apply negligence principles and reject true strict liability principles in failure to warn cases concerning prescription drugs. In *Feldman v Lederle Laboratories*,[12] the New Jersey Supreme Court, while deciding that the principles of strict liability were applicable to the manufacturers of prescription drugs,[13] and that a manufacturer would be strictly liable for failing to warn of risks of which he knew or should have known,[14] held that a manufacturer would not be liable for failure to warn of risks which were unknown and unknowable at the time of manufacture. Schreiber J declared:[15]

> If *Beshada*[16] were deemed to hold generally or in all cases, particularly with respect to a situation like the present one involving drugs vital to health, that in a warning context knowledge of the unknowable is irrelevant in determining the applicability of strict liability, we would not agree.

The Court endorsed the restriction in comment *j* of § 402A of the *Restatement, Second, Torts* that the duty to warn extended only to *foreseeable* risks and adopted the traditional negligence approach of constructive knowledge, namely '[d]id the defendant know, or should he have known of the danger'.[17]

The application of strict liability to unknown and unknowable defects in the context of medicinal products (including diethylstilbestrol) was also rejected by the California Supreme Court in *Brown v Superior Court (Abbott Laboratories)*,[18] where the Court held that a drug manufacturer should not be strictly liable for failure to warn of defects inherent in a drug of which it neither knew nor could have known by the application of scientific knowledge available at the time of distribution.[19] A manufacturer of drugs thus has a duty to warn physicians 'about any known or reasonably knowable dangerous side effects'.[20] The same court extended the decision in *Brown* beyond prescription drugs to products generally in *Anderson v Owens-Corning Fiberglas Corp*,[21] holding that knowledge or knowability was a component of strict liability for failure to warn. It reaffirmed this position in the context of failure to warn and prescription drugs in *Carlin v Superior Court*,[22] holding that '[d]rug manufacturers need only warn of risks that are *actually known or scientifically knowable*'.[23] In spite of the firm statement of principle in the *Sternhagen* decision, it seems, as Professor Owen has put it, that 'the tide had sharply turned against a duty to warn of

---

[12] *Feldman v Lederle Laboratories* 479 A 2d 374, 388 (1982). Cf *Beshada v Johns-Manville Products Corporation* 447 A 2d 539, 546–49 (NJ 1984) (imposing strict liability for failure to warn of dangers undiscoverable at the time of manufacture, and holding unknowability of the dangers of asbestos as irrelevant in a strict liability claim). For further discussion of *Beshada*, see Miller and Goldberg (above, n 2) paras 12.30, 13.68–13.70.

[13] Ibid 380.

[14] Ibid 386.

[15] Ibid 387.

[16] See above, n 12.

[17] Ibid 386. However, in strict liability, as opposed to negligence, the burden of proof lay on the defendant to establish that he lacked actual or constructive knowledge: ibid 388.

[18] *Brown v Superior Court (Abbott Laboratories)* 751 P 2d 470 (Cal 1988).

[19] Ibid 480–81.

[20] *Dorsett v Sandoz, Inc* 699 F Supp 2d 1142, 1163 (CD Cal 2010); *Motus v Pfizer, Inc* 196 F Supp 2d 984, 990–91 (CD Cal 2001).

[21] *Anderson v Owens-Corning Fiberglas Corp* 810 P 2d 549, 550, 556–57 (1991).

[22] *Carlin v Superior Court* 920 P 2d 1347 (Cal 1996).

[23] Ibid 1354.

unknowable product risks'.[24] The decisions in the higher courts of four other States have supported the view that there is no duty to warn of unknowable risks, two in respect of prescription pharmaceutical products,[25] and two in respect of products generally.[26]

The decision of the Supreme Judicial Court of Massachusetts in *Vassalo v Baxter Healthcare Corp*,[27] is indicative of the trend. The background was a claim in negligence and for alleged breach of the implied warranty of merchantability[28] against a silicone implant manufacturer for auto-immune disease suffered by the plaintiff in whom such products had been implanted. The trial court had declined the defendant's request for a jury instruction that a manufacturer need warn only of known or knowable risks and had followed the imputed knowledge doctrine.[29] The Court took the opportunity to reconsider its duty to warn rule, which had 'presum[ed] that a manufacturer was fully informed of all risks associated with the product at issue, regardless of the state of the art at the time of the sale'.[30] The Court recognised that Massachusetts was 'among a distinct minority of States that applie[d] a hindsight analysis to the duty to warn',[31] that the majority of States followed the rule which limits the duty to warn to foreseeable dangers as reflected in *Restatement, Second, Torts* § 402A, comment *j* and in *Restatement, Third, Torts: Products Liability* § 2(c), comment *m*;[32] that the goal of inducing product safety was not advanced by imposing liability for failure to warn of the unknowable; and that the hindsight approach to duty to warn of risks associated with a product had received substantial criticism in the literature. It concluded that, in recognition of the clear judicial trend and the principles in *Restatement, Third, Torts: Products Liability* § 2(c) and comment *m*, recently approved by the American Law Institute, Massachusetts law should be revised to state that a manufacturer will not be held liable under an implied warranty of merchantability for failure to warn or provide instructions about risks which were unforeseeable at the time of sale or undiscoverable by way of reasonable testing prior to marketing.[33] As the Court in *Vassallo* noted, several respected legal scholars who acted as advisors to the *Restatement, Second, Torts* and Reporters to the *Restatement Third, Torts: Products Liability* have concluded that

---

[24] DG Owen, 'Bending Nature, Bending Law' (2010) 62 *Florida Law Review* 569, 599; see also *Madden & Owen on Products Liability*, 3rd edn § 10:6.

[25] *Young for Young v Key Pharmaceuticals Inc* 922 P 2d 59, 63–64 (1996) (Wash Sup Ct) (prescription drug theophyilline administered to treat asthma was an unavoidably unsafe product within the scope of *Restatement, Second, Torts* § 402A, comment *k* and thus its manufacturer could not be liable for failure to warn of effect of viral illnesses on the body's ability to metabolise the drug of which it neither knew nor should have known based on the studies and medical literature available at the time); *Wagner v Roche Laboratories* 671 NE 2d 252, 256 (1996) (Ohio Sup Ct) (manufacturer of unavoidably unsafe prescription drug, Accutane, is not strictly liable in tort to a consumer where the manufacturer has provided adequate warning to the medical profession of all potential adverse reactions inherent in the use of the drug of which the manufacturer knew or should have known at the time of marketing).

[26] *Owens-Illinois Inc v Zenobia* 601 A 2d 633, 641 (Md Sup Ct 1992) (no liability for failure to warn if there is insufficient knowledge on the part of the manufacturer or in the scientific field involved; burden of proof of knowability remains on the plaintiff); *Vassalo v Baxter Healthcare Corp* 696 NE 2d 909 (1998).

[27] Ibid.

[28] Massachusetts never adopted a doctrine of strict liability in tort and it used the implied warranty of merchantability as a vehicle for strict products liability: *Madden & Owen on Products Liability*, 3rd edn (Thomson/West, 2000) § 10:6.

[29] 696 NE 2d 909, 922.

[30] Ibid.

[31] Ibid.

[32] See Miller and Goldberg (above, n 2) para 13.75.

[33] 696 NE 2d 909, 923.

liability for failure to warn should not be imposed without showing that a defendant knew or should have known of the risk at the time of the product's sale.[34]

The absence of a duty to warn of unknowable risks in the context of medicinal products may also be important in respect of brand manufacturers who cease distribution of a drug before an adverse reaction is reported to the FDA's Adverse Event Reporting System (AERS) or is discussed in the literature. This scenario transpired in *Wendell v Johnson & Johnson*,[35] where GlaxoSmithKline (GSK), the original brand manufacturer, were held not strictly liable for failure to warn of the risk of hepatosplenic T-cell lymphoma associated with Purinethol. Information concerning the occurrence of this adverse effect was not reported to AERS or discussed in the literature until after GSK had ceased to distribute the drug in July 2003.[36]

Accordingly, while the majority of courts have continued to apply strict liability by name in warning cases involving prescription drugs, the principles applied 'are nothing more than negligence'.[37] This use of negligence principles in failure to warn cases involving prescription drugs is reflected in *Restatement, Third, Torts: Products Liability*, § 6(d), which limits the responsibility in prescription drug cases to a duty to provide 'reasonable instructions or warnings regarding foreseeable risks of harm'. It should, however, be noted that a negligence standard for failure to warn of adverse effects of prescription drugs must be viewed against a background of a strict form of regulation by the FDA, which regulates both the safety and effectiveness of prescription drugs, and approves all information a manufacturer intends to provide physicians on a drug's recommended use, contraindications, risks and adverse effects.[38]

C. Adequacy

When an unreasonable foreseeable risk exists, and there is a feasible means of abating that risk by warnings, a manufacturer's failure to warn against the risk will, other things being equal, result in liability.[39] The Reporters for the *Restatement, Third, Torts: Products Liability* observe that in assessing the adequacy of the instructions or warnings, there is '[n]o easy guideline' in existence for the courts to adopt; accordingly, the courts focus on several factors, including 'content and comprehensibility, intensity of expression, and the characteristics of expected user groups'.[40]

---

[34] Ibid 923, fn 18, citing DG Owen, 'Defectiveness Restated: Exploding the "Strict" Products Liability Myth' (1996) *University of Illinois Law Review* 743, 782–84; JA Henderson Jr, 'Doctrinal Collapse in Products Liability: the Empty Shell of Failure to Warn' (1990) 65 *NYU Law Review* 265, 273–75 (holding manufacturers strictly liable for unknowable risks prevents the achievement of the tort law objectives of fairness and efficiency).

[35] *Wendell v Johnson & Johnson*, 2012 WL 3042302 (ND Cal) (CD Cal July 25, 2012).

[36] Ibid at *12.

[37] DG Owen, 'Dangers in Prescription Drugs: Filling a Private Law Gap in the Healthcare Debate' (2010) 42 *Conneticut Law Review* 733, 753.

[38] See Federal Food, Drug, and Cosmetic Act, 21 USC §§ 301–392 (2006), originally enacted in 1938; the requirements for warnings and instructions are addressed in ibid §§ 352–353; see further, ibid 753–54.

[39] MS Madden, 'The Duty to Warn in Products Liability: Contours and Criticism' (1987) 89 *West Virginia Law Review* 221, 234.

[40] *Restatement, Third, Torts: Products Liability*, § 2(c) cmt *i*.

A manufacturer of drugs must warn doctors of all material risks, ie those to which a reasonable patient would be likely to attach significance in deciding whether to take the drug.[41] For a warning to be adequate in a prescription drug liability case, it must: '(1) indicate the scope of the danger; (2) communicate the extent or seriousness of the potential danger; (3) alert a reasonably prudent practitioner to the danger; and (4) be conveyed in a satisfactory manner'.[42] In order for a warning to be adequate, it must also be timely. Importantly, there may be a duty to warn of a side-effect *even though a causal relationship has not been clearly proved*.[43] Such a warning must be provided as soon as the risks are identified in reputable journals.[44] This suggests that RR > 2 is not a general threshold to be applied in all cases in determining whether a warning should be given.

Two important aspects of a drug warning's adequacy are the undermining of a drug's effectiveness through over-promotion of a drug's safety and the issue of whether a manufacturer should consider giving bilingual warnings. The undermining of the effectiveness of an otherwise adequate warning may result in a finding that the warning was inadequate. In *Incollingo v Ewing*,[45] the Supreme Court of Pennsylvania held that evidence was properly admitted that detail men working for a pharmaceutical manufacturer over-promoted the antibiotic Chloromycetin by 'minimiz[ing] the dangers of the drug while emphasizing its effectiveness, wide acceptance and use, and lack of certain objectionable side-effects associated with other drugs'.[46]

The matter of whether a manufacturer should provide foreign language warnings is due to the concern that exclusively English usage may fail to provide adequate information to persons who cannot read English, or for whom English is not their principal language. This has resulted in litigation in the US involving persons of Latino origin. In *Ramirez v Plough Inc*,[47] the Supreme Court of California held that any duty of a manufacturer of children's aspirin to provide a warning in respect of the dangers of young children using the product suffering from respiratory illnesses extended merely to the provision of warnings in English as required under Food and Drug Administration regulations, and that there was no duty to provide a Spanish language warning.[48]

[41] *Perez v Wyeth Laboratories Inc* 734 A 2d 1245, 1257 (NJ 1999).

[42] *Madsen v American Home Products Corp* 477 F Supp 2d 1025, 1035 (ED Mo 2007); see also *Martin v Hacker* 628 NE 2d 1308, 1312–15 (NY 1993) (factors include whether the warning is accurate, clear and consistent on its face and whether it portrays with sufficient intensity the risk involved in taking the drug; held insert adequately warned against risk of depression-caused suicide).

[43] *Basko v Sterling Drug, Inc* 416 F 2d 417, 426 (1969); *Sterling Drug, Inc v Cornish* 370 F 2d 82, 85 (1966); *Seley v GD Searle & Co* 423 NE 2d 831, 836–37 (1981) (consumer of ethical birth control drug who suffered stroke alleging Searle was strictly liable for failing to provide proper warnings of risks associated with ingestion of Ovulen by women with a prior medical history of toxaemia during pregnancy).

[44] *Schenebeck v Sterling Drug, Inc* 423 F 2d 919, 921–23 (8th Cir 1970) (failure to warn in 1961 of serious ocular side-effects in patients using chloroquine therapy, despite an American Medical Association publication of that year calling attention to permanent eye damage incurred by a 'few' patients as a result of using the defendant's prescription drug Aralen).

[45] 282 A 2d 206 (Pa 1971).

[46] 282 A 2d 206, 221 (Pa 1971). A plaintiff may utilise an over-promotion theory in order to overcome a manufacturer's argument either that it provided adequate warnings or that a doctor's decision to prescribe a drug notwithstanding his awareness of its dangers was an intervening cause: *Motus v Pfizer, Inc* 196 F Supp 2d 984, 998 (CD Cal 2001), aff'd, 358 F 3d 659, 660–61 (9th Cir 2004). Over-promotion can include the manufacturer's promotion of illegal off-label use, not approved by the FDA: *Ebel v Eli Lilly & Co* 536 F Supp 2d 767, 775 (SD Tex 2008).

[47] *Ramirez v Plough Inc* 863 P 2d 167 (1993).

[48] Ibid 168, 177.

D. Learned Intermediary Doctrine

(i) General Rule

The learned intermediary doctrine provides an exception to the general rule that imposes liability on a manufacturer for failing to warn an end user of the known risks or hazards of its products when it is reasonably foreseeable that they may be injured by them and a warning might be expected to be effective to eliminate or reduce the risk. It allows the manufacturer of a prescription drug to discharge his duty to warn by providing the relevant information to a responsible intermediary, ie to the prescribing physician or other health care provider.[49]

In the United States, the general, although not universal,[50] rule is that a manufacturer of prescription products fulfils its legal duty to warn the patient by conveying an adequate warning to a prescribing physician[51] or other health care provider[52] as an informed intermediary. As the Supreme Court of Oregon stated in *McEwan v Ortho Pharmaceutical Corp*:

> It is well settled ... that the manufacturer of ethical drugs bears the ... duty of making timely and adequate warnings to the medical profession of any dangerous side effects produced by its drugs of which it knows, or has reason to know.[53]

The general rule was followed in *Ortho Pharmaceutical Corp v Chapman*,[54] where the Court explained that where drugs were available only on prescription, a manufacturer's duty to warn extended only to the medical profession, and not to the ultimate users[55] and that since prescription drugs were 'likely to be complex medicines, esoteric in formula and varied in effect', the prescribing physician was able to weigh the benefits and risks of the medication and to make an informed choice—'an individualized medical judgment buttressed on a knowledge of both patient and palliative'.[56] It held that a proper warning by a manufacturer 'communicates a risk attendant on the product's use which is known to experts in the field during the period in which the product is used' and 'need only be directed to doctors, not patients who are the ultimate users'.[57]

Accordingly, the principal rationale behind the learned intermediary rule is that only medical professionals have the 'requisite knowledge, training and judgment' to match

---

[49] *Dietz v Smithkline Beecham Corp* 598 F 3d 812, 815 (11th Cir 2010).

[50] See eg *Griffiths v Blatt* 51 P 3d 1256, 1262 (Or 2002).

[51] *Sterling Drug Inc v Cornish* 370 F 2d 82, 85 (8th Cir 1966); *MacDonald v Ortho Pharmaceutical Corp* 475 NE 2d 65, 69 (Mass 1985): 'The rule in jurisdictions that have addressed the question of the extent of a manufacturer's duty to warn in cases involving prescription drugs is that the prescribing physician acts as a "learned intermediary" between the manufacturer and the patient, and "the duty of the ethical drug manufacturer is to warn the doctor, rather than the patient [although] the manufacturer is directly liable to the patient for a breach of such duty"', citing *McEwan v Ortho Pharmaceutical Corp* 528 P 2d 522, 529 (1974); *Vitanza v Upjohn Co* 428 F Supp 2d 124 (D Conn 1999).

[52] *Walker v Merck & Co Inc* 648 F Supp 931, 934–5 (MD Ga 1986), judgment aff'd 831 F 2d 1069 (11th Cir 1987) (manufacturer fulfilled duty to warn licensed practical nurse who administered vaccine of dangers inherent in measles, mumps and rubella vaccine).

[53] *McEwan v Ortho Pharmaceutical Corp* 528 P 2d 522, 528 (1974).

[54] *Ortho Pharmaceutical Corp v Chapman* 388 NE 2d 541 (1st Dist 1979).

[55] Ibid 548.

[56] Ibid 549.

[57] Ibid.

properly particular drugs with distinctive benefits and dangers to particular patients possessing distinctive constitutions and medical conditions, and to monitor the results thereafter.[58] If manufacturers fulfil their obligations to provide full and fair information to such medical professionals, those professionals should be able to make treatment decisions which are reasonably safe and effective.[59] Other basic rationales have been articulated to support the rule, viz: (1) that the prescribing physician is in a superior position to impart appropriate warnings to their patients; (2) that manufacturers lack effective means to communicate directly with each patient; and (3) that imposing a duty to warn upon the manufacturer would unduly interfere with the physician-patient relationship.[60] There is a strong trend in prescription drug failure to warn cases of adopting this well-established doctrine, which appears to have been adopted by the vast majority of States.[61] However, these figures were subject to challenge by the West Virginia Supreme Court of Appeals in *State, ex rel Johnson & Johnson Corporation v Karl*,[62] which concluded, in rejecting the learned intermediary doctrine for all prescription drugs, that only 22 jurisdictions recognised the learned intermediary doctrine, either by decision or statute.[63]

Texas had been an important jurisdiction without State Supreme Court precedent on the learned intermediary doctrine in cases involving prescription drugs. The matter was resolved in *Centocar, Inc v Hamilton*,[64] where the Texas Supreme Court adopted the doctrine and held that a prescription drug manufacturer fulfils its duty to warn end users of its product's risks by providing adequate warnings to the prescribing physician. It observed that the underlying rationale for the validity of the doctrine, viz that 'the prescribing physician is best suited to weigh the risks and benefits of the prescription drug', remains viable today.[65] The Court stressed that the decision to apply the learned intermediary doctrine placed it alongside the majority of other jurisdictions that had considered the issue,[66]

---

[58] *Reyes v Wyeth Laboratories* 498 F 2d 1264, 1276 (5th Cir 1974), cert denied, 419 US 1096, 95 S Ct 687, 42 L Ed 2d 688 (1974); *Centocar, Inc v Hamilton* 372 SW 3d 140, 158–59 (Tex 2012).

[59] DG Owen, 'Dangers in Prescription Drugs: Filling a Private Law Gap in the Healthcare Debate' (2010) 42 *Conneticut Law Review* 733, 760; and, further, *Dietz v Smithkline Beecham Corp* 598 F 3d 812, 815 (11th Cir 2010); *In re Zyprexa Products Liability Litigation*, 2009 WL 2487305 at *13 (EDNY).

[60] *Larkin v Pfizer, Inc* 153 SW 3d 758, 763–64 (Ky 2004); see further, *State, ex rel Johnson & Johnson Corporation v Karl* 647 SE 2d 899, 905 (W Va 2007), where the Supreme Court of Appeals noted five justifications for the learned intermediary rule, viz (1) the difficulty manufacturers encounter in trying to provide warnings to the ultimate users of prescription drugs; (2) patients' reliance on their treating physicians' judgement in selecting appropriate prescription drugs; (3) the fact that it is physicians who exercise their professional judgement in selecting appropriate drugs; (4) the prescribing physician is in the best position to impart appropriate warnings to their patients; and (5) the concern that imposing a duty to warn directly the ultimate consumers upon the manufacturer would unduly interfere with the doctor patient relationship.

[61] *In re Norplant Contraceptive Prods Liability Litigation* 215 F Supp 2d 795, 806 (ED Tex 2002) (doctrine applying in 48 States, District of Columbia and Puerto Rico); *Vitanza v Upjohn Co* 778 A 2d 829, 838, fn 11 (Conn 2001) (doctrine adopted in 44 jurisdictions); *Larkin v Pfizer, Inc* 153 SW 3d 758, 767, fn 3 (Ky 2004) (34 States specifically adopted learned intermediary rule); *Motus v Pfizer Inc* 358 F 3d 659, 661 (9th Cir 2004); *Ebel v Eli Lilly & Co* 536 F Supp 2d 767, 772–73 (SD Tex 2008), aff'd No 08-40170, 2009 WL 837325 (5th Cir March 30, 2009); *La Meridia Products Liability Litigation v Abbott Laboratories* 447 F 3d 861, 867 (6th Cir 2006).

[62] *State, ex rel Johnson & Johnson Corporation v Karl* 647 SE 2d 899 (W Va 2007).

[63] *State, ex rel Johnson & Johnson Corporation v Karl* 647 SE 2d 899, 900–901, 903–4, 914 (W Va 2007). Their research concluded that the highest courts of 22 States had not adopted the learned intermediary doctrine, although the States cited in fact add up to a total of 21: ibid 903–4.

[64] *Centocar, Inc v Hamilton* 372 SW 3d 140 (Tex 2012).

[65] *Centocar, Inc v Hamilton* 372 SW 3d 140, 158–59 (Tex 2012), citing *Reyes v Wyeth Laboratories* 498 F 2d 1264, 1276 (5th Cir 1974), cert denied, 419 US 1096, 95 S Ct 687, 42 L Ed 2d 688 (1974).

[66] Ibid 157–58.

noting that the highest courts of at least 35 States had adopted some form of the doctrine in the prescription drug products liability context, or referred favourably in decisions to its application within that context.[67]

(ii) Exceptions

In the absence of a conventional physician-patient relationship, exceptions to the learned intermediary rule may operate. In the leading decision of *MacDonald v Ortho Pharmaceutical Corp*,[68] it was held that a manufacturer of oral contraceptives owed a direct duty to the ultimate user to warn her of dangers inherent in the use of the pill. The learned intermediary doctrine was held not to apply to contraceptives, which warranted the imposition of a common law duty on a manufacturer to warn users directly of associated risks.[69] In *MacDonald*, a woman who had used Ortho Novum contraceptive pills for three years brought an action against Ortho, alleging that her stroke and consequent disablement had been caused by the pills. The Court observed that oral contraceptives were distinguishable from other prescription drugs in the light of 'the heightened participation of patients in decisions relating to use of "the pill"'; the substantial risks connected with the pill; the feasibility of direct warnings by the manufacturer to the user; the limited annual prescribing of the physician; and the possibility that oral communications between physicians and consumers were 'insufficient or too scanty ... to apprise consumers of the product's dangers'.[70] However, the majority of jurisdictions have declined to follow the *MacDonald* approach and have continued to adhere to the learned intermediary doctrine.[71] Other exceptions to the learned intermediary rule concern vaccines administered en masse at public health clinics[72] and direct marketing of prescription drugs to consumers.

(iii) Direct Marketing of Prescription Drugs

An exception has developed in recent times in response to the proliferation in the United States of direct-to-consumer advertising. The view is taken by some commentators that the learned intermediary doctrine is anachronistic in the modern medical world where prescription drug manufacturers now 'jump over' physicians to consumers via television

---

[67] Ibid 157, fn 17.

[68] *MacDonald v Ortho Pharmaceutical Corp* 475 NE 2d 65 (Mass 1985).

[69] Ibid 68.

[70] Ibid 70; see also *Odgers v Ortho Pharmaceutical Corp* 609 F Supp 867, 878–79 (DC Mich 1985). Cf *Kociemba v GD Searle & Co* 680 F Supp 1293, 1306 (D Minn 1988) (intrauterine device (IUD) manufacturer had no duty to warn device user directly of the risks and hazards associated with the Cu-7 IUD, when manufacturer had provided warnings and information to the plaintiff's physician, who, 'as the prescriber of a drug, [was] in the best position to give a highly individualized warning to a patient based on the physician's knowledge of the patient and the inherent risk of the drug': ibid 1305).

[71] See eg *MacPherson v Searle & Co* 775 F Supp 417, 425 (DDC 1991).

[72] *Davis v Wyeth Lab Inc* 399 F 2d 121, 131 (9th Cir 1968); *Reyes v Wyeth Laboratories* 498 F 2d 1264, 1276–77 (1974) (where vaccine dispensed 'to all comers in an assembly line fashion', precluding the ability of medical personnel 'to make an individualized medical judgment of the vaccinee's needs or susceptibilities', Wyeth was under a duty to warn vaccinees' parents of the danger inherent in its vaccine: ibid 1277); *Givens v Lederle* 556 F 2d 1341, 1345 (1977). Cf vaccines administered under a local programme which continue to fall within the scope of the learned intermediary rule: *Walker v Merck & Co Inc* 648 F Supp 931, 934–5 (MD Ga 1986).

and other forms of mass advertising.[73] Consequently, it has been held that the learned intermediary doctrine does not apply to the direct marketing of prescription drugs to consumers. In *Perez v Wyeth Laboratories Inc*,[74] patients who had undergone the surgical insertion of Norplant, an FDA-approved reversible contraceptive, brought a products liability action against the manufacturer of the drug. They alleged that the defendants had conducted a 'massive' advertising campaign for Norplant, which was directed at women rather than at their doctors, advertising on television, and in women's magazines. The plaintiffs' principal claim alleged that the defendant had failed to warn adequately about the side-effects associated with Norplant. It was held by the Supreme Court of New Jersey that since the premises justifying the learned intermediary doctrine, viz reluctance to undermine the doctor-patient relationship; the absence of the need for patient's informed consent; inability of a drug manufacturer to communicate with patients; and the complexity of the subject, were belied by advertisement of pharmaceuticals directed at consumers, the doctrine did not apply to the direct marketing of drugs to consumers.[75] In addition, the Court held that, in the context of direct-to-consumer advertising of pharmaceuticals, a rebuttable presumption existed that when a manufacturer complied with FDA advertising, labelling and warning requirements it would be taken to have had satisfied its duty to warn the physician about potentially harmful side-effects of its product. The presumption was not absolute, but compliance with FDA regulations served as 'compelling evidence' that a manufacturer had satisfied its duty to warn.[76] The New Jersey Supreme Court also ruled that where a manufacturer of drugs had directly advertised the drug to consumers, neither the physician nor the manufacturer should be entirely relieved of their respective duties to warn of adverse effects. Thus the role of the physician in prescribing the drug did not break the chain of causation in respect of the manufacturer's failure to warn of such effects.[77]

Until 2007, all courts considering the learned intermediary doctrine in the context of direct-to-consumer advertising continued to apply the doctrine, rejecting *Perez*.[78] However, in 2007, a majority of the West Virginia Supreme Court of Appeals, as a matter of first impression, relied extensively on *Perez* in declining to adopt the learned intermediary doctrine for *all* prescription drugs in *State ex rel Johnson & Johnson Corp v Karl*.[79] It followed *Perez* in finding the justifications for the learned intermediary doctrine to be 'largely outdated and unpersuasive'.[80] The primary reasons for this conclusion were '[s]ignificant changes in the drug industry' subsequent to the doctrine's adoption, in particular, 'the initiation and intense proliferation of direct-to-consumer advertising, along with its impact on the physician/patient relationship, and the development of the internet as a common

---

[73] DG Owen, 'Dangers in Prescription Drugs: Filling a Private Law Gap in the Healthcare Debate' (2010) 42 *Connecticut Law Review* 733, 765.

[74] 734 A 2d 1245 (NJ 1999).

[75] Ibid 1255–57.

[76] Ibid 1257.

[77] Ibid 1262–63.

[78] See, esp *In re Norplant Contraceptive Products Liability Litigation* 165 F 3d 374, 379–80 (5th Cir 1999); *Beale v Biomet, Inc* 492 F Supp 2d 1360, 1376–77 (SD Fla 2007); *Colacicco v Apotex, Inc* 432 F Supp 2d 514, 547 fn 30 (ED Pa 2006), aff'd, 521 F 3d 253, 276 (3rd Cir 2008); *In re Meridia Products Liability Litigation* 328 F Supp 2d 791, 812 fn 19 (ND Ohio 2004), aff'd, 447 F 3d 861 (6th Cir 2006); *Heindel v Pfizer, Inc* 381 F Supp 2d 364, 378 (DNJ 2004).

[79] *State, ex rel Johnson & Johnson Corporation v Karl* 647 SE 2d 899, 908, 910–11 (W Va 2007).

[80] Ibid 906.

method of dispensing and obtaining prescription drug information'.[81] On a public policy and public interest basis, a majority of the Court held that manufacturers of prescription drugs were subject to the same duty to warn consumers about the risks of their products as other manufacturers and declined to adopt the learned intermediary exception to this general rule.[82] By the courts' declining to recognise the learned intermediary rule, patients would be able to make an informed decision about their medical treatment.[83] However, the dissenting judges argued that the majority had been 'shortsighted' in deciding that the doctrine had completely outlived its purpose. By attaching undue influence to the effect of direct marketing, the majority had overlooked the useful purpose served by the doctrine for prescription drugs that were not heavily marketed and had downplayed the circumstances where the physician *did* assume the learned intermediary role in deciding which prescription drugs were appropriate for a given patient, based upon a particular individual's specific medical needs.[84]

It has been suggested that the support for *Perez* in *Karl* may herald an abandonment of 'a rigid paternalistic doctrine' that developed under very different circumstances.[85] Indeed, it has been predicted that the New Mexico Supreme Court would follow suit.[86] However, Professor Owen cautions against the idea that the two cases reflect a trend in recognition by the courts of 'the wisdom of broadening the duty of pharmaceutical manufacturers to share vital information about drug risks directly with consumers'.[87] Nevertheless, he submits that in order to enhance choice, private law should abolish the learned intermediary doctrine. So doing would 'provide both manufacturers and pharmacists with duties to communicate useful cost–benefit information about drug dangers'.[88] Abolishing the doctrine should

---

[81] Ibid 907.

[82] Ibid 914, Davies CJ (Maynard and Starcher JJ, concurring).

[83] Ibid 918, Maynard J, and 919, Starcher J. They 'can read the labels, instructions and warnings, and if the manufacturer makes them clear enough, the patients can be proactive in working with their doctors to receive the best care': ibid 919, Starcher J.

[84] Ibid 914–15, 917, Albright J (joined by Benjamin J).

[85] DG Owen, 'Dangers in Prescription Drugs: Filling a Private Law Gap in the Healthcare Debate' (2010) 42 *Conneticut Law Review* 733, 767.

[86] *Rimbert v Eli Lilly & Co* 577 F Supp 2d, 1174, 1214–24 (DNM 2008) (predicting that the New Mexico Supreme Court would not adopt the learned intermediary rule).

[87] DG Owen, 'Dangers in Prescription Drugs: Filling a Private Law Gap in the Healthcare Debate' (2010) 42 *Connecticut Law Review* 733, 767. That this is true is reflected in the recent decision of the Texas Supreme Court in *Centocar, Inc v Hamilton* 372 SW 3d 140 (Tex 2012). Without determining whether Texas law should recognise a direct-to-consumer (DTC) advertising exception when a prescription drug manufacturer distributes intentionally misleading information directly to patients or prospective patients, the Court held that there was no reason to adopt the exception where the physician-patient relationship existed, the manufacturer provided warnings to the prescribing physician that the drug had the possible side effect in issue of which the patient complained (lupus-like syndrome), and the patient had been prescribed the drug before she saw the informational materials at issue (a video which was part of a 'treatment companion kit', intended to educate the patient regarding the medication): ibid 164. It is submitted that this is the correct decision as to have accepted the DTC advertising exception would be likely to make manufacturers reluctant to provide patient care materials to prescribers.

[88] Ibid 775. A pharmacist has a general duty to warn physicians (or customers) of susceptibilities of those particular customers of the pharmacy to side-effects of a drug that it sells them, either because of other drugs the pharmacy knows the customer is taking or because of a pre-existing physical or mental condition known to the pharmacy that makes the drug contraindicated for the customer: *Walton v Bayer Corp* 643 F 3d 994, 1000–1001 (7th Cir 2011). However, a pharmacist has been held to be under no duty to warn a customer of a potential inter-action between two drugs under the learned intermediary doctrine. The court reasoned that '[t]o hold otherwise would impose a greater duty on the pharmacist than on the drug's manufacturer, as the duty of extending warn-ings concerning prescription drugs belongs with physicians': *Digiovanni v Albertson's Inc* 940 NE 2d 73, 76 (Ill Ct App 2010). Nonetheless, a pharmacist may be under a duty to notify a customer that there has been a change in

increase the amount of information on drug dangers provided to consumers, improving their opportunity for an intelligent final say on what types of dangerous pharmaceuticals, if any, they chose to consume.[89] However, how Professor Owen would achieve this provision of information to the consumer remains unclear. There is a distinct difference between the provision of information to patients for advertising purposes and that for labelling purposes, since the latter is directed primarily to health care professionals.[90] If this provision of information to consumers was through patient package inserts, it is difficult to see how this information would be seen by the consumer prior to consultation with the doctor. The only feasible way in which such information could be communicated by manufacturers to provide effective information about various drug choices would be at the direct-to-consumer advertising stage. This is suggested by Owen's view that such manufacturers 'will be better positioned to help doctors determine *initially*, which (if any) drugs are best suited to their particular conditions and constituents'.[91] However, while under the current law physicians often fail to engage in meaningful discussion with patients, imposing an obligation on manufacturers to warn patients direct could further reduce incentives of conscientious physicians even to try.[92] Moreover, in a world where the provision of medication is becoming increasingly personalised, it is arguable that the learned intermediary rule should be retained: while manufacturers of prescription drugs can develop drugs for specific genetic profiles, they are unable to make warnings that pertain to all individuals with such profiles.[93] In any event, even if full risk information on a prescription drug were provided by its manufacturer directly to consumers, this would only offer limited assistance to patients: such patients would need to be provided with 'equally clear information about all of the other products and procedures that might serve the same purpose'.[94] Such a broad duty to educate is not part of a manufacturer's duty to warn of the risks associated with its product.[95]

There are also certain legal differences between the law in the United Kingdom/European Community and in the United States, which would make the outcome in *Perez* unlikely to be the same under the Directive. First, in the European Community all advertising to the general public of prescription only medicines is prohibited.[96] Secondly, the fact that a competent regulatory authority in the European Community has not refused a marketing

strength of *dosage* of a prescription drug since such a notification 'does not infringe upon the physician-patient relationship': *Nail v Publix Super Markets, Inc* 72 So 3d 608, 616 (Ala 2011) (Supreme Court of Alabama).

[89] Ibid. But cf HR 542: Consumer Protection Act of 2011, '[t]o eliminate the learned intermediary defence to tort claims based on product liability, and for other purposes'. See n 104 below.

[90] See 21 CFR §201.5 (2007) (advertising regulations) and 21 CFR § 201.5 (2007) (labelling regulations); JL Peters, Note, 'State v. Karl: An Unreasonable Rejection of the Learned Intermediary Doctrine' (2008) 48 *Jurimetrics Journal* 285, 297–98.

[91] DG Owen (above, n 87) (2010) 42 *Conneticut Law Review* 733, 775–76.

[92] L Noah, 'This is Your Products Liability Restatement on Drugs' (2009) 74 *Brooklyn Law Review* 839, 899; see further, JL Peters, (2008) 48 *Jurimetrics Journal* 285, 299–305, 308.

[93] JL Peters (above, n 90) (2008) 48 *Jurimetrics Journal* 285, 304–5.

[94] L Noah (above, n 92) (2009) 74 *Brooklyn Law Review* 839, 903.

[95] Ibid.

[96] Dir 2001/83/EEC on the Community Code Relating to Medicinal Products for Human Use [2001] OJ L311/67, as amended by Dir 2004/27/EC [2004] OJ L136/34, Art 88(1); Human Medicines Regulations 2012, SI 2012/1916, reg 284.

authorisation pursuant to labelling or package leaflet requirements 'does not alter the general legal liability of the manufacturer'.[97]

(iv) Regulatory Exceptions

There are important American regulatory exceptions to the learned intermediary rule. In respect of oral contraceptives, the FDA has issued detailed requirements for the patient package inserts accompanying the product received by the user,[98] and similar requirements have been laid down for intrauterine devices.[99] In the United Kingdom and indeed throughout the European Union the provision of package leaflets for human medicinal products is obligatory unless all the required information is on the container or on the packaging.[100]

(v) Restatement, Third, Torts: Products Liability

The *Restatement, Third, Torts: Products Liability* § 6(d)(1) and (2), follow the majority of jurisdictions by adopting both the learned intermediary doctrine (§ 6 (d)(1)) and the mass immunisation exception (§ 6(d)(2)). Section 6(d)(1) preserves the learned intermediary rule by permitting the manufacturer of a prescription drug to discharge its duty to warn by providing adequate warnings or instructions to 'prescribing and other health-care providers[101] who are in a position to reduce the risks of harm in accordance with the instructions or warnings'. Section 6(d)(2) preserves the exception to the learned intermediary rule by affirming the manufacturer's duty to provide warning and instruction information directly to the patient 'when the manufacturer knows or has reason to know that health-care providers will not be in a position to reduce the risks of harm in accordance with the instructions or warnings'. As has been noted, the latter exception, where a manufacturer has a duty to provide a warning direct to a patient, has been associated with mass immunisations, a limited number of situations concerning direct manufacturer to consumer advertising, and certain situations where physician-patient contact is in practice restricted, including

---

[97] Dir 2001/83/EC, Art 61(4).

[98] *Madden & Owen on Products Liability*, 3rd edn, (2011), § 22:10, citing Code of Federal Regulations, Title 21–Food and Drugs, 21 CFR § 310.501.

[99] 21 CFR § 310.502.

[100] Dir 2001/83/EC on the Community Code Relating to Medicinal Products for Human Use [2001] OJ L311/67, as amended by Dir 2004/27/EC [2004] OJ L136/34, Art 58; Medicines Act 1968, s 86; (see generally, Dir 2001/83/EC, Title V, labelling and package leaflets, Arts 54–69). Note that in the US, a 'hybrid' model has been advocated to promote safe and effective prescription drug therapy by adopting (a) the learned intermediary doctrine as the legal standard of liability for drug manufacturer's in their product warnings; and (b) an FDA-mandated system of patient package inserts (PPIs) for all prescription drugs to supplement the information a patient receives from his doctor: CA Paytash, Note, 'The Learned Intermediary Doctrine and Patient Package Inserts: A Balanced Approach To Preventing Drug-Related Injury' (1999) 51 *Stanford Law Review* 1343,1367, 1368–71.

[101] Note that an obligation to provide warnings to physicians *other* than a prescribing physician could amount to a potential expansion of a duty to warn. There have been dicta (albeit not controlling) supporting *Restatement, Third, Torts: Products Liability* § 6(d)(1) as not inconsistent with Montana law, where a health care provider other than the prescribing physician was actually responsible for making decisions related to the patient's case, such that the warnings should be provided to that other health care professional as well: *Stevens v Novartis Pharmaceuticals Corp* 246 P 3d 244, 259–60 (Mont 2010).

prescriptions for birth control medicines. The *Restatement* 'leaves to developing case law' the recognition of exceptions to the learned intermediary rule.[102]

Notwithstanding Professor Owen's radical proposal that American private law should abolish the learned intermediary rule,[103] it appears that the learned intermediary doctrine is operative and continues to play an important role in American law.[104] Some uncertainty has, however, arisen as to whether the doctrine is available only where the claim is in negligence, or is available under strict liability. On a failure to warn claim, Oregon's Strict Products Liability Statute, construed in accordance with *Restatement, Second, Torts* § 402A, and its comments *h* and *j*, has been held not to leave room for the learned intermediary doctrine, which is regarded as operative only in claims based on the common law of negligence.[105] Similarly, it will be seen[106] that in the United Kingdom there has also been uncertainty as to whether the doctrine is available only where the claim is in negligence, or is available also under the strict liability regime of the Product Liability Directive and the Consumer Protection Act 1987.

III. WARNING AND INSTRUCTION DEFECTS AND PHARMACEUTICAL PRODUCTS UNDER THE PRODUCT LIABILITY DIRECTIVE

A. A Fault-based Form of Liability

(i) *Reasonableness Standard: Feasibility of Warning*

The position under the Directive in respect of warning defects is an uncertain one. However, most commentators who have explored the issue suggest that the matter is essentially no different from that of negligence. In viewing warning defects as fault based, Professor Stapleton considers that a claim for failure to have a warning about a drug's side-effect is 'inexorably linked to the reasonable *feasibility* of warning, given an alert understanding of the world and the state of the art in acquiring information such as the epidemiological data needed to justify such a warning' (emphasis added).[107]

---

[102] *Restatement, Third, Torts: Products Liability* § 6(d), comment *e*, p 149.

[103] DG Owen (above, n 87) (2010) 42 *Conneticut Law Review* 733, 775.

[104] A Bill was introduced into Congress (HR 542: Consumer Protection Act of 2011) by Representative Bob Filner (D-CA) '[t]o eliminate the learned intermediary defence to tort claims based on product liability, and for other purposes'. The Bill provides that it 'shall not be a defence to any tort claim in any court in the United States that a manufacturer of a product has fulfilled that manufacturer's duty of care when the manufacturer provides all the necessary information to a learned intermediary who then interacts with the consumer of the product'. Although the defence is presumed to apply to pharmaceutical manufacturers, the Bill is not limited to prescription drugs, referring broadly to products. It is highly unlikely that the Bill will ever make it out of Committee, let alone pass, in the light of the current Republican majority in the House: See, further, CM Dickenson, 'Issues and Trends in Drug Product Labelling' in *Recent Developments in Food and Drug Law: 2012 Edition* (Thomson Reuters/Aspatore, 2011) 80–81.

[105] *Griffith v Blatt* 51 P 3d 1256, 1262 (2002). This may increase the uncertainty surrounding the basis of the learned intermediary doctrine.

[106] As to which, see below, pp 74–77.

[107] J Stapleton, 'Liability for Drugs in the US and EU: Rhetoric and Reality' (2007) 26 *Review of Litigation* 991, 1019.

(ii) Use of Epidemiological Data in Exercising the Reasonableness Standard

There is much to be unpacked in Stapleton's analysis, but there is a clear suggestion that there is a link between the reasonableness of including a warning and 'the state of the art of the epidemiological data relating to the drug'.[108] She argues that in determining whether a warning of a side-effect is necessary, there needs to be a 'scientific consensus of a causal link', formed on the accumulation of enough data to be 'sufficiently scientifically significant'.[109] The danger with this approach is that it might suggest supremacy of statistical significance in determining failure to warn, and that a warning of a suspected side-effect should only be provided when a risk is statistically significant, ie where the relative risk of an association is greater than two. Such an approach is arguably designed to insert an epidemiological threshold into both defectiveness and causation, and it is submitted that this could be seen as part of what one leading claimant solicitor describes as a defendant-based strategy of presenting 'all issues of defect and causation as intrinsically dependent'.[110] However, Stapleton concedes, and surely correctly, that, in some circumstances a drug may be defective by virtue of not having a warning about a possible adverse effect, 'even where evidence for a causal link is "immature"'.[111] The latter approach would be consistent with the position in the US, where, as we have seen, there may be a duty to warn of a side-effect *even though a causal relationship has not been clearly proved*.[112] A recent illustration of this approach is the decision of the Full Federal Court of Australia in *Merck Sharp & Dohme (Australia) Pty Limited v Peterson*,[113] where it upheld the decision of the trial judge that the anti-inflammatory drug Vioxx had a defect[114] in that in some people, by some unknown mechanism, it increased the risk of myocardial infarction (MI) and the defendant had provided no information, advice or warning as to this effect.[115] The Full Court came to this decision, despite acknowledging the problems in drawing definite conclusions from a major study into Vioxx—the VIGOR study—about the risk of MI from the consumption of Vioxx.[116]

---

[108]   Ibid 1017.

[109]   Ibid 1014.

[110]   D Body, 'Product Liability Claims Under the Consumer Protection Act 1987: Some Practical Problems' [2012] *Journal of Personal Injury Law* 79, 84.

[111]   J Stapleton, 'Liability for Drugs in the US and EU: Rhetoric and Reality' (2007) 26 *Review of Litigation* 991, 1017.

[112]   *Basko v Sterling Drug, Inc* 416 F 2d 417, 426 (1969); *Sterling Drug, Inc v Cornish* 370 F 2d 82, 85 (1966).

[113]   *Merck Sharp & Dohme (Australia) Pty Ltd v Peterson* [2011] FCAFC 128, leave to appeal refused, [2012] HCATrans 105.

[114]   Section 75AD of Part VA of the Trade Practices Act 1974 (Cth) (now s 138 of Sch 2 of the Competition and Consumer Act 2010 (Cth)) gives individuals the right to be compensated by a manufacturer for loss suffered by the individual as a result of injury caused by defective goods. Part VA introduced strict liability based on the Product Liability Directive. Section 75AC of the Trade Practices Act (now s 9 of Sch 2 of the Competition and Consumer Act 2010 (Cth)) similarly defines goods (its equivalent to a product) as being defective 'if their safety is not such as persons generally are entitled to expect'.

[115]   *Merck Sharp & Dohme (Australia) Pty Limited v Peterson* [2011] FCAFC 128, [201].

[116]   Ibid [200]. See further, [48]. The trial judge held that across a population the consumption of Vioxx did involve an increase in risk but that the extent of the risk in a particular case would be dependent on the conditions presumptively existing in the patient's vasculature. Thus, for a patient in a reasonably advanced state of atherosclerosis, the risk was more pronounced: [2010] FCA 180, (2010) 184 FCR 1, [916]. Accordingly, he concluded that '[a]bsent the provision of any information advice or warning ... the risk ... made the safety of Vioxx less than what persons generally were entitled to expect': ibid [917]. See generally, C Newman-Martin, 'Manufacturers' liability for undiscoverable design flaws in prescription drugs: A Merck-Y area of the law' (2011) 19 *Torts Law Journal* 26.

B. Impossibility of Warning: Undiscoverability or Unknowability of Risk Versus Foreseeability of Risk

Given the sensitivity of Member States to the manner in which the state of the art develops, and their commitment in Recital 7 of the Directive to a fair apportionment of the risks inherent in modern technological production', Stapleton suggests that the claim of defect must fail where such a warning was 'impossible', in the light of the state of the art of the epidemiological data relating to the drug at the time of its supply.[117]

The meaning of impossible in this context is significant. Stapleton submits that a failure to warn could only be 'impossible' if the risk or hazard in question is 'undiscoverable' or 'scientifically unknowable' at the time of supply.[118] While this would seem to be correct, it is perhaps easier to see these issues as matters of *foreseeability* of risk. This would be consistent not only with the endorsement by the US courts of comment *j* of § 402A of the *Restatement, Second, Torts* that the duty to warn extended only to foreseeable risks,[119] but also with *Restatement, Third, Torts: Products Liability*, § 6(d), which limits the responsibility in prescription drug cases to a duty to provide 'reasonable instructions or warnings regarding foreseeable risks of harm'.

An objectification of this foreseeability of risk approach is reflected in Christopher Newdick's helpful and wide-ranging analysis of strict liability for medicinal products prior to the Consumer Protection Act's entry into force.[120] Newdick submits that an overreliance on warnings under a consumer expectation approach, 'as if under a theory of volenti', may conceal a range of circumstances in which it is unreasonable to assume the patient to have consented to the risk of the damage in question, and, without cautious treatment, could seriously undermine the notion on which strict liability is based.[121] To circumvent the problems of an *over-subjective* approach to the use of foresight as a test by which patients have to tolerate untoward side-effects of drugs, Newdick adopts an *objective* approach to three categories of risk associated with medicinal products, viz (i) foreseen risks to foreseeable individuals; (ii) foreseen risks to unforeseeable individuals; and (iii) unforeseeable injuries.[122]

In respect of foreseen risks to foreseeable individuals, since warnings are passed to patients 'only in the most variable and inconsistent fashion',[123] he has suggested that an objective test replace the notion of consent, 'based on the needs of all patients to tolerate

---

[117] J Stapleton, (2007) 26 *Review of Litigation* 991, 1010–11, 1029–30.

[118] Ibid 1010–11. Cf, per contra, Decision 442/2011 by the Supreme Court of Spain, 17 June (LA LEY 91051/2011), noted in SP Romero and CR Belda, 'Failure to provide adverse event information both to patients and to doctors can render the medicine defective (even if the adverse event was not known at the time of the launch' (2011) 45 *International Product Liability Review* 16. The Supreme Court held that the omission from the Patient Information Leaflet (PIL) of information about a medicine's adverse effects which was *unknown* at the time of the medicine's launch impacted on the safety of the medicinal product and rendered the product defective under the Spanish General Consumers Act (Royal Decree 1/2007 of 16 November), the Spanish legislation implementing the Product Liability Directive. *Sed quere?*

[119] *Feldman v Lederle Laboratories* 479 A 2d 374, 387 (NJ 1984).

[120] C Newdick, 'Strict Liability for Defective Drugs in the Pharmaceutical Industry' (1985) 101 *Law Quarterly Review* 405, 412–20.

[121] Ibid 411.

[122] Ibid 412–20.

[123] Ibid 414.

the danger of some degree of loss from risks that have been taken reasonably'.[124] Such an approach would depend upon a patient undertaking a reasonable risk, following recommended treatment and submitting to the reasonable costs inevitably attaching to any decision to have treatment by drugs.[125] Regard would be had 'to the seriousness of the side-effect relative to the extent or nature of the illness under treatment', and accordingly, the 'graver the consequences of illness, the greater should be the patient's willingness to risk suffering a reaction from the drug as a cost of recuperation'.[126] Thus, in the case of cancer the gravity of such a disease would allow one to consider the possibility of an adverse reaction to the drug of a certain severity being acceptable, but in the case of a sore throat one would not accept adverse side-effects of such severity.[127]

In the context of foreseen risks to unforeseeable individuals, following *Sidaway v Governors of Bethlem Royal Hospital*,[128] Newdick submits that those risks regarded as too remote to form the basis of a rational judgement by the patient would not require disclosure:[129] in effect, this would suggest a negligence approach within a strict liability system. Moreover, the subsequent decision of the House of Lords in *Bolitho v City & Hackney HA*[130] has enabled courts more readily to assess the reasonableness of clinical judgement on a risk–benefit basis in the light of their own assessment of expert opinion.[131] It could therefore be argued that there is an inevitability about the connection between a risk–benefit approach, along with a *Sidaway/Bolitho* negligence standard of the warnings of adverse effects, in the determination of whether a product is defective under the Act. This appears to be especially true in cases of medical emergency. Yet the very scenario of an emergency points to the practical difficulties of warnings: in particular, how should, and in what circumstances can, the public be warned of risks such as hepatitis C? Should the

---

[124] Ibid 414–15.

[125] Ibid.

[126] Ibid 415.

[127] Miller and Goldberg (above, n 2) para 12.19. cf the decision of the Paris Court of Appeal that in the absence of a specific warning, a drug will be considered defective each time an adverse reaction takes place in relation to a known risk, even where the adverse reaction is serious or extremely rare: CA Paris 23 September 2004, *Société Ferring* n° 02/16713, Dalloz 2005 p1012. See T Rouhette and T d'Honincthun, 'The expanding obligation to provide information on the undersirable effects of medication' (2005) 19 *European Product Liability Review* 29 (criticising the Paris Court of Appeal for stating that had it not applied the development risk defence, the manufacturer would have been liable for failing to warn the user or prescribing physician about potential, even very unusual side effects, and questioning the appropriateness of increasing the list of undesirable effects on packaging leaflets); and, further, chapter 8 of this volume, p 184–85. Professor Newdick has argued that there may be scope for extending a doctor's obligation to disclose risks by making available medicinal products (presumably on a named-patient basis) that are currently considered too dangerous to market, on the understanding that there will be greater discussion of such relative risks and benefits: C Newdick, 'Special Problems of Compensating Those Damaged by Medicinal Products' in SAM McLean (ed), *Compensation for Damage: An International Perspective* (Aldershot, Dartmouth, 1993) 13.

[128] *Sidaway v Governors of Bethlem Royal Hospital* [1985] AC 871, [1985] 1 All ER 643. A doctor owes a legal duty to a patient to warn in general terms of possible serious risks involved in the medical procedure. The concept of 'medical paternalism' has been rejected and a patient has a prima facie right to be informed of any risk of serious injury which might result, even if that risk is small, providing it is well-established as a risk: *Chester v Afsher* [2004] UKHL 41, [2005] 1 AC 134 at [16] per Lord Steyn.

[129] Newdick (1985) 101 *Law Quarterly Review* 405, 416.

[130] *Bolitho v City & Hackney Health Authority* [1998] AC 232, [1997] 4 All ER 771.

[131] Ibid 241–43, 777–80, Lord Browne-Wilkinson. See also *Pearce v United Bristol Healthcare NHS Trust* (1998) 48 BMLR 118, CA, and, for a somewhat different approach, *Rogers v Whittaker* (1992) 109 ALR 625 (Australian High Ct); also S Deakin, A Johnston and B Markesinis, *Markesinis and Deakin's Tort Law*, 6th edn (Oxford, Oxford University Press, 2008) 233–35; Winfield and Jolowicz, *Tort*, paras 5.56 and 25.4.

warnings be given to each individual patient who is given blood?[132] '[T]he patient is likely to be unconscious when the units of blood, bearing a [warning] on the label, arrive'.[133] It also seems apparent from the judgment in *A v National Blood Authority*[134] that even warning the public of possible hepatitis C contamination in blood, together with express warnings on the bags of blood, would not necessarily have been sufficient to ensure that the blood was not defective.[135]

Although Stapleton correctly concludes that under Article 6, which suspected adverse effects must be warned about and when in order for a drug to provide the safety to which we are legally entitled 'taking all circumstances into account', is 'a matter of degree and judgment',[136] it is submitted that the Newdick objectification of the foreseeability of risk approach provides greater clarity of guidance on when an allegation of a failure to warn defect becomes viable than the reasonableness standard of feasibility of warning.

C. Unforeseeable Injuries: Is There a Role for the Article 7(e) Defence in Failure to Warn Claims?

In the context of unforeseeable injuries, Newdick argues that no question of consent complicates the issues. In his view, such injuries would probably fall within the development risk defence of Article 7(e) of the Directive,[137] which provides that:

> The producer shall not be liable as a result of this Directive if he proves ... that the state of scientific and technical knowledge at the time when he put the product into circulation was not such as to enable the existence of the defect to be discovered.[138]

However, this is not accepted by Stapleton, who considers that there is no role for the defence in failure to warn cases. In her view, since a failure to warn claim is assessed according to the reasonableness of including a warning at the time of supply, there will therefore be no role for the Article 7(e) defence, and Article 7(e) only has a role in the context of design defect claims.[139] This view is controversial, and appears to be at least partly based on an eliding of the concepts of the state of the art and the state of scientific and technical knowledge, in determining whether a product is defective because of failure to warn, thus rendering the role of the defence otiose. This elision occurs through her suggestion that

---

[132] R Goldberg, 'Paying for Bad Blood: Strict Product Liability After the Hepatitis C Litigation' (2002) 10 *Medical Law Review* 165, 185.

[133] Cf MA Franklin, 'Tort Liability for Hepatitis: An Analysis and a Proposal' (1972) 24 *Stanford Law Review* 439, 473.

[134] *A v National Blood Authority* [2001] 3 All ER 289, para 65.

[135] Ibid. Burton J noted that this was particularly so in the light of the no-waiver of liability provision in Art 12 of the Directive. It has been submitted that the warning of possible hepatitis C contamination in blood with express warnings on the bags would not amount to a provision limiting or exempting from liability, contrary to Art 12. Warnings about dangers are not the same as an attempt to *exclude* liability in respect of them: Miller and Goldberg (above n 2) para 12.20, fn 82. Nonetheless, it has been observed that '[a] court might, exceptionally, hold that, since many patients receiving blood are incapable of giving consent, the provision of a warning in the product information would be an Article 6 circumstance rendering the product defective in any event': C Hodges, Note, 'Compensating Patients' (2001) 117 *Law Quarterly Review* 528, 529.

[136] J Stapleton, (2007) 26 *Review of Litigation* 991, 1014–15.

[137] Newdick (1985) 101 *Law Quarterly Review* 405, 419–20.

[138] For discussion of the development risk defence and medicinal products, see chapter 8 of this volume.

[139] J Stapleton, (2007) 26 *Review of Litigation* 991, 1018.

there is a role for the state of scientific knowledge at the time of supply in ascertaining whether a medicinal product is defective.[140]

While both section 3(2)(c) of the Consumer Protection Act 1987 and Article 6(1) (c) and 6(2) of the Directive recognise that the level of safety which has to be assessed in determining what persons generally are entitled to expect is the one which was considered appropriate at the time when the product was supplied by its producer to another, there is also a need in this context to distinguish section 3(2)(c)/Article 6(1) (c) from the development risk defence of section 4(1)(e)/Article 7(e). The term 'development risk' refers to defects undiscoverable in the light of the state of scientific and technical knowledge at the time of supply, whereas section 3(2)(c) focuses on the state of the art, which is the relative standard of safety required to ascertain whether a product was defective at the time of supply.[141] This view was reaffirmed by the trial judge in the Vioxx class action, *Merck Sharp & Dohme (Australia) Pty Limited v Peterson*,[142] who opined that section 75AK(1)(c) of the Trade Practices Act 1974 (the equivalent of section 4(1)(e)/Article 7(e)) contemplated the existence of a defect capable of being discovered by reference to the current state of scientific or technical knowledge.[143] It was 'not concerned with the kind of contextual circumstances referred to in s 75AC (2) [the Australian equivalent of section 3(2)/Article 6(1)]'.[144] An attempt to elide some of the issues relevant to the state of the art and to development risks was presented in the defendant's arguments in *Abouzaid v Mothercare (UK) Ltd*.[145] In particular, it appears to have been suggested that there was a role for the state of scientific and technical knowledge at the time of supply in ascertaining whether a product was defective when in fact it was relevant only to the availability of the development risk defence. The defendant's suggestion was rejected by Chadwick LJ. He emphasised that, in determining whether the product was defective under strict liability, the test was what level of safety persons generally were entitled to expect and not, as an expert witness appeared to assume, the level of safety which consumers could reasonably expect. Thus, it was irrelevant whether the hazard causing the damage had come, or ought reasonably to have come, to the producer's attention before the accident occurred. To hold otherwise would reintroduce negligence concepts into the strict liability regime which gave effect to the Product Liability Directive.[146]

Although Stapleton is seemingly persuasive in suggesting that there is no role for Article 7(e) in failure to warn claims, her elision of state of the art and state of scientific and technical knowledge is so doing is controversial. A better way to think of these issues is in terms

---

[140] Ibid 1007–11. This elision of state of the art and state of scientific and technical knowledge is particularly evident in the following: '[I]t is manifestly clear that Member States did not intend to impose liability on a manufacturer who can establish that "the state of scientific and technical knowledge at the time when he put the product into circulation was not such as to enable the existence of the" *hazard* in his product to be discovered. It would therefore be absurd if in such a case a plaintiff could establish liability merely by formulating her Article 6 claim as one of "defectiveness" due to failure to warn of that hazard. It follows that where the alleged "defect" consists of a failure to warn of a risk, and where such warning was impossible given the state of the art of the epidemiological data relating to the drug at the time it was supplied, the claim of "defect" will fail': ibid 1011.

[141] Miller and Goldberg (above, n 2) paras 10.62, 10.66.

[142] *Merck Sharp & Dohme (Australia) Pty Limited v Peterson* (2010) 184 FCR 1.

[143] Ibid [929].

[144] Ibid.

[145] *Abouzaid v Mothercare (UK) Ltd* [2000] All ER (D) 2436; *The Times*, 20 February 2001.

[146] [2000] All ER (D) 2436, Chadwick LJ, paras 43–44.

of foreseeability of risk. If the injury or risk is *unforeseeable*, then it might be concluded that there the claim for a defect on the grounds of failure to warn will fail. The product is simply not defective and the defence would be rendered otiose.[147] However, the position as to warnings under the Directive remains an uncertain one.

In such circumstances, there is arguably a need to expressly define when a prescription drug is defective through failure to warn. The approach of the *Restatement, Third, Torts: Products Liability*, § 6(d) is to define prescription drugs as 'not reasonably safe as to inadequate instructions or warnings' where there has been a failure on behalf of a manufacturer to provide 'reasonable instructions or warnings regarding foreseeable risks of harm'. The § 6(d) standard would seem to be the most appropriate in determining failure to warn defects in prescription drugs. However, the issue of to whom such warnings should be provided emerges. In particular, should the Directive recognise the status of the learned intermediary rule as a defence to a strict liability action in the same way that § 6(d)(1) does? It is to that question that we know turn.

D. Adequacy

Whilst the Directive is silent on the issue, the adequacy of the warning is clearly relevant in determining whether, having regard to the presentation of a medicinal product, it has achieved the level of safety which persons are entitled to expect.[148] The factors which will need to be considered to determine adequacy are the likelihood and probable severity of damage (since the greater the likelihood or probable severity and the more practicable the measures to guard against it, the more comprehensive should the warning be),[149] and whether the warning is sufficiently comprehensive to remove or reduce the danger associated with the product or sever the causative link between the product's marketing and the injury or damage.[150]

A warning's adequacy may also depend on its wording, intensity, and location. The High Court decision in *Worsley v Tambrands Ltd*[151] turned on the nature and extent of the warning and information accompanying tampons and whether they were adequate to warn the claimant of the potential of toxic shock syndrome (TSS) associated with tampon use, having regard to the nature of the risk and potentially life-threatening consequences of TSS. The claimant alleged that the product was defective within the meaning of section 3 of the Consumer Protection Act 1987 by virtue of inadequate warnings of the danger and, in particular, that the defendant ought to have foreseen that the internal leaflet which came with the product might not be kept and/or read, and that the health warning, including the list of likely symptoms and advice on how to react to them, ought to have been printed in full on the outside of the package. Her main complaint was that the United Kingdom

---

[147] For a defence of the continued use of a robust and flexible principle of foreseeability at the heart of private law to define the proper boundaries of responsibility for harm in a brave new world of scientific and technical advancement, see DG Owen, 'Bending Nature, Bending Law' (2010) 62 *Florida Law Review* 569, 573.

[148] See Art 6(1)(a).

[149] The need to avoid alarming the public unduly might well be a relevant consideration: *Thompson v Johnson & Johnson Pty Ltd* [1991] 2 VR 449, 491 (Vict Sup Ct).

[150] See, generally, Miller and Goldberg (above, n 2) paras 12.65–12.69.

[151] *Worsley v Tambrands Ltd* [2000] PIQR P95.

leaflet was designed in such a way that it did not have a sufficient impact upon her, whereas American warnings were more prominent, fuller, and would have had such an impact.[152] Ebsworth J adopted a pragmatic approach to the issue in holding that the defectiveness of the leaflet had to be determined according to a minimum standard. She explained that the fact that the American warning was more effective than the UK one was not the issue. The key issue was the minimum standard of defectiveness:[153]

> It is true that the 1994 United States leaflet is a single-language document with the warning in larger type than the contemporary United Kingdom leaflet. It also contains advice on how to reduce the risks of TSS by alternating tampon and towel use, or by not using tampons at all. As a design, I accept that the United States model is better than the United Kingdom one. But that is not the point. The issue is not whether the United Kingdom pattern could have replicated the United States one (I am prepared to accept that it could, in the absence of evidence to the contrary), but whether the United Kingdom one falls below the statutory or common law standard by reason of its design and/or contents, and if it did, whether a different design would have caused the claimant to have acted differently.

Ebsworth J was also pragmatic in allowing the main warning of the risk on the box to refer to the details in the internal leaflet. Accordingly, she held that neither the box nor the leaflet were defective since the manufacturers had provided a 'clearly legible warning' of the risk of TSS on the outside of the box, directing the user to an internal leaflet which was 'legible, literate, unambiguous and [which] contained all the material' necessary to convey both the warning signs and the action required if any such signs were present.[154]

E. Learned Intermediary Doctrine

(i) Nature of the Doctrine

The learned intermediary doctrine provides an exception to the general rule that there is a duty to warn users of products when it is reasonably foreseeable that they may be injured by them and a warning might be expected to be effective to eliminate or reduce the risk. It allows the manufacturer to discharge his duty to warn by providing the relevant information to a responsible intermediary. Historically, the doctrine has been applicable under the common law,[155] but it has also been submitted that its existence is not affected by the subsequent transposition of the Directive by the 1987 Act.[156]

---

[152] Ibid P103.

[153] Ibid. The justification for the difference between the UK and American leaflets was that the UK leaflet was multilingual. But note Stapleton's questioning of whether an accurate warning of risk is sufficient, particularly when people may not notice a warning or be able to understand or read it: Stapleton, *Product Liability* (London, Butterworths, 1994) 254. See further, Miller and Goldberg (above, n 2) paras 12.75–12.76, 12.78–12.79.

[154] [2000] PIQR P95, 104. See also *Thompson v Johnson & Johnson Pty Ltd* [1991] 2 VR 449 (Vict Sup Ct).

[155] See eg *Kubach v Hollands* [1937] 3 All ER 907, 911; *Holmes v Ashford and Others* [1950] 2 All ER 76, 80, CA; *Buchan v Ortho Pharmaceutical (Canada) Ltd* (1986) 25 DLR (4th) 658, 668–69, 680–81; *Hollis v Dow Corning Corp* (1995) 129 DLR (4th) 609, 623–24; *Bow Valley Huskey (Bermuda Ltd) v Saint John Shipbuilding Ltd* (1997) 153 DLR (4th) 385, 401–2; *Park v B & B Electronics Ltd* 2003 Carswell Alta 985 (Alb Ct of Queen's Bench), paras 189–93 and, in general, Miller and Goldberg (above, n 2), paras 14.109–14.114. Cf *H v Royal Alexandra Hospital for Children* (1990) 1 Med LR 297, 316–17.

[156] CJ Hodges, *Product Liability: European Laws and Practice* (London, Sweet & Maxwell, 1993) para 3-048.

The doctrine is most commonly applicable where a manufacturer of medicinal products provides information on a product's risk to a doctor. It is therefore argued that the product is not defective when supplied to a physician since the product was accompanied by adequate warnings. In such circumstances, the claimant patient would submit that the manufacturer had failed to provide warnings to him personally on the product label or in a leaflet. In such circumstances, the test of causation appears to be subjective, and dependent on the response which the actual claimant (as opposed to some hypothetical reasonable claimant) would have adopted if a proper warning had been provided.[157] It is likely that the courts would accept that the patient would place more credence on their doctor's advice than on the producer's warning.[158]

(ii) Defence to a Strict Liability Action

The status of the learned intermediary rule as a defence to a strict liability action was not addressed directly in *A v National Blood Authority*.[159] However, in the context of discussing so-called 'non-standard' products,[160] Burton J concedes the sole situation where risk–utility or risk–benefit would be relevant to the question of defectiveness, as being 'whether with full information and proper knowledge—the public does and ought to accept the risk'.[161] In his judgement, it was not arguable that consumers had knowledge that they were likely to be infected with hepatitis C. As he observed:

> Doctors and surgeons knew, but did not tell their patients unless asked, and were very rarely asked. It was certainly … not known and accepted by society that there was such a risk, which was thus not … [socially acceptable].[162]

It has been argued by Christopher Hodges that this amounts to a summary dismissal by Burton J of the possibility of the operation of the learned intermediary rule as a defence to a strict liability action and that the application of the rule requires to be 'given greater consideration'.[163] He suggests that:

> it could be a relevant Article 6 circumstance that the product was used and was intended to be used, only where learned intermediaries would interpose between the producer and consumer, and that it was generally recognised to be the function of such intermediaries to warn consumers as fully as should be necessary of the risks involved in the selection for use of a particular product, often from a number of other products.[164]

As a general proposition the above suggestion must surely be correct.[165] Obviously, there are, as Hodges observes, further problems where individual consumers are incapable

---

[157] *Buchan v Ortho Pharmaceuticals Canada Ltd* (1986) 25 DLR (4th) 658, 685–87; *Hollis v Dow Corning Corp* (1995) 129 DLR (4th) 609, 632.

[158] G Howells in Howells (ed), *The Law of Product Liability*, 2nd edn (London, LexisNexis Butterworths, 2007) para 4.202.

[159] [2001] 3 All ER 289.

[160] For the distinction between 'non-standard' and 'standard' products, see above, chapter 4 of this volume, text to fns 92–102.

[161] Ibid [68].

[162] Ibid [55].

[163] C Hodges, Note, 'Compensating Patients' (2001) 117 *Law Quarterly Review* 528, 532.

[164] Ibid.

[165] Miller and Goldberg (above, n 2) para 12.49.

of giving consent (for example, because they are unconscious) and clearly it would be contemplated that transfused blood will be used in such circumstances, as well as in ones in which the consent of the patient is 'freely' given. It has already been submitted that Burton J was wrong to classify infected blood as a 'non-standard' product, and to conclude that with such products a weighing of risks and benefits was not permissible when determining what the public generally was entitled to expect unless the risk was known to the generality of the public and socially acceptable.[166] However, the narrower point that should be made here is that it would, in any event, be wrong to treat the decision as authoritatively denying the potential application of the learned intermediary rule in a strict liability context. It was simply not addressed in any systematic way.[167] In an important Canadian decision, *Buchan v Ortho Pharmaceutical (Canada) Ltd*,[168] the Ontario Court of Appeal, in discussing a manufacturer's duty to warn with respect to over-the-counter or prescription drugs and the learned intermediary rule, indicated that the plaintiff had sought relief on the alternative ground of strict liability. However, Robins JA, in delivering the judgment of the Court, stated that on his view of the case he considered it unnecessary to discuss any such liability.

(iii) Support for Retention of the Doctrine

It is submitted that the principal reason why the doctrine should be retained in the UK is the fact that prescription drugs continue to require the intervention of a medical practitioner. Almost all of the prescribing of drugs in the community is carried out by general practitioners.[169] In such circumstances, the focus of the law should continue to be on the duty of such practitioners to engage in the informed consent process by discussing the risks and benefits of prescription drugs with their patients when selecting the appropriate medication.[170] The main benefit of the learned intermediary doctrine is that it encourages this activity.[171] As has been previously noted,[172] the abolition of the doctrine and its

---

[166] See chapter 2 of this volume, pp 32–37.

[167] Ibid. In its Fourth Report on the application of the Product Liability Directive, the European Commission noted concern amongst the pharmaceutical industry that since a medicinal product 'is generally subject to external examination by health professionals (including doctors, nurses or pharmacists) and that the producer does not have any control over the way in which medicines are prescribed or administered', this should be taken into consideration 'when analysing the defect of the product and the producer's liability': Fourth Report from the Commission on the Application of Council Directive 85/374/EEC on Liability for Defective Products, amended by Directive 1999/34/EC, Brussels, COM(2011) 547 final (8 September 2011) 8. The comments seem to suggest support for the learned intermediary rule in determining whether a medicinal product is defective in terms of Art 6, though they are made in the context of discussion of Art 7(d). The Explanatory Memorandum to the Trade Practices Amendment Bill 1992, para 24 explicitly mentions the need to take account of the learned intermediary and the detailed product information provided to doctors and pharmacists in determining whether a pharmaceutical is defective, especially where a claim of defect in information is made.

[168] *Buchan v Ortho Pharmaceutical (Canada) Ltd* (1986) 25 DLR (4th) 658, 668.

[169] B Guthrie, C McCowan, P Davey, CR Simpson, T Dreischulte and K Barnett, 'High risk prescribing in primary care patients particularly vulnerable to adverse drug events: cross sectional population database analysis in Scottish general practice' (2011) 342 *British Medical Journal* d3514. Independent prescribing rights have also been extended to suitably qualified pharmacists and nurses: Health and Social Care Act 2001, s 63; National Health Service (Miscellaneous Amendments Relating to Independent Prescribing) Regulations 2006, SI 2006/913 and Medicines for Human Use (Prescribing) (Miscellaneous Amendments) Order 2006, SI 2006/915.

[170] L Noah (above, n 92) (2009) 74 *Brooklyn Law Review* 839, 905.

[171] JL Peters (above, n 90) (2008) 48 *Jurimetrics Journal* 285, 299–91.

[172] See above, text to n 92.

replacement with an obligation imposed on manufacturers to warn patients direct could further reduce incentives to conscientious physicians. This is particularly important in the primary care environment when there is now evidence of a need to improve the safety of prescribing by general practitioners.[173] Finally, it should be remembered that in the European context, the significance of the learned intermediary rule has to some extent been reduced in the case of medicinal products, since, unless all the required information is on the container or on the packaging, the provision of package leaflets for human medicinal products is obligatory.[174]

F. The Requirement of Causation

(i) General Comments

In the case of instructions as to how to use products safely and warnings which focus on the risks associated with their use, causation remains central to the claim.[175] Under the Product Liability Directive's strict liability regime, the person injured by a defective product must prove the damage, the defect, and the causal relationship between defect and damage.[176] Accordingly, whereas a breach of duty in a negligence action must cause the harm, it is the defect under the Directive and hence the 1987 Act which must cause the damage. Translated into the context of drug defects through an alleged failure to warn, the causation requirement necessitates not only that claimants prove the feasibility of a warning, but also that, had a warning been provided, they would have heeded it, thus avoiding the injury.[177]

---

[173] See B Guthrie, C McCowan, P Davey, CR Simpson, T Dreischulte and K Barnett, 'High risk prescribing in primary care patients particularly vulnerable to adverse drug events: cross sectional population database analysis in Scottish general practice' (2011) 342 *British Medical Journal* d3514 (cross sectional population database analysis of high-risk prescribing in Scottish primary care patients, ie potentially inappropriate prescribing of drugs to primary care patients particularly vulnerable to adverse drug reactions. Data from 315 Scottish general practices was examined with 1.76 million registered patients. Of that number, 139,404 (7.9%) were defined as particularly vulnerable to adverse drug reactions, and 13.9% of these patients were found to have been prescribed one or more high-risk drugs).

[174] Dir 2001/83/EC on the Community Code Relating to Medicinal Products for Human Use [2001] OJ L311/67, as amended by Dir 2004/27/EC [2004] OJ L136/34, Art 58; Medicines Act 1968, s 86; (see generally, Dir 2001/83/EC, Title V, labelling and package leaflets, Arts 54–69). Note that in the US, a 'hybrid' model has been advocated to promote safe and effective prescription drug therapy by adopting (a) the learned intermediary doctrine as the legal standard of liability for drug manufacturer's in their product warnings; and (b) an FDA-mandated system of patient package inserts (PPIs) for all prescription drugs to supplement the information a patient receives from his doctor: CA Paytash, Note, 'The Learned Intermediary Doctrine and Patient Package Inserts: A Balanced Approach To Preventing Drug-Related Injury' (1999) 51 *Stanford Law Review* 1343, 1367, 1368–71.

[175] J Stapleton, *Product Liability* (above n 153) 252.

[176] Dir 85/374/EEC, Art 4. Thus in *Merck Sharp & Dohme (Australia) Pty Limited v Peterson* [2011] FCAFC 128, while the Full Court upheld the decision of the trial judge that the anti-inflammatory drug Vioxx had a defect within the meaning of s 75AC Trade Practices Act 1974, in that in some people, by some unknown mechanism, it increased the risk of myocardial infarction (MI) and provided no information, advice or warning as to this effect, it held that Mr Peterson had failed on causation as he was unable to show, as required by s 75AD (c), that the injury he had suffered (MI) had been caused by the defect in Vioxx: ibid [201].

[177] Cf *McWilliams v Sir William Arrol & Co* [1962] 1 WLR 295, 306, HL, Lord Reid.

(ii) Consumers' Inattention to Warnings

Notwithstanding the importance attached to warnings, both behavioural and scientific research indicates that the majority of people do not heed them.[178] Since inattention to warnings is very common, it has been argued that courts should not permit manufacturers to shift the burden of taking precautions when safer product designs or marketing strategies could feasibly reduce the risk of accidents. In the United States, it has therefore been submitted that courts should impose the burden of a greater proportion of product-related accidents on manufacturers by adopting a 'true strict liability rule', whereby manufacturers will be liable for any injuries proximately caused by their products. It is said that such an approach would create incentives for producers to minimise accidents through the most cost-effective means, whether through improved product designs, selective warnings, safer marketing strategies, or a combination of all of these.[179] It has also been argued that if it is foreseeable that the user might be *unable* to heed a warning, then the provision of a warning would not exculpate the manufacturer.[180] Indeed, it was suggested by Burton J in *A v National Blood Authority*[181] that even warning the public of possible hepatitis contamination in blood, together with express warnings on bags of blood, would not necessarily have been sufficient to ensure that the blood was not defective, particularly in the light of the no-waiver of liability provision in Article 12 of the Directive. However, the relevance of Article 12 is unclear since the function of a warning is not to limit or exclude liability but to discharge the underlying obligation.[182] This is, of course, without prejudice to an argument that a court might exceptionally hold that since many patients receiving blood are incapable of giving consent, the provision of warnings in product information would be ineffective in any event.[183] Alternatively, it could be argued that warnings to the medical profession should be sufficient, but even accepting this view, there remains uncertainty as to how far current warnings—largely distributed by means of patient and doctor/nurse information leaflets and small warnings on blood bags—will be considered to be adequate.[184]

---

[178] H Latin, '"Good" Warnings, Bad Products and Cognitive Limitations' (1994) 41 *UCLA Law Review* 1193, 1206–57; see also reference to a decision of a German Court which found it unlikely that a consumer would have heeded a warning about the risk associated with the use of an insect repellent in the light of the value of using that product in Africa: OLG Köln-20 u 26/93 [1994] NJW-RR 91, 17 September 1993, cited by G Howells in Howells (ed), *The Law of Product Liability*, 1st edn London, Butterworths, 2000) para 4.165; Miller and Goldberg (above, n 2) para 12.78.

[179] H Latin, '"Good" Warnings, Bad Products and Cognitive Limitations' (1994) 41 *UCLA Law Review* 1193, 1199, 1293–94; and see further, JD Hanson and DA Kysar, 'Taking Behaviouralism Seriously: The Problem of Market Manipulation' (1999) 74 *NYU Law Review* 630; 'Taking Behaviouralism Seriously: Some Evidence of Market Manipulation' (1999) 112 *Harvard Law Review* 1422.

[180] AM Clark, *Product Liability* (London, Sweet & Maxwell, 1989) 101–2.

[181] [2001] 3 All ER 289, [65].

[182] Art 12 provides that: 'The liability of the producer arising from this Directive may not, in relation to the injured person, be limited or excluded by a provision limiting his liability or exempting him from liability'. For implementation, see s 7 of the 1987 Act. In the context of personal injury litigation the distinction between warnings and exclusion or limitation clauses is apparent also in the case of occupiers' liability: see Occupiers' Liability Act 1957, s 2(4)(a) (warnings) and Unfair Contract Terms Act 1977, s 2(1) (exclusion of liability).

[183] CJS Hodges, Note, 'Compensating Patients' (2001) 117 *Law Quarterly Review* 528, 531.

[184] Personal communication from Professor Ian Franklin, Scottish National Blood Transfusion Service, March 2010.

(iii) A Subjective Test?

The causation requirement appears to be determined on a subjective basis. In other words, the question is whether the claimant would have acted differently if proper warnings or instructions had been given and not whether a reasonable person would have done so. At least this was the position adopted by the Ontario Court of Appeal in *Buchan v Ortho Pharmaceutical (Canada) Ltd*, where in the context of a claim involving an oral contraceptive and a stroke, Robins JA, said:[185]

> When a manufacturer's breach of the duty to warn is found to have influenced a physician's opinion as to the safety of a drug thereby contributing to the physician's non-disclosure of a material risk and the consumer's ingestion of the drug, the *manufacturer is not entitled to require the injured consumer to prove that a reasonable consumer in her position would not have taken the drug if properly warned.* (emphasis added)[186]

The Court continued: 'Whether the particular consumer would have taken the drug even with a proper warning is a matter to be decided by the trier of fact on all the relevant evidence.'[187] In principle, the onus lies on the claimant to establish the point,[188] and, in the context of prescription drugs, there is important authority in the United States rejecting a rebuttable presumption that a warning will be heeded.[189] The subjective approach was commended in *Buchan* on the grounds of principle and policy because it facilitated

---

[185] *Buchan v Ortho Pharmaceutical (Canada) Ltd* (1986) 25 DLR (4th) 658, 686.

[186] See also *Hollis v Dow Corning Corp* (1996) 129 DLR (4th) 609, 632–33, La Forest J (Can Sup Ct) (upholding the subjective test of causation in product liability cases in an action against a breast implant manufacturer when determining whether a breach of the duty to warn of the risk associated with implants caused the plaintiff's injury).

[187] (1986) 25 DLR (4th) 658, 686.

[188] See, albeit in a different context, *McWilliams v Sir William Arrol & Co* [1962] 1 WLR 295, 306, Lord Reid; *Goorkani v Tayside Health Board* 1991 SLT 94, 95. In cases involving learned intermediaries it was said in *Buchan* that the presumption is that the intermediary would have acted on the warning and that it should not be incumbent on the plaintiff to prove this as part of her case (above, n 185) (1986) 25 DLR (4th) 658, 681–83. However, in an unreported judgment of Ian Kennedy J in the English *Benzodiazepine* litigation, where the cause of action was based on negligence, it was decided that while evidence of the effect of a different warning on a reasonable practitioner might not be strictly inadmissible, such evidence would be given less weight than evidence addressed directly to the circumstances of the case: see M Mildred, 'Group Litigation' in Miller, *Product Liability and Safety Encyclopaedia*, Div IIIA, para 176. This seems to suggest that the claimant may be required to produce evidence of what her actual doctor would have done, but not evidence of what a reasonable practitioner would have done.

[189] *Thomas v Hoffman La-Roche Inc* 949 F 2d 806, 814 (5th Cir 1992) (rebuttable presumption in *Reyes v Wyeth Laboratories* 498 F 2d 1264, 1281 (5th Cir), cert denied 419 US 1096 (1974), namely, that a consumer would have read any warning provided by a manufacturer and acted so as to minimise the risks, rejected under Mississippi law). The Fifth Circuit held that the plaintiff had to show that an adequate warning would have convinced the prescribing physician not to prescribe an acne medication, Accutane, and that the injury would not have occurred had the drug not been administered. In the light of the fact that the subsequent release of an adequate warning had no effect on the overall use of Accutane, and that the possibility that the plaintiff's doctor would have changed his decision had he been warned was remote, the plaintiff failed to establish a cause of action for failure to warn: 949 F 2d 806, 817 (5th Cir 1992). Note also the lack of any 'heeding' presumption in favour of causation in the context of prescription drugs and medical devices in § 6(d) of the *Restatement, Third, Torts: Products Liability*: TM Schwartz, 'The Impact of the New Products Liability Restatement on Prescription Products' (1995) 50 *Food and Drug Law Journal* 399, 404. Proximate causation was not established in a failure to warn claim where a physician maintained that he would not have prescribed a drug if he had been informed of a risk of disease required by the FDA as a black-box warning (valvular heart disease (VHD)), but the patient sustained a separate disease (primary pulmonary hypertension (PPH)) of which the manufacturer had adequately disclosed the risk. Finding the issues of informed consent and failure to warn analogous, the court held that 'a plaintiff cannot establish causation where the non-disclosed risk never materialized into an injury': *Cochran v Wyeth, Inc* 3 A 3d 673, 679–81 (Pa Super Ct 2010). Before a plaintiff could prove that a non-disclosed risk would have changed the physician's

meaningful consumer choice and encouraged full disclosure.[190] It also appears to have been generally accepted in the context of medical negligence cases, both in English and Australian courts, which focus on what a particular patient, as opposed to a reasonable patient, would have done if warned.[191] In particular, the issue was addressed in the decision of the House of Lords in *Chester v Afshar*,[192] where it was held that a claimant could recover against a defendant surgeon for failure to warn of the risk of injury through surgery (here, a one to two per cent risk of cauda equina syndrome), where the injury transpired, notwithstanding the fact that the risk was neither created nor increased by the failure to warn, and despite the claimant's inability to show that she would never have undergone surgery carrying the same risk at a later date. While their Lordships held that on conventional causation grounds, failure to warn did not cause the claimant's injury,[193] a majority of their Lordships relied on the policy factors underlying the scope of the defendant's duty to warn his patient of the risk of injury, to modify the normal approach to causation.[194] Since the injury was 'intimately involved with'[195] and was within the scope of the very risk that she should have been warned about when her consent to the operation was obtained, the injury could be regarded as having been caused, in the legal sense, by the defendant's breach of duty.[196] It has been submitted that this 'more relaxed approach to causation' could be applied to failure to warn in the context of medicinal products.[197]

---

decision to prescribe a drug, the plaintiff had to first show that he suffered from the precise injury that the manufacturer allegedly failed to disclose: ibid.

[190] (1986) 25 DLR (4th) 658, 687.

[191] *Chatterton v Gerson* [1981] QB 432; *Chester v Afshar* [2004] UKHL 41, [2005] 1 AC 134; See *Smith v Barking, Havering and Brentwood Health Authority* [1994] 5 Med LR 285 and *Smith v Tunbridge Wells Health Authority* [1994] 5 Med LR 334; *Chappel v Hart* (1998) 195 CLR 232, 246, McHugh J, 257, Gummow J, 272 Kirby J.

[192] *Chester v Afshar* [2005] 1 AC 134.

[193] Ibid [81], Lord Hope.

[194] Ibid [24]–[25], Lord Steyn, paras 85–88, Lord Hope, para 93, Lord Walker. Cf the dissenting judgments of Lord Bingham (at para 8) and Lord Hoffmann (at paras 29 and 31), concluding that the claimant had failed to establish that 'but for' the failure to warn, she would have not undergone surgery. Lord Hoffmann criticised the claimant's argument that it was sufficient that she would not have had the operation at that time or by another surgeon, as being 'about as logical as saying that if one had been told, on entering a casino, that the odds on the number 7 coming up at roulette were only 1 in 37, one would have gone away and come back next week or gone to a different casino': para 31. He added: 'The question is whether one would have taken the opportunity to avoid or reduce the risk, not whether one would have changed the scenario in some irrelevant detail'. For criticism of this reasoning, and for the view that there was sufficient evidence to satisfy the 'but for' test (since Miss Chester would have had the operation, if at all, at a different time, and the a priori estimate of the risk would have been one to two per cent, so that it would have been more than likely than not that, but for the breach, she would not have suffered the syndrome), see J Stapleton 'Occam's Razor Reveals an Orthodox Basis for Chester v Afsher' (2006) 122 *Law Quarterly Review* 426, 428, 429–30. However, in order successfully to argue that an orthodox approach is an adequate one, Professor Stapleton considers that it is necessary to move from the three-step approach to causation as championed by Hart and Honoré (historical fact, causal connection and remoteness) to a two-step analysis, viz factual historical involvement and scope of liability for consequences of breach): (2006) 122 *Law Quarterly Review* 426, 426, 436–48.

[195] [2005] 1 AC 134, [87], Lord Hope.

[196] Ibid [87]–[88].

[197] H Teff, 'Products Liability in the Pharmaceutical Industry at Common Law' (1974) 20 *McGill Law Journal* 102, 105 and 'Products Liability' in A Grubb, J Lang and J McHale (eds), *Principles of Medical Law*, 3rd edn (Oxford, Oxford University Press, 2010) para 18.33. But note that the High Court of New Zealand has held that *Chester* is inapplicable to cases involving product liability and failure to warn, especially where the product is manufactured for the mass market and there is no direct relationship between the manufacturer and the ultimate consumer: *Pou v British American Tobacco* HC AK CIV-2002-404-1729 [2006] NZHC 451 (3 May 2006) paras 322, 325 Lang J.

Professor Stapleton has argued that while the general approach of the English courts in the tort of negligence is to reject liability for coincidental consequences of breach, the claimant's outcome in *Chester* was not a coincidental occurrence.[198] In her view, in the context of medical failure to warn cases, 'the deleterious outcome of breaches are not coincidental outcomes ... because ... breaches of the obligation to warn patients will tend to increase the incidence of the medical risk occurring'.[199] By way of example, she cites the case of failure to warn of a generic risk in a product such as the adverse effect of a medicinal product. She explains: '[T]he warned consumer may choose not to use that product so while the *riskiness* of the product would remain the same, the overall *incidence* of that side effect eventuating would be affected by whether or not consumers are warned'.[200] However, it is submitted that this argument is questionable,[201] since the *riskiness* of a product causing a disease is measured by its *incidence* rate, which is the number of new cases of a disease divided by the sum of the different times each individual was exposed to the disease. This enables incidence to be a measure of risk. Accordingly, the overall incidence of that side-effect will therefore not be affected by whether or not consumers are warned. What will be affected is not the *incidence* of a side-effect eventuating, but arguably the *prevalence* of the side-effect eventuating, which is the proportion of the population with the side-effect (ie the number of individuals with the side-effect in the population, divided by the number of population).[202] Whatever terminology is used, from the perspective of the statistician, the determination of whether an occurrence is coincidental or not is likely to focus on *risk* and *incidence* rate, as opposed to prevalence.[203] It is submitted, therefore, that the injury to Miss Afsher is still likely to be characterised as a random occurrence.[204] Perhaps a preferable approach is to say that if the claimant's damage is considered to be 'the *physical consequences* of the materialisation of the risk, rather than simply being exposed to the risk', the but for test for causation 'was readily established'.[205] However, if the physical consequences of the materialisation of the risk remain random, it is arguable that there should be no liability for such a coincidental consequence. In other words, while the 'but for' test of causation is satisfied, the scope-of-liability-for-consequences test should reject liability.[206] While the subjective approach has been criticised in the negligence context as an increasing use of causation as a 'proxy for moral accountability',[207] it is arguable that it is appropriate

---

[198] J Stapleton 'Occam's Razor Reveals an Orthodox Basis for Chester v Afsher' (2006) 122 *Law Quarterly Review* 426, 441.

[199] Ibid 443.

[200] Ibid 443.

[201] R Goldberg, 'Causation' in G Howells (ed), *The Law of Product Liability*, 2nd edn (London, LexisNexis, 2007) para 5.33.

[202] For the distinction between prevalence and incidence, see KJ Rothman, S Greenland and TL Lash, *Modern Epidemiology*, 3rd edn (Philadelphia, PA, Lippincott, Williams & Wilkins, 2008) 46–48.

[203] 'Seldom is prevalence of direct interest in etiologic applications of epidemiologic research': ibid 46.

[204] 'The evidence indicated that [the injury] was also likely to occur at random, irrespective of the degree of care and skill with which the operation was conducted by the surgeon. This means that the risk would have been the same whenever and at whoever's hands she had the operation': [2005] 1 AC 134, para 61, Lord Hope.

[205] *Clerk and Lindsell on Torts*, 20th edn (London, Sweet & Maxell, 2010) para 2-17.

[206] Cf the view of Professor Stapleton that Miss Chester's syndrome was a coincidental occurrence: J Stapleton 'Occam's Razor Reveals an Orthodox Basis for Chester v Afsher' (2006) 122 *Law Quarterly Review* 426, 441–44.

[207] K Amirthalingam, Note 'Medical Non-Disclosure, Causation and Autonomy' (2002) 128 *Law Quarterly Review* 540, 542.

within a strict liability regime.[208] Needless to say, it is possible for courts to disbelieve a claimant[209] or for a claimant not to overcome the burden of proof in each case.[210]

IV. CONCLUSIONS

Notwithstanding the fact that the category of warnings about risks and instructions for use is the most significant factor relevant to determining the expectation of safety with medicinal products, the position of warnings under the Product Liability Directive remains uncertain.

It has been submitted that most commentators are correct in viewing warning defects as fault based, and that there is much to Stapleton's analysis of a claim for failure to have a warning about a drug's side-effect as being one 'inexorably linked to the reasonable *feasibility* of warning'. Nonetheless, her argument that in determining whether a warning of a side-effect is necessary, there needs to be a 'scientific consensus of a causal link', formed on the accumulation of enough data to be 'sufficiently scientifically significant' should be viewed with an element of caution. The danger with such an approach is that it might suggest supremacy of statistical significance in determining failure to warn, and that a warning of a suspected side-effect should only be provided when a risk is statistically significant, ie where the relative risk of an association is greater than two. Indeed, it is clear that there may be a duty to warn of a side-effect even though a causal relationship has not been clearly proved, and this has been recognised both in the United States and in the recent Vioxx litigation in Australia.

While Stapleton correctly submits that a failure to warn could only be 'impossible' if the risk or hazard in question is 'undiscoverable' or scientifically unknowable" in the light of the state of the art of the epidemiological data relating to the drug at the time if its supply, it is perhaps easier to see these issues as matters of *foreseeability* of risk. This would be consistent not only with the endorsement by the US courts of comment *j* of § 402A of the *Restatement, Second, Torts* that the duty to warn extended only to foreseeable risks, but also with *Restatement, Third, Torts: Products Liability*, § 6(d), which limits the responsibility in prescription drug cases to a duty to provide 'reasonable instructions or warnings regarding foreseeable risks of harm'. Although Stapleton correctly concludes that under Article 6, which suspected adverse effects must be warned about and when in order for a drug to provide the safety to which we are legally entitled 'taking all circumstances into account, is 'a matter of degree and judgment', Newdick's objectification of the foreseeability of risk approach provides greater clarity of guidance as to when an allegation of a failure to warn defect becomes viable than the reasonableness standard of feasibility of warning.

---

[208]   Miller and Goldberg (above, n 2) para 12.80.

[209]   The judge may reject a patient's evidence that if there had been any risk they would not have had treatment as self-serving and lacking credibility: *Rosenberg v Percival* (2001) 205 CLR 434 (High Court of Australia upholding trial judge's rejection of patient's evidence that they would never have gone ahead with dental surgery, had she been warned of the risks following such surgery).

[210]   *H v The Royal Alexandra Hospital for Children and the Commonwealth Serum Laboratories Commission and the Australian Red Cross* (NSW, Division) [1990] 1 Med LR 297, 317. Note, however, that there is no principle of law requiring a plaintiff to give evidence personally about what would or would not have happened if he had been properly informed of the facts before making a decision: *Webb v Barclays Bank plc and Portsmouth Hospitals* [2001] Lloyd's Rep Med 500, [2002] *PIQR* P8, para 42.

Notwithstanding Stapleton's persuasiveness in suggesting that there is no role for Article 7(e) in failure to warn claims, her elision of state of the art and state of scientific and technical knowledge in so doing is controversial. A better way to think of these issues is in terms of foreseeability of risk. If the injury or risk is *unforeseeable*, then it might be concluded that there the claim for a defect on the grounds of failure to warn will fail. The product is simply not defective and the defence would be rendered otiose.

In the light of the uncertainties as to the position as to warnings under the Directive, there is arguably a need to define expressly when a medicinal product is defective through failure to warn. The approach of the *Restatement, Third, Torts: Products Liability*, § 6 (d) is to define prescription drugs as 'not reasonably safe as to inadequate instructions or warnings' where there has been a failure on behalf of a manufacturer to provide 'reasonable instructions or warnings regarding foreseeable risks of harm'. It has been submitted that the § 6(d) standard would seem to be the most appropriate one for the EU to follow in determining failure to warn defects in prescription drugs and that the Directive should recognise the status of the learned intermediary rule as a defence to a strict liability action in the same way that § 6(d)(1) does.

Even if the Directive was not amended to recognise expressly the learned intermediary rule as a defence, it is arguable that its existence is not affected by the subsequent transposition of the Directive by the 1987 Act. The principal reason why the doctrine should be retained in the UK, and arguably in the other Member States too, is the fact that prescription drugs continue to require the intervention of a medical practitioner. In the UK, almost all of the prescribing of drugs in the community is carried out by general practitioners. In such circumstances, the focus of the law should continue to be on the duty of such practitioners to engage in the informed consent process by discussing the risks and benefits of prescription drugs with their patients when selecting the appropriate medication. The abolition of the doctrine and its replacement with Professor Owen's radical proposal that an obligation imposed on manufacturers to warn patients direct could further reduce incentives of conscientious physicians. This is particularly important in the primary care environment when there is now evidence of a need to improve the safety of prescribing by general practitioners. In any event, it should be remembered that in the European context, the significance of the learned intermediary rule has to some extent been reduced in the case of medicinal products, since, unless all the required information is on the container or on the packaging, the provision of package leaflets for human medicinal products is obligatory.

Finally, in the context of drug defects through an alleged failure to warn, the requirement of causation necessitates not only that claimants prove the feasibility of a warning, but also that, had a warning been provided, they would have heeded it, thus avoiding the injury. It is arguable that the amenable approach to causation suggested by *Chester v Afshar* could be applied to failure to warn in the context of medicinal products.

5

Causation, Risk and Epidemiological Evidence in Medicinal Product Liability Litigation: Law's Coming of Age[*]

I. INTRODUCTION

Proof of causation in toxic tort litigation is an inherently difficult problem, which regularly requires time-consuming analysis of complex scientific evidence.[1] The difficulties in proving both general causation (whether the product was capable of causing the damage alleged) and specific causation (whether the product did so in the individual case) are magnified in the context of medicinal products.[2] As Teff and Munro have highlighted:

> Drugs are always potentially dangerous due to their toxicity. They are often taken by people who are already ill and who may be unusually susceptible to further ailments. Unlike many other products, they may cause injury in unpredictable ways, depending on the individual user's constitution. They may not be taken according to the instructions. The user may be allergic to a particular drug. Alternatively, what appears to be an allergy may in fact be a toxic reaction.[3]

With a multitude of new kinds of drugs emerging as a harvest of the scientific and technological revolutions of both the twentieth and early twenty-first centuries, the cases have become even more complex, demanding much from lawyers and scientific experts on both sides and the judges themselves.[4] The practical significance of establishing causation in a

[*] An earlier draft of this chapter was delivered to the Department of Epidemiology, Biostatistics and Occupational Health, Faculty of Medicine, McGill University, Montreal, April 2011 under a Carnegie Research Grant. The author wishes to thank Professor Philip Dawid, Professor David Goldberg, Professor Mike Green and Professor Joseph Sanders for helpful discussions.

[1] CJ Miller and RS Goldberg, *Product Liability*, 2nd edn (Oxford, Oxford University Press, 2004) para 17.05.

[2] R Goldberg, *Causation and Risk in the Law of Torts: Scientific Evidence and Medicinal Product Liability* (Oxford, Hart Publishing, 1999) 5, et seq.

[3] H Teff and C Munro, *Thalidomide: The legal aftermath* (Farnborough, Saxon House, 1976) 135–36. 'Clearly it is often harder to prove that one's injuries are due to an adverse drug reaction than that they have been caused by a faulty machine': Teff, 'Regulation Under the Medicines Act 1968: A Continuing Prescription for Health' (1984) 47 *Modern Law Review* 303, 322. Professor Teff also notes '[t]he synergistic effects of certain combinations (for example, barbiturates and alcohol, anti-histamines and cheese)': H Teff, 'Products Liability in the Pharmaceutical Industry at Common Law' (1974) 20 *McGill Law Journal* 102, 115.

[4] See, eg, *Bonthrone v Millan*, cited in D Brahams, 'Pertussis Vaccine and Brain Damage: Two Claims Before the Courts' [1985] 2 *The Lancet* 1137 (Lord Jauncey) (existence of cryptogenic (unknown) causes to eliminate possible causal connection between pertussis vaccine and brain damage); *Loveday v Renton* [1990] 1 Med LR 117, where Stuart-Smith LJ, after examining complex scientific evidence and arguments, held that the plaintiff had failed to prove on a balance of probabilities that the pertussis (whooping cough) vaccine could cause permanent

medicinal product liability case cannot be overstated. Whether the claim is in negligence or under the Product Liability Directive,[5] proof of causation will often lead to either a settlement or a successful claim.[6] Conversely, a failure to establish a causal link between a medicinal product and, for example, the alleged medical conditions of claimants, may lead to such claims being struck out as an abuse of the process of the court on the basis that each claim has no real prospect of success.[7]

---

brain damage in young children: [1990] 1 Med LR 117, 185 (discussed in: R Goldberg, *Causation and Risk in the Law of Torts: Scientific Evidence and Medicinal Product Liability* (Oxford, Hart Publishing, 1999) 137–43); *Kay v Ayrshire and Arran Health Board* [1987] 2 All ER 417 (penicillin overdose not capable of causing or aggravating deafness). Cf the US mass tort litigation concerning Bendectin (Debendox), the anti-nausea drug used in pregnancy. In contrast to thalidomide, where many lines of evidence showed that the drug caused phocomelia malformations (see H Sjöström and R Nilsson, *Thalidomide and the Power of Drug Companies* (Harmondsworth, Penguin, 1972) 156–59), no causal link has ever been scientifically established between Bendectin and birth defects. The Bendectin Litigation demonstrated a persistent failure by plaintiffs' lawyers to prove causation: see the seminal paper on this topic, J Sanders, 'The Bendectin Litigation: A Case Study in the Life Cycle of Mass Torts' (1992) 43 *Hastings Law Journal* 301 and, for its implications in the UK, see R Goldberg, *Causation and Risk in the Law of Torts: Scientific Evidence and Medicinal Product Liability* (see above) 102–31. The litigation spawned two formative monographs (M Green, *Bendectin and Birth Defects: The Challenges of Mass Toxic Substances Litigation* (Philadelphia, PA, University of Pennsylvania Press, 1996); and J Sanders, *Bendectin on Trial: A Study of Mass Tort Litigation* (Ann Arbor, MI, The University of Michigan Press, 1998)). 30 years after Bendectin's withdrawal from the market, the drug (now renamed Diclegis) has won Food and Drug Administration approval as the only FDA-approved treatment for morning sickness: www.fda.gov/NewsEvents/Newsroom/PressAnnouncements/ucm347087.htm, accessed 13 April 2013; Associated Press, 'Morning Sickness Drug Returns', *New York Times*, 8 April 2013, www.nytimes.com/2013/04/09/us/morning-sickness-drug-returns.html?emc=tnt&tntemail1=y&_r=0&pagewanted=print, accessed 13 April 2013.

[5] By Article 4 of the Directive, and s 2(1) of the 1987 Consumer Protection Act, the person injured by a defective medicinal product must prove the damage, the defect, and the causal relationship between them: See Dir 85/374/EEC, Art 4. The damage must have been caused 'wholly or partly by a defect' in the medicinal product: s 2(1) of the 1987 Act. Thus the formal distinction between negligence and strict liability is that with negligence it must be proved that the breach of duty caused the harm, whereas under the 1987 Act it must be proved that the defect caused the damage. Cf P Ferguson, *Drug Injuries and the Pursuit of Compensation* (London, Sweet & Maxwell, 1996) 125. It appears that each Member State will rely on its own theory of causation as established in its civil liability system, though it has been observed that some kind of semi-autonomous European understanding of causation could be established from common elements of the Member States' legal systems: S Whittaker, 'The EEC Directive on Product Liability' (1985) 5 *Yearbook of European Law* 233, 247. The argument that causation is likely to be defined and interpreted by national law and assessed by national courts is strengthened by the decision of the European Court of Justice, Case C-203/99, *Henning Veedfald v Århus Amtskommune* [2001] ECR I-3569, where the Court concluded that it was for the national court to decide whether a claim was to be categorised in respect of personal injury, property damage, or non-material damage: ibid paras 27–28. This is subject to a qualification founded on the principle of effectiveness, in that national laws must not by their interpretation of causation either render ineffective the protection of injured persons or the restraints on liability of producers, since both reflect the 'fair apportionment of risk' of the Directive. In so doing, however, courts will take into consideration the extent to which these causal issues combine issues of fact and their evaluation and questions of law: S Whittaker, *Liability for Products: English Law, French Law, and European Harmonisation* (Oxford, Oxford University Press, 2005) 512–13. The Fourth Commission Report of 8 September 2011 on the Application of Directive 85/374 on liability for defective products, COM(2011) 547 final 11 has noted the European Commission's belief that 'injured parties can establish the causal link in cases where a defective product causes damage irrespective of the differences between national procedural rules', though it has noted the views of consumers that there is difficulty in 'proving the causal link between the defect and damage when such damage is complex in nature': ibid 7. Consumers believe that the burden of proof should be reversed: ibid.

[6] M Mildred, 'Representing the plaintiff' in G Howells (ed), *Product Liability, Insurance and the Pharmaceutical Industry: An Anglo-American Comparison* (Manchester, Manchester University Press, 1991) 27.

[7] CJ Miller and RS Goldberg, *Product Liability*, 2nd edn (Oxford, Oxford University Press, 2004) para 17.02. In *D and R v Schering Chemicals* (2 July 1982, unreported), counsel for the plaintiffs obtained leave from Bingham J (as he then was) to discontinue actions alleging that, as a result of the hormone pregnancy test drug Primodos taken by mothers during pregnancy, their children were born with serious congenital defects. The basis of Bingham J's decision was that, after an exchange of expert evidence, counsel for the plaintiffs concluded that on

Epidemiology is defined as 'the field of public health and medicine that studies the incidence, distribution and aetiology of disease in human populations'.[8] Epidemiological evidence is regularly presented to courts in determining proof of causation in medicinal product liability litigation. Building on the foundations of the author's previous monograph, which supported the use of epidemiological evidence in dealing with problems of proof of causation in alleged cases of adverse drug reactions,[9] this chapter revisits this perennial problem of the role of epidemiological evidence in assessing causation in product liability cases in a twenty-first-century context, examining the recent cases involving the role of epidemiological evidence in assessing causation in product liability cases in the United Kingdom, United States, Australia and in Canada. In essence, it seeks to determine the extent to which the courts in the highlighted cases have been pragmatic and fair in their interpretation and utilisation of epidemiological evidence from the perspective of both consumers and pharmaceutical manufacturers.[10]

In order to establish factual causation in the context of medicinal product liability, claimants must prove both general causation ('whether a substance is capable of causing a particular injury or condition in the general population')[11] and specific causation ('whether a substance caused a particular individual's injury').[12] Since epidemiology is based on the study of populations and not individuals, it focuses on the question of general causation rather than specific causation.[13] Epidemiological evidence may identify an association between a drug and a disease, but whether such an association is causal requires an evaluation of the evidence, with emphasis on the extent to which weaknesses of the study's design and implementation compromise its findings and allow inferences about

---

the evidence available the actions stood no reasonable prospect of establishing that the products were teratogenic as alleged: ibid Bingham J at 2, 3 of Official Transcript.

[8] MD Green, DM Freedman & L Gordis, 'Reference Guide on Epidemiology' in *Reference Manual on Scientific Evidence*, 3rd edn (Washington, DC, National Academies Press 2011) 551.

[9] See, generally, R Goldberg, *Causation and Risk in the Law of Torts: Scientific Evidence and Medicinal Product Liability* (Oxford, Hart Publishing, 1999).

[10] The chapter does not seek to explore the problem of proving that the defendant is the manufacturer of the medicinal product in issue, and the related issue as to whether *Fairchild v Glenhaven Funeral Services Ltd* [2003] 1 AC 32 provides a basis for the introduction of market share or alternative liability into English law. For details of that discussion, see CJ Miller and RS Goldberg, *Product Liability*, 2nd edn (Oxford, Oxford University Press, 2004) paras 17.45–17.56; cf I Dodds-Smith, M Spencer and J Bore, 'Product Liability for Medicinal Products' in MJ Powers, NH Harris and A Barton (eds), *Clinical Negligence*, 4th edn (London, Tottel Publishing, 2008) paras 24.22–24.31 (doubting the ability of *Fairchild* to assist under negligence, and arguing that relaxation of the legal requirement to prove causation under the Product Liability Directive, Art 4 and the Consumer Protection Act 1987, s 2(1) would be inappropriate in the context of the strict liability regime); cf S Whittaker, *Liability for Products: English Law, French Law, and European Harmonisation* (Oxford, Oxford University Press, 2005) 513 (suggesting a similar case to *Fairchild* in the medicinal product context, and arguing that *Fairchild* could be followed on the basis that while prima facie the 'fair apportionment of risks' is upset by applying such an approach, since such a case involves special difficulties for causation, which are well-known in other Member States, these should not be permitted to bar recovery). R Goldberg, *Causation and Risk in the Law of Torts: Scientific Evidence and Medicinal Product Liability* (above, n 9) 55–101.

[11] *Merck & Co., Inc v Garza*, 347 SW3d 256, 262 (Tex 2011), citing. *Merrell Dow Pharmaceuticals, Inc v Havner* 953 S.W. 2d 706, 714 (Tex. 1997).

[12] Ibid. See, further, M Green, 'The Future of Proportional Liability: The Lessons of Toxic Substances Causation' in S Madden (ed), *Exploring Tort Law* (New York, Cambridge University Press, 2005) 366.

[13] Ibid, 552; S Gold, 'Causation in Toxic Torts: Burdens of Proof, Standards of Persuasion, and Statistical Evidence' (1986) 90 *Yale Law Journal* 376, 379–380.

causation.[14] The results of epidemiological studies cannot *per se* conclusively prove specific causation. However, several cases have focused on the role that epidemiologic evidence plays in determining proof of specific causation, which is a legal question addressed by courts.[15] This chapter explores the ways in which probabilistic methods, including statistical refining with individual risk factors, can be used in conjunction with epidemiologic evidence to determine specific causation.

Part IIA explores the apparent tension between the levels of proof required in law and science, including the relationship between levels of statistical significance and the claimant's burden of proof, and is followed in Part IIB by an assessment of the wisdom of using a doubling of the risk rule as a threshold to any recovery. Notwithstanding the problems with the doubling of risk theory in the US, its existence appears to be gaining ground in the UK. In particular, these matters have come to recent attention in the context of the utilisation and value of epidemiological or statistical evidence alone in determining causation on a balance of probabilities, with discussion in the Supreme Court in *Sienkiewicz v Greif*.[16] A cautious attitude towards the utilisation of the doubling of risk rule in the context of both general and specific causation is seen from the case law, which is explored in this part. In examining the distinction between association and causation, Part IIC discerns two main reasons for judicial scepticism about epidemiologic evidence emerging from the case law, namely the propriety of drawing causal inferences from observed associations (a general causation issue) and the propriety of drawing causal inferences in individual cases from concededly causal associations observed in samples of populations (a 'specific causation' issue). These reasons are discussed in an analysis of the controversial Scottish case of *McTear v Imperial Tobacco Limited*,[17] and the decision of the Federal Full Court of Australia in the Vioxx case, *Merck Sharp & Dohme (Australia) Pty Limited v Peterson*.[18] In the context of *McTear*, Part IID discusses the necessity of requiring something more than a doubling of the risk to permit the claimant to recover, and the role of judges in playing an active role in resolving this issue. Part IIE notes the implications of the fact that epidemiology is based on the study of populations and not individuals on the question of specific causation in the context of *McTear*. It suggests that the limitations of epidemiologic evidence in determining specific causation as described by the trial judge are somewhat inaccurate, since epidemiologists can and do adjust for these potentially confounding factors through logistic regression statistical techniques and other forms of statistical refining mechanisms in determining specific causation. Part IIF concludes with an examination of such statistical refining methods in determining specific causation in medicinal product liability cases, including the use of Bayes theorem to help us understand how statistical risks can be refined using personal risk factors. However, the chapter does not argue that Bayes' theorem is necessarily the answer to the problem of establishing specific causation in the context of epidemiological evidence. Nonetheless, while recognising the limitations of Bayes' theorem, the chapter supports the view that logistic regression statistical techniques and

---

[14] MD Green, DM Freedman & L Gordis, 'Reference Guide on Epidemiology' in *Reference Manual on Scientific Evidence* (above, n 8) 552–553, 598.

[15] Ibid, 609.

[16] *Sienkiewicz v Greif* [2011] UK SC 10, [2011] 2 WLR 523.

[17] *McTear v Imperial Tobacco Ltd* 2005 2 SC 1.

[18] *Merck Sharp & Dohme (Australia) Pty Ltd v Peterson* [2011] FCAFC 128, leave to appeal refused, [2012] HCATrans 105.

other forms of statistical refining mechanisms using specific risk factors can and do help in the process of giving quantitative or quasi-quantitative expression to conclusions about the cause of disease in an individual drug product liability claim that is based on epidemiological evidence. Finally, it illustrates the increasing support for the refining and personalising of epidemiological evidence in cases of individual causation involving medicinal products with the the decision of the Ontario Supreme Court of Justice in *Anderson v St Jude*.[19]

II. RECONCILING THE STANDARDS OF PROOF
IN LAW AND SCIENCE IN THE UK

A. Evidence of Causation for Purposes of Science and for Purposes of Law

There is an apparent tension between what are regarded as levels of proof required in law and in science. For the law of negligence, it is sufficient to show that the balance of probabilities—meaning more than 50 per cent, or on a preponderance of the evidence—indicates a causal connection. It is sometimes erroneously assumed by lawyers that scientists regard an association as causal if it is 95 per cent certain.[20] However, this is a misinterpretation of the so-called p value, which is merely the level of statistical significance used to exclude the possibility that when something transpires in a cohort of cases, it does so by chance (ie the null hypothesis). When the p value falls below the threshold of 0.05, the investigator is able to reject the null hypothesis since there is a less than 1 in 20 chance that the link between exposure and disease is random.[21] While there is no generally accepted standard of scientific proof for causation,[22] and neither the claimant nor the defendant is required to apply scientific standards of proof when determining causation on a balance of probabilities, [23] such a standard must be 'more than marginal'.[24] In light of this apparent tension between the balance of probabilities standard and the standard of statistical significance, courts

---

[19] *Anderson v St Jude Medical Inc* 2012 Carswell Ont 8061, 2012 ONSC 3660, 219 ACWS (3d) 725. [542], [544], [555], [558]–[559].

[20] See MD Green, DM Freedman & L Gordis, 'Reference Guide on Epidemiology' in *Reference Manual on Scientific Evidence* (above, n 8) 576–577; equating statistical significance with the legal burden of proof has been described as being 'like trying to find the shortest path from Oxford to Cambridge by scrutinizing a map of London': David H. Kaye, 'Apples and Oranges: Confidence Coefficients and the Burden of Persuasion' (1987) 73 *Cornell Law Review* 54, 66. Kay demonstrates the distinction between statistical significance and the civil burden of persuasion by utilising a hypothetical case: ibid 66–73, esp 72. There is often judicial reference to a statement that the level of 0.05 for statistical significance is a much higher burden of proof than the civil burden of a preponderance of the evidence or balance of probabilities (viz greater than 50%) MD Green, DM Freedman & L Gordis, 'Reference Guide on Epidemiology' in *Reference Manual on Scientific Evidence* (above, n 8) 577, citing *In re Ephedra Prods Liab Litig*, 393 F. Supp. 2d 181, 193 (SDNY 2005); *Marmo v IBP, Inc*, 360 F. Supp. 2d 1019, 1021 (D Neb 2005); P Feldschreiber, L Mulcahy and S Day, 'Biostatistics and Causation in Medicinal Product Liability Suits', in R Goldberg (ed), *Perspectives on Causation* (Oxford, Hart Publishing, 2011) 190. Recent case law has referred to Wyeth's citation of the Reference Manual on Scientific Evidence to point to the erroneous nature of this approach: *Giles v Wyeth, Inc*, 500 F. Supp. 2d 1048, 1056–1057 (SD Ill 2007).

[21] P Feldschreiber, L Mulcahy and S Day, 'Biostatistics and Causation in Medicinal Product Liability Suits', in R Goldberg (ed), *Perspectives on Causation* (Oxford, Hart Publishing, 2011) 184, 190.

[22] *Loveday v Renton & anr* [1990] 1 Med LR 117, 124, Stuart-Smith LJ.

[23] *Carter v Basildon and Thurrock University Hospitals NHS Foundation Trust* [2007] EWHC 1882 (QB), [2007] LS Law Medical 657, [92].

[24] *Dingley v Chief Constable, Strathclyde Police* 1998 SC 548, 603, per Lord Prosser, cited in *Sienkiewicz v Greif (UK) Ltd* [2011] UKSC 10, [2011] 2 AC 229, [9], per Lord Phillips of Worth Matravers PSC.

must be alert to the problem that may be faced by an expert 'in readjusting his focus from the 95 per cent confidence limits approach to the balance of probabilities test'.[25] However, in *Vadera v Shaw*[26] the Court of Appeal reconciled the legal standard of proof of a balance of probabilities with the scientific standard of statistical significance in showing that a failure to establish a statistically significant connection between the oral contraceptive Logynon and strokes was fatal to the establishment of proof of causation on a balance of probabilities. Henry LJ stated:

> The judge concluded, and in our respectful view was right on the evidence to conclude, that the studies carried out and referred to by Dr Lidegaard [for the plaintiff] did not establish a statistically significant connection between Logynon and strokes. Such evidence cannot be ignored by a judge. It is as common sense a conclusion as one could wish to say that if the connection between 'a' and 'b' cannot be shown with confidence to be other than a coincidence, then it cannot be held on a balance of probabilities that 'a' caused 'b'. This is not to allow scientists or statisticians to usurp the judge's function, but rather to permit him to use their skills to discern a connection, or lack of connection between the two phenomena.[27]

B. 'Doubling of Risk' Theory

Epidemiologists investigating disease causation measure the association between exposure to an agent and the incidence of disease, using the concept of relative risk. Relative risk is defined as the ratio of the incidence of a disease in a population exposed to the agent to the incidence of disease in a population that has not been exposed.[28] For example, if 10 per cent of all people exposed to a drug develop a disease, compared with 5 per cent of people who are unexposed, the disease occurs twice as frequently among the exposed people. The relative risk is 10 per cent/5 per cent, ie 2. A relative risk of 1 shows no association between exposure and disease.[29] A significant attempt to reconcile the apparent tension between the balance of probabilities standard and the standard for epidemiology has emerged with the theory that causation can be proved on the balance of probabilities by reference to the doubling of risk of injury. That theory has long been recognised in the United States,[30] where

---

[25] *Carter v Basildon and Thurrock University Hospitals NHS Foundation Trust* [2007] EWHC 1882 (QB), [2007] LS Law Medical 657, [97]. A confidence interval or confidence limit is a range of values within which the true value is likely to fall: MD Green, DM Freedman & L Gordis, 'Reference Guide on Epidemiology' in *Reference Manual on Scientific Evidence* (above, n 8) 621; R Goldberg, *Causation and Risk in the Law of Torts: Scientific Evidence and Medicinal Product Liability* (above, n 4) 137; American Law Institute Reporters' Study, *Enterprise Responsibility for Personal Injury Vol II: Approaches to Legal and Institutional Change* (Philadelphia, PA, American Law Institute, 1991) 324–28.

[26] *Vadera v Shaw* (1998) 45 BMLR 162 (CA).

[27] Ibid 164. However, it is suggested that there was a failure by the trial judge and the Court of Appeal to scrutinise adequately the scientific evidence in respect of causation in this case: R Goldberg, 'The Contraceptive Pill, Negligence and Causation: Views on *Vadera v Shaw*' (2000) 8 *Medical Law Review* 316, 331–35.

[28] MD Green, DM Freedman & L Gordis, 'Reference Guide on Epidemiology' in *Reference Manual on Scientific Evidence* (above, n 8) 566, 627; M Green, 'The Future of Proportional Liability: The Lessons of Toxic Substances Causation' in S Madden (ed), *Exploring Tort Law* (New York, Cambridge University Press, 2005) 366.

[29] Ibid.

[30] See, in particular, *Daubert v Merrell Dow Pharmaceuticals, Inc* 43 F 3d 1311 (9th Cir 1995), cert denied, 116 S Ct 189 (1995) (*Daubert II*). In that case, the court of appeals, on remand from the Supreme Court of the United States held that the plaintiffs had to show not merely that Bendectin increased the likelihood of injury but more likely than not caused their injuries. In terms of statistical proof, it had to be shown that their mothers'

it has been said that '[t]he use of scientifically reliable epidemiological studies and the requirement of more than a doubling of the risk strikes a balance between the needs of our legal system and the limits of science'.[31] However, the theory has also been subject to trenchant criticism.[32] In particular, it has been submitted that judges have adopted 'substantive changes in causation law through the rubric of evidentiary admissibility decisions',[33] and have frequently conflated admissibility decisions and sufficiency of evidence decisions.[34] Those courts which require plaintiffs to produce epidemiological studies with a relative risk of two are making a 'legal policy determination to equate epidemiology, relative risk, general causation, and the burden of proof on individual causation'.[35] Moreover, while the total number of judicial opinions that at least mention the concept of doubling of risk has increased, the US courts disagree as to the proper role of the doubling of risk theory in deciding questions of both sufficiency and admissibility of scientific evidence of causation in toxic tort cases. They do not agree on whether to adopt the doubling of risk as a threshold, nor do they agree on the meaning of such a threshold.[36] As the reporters for the American Law Institute's *Restatement Third of Torts* have noted:[37]

> Many courts accept the doubling of the incidence of disease in group studies; some courts insist on doubling of risk as a minimum threshold for establishing specific causation. Others have recognised that if other known causes can be identified and eliminated, something less than a doubling would still be sufficient to find specific causation.

ingestion of Bendectin more than doubled the likelihood of birth defects: ibid 1320. This was reaffirmed by the Supreme Court of Texas in *Merrell Dow Pharmaceuticals, Inc v Havner* 953 SW 2d 706, 716–18 (Tex 1997). The Texas Supreme Court has now expanded on its holding in *Havner* and adopted the position that a doubling of risk is a necessary but not sufficient condition to prove causation: *Merck & Co., Inc v Garza*, 347 SW3d 256, 265 (Tex 2011). Vermont has also adopted the doubling of risk theory in a slightly diluted form in the context of specific causation: *Blanchard v Goodyear Tire & Rubber Co*, 30 A3d 1271, 1275–1277 (Vt 2011) For an insightful discussion of the implications of both cases, see S Gold, 'Revisiting Relative Risk Rules: *Garza, Blanchard*, and the Ever Evolving Role of Epidemiological Proof in Toxic Tort Cases', (2012) 40 *Product Safety & Liability Reporter* 50.

[31] *Merrell Dow Pharmaceuticals, Inc v Havner* 953 SW 2d 706, 718 (Tex 1997) (echoing the views of the court of appeals in *Daubert v Merrell Dow Pharmaceuticals, Inc* 43 F 3d 1311, 1320 (9th Cir 1995) (*Daubert II*)).

[32] See, eg, LM Finley, 'Guarding the Gate to the Courthouse: How Trial Judges Are Using their Evidentiary Screening Role to Remake Tort Causation Rules' (1999) 49 *DePaul Law Review* 335, 336, 348 (criticism of the doubling of risk evidentiary requirement for epidemiological proof, describing the trend as 'seriously scientifically and legally misguided'); MA Berger, 'Upsetting the Balance Between Adverse Interests: The Impact of the Supreme Court's trilogy on Expert Testimony in Toxic Tort Litigation' (2001) 64 *Law & Contemporary Problems* 289, 304–6 (criticism of the doubling of risk rule as 'a legal invention that creates a hard and fast rule that disposes of cases efficiently but rests on assumptions that cannot be scientifically validated at this time'); S Greenland and JM Robins, 'Epidemiology, Justice, and the Probability of Causation' (2000) 40 *Jurimetrics Journal* 321, 325–326. Cf M Geistfeld, 'Scientific Uncertainty and Causation in Tort Law' (2001) 54 *Vanderbilt Law Review* 1011, 1015, 1018, 1020.

[33] Ibid 336, 347.

[34] Ibid 336; supported by JM Eggen, 'Clinical Medical Evidence of Causation in Toxic Tort Cases: Into the Crucible of *Daubert*' (2001) 38 *Houston Law Review* 369, 378–79; M Green, 'The Future of Proportional Liability: The Lessons of Toxic Substances Causation' in S Madden (ed), *Exploring Tort Law* (New York, Cambridge University Press, 2005) 368–69. A recent instance of the conflation of both admissibility and sufficiency of evidence requirements is *Merck & Co v Garza*, 347 SW 3d 256, 265–266 (Tex 2011), discussed in S Gold, 'Revisiting Relative Risk Rules: *Garza, Blanchard*, and the Ever Evolving Role of Epidemiological Proof in Toxic Tort Cases', (2012) 40 *Product Safety & Liability Reporter* (framing a totality of evidence test as a matter of reliability, *Garza* explicitly conflated rules of admissibility and substantive sufficiency (weighing of evidence)).

[35] Ibid 362.

[36] RS Carruth and RD Goldstein, 'Relative Risk Greater than Two in Proof of Causation in Toxic Tort Litigation' (2001) 41 *Jurimetrics Journal* 195, 199, 202–3.

[37] *Restatement of the Law Third, Torts: Liability for Physical and Emotional Harm* [Restatement Third] (St Paul, MN, American Law Institute, 2010) §28(a), Reporters' Notes to cmt *c*, pp 450–52.

Accordingly, the requirement of a relative risk of two for the admissibility or sufficiency of epidemiological evidence has been subject to much scepticism:[38] and the reporters for the *Restatement Third of Torts*, in discussing the considerations which affect the appropriateness of determining the probability of specific causation based on the outcome of group studies, have concluded that a judicial requirement that plaintiffs must show a threshold increase in risk or a doubling of incidence in a group study to satisfy the burden of proof of specific causation is 'usually inappropriate'.[39]

Notwithstanding the problems with the doubling of risk theory in the US, its existence appears to be gaining ground in the UK. Of particular significance was the case of *XYZ v Schering Health Care Ltd*,[40] a trial of seven lead cases in group litigation against three pharmaceutical companies in respect of cardiovascular injuries, coming under the collective description of venous thromboembolism (VTE), which the claimants alleged were caused by taking the defendants' different brands of third generation combined oral contraceptives. The claimants alleged that the products they took were defective under the Consumer Protection Act 1987 and the Product Liability Directive: while the cause of action was based on strict liability, the requirement common to both negligence and strict liability of proving a causal link between the product and the damage emerged as the first central issue requiring determination (ie an issue of general causation).

Mackay J stated that the claimant could prove that an exposure to risk caused injury if that exposure had more than doubled the risk of the injury occurring.[41] This method of proving causation was applied in a case of bladder cancer where the claimant had been tortiously exposed to carcinogens and non-tortiously exposed to cigarette smoke, both of which are potent causes of the condition.[42] However, it has been argued that since the doubling of risk approach is only valid where the risk estimates represent '*mutually exclusive ways in which the injury may have been caused*', and it is sought 'to estimate the likelihood it was one way which had operated in a particular case rather than one of the other potential ways',[43] since the mechanism by which amines cause cancer is unknown,

---

[38] C Cranor, *Toxic Torts: Science, Law, and the Possibility of Justice* (Cambridge, Cambridge University Press, 2007) 234–38, 281.

[39] *Restatement of the Law Third, Torts: Liability for Physical and Emotional Harm* [Restatement Third] (St Paul, MN, American Law Institute, 2010) § 28(a) cmt c(4), p 409.

[40] *XYZ v Schering Health Care Ltd* [2002] EWHC 1420, (2002) 70 BMLR 88 (QB).

[41] Ibid [21] Mackay J. See, further, CJ Miller and RS Goldberg, *Product Liability*, 2nd edn (Oxford, Oxford University Press, 2004) paras 17.06–17.08.

[42] *Novartis Grimsby Ltd v Cookson* [2007] EWCA Civ 1261, [74] Smith LJ. See also *AB v Ministry of Defence* [2010] EWCA Civ 1317, (2011) 117 BMLR 101, [151] (doubling of risk theory relevant in the context of examining strength of claimants' cases on causation in determining the exercise of discretion under Limitation Act 1980, s 33; trial judge had wrongly exercised his discretion). In dismissing the claimants' appeals, the Supreme Court observed that it was undesirable that a court which conducts an inquiry into whether a claim is time-barred should, even when it considers its power under s 33 of the 1980 Act, have detailed regard to the evidence with which the claimant aspires to prove its case. Nonetheless, because of the complexity of the claims placed before the trial judge and the nature of the submissions about knowledge in s 14(1) of the 1980 Act, the trial judge was able to make a 'microscopic survey of the written evidence', especially in respect of causation. The Court of Appeal had been unusually well-placed in exercising its discretion under s 33 to assess the claimants' prospects of establishing causation. Since the Court of Appeal had concluded that the claimants' faced 'very great difficulties' in establishing causation, and the claimants had no real prospects of success, it had been correct not to exercise its discretion to allow the claims to proceed: to have done so would have been absurd: [2012] UKSC 9, [2013] 1 AC 78, [27], Lord Wilson JSC, [65], Lord Walker of Gestingthorpe JSC, [89], Lord Mance JSC.

[43] J Stapleton, 'Factual Causation, Mesothelioma and Statistical Validity' (2012) 128 *Law Quarterly Review* 221, 223–25.

the doubling of risk approach is not validly applicable as a method. By contrast, such comparisons of risk estimates in the doubling of risk approach are statistically valid where the estimates relate to mechanisms, which even if their details remain not understood, are known to involve different agents, such as a birth defect which may be attributable either to a medicinal product or a background risk.[44]

The utilisation and value of epidemiological or statistical evidence alone in determining causation on a balance of probabilities was subject to some interesting debate in the Supreme Court in *Sienkiewicz v Greif*.[45] The reason for this discussion, as pointed out by Baroness Hale,[46] was the presence of an obiter observation of Smith LJ in her judgment in *Sienkiewicz* that 'in a case of multiple potential causes, a claimant can demonstrate causation by showing that the tortious exposure has at least doubled the risk arising from the non-tortious cause or causes'.[47] Their Lordships were postulating the scenario where, having established general causation between the toxic agent and the disease, epidemiological evidence might be utilised in establishing specific causation, ie whether the claimant's injury was caused by the product in question. While there was unanimity in their Lordships holding that there was no room for introducing the doubling of risk approach to 'single exposure'[48] mesothelioma cases or multiple defendant mesothelioma cases,[49] the differences in view emerged with the obiter discussion of the general applicability of the doubling of risk theory using epidemiological evidence to determine proof of causation in personal injury cases.

Lord Phillips discussed the decision of *XYZ v Schering Health Care Ltd*,[50] and took the view that, while the case contained 'a detailed and illuminating discussion of epidemiology', it did not afford any direct assistance to the question of whether the 'doubles the risk' test—as he called it—was an appropriate test for determining causation in a case of multiple potential causes.[51] His reasoning was somewhat obscured by his misclassification of the contraceptives in this case. He stated that the issue

> was whether a second generation of oral contraceptives more than doubled the risk of causing deep vein thrombosis (DVT) that was created by the first generation of contraceptives ... It was

---

[44] Ibid 223.

[45] *Sienkiewicz v Greif* [2011] UK SC 10, [2011] 2 AC 229 (SC). See R Goldberg, 'Using Scientific Evidence to Resolve Causation Problems in Product Liability: UK, US and French Experiences' in R Goldberg (ed), *Perspectives on Causation* (Oxford, Hart Publishing, 2011) 153–55 and RW Wright, Proving Causation: Probability versus Belief' in R Goldberg (ed), *Perspectives on Causation* (Oxford, Hart Publishing, 2011) 199–205. Cf J Stapleton, (2012) 128 *Law Quarterly Review* 221, 223–25, who considers it regrettable that the Supreme Court speculated on the appropriate role of epidemiological evidence.

[46] Ibid [169].

[47] *Sienkiewicz v Greif (UK) Ltd* [2009] EWCA Civ 1159, [2010] QB 370, [23] Smith LJ.

[48] *Sienkiewicz v Greif* [2011] UK SC 10, [67]. As Lord Kerr has noted, '[t]he use of the expression "single exposure" may be misleading in this context': ibid [199]. It is probably better expressed as 'single tortious exposure cases': ibid [173], Baroness Hale. These are cases where only one defendant exposed the victim to asbestos and there was only one possible tortious source for the exposure, and the only other exposure creating a risk of developing mesothelioma was environmental exposure to low level asbestos dust in the general atmosphere: ibid [113], Lord Rodger; [199], Lord Kerr, [207], Lord Dyson.

[49] Ibid [106], Lord Phillips, [160], Lord Rodger, [169], Baroness Hale, [188], Lord Mance, [2003], Lord Kerr, [220], Lord Dyson. Cf Stapleton (2012) 128 *Law Quarterly Review* 221, 224–25, who states that both propositions (using the doubling of risk approach in mesothelioma cases where there was a single exposure or one with multiple defendants) could have been rejected as invalid on elementary statistical principles.

[50] *XYZ v Schering Health Care Ltd* [2002] EWHC 1420, (2002) 70 BMLR 88 (QB).

[51] *Sienkiewicz v Greif* [2011] UKSC 10, [74], Lord Phillips.

not whether the DVT suffered by the claimants had been caused by the second generation of oral contraceptives.[52]

In fact, the issue was whether the claimants had proved that *third* generation combined oral contraceptives caused a true excess risk of Venous Thromboembolism (VTE), which was more than twice that caused by *second* generation combined oral contraceptives. This had been suggested in three unpublished studies highlighted in a 'Dear Doctor' letter sent to prescribers by the Committee on Safety of Medicines (CSM) on 18 October 1995. Both sides agreed that if the claimants failed to prove this, the action would go no further, as it could not succeed. The reason for this utilisation of doubling of risk theory in fact related to proving that the third generation contraceptives were defective. Both parties had agreed that if the claimants could prove a true excess risk of VTE, they would also succeed on the second issue, which was whether the relevant products were defective within the meaning of section 3 of the Consumer Protection Act 1987, ie that their safety would not be such as persons generally were entitled to expect. The test of defectiveness under section 3 includes consideration of instructions or warnings associated with the product. The reasoning behind the doubling of risk theory's relevance to establishing that the third generation contraceptives were defective was that if the Court ruled that the true risk of VTE was more than doubled with third generation combined oral contraceptives, women and their prescribers were entitled to be told this before making their decisions or giving their advice, and they had not been.[53] However, Lord Phillips' reasoning seems to ignore the fact that causation was *inherently behind* the court's approach. As Mackay J explained in *XYZ*:

> The reason why the Claimants accept through Lord Brennan QC that this first issue is capable of disposing of the claims should be set out. It is not because an increase of less than 2 would fail to render the product defective within the meaning of the Act, though the Defendants would so argue if they had to. It is for reasons of *causation* that he accepts this burden, correctly in my view. If factor X increases the risk of condition Y by more than 2 when compared with factor Z it can then be said, of a group of say 100 with both exposure to factor X and the condition, that as a matter of probability more than 50 would not have suffered Y without being exposed to X. If medical science cannot identify the members of the group who would and who would not have suffered Y, it can nevertheless be said of each member that she was more likely than not to have avoided Y had she not been exposed to X (emphasis added).[54]

While Lord Phillips concluded[55] that there was no scope for the doubling of risk test in cases where two agents operated cumulatively and simultaneously in causing the onset of the disease, since in such cases the material contribution rule in *Bonnington Castings v Wardlaw*[56] would apply, he submitted[57] that there was no reason in principle why the 'doubles the risk test' should not be applied where the initiation of a disease was dose related and there had been consecutive exposures to an agent or agents that cause the disease, eg *McGhee v*

[52] Ibid.
[53] *XYZ v Schering Health Care Ltd* [2002] EWHC 1420, (2002) 70 BMLR 88 (QB), [20]–[21]. See, further, CJ Miller and RS Goldberg, *Product Liability*, 2nd edn (Oxford, Oxford University Press, 2004) paras 17.06–17.08.
[54] *XYZ v Schering Health Care Ltd* [2002] EWHC 1420, (2002) 70 BMLR 88 (QB), [21].
[55] *Sienkiewicz v Greif* [2011] UKSC 10, [91], Lord Phillips.
[56] *Bonnington Castings v Wardlaw* [1956] AC 613, 620, Lord Reid.
[57] *Sienkiewicz v Greif* [2011] UKSC 10, [92], Lord Phillips.

National Coal Board.[58] He also considered[59] that there was no reason in principle why the 'doubles the risk' test should not apply to competing alternative, rather than cumulative potential causes of a disease or injury, such as *Hotson v East Berks Area Health Authority*.[60] However, neither Lord Rodger nor Baroness Hale took such a view, and both thought that a doubling of risk approach was not an appropriate test of causation.[61] Lord Rodger stressed that where statistical evidence established that exposure to a substance more than doubled the risk of a disease, this would not amount to proof, on the balance of probability, that the exposure actually caused the disease.[62] While Lord Dyson felt it 'unnecessary to decide whether there [were] any circumstances in which, as a matter of English law, causation [could] be proved on the basis of epidemiological evidence alone',[63] he expressed the view that 'there [was] no *a priori* reason why, if the epidemiological evidence [was] cogent enough, it should not be sufficient to enable a claimant to prove his case without more'.[64] By contrast, Lord Kerr stressed the need to treat the use of epidemiological evidence to seek to establish any specific proposition in an individual case with great caution.[65] He felt that there was a real danger that 'so-called "epidemiological evidence" [would] carry a false air of authority'.[66] Lord Mance felt that whether and if so when epidemiological evidence could, per se, prove a case, was 'a question best considered not in the abstract but in a particular case, when and if that question [arose]'.[67] If it could, he would hope and expect that this would only occur in the rarest of cases.[68] Ultimately, the question of whether the law should allow reliance solely on a doubling of risk approach is one of judicial policy,[69] so it is unsurprising that the Court took a generally cautious approach.

This generally cautious attitude towards the utilisation of the doubling of risk rule in the context of specific causation has been reflected in medicinal product liability litigation concerning the anti-inflammatory drug Vioxx. In *Merck Sharp & Dohme (Australia) Pty Limited v Peterson*,[70] it was alleged in representative proceedings that consumption of Vioxx

---

[58] *McGhee v National Coal Board* [1973] 1 WLR 1. Yet as Professor Stapleton has observed, the basis for the validity of the doubling-of-the-risk approach in this instance would be absent. By way of illustration, she cites the example of a person injured in a road accident who is administered an emergency dose of a medicinal product. The injured person is immediately transferred to a hospital, where the admitting doctor, failing to discover what medications had been administered to the victim, negligently administers a smaller dose of the medication. In that scenario, it is likely that the causal mechanism required a commingling of molecules from the later smaller dose with the innocent molecules, and thus the tortious administration of the medication by the admitting doctor would have made a causal contribution to the death, even though another larger and earlier dose would have been sufficient to cause death: J Stapleton, 'Factual Causation, Mesothelioma and Statistical Validity' (2012) 128 *Law Quarterly Review* 221, 228–29; see, further, J Stapleton, 'Unnecessary Causes' (2013) 129 *Law Quarterly Review* 39, 55–56.

[59] *Sienkiewicz v Greif* [2011] UKSC 10, [93], Lord Phillips.

[60] *Hotson v East Berks Area Health Authority* [1987] AC 750.

[61] *Sienkiewicz v Greif* [2011] UKSC 10, [156], [158], [162], Lord Rodger, [170], [172]–[173], Baroness Hale.

[62] Ibid [156], [158], Lord Rodger.

[63] *Sienkiewicz v Greif* [2011] UKSC 10, [221], Lord Dyson.

[64] Ibid [222], Lord Dyson.

[65] Ibid [205], Lord Kerr.

[66] Ibid [206].

[67] Ibid [192].

[68] Ibid.

[69] J Stapleton, 'Factual Causation, Mesothelioma and Statistical Validity' (2012) 128 *Law Quarterly Review* 221, 223, 229–30.

[70] *Merck Sharp & Dohme (Australia) Pty Ltd v Peterson* [2011] FCAFC 128, leave to appeal refused, [2012] HCATrans 105. Special leave to appeal to the High Court of Australia was refused since the applications were deemed not suitable vehicles for the consideration of the relevant questions of principle that would warrant

increased the risk of a myocardial infarction (heart attack) and that Vioxx had caused or contributed to the myocardial infarction of the class representative, Mr Peterson.[71] The trial judge, Jessup J, had held that the epidemiological evidence demonstrated that Vioxx had doubled the risk of heart attack across the population as a whole,[72] and that consumption of Vioxx materially contributed to Peterson's heart attack.[73] In upholding Merck Australia's appeal on the issue of causation, the Full Court criticised the doubling of risk approach as being 'apt to mandate an award of compensation to applicants who have not, in truth, been injured by the respondent'.[74] It also noted that, while a relative risk of two might imply a 50 per cent probability that the risk had come home in a typical case, a relative risk of less than two would imply a probability of less than 50 per cent, ie less probable than not; the trial judge's finding of relative risk was 'about two'.[75]

C. Association Versus Causation

It is suggested that it would be an oversimplification to think that the views of Lord Phillips in *Sienkiewicz* will help to signal a green light to the establishment of proof of causation on a balance of probabilities by a mere doubling of relative risk. The matter was addressed in *Merrell Dow Pharmaceuticals, Inc v Havner*[76] where, having stated that the balance between the needs of the legal system and the limits of science could be shown by the use of scientifically reliable epidemiological studies and the requirement of more than doubling the risk, the Supreme Court of Texas added the caveat:

> We do not hold, however that a relative risk of more than 2.0 is a litmus test or that a single epidemiological test is legally sufficient evidence of causation. Other factors must be considered. As already noted, epidemiological studies only show an association. There may in fact be no causal relationship even if the relative risk is high.[77]

---

the grant of leave, 'having regard to the findings of fact of the primary judge and the Full Court's treatment of them'.

[71] *Merck Sharp & Dohme (Australia) Pty Ltd v Peterson* [2011] FCAFC 128, [2].

[72] *Merck Sharp & Dohme (Australia) Pty Ltd v Peterson* [2010] FCR 1, [570]; see, generally, C. Newman-Martin, 'Manufacturers' liability for undiscoverable design flaws in prescription drugs: A Merck-Y area of the law' (2011) 19 *Torts Law Journal* 26.

[73] Ibid [772].

[74] *Merck Sharp & Dohme (Australia) Pty Ltd v Peterson* [2011] FCAFC 128, [110]. This would be the case since 'those applicants who were actually injured by causes other than the respondent's actionable conduct will be able to recover compensation because, for them too, a relative risk of greater than 2 can be said to imply probability of greater than 50% that the respondent's actionable conduct was the cause of their loss'. It is submitted that this criticism is misconceived since the problem of compensation to those not injured by a defendant is generic in any system that uses a preponderance of the evidence rule and has no relevance to the type of evidence employed to determine whether the plaintiff has met the preponderance threshold.

[75] Ibid [111]. Cf *Seltsam Pty Limited v McGuiness* [2000] NSWCA 29 at [137], Spigelman CJ at [137], who noted that while in Australian law the test of actual persuasion did not require epidemiological studies to reach the level of risk of two, 'the closer the ratio approaches two, the greater the significance that can be attached to the studies for the purposes of drawing an inference of causation in an individual case. The "strands in the cable" must be capable of bearing the weight of the ultimate inference'.

[76] *Merrell Dow Pharmaceuticals, Inc v Havner* 953 SW 2d 706 (Tex, 1997).

[77] Ibid 718.

The latter sentence is of particular importance, and while Lord Phillips referred to the remainder of this caveat in his speech in *Sienkiewicz*,[78] he omitted the last sentence, and ignored its import in his final analysis. Unlike Lord Phillips, Lord Rodger stressed the importance of the distinction between association and causation. In this context, Lord Rodger's reason for scepticism about epidemiologic evidence concerns the propriety of drawing causal inferences from observed associations (a general causation issue); yet there is seemingly a further reason for scepticism in his speech, viz the propriety of drawing causal inferences in individual cases from concededly causal associations observed in samples of populations. (a 'specific causation' issue).[79] Lord Rodger's speech is more compelling in that it shows a greater understanding of both the significance and limitations of epidemiological evidence and demonstrates a reluctance to support the general applicability of the doubling of risk theory using epidemiological evidence to determine proof of both general and specific causation in personal injury cases.[80] Lord Rodger accepted that epidemiological and statistical evidence may form an important element in proof of causation, and he supported the utilisation and value of epidemiological evidence where a claimant was required to prove his case on a balance of probabilities.[81] However, he emphasised that, since by its very nature the statistical evidence does not deal with the individual case, the court should not proceed to find a causal relationship *in that particular case* without further, non-statistical evidence, e.g. temporality.[82] In so doing, he cited *Phipson on Evidence*, which states that '[w]here there is epidemiological evidence of association, the court should not proceed to find a causal relationship without further, non-statistical evidence'.[83] Lord Rodger illustrated his example of evidence of temporality in the context of a medicinal product and an adverse effect, where there was 'a strong epidemiological association between a drug and some condition that could have been caused in some other way'.[84] He submitted that that epidemiological evidence, 'along with evidence that the claimant developed the condition immediately after taking the drug' could be sufficient to allow the judge to conclude that the drug caused the condition on the balance of probability.[85]

---

[78] *Sienkiewicz v Greif* [2011] UKSC 10, [88], Lord Phillips.

[79] This can be contrasted with the other reason for judicial scepticism about epidemiologic evidence, viz the propriety of drawing causal inferences from observed associations (a 'general causation' issue). It is often difficult to tease out from the decisions as to which form of judicial treatment is taking place.

[80] Ibid [162], Lord Rodger, [170], [173], Baroness Hale.

[81] Ibid [163], Lord Rodger.

[82] Ibid; see also, Baroness Hale, who opined that 'the existence of a statistically significant association between factor X and disease Y does not prove that in the individual case it is more likely than not that factor X caused disease Y': ibid [170]. Lord Mance accepted that epidemiological evidence, used with proper caution, could be admissible and relevant in conjunction with specific evidence related to the individual circumstances and parties. The significance a court might attach to it depended 'on the nature of the epidemiological evidence, and of the particular factual issues before the court': ibid [191]. Lord Kerr considered that '[i]t is an essential and minimum requirement ... that there be evidence connecting avowedly relevant statistical information produced by the epidemiological studies to the facts of the case': ibid [205]. Lord Dyson also stressed the association/causation dichotomy, stating that 'epidemiology ... seeks to establish associations between alleged causes and effects ... However, in an individual case, epidemiology alone cannot *conclusively* prove causation': ibid [218]; see, further, the recent discussion by the High Court of Australia in *Amaca Pty Ltd v Booth; Amaba Pty Ltd v Booth* [2011] HCA 53, [49], French CJ (distinguishing between mere statistical correlation between conduct and injury and the need to establish causal connection between the conduct and injury).

[83] HM Malek (ed), *Phipson on Evidence*, 17th edn (London, Sweet & Maxwell, 2010) 34-27.

[84] [2011] UK SC 10, [163], Lord Rodger.

[85] Ibid.

A further instance of a court which is sceptical of inference from population to individual in the context of medicinal products is the decision of the Federal Full Court of Australia in *Merck Sharp & Dohme (Australia) Pty Limited v Peterson*.[86] There the Full Court upheld the 'but for' test of causation, and that the trial judge's findings of fact were insufficient to sustain the position that, on the balance of probabilities, 'but for' the consumption of Vioxx, Peterson's myocardial infarction would not have occurred.[87] It concluded that while the epidemiological evidence meant that it was *possible* Vioxx caused Peterson's myocardial infarction, there were other strong potential causes, viz age, gender, hypertension, hyperlipidaemia, obesity, left ventricular hypertrophy and a history of smoking.[88] Peterson was therefore a member of a group within the community, 25 per cent of whom were expected by cardiologists to suffer a heart attack within five years.[89] These personal circumstances seriously diminished the strength of the epidemiological evidence as a strand in the cable of circumstantial proof.[90] Accordingly, the Full Court held that it was not more probable than not that Vioxx, whether alone or in combination with Peterson's personal risk factors, was a necessary condition of the occurrence of his heart attack.[91] While a relative risk of two could be converted into a statistical likelihood of 50 per cent that Vioxx was causally implicated in the occurrence of a myocardial infarction, there were other candidates as causes of the jury. The strength of the epidemiological strand did not rise above the possibility that it was 'in the mix' of factors which may have caused Peterson's heart attack.[92] While the fact that the plaintiff in *Peterson* suffered from several personal risk factors prima facie cuts against recovery, this mere fact alone does not resolve the import of the epidemiological evidence. The difficulty lies with the fact that epidemiological evidence conflates people with different underlying conditions and it may not be known what the relative risk is for those individuals with no history of heart disease and individuals like Peterson, with a long history of heart disease. Indeed, there is a strong argument, based upon Merck's own VIGOR study of Vioxx, that the relative risk of taking Vioxx is equally strong in both subgroups and that Vioxx could have caused a heart attack, even in someone with a history of heart disease.[93] It is submitted that there is no data to support the court's conclusion that personal circumstances seriously diminishes the strength of the epidemiological evidence. Accordingly, the court's approach is arguably a guess by a sceptical court that Vioxx

---

[86] *Merck Sharp & Dohme (Australia) Pty Ltd v Peterson* [2011] FCAFC 128.

[87] Ibid [103]–[105].

[88] Ibid [120].

[89] Ibid.

[90] Ibid [113].

[91] Ibid [120].

[92] Ibid [123]. Special leave to appeal to the High Court of Australia was refused since the applications were deemed not suitable vehicles for the consideration of the relevant questions of principle that would warrant the grant of leave, 'having regard to the findings of fact of the primary judge and the Full Court's treatment of them': [2012] HCATrans 105.

[93] *See McDarby v Merck & Co*, 949 A2d 223, 234 (NJ Super 2008) (noting that the results of the VIGOR study in March 2000 revealed a higher incidence of adverse cardiovascular events with those who received rofecoxib (Vioxx) than those patients who received naproxen, 'in patients with and without a history of atherosclerotic cardiovascular disease, and in patients with or without classic risk factors for cardiovascular disease'); and, further, Steve Gold, 'Revisiting Relative Risk Rules: *Garza, Blanchard*, and the Ever Evolving Role of Epidemiological Proof in Toxic Tort Cases' (2012) 40 *Product Safety & Liability Reporter*, 50, 2. Consider the following hypothetical. For those with no pre-existing heart problems, taking Vioxx raises the risk of heart attacks 101% (more than double) from 1% to 2.01%. For those with pre-existing heart conditions like Peterson, taking Vioxx raises the risk of heart attacks 101% from 10% to 20.01%. Vioxx is identically implicated in both scenarios.

is incapable of being identically implicated in both cases of those with pre-existing heart problems and those without.

In the light of Lord Rodger's observations in *Sienkiewicz*, and from the perspective of the propriety of drawing causal inferences from observed associations (a general causation issue), the mere existence of a statistically significant association is insufficient to establish a causal relationship without the presence of further non-statistical evidence, and, in order to do so, factors such as those adumbrated by Sir Austin Bradford Hill would need to be utilised to determine whether a reported association is causal.[94] This point was emphasised by the Scottish Court of Session in *McTear v Imperial Tobacco Limited*,[95] a decision which takes a cautious approach to the use of epidemiological evidence, and stresses the impossibility of applying epidemiological studies to determine causation in individual cases. While the case concerns tobacco products, its implications are particularly pertinent to problems involving medicinal products, where the role of epidemiological evidence in proving both general and specific causation is prominent.

UK developments in this area have often focused on the difficulty in proving general and specific causation between a product and damage using epidemiological evidence[96] derived from trends in general populations, and this was graphically illustrated by *McTear*. In that case, the pursuer, the widow of a smoker, sought to recover damages from the defenders, manufacturers of John Player brand cigarettes, which were smoked by her late husband. Her husband had contracted squamous cell carcinoma of the lung, and the pursuer averred that cigarette smoking could cause lung cancer (an issue of general causation), and that her husband's lung cancer was caused by his smoking (an issue of individual or specific causation).

The problem of establishing a general causal link between cigarette smoking and cancer was exacerbated by the fact that, unlike all the US cigarette companies, and all the other UK cigarette companies, Imperial Tobacco Ltd had not accepted that there was a causal link between smoking and disease, especially lung cancer.[97] In respect of establishing general causation, Lord Nimmo Smith concluded that, in the absence of such an admission, and

---

[94] See A Bradford Hill, 'The Environment and Disease: Association or Causation' (1965) 58 *Proceedings of the Royal Society of Medicine* 295–300. These aspects of association (viz strength of association, consistency, specificity, temporality, biological gradient, plausibility, coherence, experiment and analogy) are utilised to determine whether a reported association is causal or non-genuine. For recent support for the Bradford Hill factors as providing a guide to the kind of considerations that lead to an inference of causal association, see *Amaca Pty Ltd v Booth; Amaba Pty Ltd v Booth* [2011] HCA 53, [49], French CJ.

[95] *McTear v Imperial Tobacco Limited* 2005 2 SC 1, [6.158]. However, the presentation of the list of factors in textbooks as 'criteria' for inferring causality or associations in a way as to imply that all the conditions are necessary has been described as 'unfortunate': S Greenland (ed), *The Evolution of Epidemiological Ideas: Annotated Readings on Concepts and Methods* (Newton Lower Falls, MA, Epidemiology Resources, Inc, 1987) 14. As Greenland correctly observes, Hill expressly stated that he did not intend to lay down 'hard-and-fast rules of evidence that *must* be obeyed before we accept cause and effect': AB Hill, 'The Environment and Disease: Association or Causation' (1965) 58 *Proceedings of the Royal Society of Medicine* 295, 299. He added that '[n]one of [his] nine viewpoints can bring indisputable evidence for and against the cause and effect hypothesis and none can be required as a *sine qua non*': ibid. See, further, C Cranor, *Toxic Torts: Science, Law, and the Possibility of Justice* (above, n 28) 102–5.

[96] Epidemiology has been defined as 'the study of patterns of disease occurring in human populations and the factors that influence these patterns': *McTear v Imperial Tobacco Limited* 2005 2 SC 1, [6.157].

[97] 2005 2 SC 1, [2.58], [2.76], [6.30]. This was notwithstanding the generally accepted view for over 50 years that cigarette smoking could cause lung cancer: R Doll and AB Hill 'Smoking and carcinoma of the lung: Preliminary report' (1950) 2 *British Medical Journal* 739–48; R Doll and AB Hill, 'The mortality of doctors in relation to their smoking habits: A preliminary report' (1954) 1 *British Medical Journal* 1451–55; 2005 2 SC 1, [5.208] (evidence of Sir Richard Doll). The defenders admitted that the World Health Organization, the United Kingdom Government and the United States Government had accepted for many years that cigarette smoking can cause lung cancer: 2005 2 SC 1, [2.7]. However, they averred that '[c]igarette smoking has not been scientifically

indeed of any evidence that this was an inference which should be drawn, the defenders were entitled to put the pursuer to proof of her averment that cigarette smoking could cause lung cancer (ie the general causation issue).[98] In the absence of support from animal experiments, proof of causation between cigarette smoking and lung cancer depended on what was proved before the court about epidemiological studies. He held that, in accordance with the Scots law of expert evidence, it was necessary to consider whether the evidence of any expert witness had imparted to him special knowledge of the subject matter of epidemiology, including published material lying within the witness's field of expertise, so as to enable the court to form its own judgment about the subject matter and the conclusions to be drawn from it. Accordingly, it was not open to the court to form its judgment on the evidence without being taught how to do the epidemiology to a sufficient extent, and without it being provided with sufficient factual material to enable it to be proved on the balance of probabilities, not only that there was an association between cigarette smoking and lung cancer, but also that the proper conclusion to be drawn from this was that there was a causal connection between them.[99] This distinction between association and causation in the context of the general causation issue lay at the heart of Lord Nimmo Smith's conclusions. In his view, while an association between an exposure and a condition was judged to be statistically significant, that *in itself* did not constitute a judgment that there was a causal connection between an exposure and a condition.[100] He explained:

> The finding of an association between an exposure and a condition or disease, even if judged to be statistically significant, does not of itself connote that a causal connection between the two is established. This is a matter for further exercise of judgment, taking account of such criteria as the consistency, the strength, the specificity, the temporal relationship and the coherence of the association ... This must, I think be especially so, when, in the view of Sir Richard Doll ... cigarette smoking is not a necessary cause nor a sufficient cause of lung cancer.[101]

He then addressed the concept of relative risk, concluding that even a relative risk derived from comparison of the incidence of lung cancer in smokers and non-smokers of a magnitude such that a positive association may be judged to be strong enough to establish causation between the two, was not such as to connote the establishment of a causal link.[102] As we shall now see, this scepticism about the epidemiologic evidence by questioning the propriety of drawing causal inferences from observed associations was not the only problem that the pursuer had in establishing general causation: the court also had to be taught the relevant epidemiology.

D. Teaching the Court the Epidemiology

In respect of general causation, Lord Nimmo Smith held that the pursuer had failed to prove, in accordance with the requirements of the Scots law of evidence relating to expert

---

established as a cause of lung cancer and, although various theories have been advanced, the cause or causes of lung cancer are unknown and the mechanism or mechanisms whereby lung cancer develops are unknown': ibid.

[98] 2005 2 SC 1, [2.78], [2.80] (OH).
[99] 2005 2 SC 1, [6.155].
[100] 2005 2 SC 1, [6.158].
[101] Ibid.
[102] Ibid, [6.159].

witnesses, that cigarette smoking could cause lung cancer.[103] This was because the pursuer had failed to lead evidence about the primary literature sufficient to impart to the court special knowledge of the subject matter (epidemiological evidence of a causal connection between cigarette smoking and lung cancer, within the expert's field of expertise) so as to enable the court to form its own judgment about it and the conclusions to be drawn from it.[104] Lord Nimmo Smith stated that 'a fundamental defect in the presentation of the pursuer's case' was the failure to take the court to any of the primary literature in which it had been concluded that there was a causal connection between cigarette smoking and lung cancer.[105] In his view, this was a missed opportunity:

> This could have been done: it is clear that the survey of British doctors, on which Sir Richard Doll and colleagues have worked for many years, is regarded as a classic of its kind, both because of the pioneering nature of the research, a preliminary report of which was published as Doll and Hill in 1950, and because this had been followed up with subsequent papers over several decades. I could at least have been shown these papers, which I assume disclosed the data, the statistical techniques and all the other considerations which led to the authors' conclusions so that I could see for myself whether these conclusions were soundly based. The opportunity was there with Sir Richard Doll in the witness box, and indeed Professor Friend for one thought that evidence would be given about this survey. Warning had been given on behalf of [Imperial Tobacco Ltd] ... that Sir Richard Doll's data were of potential interest to the court. But in the event no attempt was made to show me the data.[106]

Recent Scots law in the decision of *Smith v McNair*[107] reaffirms the very same cautious approach to the interpretation of epidemiological evidence established in previous cases.[108] It stresses the need for experts to teach the court how to do the epidemiology before it can form its reasoned judgment on interpreting the epidemiological evidence. While acknowledging that medical witnesses are entitled to refer to medical literature, in particular to refer to published papers by epidemiologists, even though they themselves are not epidemiologists,[109] Lord McEwan in *Smith* has stressed the need to look at such evidence critically because the writers of it could not be cross-examined themselves. Such scientific evidence only became a factor for consideration if it was 'intelligible, convincing and tested'.[110] Accordingly, in Scotland the cases are at one in emphasising that where a pursuer seeks to rely on epidemiological evidence of disease through an expert witness in proving causation, the pursuer must import to the court special knowledge of the subject matter of epidemiology, so that the court can form its reasoned judgment on the epidemiological evidence.[111]

---

[103] 2005 2 SC 1, [6.170]–[6.171].

[104] Ibid [6.155], [6.162]–[6.163].

[105] Ibid [6.163].

[106] Ibid [6.162].

[107] *Smith v McNair* [2008] CSOH 154; see R Goldberg, 'Causation, Idiopathic Conditions and the Limits of Epidemiology' (2009) 13 *Edinburgh Law Review* 282.

[108] See *Dingley v The Chief Constable of Strathclyde* 1998 SC 548, 555 Lord President (Rodger), at 604 Lord Prosser, aff'd 2000 SC (HL) 77; *McTear v Imperial Tobacco* 2005 2 SC 1 (OH) [5.11], Lord Nimmo Smith.

[109] *Main v McAndrew Wormald Ltd* 1988 SLT 141, 142, Lord Justice-Clerk (Ross).

[110] *Smith v McNair* [2008] CSOH 154, [18], citing *Davie v Magistrates of Edinburgh* 1953 SC 34, 40.

[111] Cf in the United States, the Advisory Committee Note (2000 Amendment) to Fed R Evidence 702. The Amendment not only stresses that the expert conducts the application of principles and methods to the facts of cases reliably, but also reiterates the 'verifiable practice of using expert testimony to educate the factfinder on general principles'. Fed R Evidence 702 Advisory Committee's Note (2000 amendment). It notes that it might be

Such a cautious approach to epidemiological evidence was central to the decision in *Smith*. While sympathetic to the experts who were 'outwith their chosen discipline and abroad in the field of epidemiology',[112] Lord McEwan concluded nonetheless that they were unable to explain the studies, which seemed to him to 'raise more questions than answers'.[113] Unlike *McTear*, however, *Smith* shows less of an impression of what Chris Miller has described as a 'dogmatic aversion'[114] to statistical evidence. Lord McEwan felt that many of the problems with the evidence might have been helped if the authors of the reports had been called and there had been some statistical evidence. Without such assistance, the judge was 'at once disabled from being able properly to evaluate the worth of the study or to draw on the proper conclusions'.[115] In his view, therefore, this was an appropriate case for epidemiologists to give evidence and for experts to explain their studies. He did not, however, believe that this was always the case, and suggested that reliance on doctors and epidemiologists 'can almost lead the court unwittingly into a kind of satellite litigation on issues away from the pursuer's case'.[116] He seemed to regard *McTear* and another Scottish decision, *Dingley*, as two recent examples of this,[117] yet it is submitted that the use of statistics in determining causation is hardly satellite litigation: in both cases it was a primary issue which required resolution in the face of scientific uncertainty. It is submitted that the concern with such a cautious approach in Scots law to epidemiological evidence is that it may make it harder to even discern that there is any reconciliation of the legal standard of proof on a balance of probabilities with the scientific standard of statistical significance.

Even more importantly, there is also concern that the mere placing of an obligation on the pursuer to teach the epidemiology to the court suggests that the court can act passively in this process. This is surely an unhelpful approach in cases such as *McTear*, and in cases involving adverse reactions allegedly caused by medicinal products, where there is a clear societal function of a judge to resolve these matters to the satisfaction of both parties. As a leading American judge has observed in cases where judges preside over non-jury trials:

> Passivity of the court is no virtue when serious scientific questions of more than passing importance are involved. The court owes an obligation to the parties, to society, and to itself to assist in obtaining the best possible answers to the scientific questions before it. That will mean forcing the parties to gather and present evidence effectively, calling upon other experts as necessary, and studying to obtain the understanding needed to maintain effective control.[118]

Had the pursuer explained the epidemiologic evidence properly, and had Lord Nimmo Smith been more receptive to the strength of evidence of relative risk, as well as taking a

---

important in some cases for an expert to *educate* the factfinder about general principles, without ever attempting to apply these principles to the specific facts of the case: ibid.

[112] [2008] CSOH 154, [81].

[113] Ibid.

[114] C Miller, 'Causation in Personal Injury; Legal or Epidemiological Common Sense' (2006) 26 *Legal Studies* 544, 566.

[115] [2008] CSOH 154, [80].

[116] Ibid [16].

[117] Ibid [16], [29].

[118] J Weinstein, 'Improving Expert Testimony' (1986) 20 *University of Richmond Law Review* 473, 495–96. Judge Weinstein also encourages judges presiding over non-jury trials 'to become familiar with the scientific background by reading about the issues and discussing them with the experts': ibid 494; noted in *Snyder v Secretary of Health & Human Services*, 01-162V, 2009 WL 332044 (Fed Cl Feb 12, 2009) at *2.

more active role in forcing the pursuers to present their evidence effectively, it would seem that general causation could have been established in this case. Moreover, the fact that the defenders admitted that the World Health Organization, the United Kingdom Government and the United States Government had accepted for many years that cigarette smoking can cause lung cancer[119] was surely important generally accepted scientific evidence to which Lord Nimmo Smith should have been given adequate weight.[120] Irrespective of the conclusions on general causation, the problem of course remained of establishing individual causation, in the context of naked statistical evidence. It is to this that we now turn.

E. The Statistical Chance/Personal Chance Dichotomy

It has been argued that there is a dichotomy between two kinds of chances—one 'statistical' and the other 'personal'. A statistical chance is a figure collected from 'previous unconnected outcomes, giving a probability of that outcome in any non-individual case', whereas a personal chance is 'peculiar to a particular individual'.[121] A statistical chance has no compensatory value, until the data is 'personalised'.[122]

The impossibility of applying statistics derived from epidemiological studies to determine causation in individual cases was cited as the principal reason for the pursuer's failure to prove individual or specific causation in *McTear*, since such evidence could not prove that it was more likely than not that but for her husband's smoking of cigarettes he would not have contacted lung cancer.[123] As Lord Nimmo Smith put it:[124]

> The information provided in an observational epidemiology is generally such that it can neither confirm nor refute a causal relationship, particularly when the exposure in question is not specifically associated with a certain condition (ie the exposure is always associated with the condition, and vice versa). Epidemiology cannot provide information on the likelihood that an exposure produced an individual's condition. The population attributable risk is a measure for populations only and does not imply a likelihood of disease occurrence within an individual, contingent upon that individual's exposure. The fact that cases and non-cases can emerge both from the unexposed and the exposed groups shows that the likelihood of the individual occurrence cannot be reliably predicted from his or her exposure group membership alone. The group estimates obscure the underlying heterogeneity of the population, so that it is entirely possible that other group memberships besides exposure, like genetic profile, socio-economic status, workplace, diet and other exposures make a major contribution to disease occurrence. The question of using epidemiological data for individual causation raises the problem of identifying a particular individual who was harmed by the exposure. While models such as the assigned share concept, derived from attribut-

---

[119] 2005 2 SC 1, [2.7], [6.30].
[120] Counsel for the pursuer had submitted (unsuccessfully) that considerable weight be placed on the fact that this proposition had come to be generally accepted: ibid [6.41].
[121] T Hill, 'A Lost Chance for Compensation in the Tort of Negligence by the House of Lords' (1991) 54 *Modern Law Review* 511, 512.
[122] Ibid 518. See *Hotson v East Berkshire AHA* [1987] 2 WLR 287, 303 CA, Croom-Johnson LJ.
[123] 2005 2 SC 1, [6.180], [6.184]–[6.185]. See also the above discussion in *Sienkiewicz v Greif* [2011] UK SC 10, [163], Lord Rodger, [170], Baroness Hale, [191], Lord Mance, [205], Lord Kerr, [218], Lord Dyson (nn 49–52). As in the UK, US courts often bifurcate both specific and general causation elements: see J Sanders, 'The Controversial Comment C: Factual Causation in Toxic-Substance and Disease Cases' (2009) 44 *Wake Forest Law Review* 1029, 1032.
[124] Ibid [6.180].

able fractions, have attempted to deal with this, they suffer from the limitations mentioned by Dr Lewis. The attempt to identify exposure as the sole cause of disease in an individual produces a statement counter to fact in that it implies that the individual would have remained healthy if the exposure had not occurred. This, as Dr Lewis said, is not provable and cannot be derived from epidemiological data.

He concluded that given there were other possible causes of lung cancer besides cigarette smoking, and that lung cancer could occur in a non-smoker, it was not possible to determine in any individual case whether but for an individual's cigarette smoking he probably would not have contracted lung cancer.[125] In doing so, he referred to '[t]he fallacy of applying statistical probability to individual causation'.[126]

However, his dicta require closer scrutiny. While Lord Nimmo Smith was correct to observe that there are limitations of epidemiological evidence, his description of such limitations of epidemiology is somewhat inaccurate. In stating that 'group estimates obscure the underlying heterogeneity of the population so that it is entirely possible that other group memberships besides exposure, like genetic profile, socio-economic status, workplace, diet and other exposures make a major contribution to disease occurrence',[127] he fails to appreciate that epidemiologists can and do adjust for these potentially confounding factors through logistic regression statistical techniques.[128]

Notwithstanding the doubts of Lord Nimmo Smith about causal proof based on population estimates of relative risk, these are relevant to individual cases, even though they do not directly measure the probability of causation in an individual case.[129] Moreover, it has been suggested that, while Lord Nimmo Smith's 'dogmatic aversion to statistical evidence' means that epidemiology alone will never secure recovery in such cases,[130] utilisation of epidemiological evidence that satisfies the Bradford Hill criteria would seem to be hard to gainsay.[131] Thus it has been argued by Chris Miller that if an individual had been one of the cases in a case control study that yields strength of association (relative risk) then, in the light of such strength of association and other Bradford Hill criteria 'it seems perverse to hold that it is less probable than not that the exposure caused that individual's condition'.[132] It is submitted that Miller is correct in concluding that a causal relationship would exist in such circumstances. Indeed, Sir Austin Bradford Hill emphasised that '[n]one of [his] nine viewpoints can bring indisputable evidence for and against the cause and effect hypothesis

[125] 2005 2 SC 1, [6.184]–[6.185].

[126] 2005 2 SC 1, [6.184]. For the need to exercise caution in the use of general statistics in establishing causation, and the importance of looking at the claimant's individual circumstances, see the observations of Brooke LJ in *Wardlaw v Farrar* [2003] 4 All ER 1358, [2004] Lloyd's Rep Med 98, [2004] *PIQR* 19 at [35]–[36]. See, further, *Amaca v Ellis* [2010] HCA 5, [62]; *Sienkiewicz v Greif* [2011] UK SC 10, [152], [163], Lord Rodger, [170], [172], Baroness Hale, [190]–[192], Lord Mance, [204]–[206], Lord Kerr.

[127] 2005 2 SC 1, [6.180].

[128] See, further, KJ Rothman, S Greenland, TL Lash, *Modern Epidemiology*, 3rd edn (Philadelphia, PA, Lippincott Williams & Wilkins, 2008) 394–95.

[129] See Steve C Gold, 'When Certainty Dissolves Into Probability: A Legal Vision of Toxic Causation for the Post Genomic Era', (2013) 70 *Washington & Lee Law Review* 237, 281, 303; and, further, S Greenland and JM Robins, 'Epidemiology, Justice, and the Probability of Causation', (2000) 40 *Jurimetrics Journal* 321, 321–322.

[130] C Miller, 'Causation in personal injury: legal or epidemiological common sense' (2006) 26 *Legal Studies* 544, 566.

[131] Ibid 566.

[132] Ibid.

and none can be required as a *sine qua non*',[133] and this has been judicially approved in the US.[134] Bradford Hill specifically cautioned against overemphasis of the importance of specificity at the expense of strength of association, and specifically referred to smoking and lung cancer in such circumstances.[135] In doing so, he provided a particularly apt example:

> Coming to modern times the prospective investigations of smoking and cancer of the lung have been criticized for not showing specificity—in other words the death rate of smokers is higher than the death rate of non-smokers from many causes of death ... But here surely one must return to my first characteristic, the strength of association. If other causes of death are raised 10, 20, or even 50% in smokers whereas cancer of the lung is raised 900–1,000% we have specificity—a specificity in the magnitude of the association ... We must also keep in mind that diseases may have more than one cause ... In short, if specificity exists we may be able to draw conclusions without hesitation; if it is not apparent, we are not thereby necessarily left sitting irresolutely on the fence.[136]

It is suggested that the importance of such a widely accepted magnitude of strength of association between cigarette smoking and cancer was underplayed by Lord Nimmo Smith in *McTear*, and that he was wrong to treat all the Bradford Hill factors as being criteria that needed to be satisfied before such an association could amount to a causal connection between smoking and lung cancer. In his discussion of the impossibility of applying statistics derived from epidemiological studies to determine causation in individual cases, Lord Nimmo Smith failed to appreciate that epidemiologists can and do adjust for potentially confounding factors through logistic regression statistical techniques and other forms of statistical refining mechanisms in determining specific causation, and it is to these techniques that we now turn.

F. Overcoming the Statistical Chance/Personal Chance Dichotomy: Statistical Refining Mechanisms Using Specific Risk Factors

The problem of utilising statistics deriving from trends in general populations to prove causation in an individual case has been recognised judicially by the House of Lords in *Hotson v East Berkshire Area Health Authority*,[137] *Gregg v Scott*[138] and by the Supreme Court in *Sienkiewicz v Greif*.[139]

Yet it is arguable that while epidemiological evidence reaches conclusions as an average in the form of relative risk, this relative risk can be refined to draw conclusions about the cause of disease in an individual using specific risk factors[140] such as were present in

---

[133] AB Hill, 'The Environment and Disease: Association or Causation' (1965) 48 *Proceedings of the Royal Society of Medicine* 295, 299.

[134] *Cook v Rockwell Intern Corp* 580 F Supp 2d 1071, 1098 (D Colo 2006).

[135] AB Hill, 'The Environment and Disease: Association or Causation' (1965) 48 *Proceedings of the Royal Society of Medicine* 295, 297. The High Court of Australia has recently stressed that reference to relative risk ratio may act as an indicator of strength of association: *Amaca Pty Ltd v Booth; Amaba Pty Ltd v Booth* [2011] HCA 53, [49], French CJ.

[136] Ibid.

[137] *Hotson v East Berkshire Area Health Authority* [1987] AC 750, 789 Lord Mackay.

[138] *Gregg v Scott* [2005] 2 AC 176, [26]–[33] Lord Nicholls and 153 Lord Phillips.

[139] *Sienkiewicz v Greif* [2011] UKSC 10, [152], [163], Lord Rodger, [170], [172], Baroness Hale, [190]–[192], Lord Mance, [204]–[206], Lord Kerr.

[140] See M Berger, 'Upsetting the Balance Between Adverse Interests: The Impact of the Supreme Court's Trilogy on Expert Testimony in Toxic Tort Litigation', (2001) 64 *Law & Contemporary Problems* 289, 306.

Mr McTear's case and in Peterson's case. This has been accepted by American courts in the context of pharmaceutical product liability litigation.[141] In the Vioxx case of *McDarby v Merck & Co, Inc*,[142] epidemiological evidence was combined by experts with the presence of personal heart attack risk factors for the plaintiff, consisting of his age, low levels of 'good' cholesterol, weight and diabetes. This was regarded as ample evidence to support an increased risk resulting from the combined effects of diabetes and Vioxx to conclude that Vioxx had been a substantial contributing factor to his heart attack.[143] In so doing, the New Jersey court applied a substantial factor standard in the context of concurrent causation, in preference to the 'but for' test.[144]

In this context, it has been submitted that statistics regarding evidence of general causal links between a drug and an injury (a 'statistical chance') could be refined into statistics establishing a specific causal link between the drug and the adverse reaction in the case in issue (a 'personal chance')[145] using logistic regression statistical techniques and other forms of statistical refining mechanisms [146]

Logistic regression techniques identify determinants of a particular outcome and assess the extent of the contribution of these determinants, adjusting for confounding factors[147] that may influence the contribution.[148] Logistic regression is also closely linked to other forms of statistical refining such as Bayes' theorem. Bayes' theorem can modify evaluations of probability based on initial assumptions in the light of more data. Bayes' theorem expresses the relationship between the probability of a proposition (A) evaluated *before* the utilisation of new data (B) (prior probability) and the probability of the same proposition evaluated *after* the utilisation of the new data (posterior probability).

[141] MD Green, DM Freedman & L Gordis, 'Reference Guide on Epidemiology' in *Reference Manual on Scientific Evidence* (above, n 8) 616, citing *Merrell Dow Pharmaceuticals, Inc v Havner* 953 S.W. 2d 706, 720 (Tex. 1997); *Smith v Wyeth Ayerst Labs Co* 278 F Supp 2d 684, 708-09 (WDNC 2003) (discussing defendant's expert's attempt to refine relative risk of epidemiological study on relationship between diet drugs and Primary Pulmonary Hypertension (PPH) to that applicable to individual plaintiff who developed PPH after taking prescription appetite suppressants based on specific risk characteristics (duration of use and timing of use), but stating that he had failed to do so).

[142] *McDarby v Merck & Co*, 949 A2d 223 (NJ Super 2008).

[143] Ibid 269–270.

[144] Ibid 271 (applying the substantial factor standard, causation was appropriately demonstrated by long term use of Vioxx and 'medical and/or scientific proof of a nexus between [that use] and ... plaintiff's condition').

[145] T Hill, 'A Lost Chance for Compensation in the Tort of Negligence by the House of Lords' (1991) 54 *Modern Law Review* 511, 518.

[146] See, for further discussion, R Goldberg *Causation and Risk in the Law of Torts: Scientific Evidence and Medicinal Product Liability* 39–40, the principles of which are adapted to meet the circumstances of *Peterson*, below.

[147] A confounding factor is a factor that is both a risk factor for the disease and one associated with the exposure in issue. Confounding refers to the situation where an association between an exposure and an outcome is all or partly due to a factor that affects the outcome but which is unaffected by the exposure: MD Green, DM Freedman & L Gordis, 'Reference Guide on Epidemiology' in *Reference Manual on Scientific Evidence* (above, n 8) 621.

[148] KJ Rothman, S Greenland, TL Lash, *Modern Epidemiology*, 3rd edn (Philadelphia, PA, Lippincott Williams & Wilkins, 2008) 394–395; O Caster, GN Norén, D Madigan and A Bate, 'Logistic regression in signal detection: another piece added to the puzzle' (2013) Clinical Pharmacology & Therapeutics, accepted article preview online 21 May 2013; doi:10.1038/clpt.2013.107.

Thus:

Posterior Probability of A given B	=	Prior Probability of A	×	Probability of B given A
		1		Unconditional Probability of B

ie $P(A/B) = P(A) \times \dfrac{P(B/A)}{P(B)}$

Prior probabilities can therefore be updated in the light of new data from epidemiologic studies as they accumulate, providing fact finders in individual product liability cases and policy makers such as the Food and Drug Administration and the European Medicines Agency with an update of the estimated risk.[149] The principal problem with such posterior probabilities is that so-called 'frequentist statisticians' who rely on epidemiological evidence regard them as necessarily subjective, since they reflect not just data but also subjective prior probabilities.[150] However, 'objective Bayesians' use Bayes' theorem without eliciting prior probabilities from subjective beliefs, avoiding the charge of subjectivism.[151] This has been supported in the pharmaceutical product liability context by Professor Joseph Gastwirth, using a first case control study or an analysis of an adverse event and case reports from two prior distributions that are consistent with the data, in order to restrict the degree of subjectivity that an analyst can insert into a Bayesian approach. This is very important in the legal context where lawyers can chose an expert who obtains a more favourable result and helps to avoid bias in their choice of prior distribution.[152] Others have also tried to apply Bayes' theorem in the evaluation of the reliability of medical and scientific evidence in toxic tort cases.[153] However, the strongest criticism of Bayes' theorem is the difficulty of arriving at a sufficiently accurate evaluation of a pre-existing probability to which experimental data can be applied.[154]

Bayes' theorem tells us that the value of a piece of evidence in testing a particular assertion is determined by its likelihood ratio. The likelihood ratio (LR) is the probability of the evidence supposing our assertion is true, divided by the probability of the evidence if

---

[149] See Joseph L Gastwirth, 'Should Law and Public Policy Adopt 'Practical Causality' as the Appropriate Criteria for Deciding Product Liability Cases and Public Policy?' (August 19, 2012). Available at SSRN: http://ssrn.com/abstract=2132163 or http://dx.doi.org/10.2139/ssrn.2132163.

[150] DH Kaye and DA Freedman, 'Reference Guide on Statistics' in *Reference Manual on Scientific Evidence*, 3rd edn (Washington, DC, National Academies Press 2011) 258, 273.

[151] Ibid, 259, n 123.

[152] Joseph L Gastwirth, 'Should Law and Public Policy Adopt 'Practical Causality' as the Appropriate Criteria for Deciding Product Liability Cases and Public Policy?' (August 19, 2012). Available at SSRN: http://ssrn.com/abstract=2132163 or http://dx.doi.org/10.2139/ssrn.2132163; and, further, P Ryan, MA Suchard, M Schuemie & D Madigan, 'Learning from Epidemiology: Interpreting Observational Database Studies for the Effects of Medical Products', (2013) *Statistics in Biopharmaceutical Research*, DOI: 10.1080/19466315.2013.791638 (supporting a Bayesian framework to interpret observational database studies for the effects of medical products, and suggesting that future work can extend the Bayesian framework to include such elements as the Bradford Hill factors (see n 101, above)).

[153] NC Stout and PA Valberg, 'Bayes Law, Sequential Uncertainties, and Evidence of Causation in Toxic Tort Cases' (2005) 38 *University of Michigan Journal of Law Reform* 781, 787 (submitting that judges should apply Bayesian probabilistic approaches in toxic tort cases when evaluating the reliability of medical and scientific evidence, and in so doing permitting the factfinder to decide only those toxic tort claims for which there is reliable and relevant scientific support for each link in the causal chain).

[154] R Eggleston, *Evidence, Proof and Probability*, 2nd edn (London, Weidenfeld and Nicholson, 1983) 171.

the assertion is not true.[155] The Centre for Evidence Based Medicine at the University of Oxford provides a helpful example of the LR in the following:

> [Yo]u have a patient with anaemia and a serum ferritin of 60mmol/l and you find in an article that 90 per cent of patients with iron deficiency anaemia have serum ferritins in the same range as your patient (=sensitivity) and that 15 per cent of patients with other causes for anaemia have serum ferritins in the same range as your patient (1 – specificity). This means that your patient's result would be six times as likely (90/15) to be seen in someone with, as opposed to someone without, iron deficiency anaemia, and this is called the LR for a positive test result.[156]

An alternative statement of Bayes' theorem is in terms of odds.[157] Bayes' theorem expresses the relationship between the odds in favour of an hypothesis *before* the utilisation of new data (prior odds) and the odds in favour of the hypothesis *after* taking account of the new data (posterior odds). The prior odds must be multiplied by the likelihood ratio of the new piece of data to generate the posterior odds.

Thus:

Posterior Odds = Prior Odds × Likelihood Ratio

A potential application to the Vioxx case, *Merck Sharp & Dohme (Australia) Pty Limited v Peterson*,[158] could be to compare 'Vioxx-induced MI' with a catch-all alternative, 'no Vioxx-induced MI', (which, a priori, ie before bringing in the evidence that Peterson has MI, would require to include both MI arising from other causes and in other ways, and no MI arising at all). Alternatively, one could compare 'Vioxx-induced MI' with some specific alternative, e.g. 'diet-induced MI', or 'totally uncaused MI' or 'no MI'. The likelihood ratio would then be the ratio of the probabilities of developing MI under these two hypotheses.[159]

A statistical chance could be refined and personalised into a personal chance using specific factors which are embodied in the likelihood ratio. The probabilities in the likelihood ratio (LR) can be decomposed into factors in the light of specific case information in respect of patient history. Such factors could include the risk factors in Peterson's case, viz his age (LR (Ag)), gender hypertension (LR (Gh)), hyperlipidaemia (LR (Hypl), obesity (LR (Ob)), left ventricular hypertrophy (LR (LVH)), and a history of smoking (LR (Hs)).[160]

The likelihood ratio is found by obtaining the product of all the individual likelihood ratio factors. Diagrammatically this can be expressed by:

LR = LR(Ag) × LR(Gh) × LR(Hypl) × LR(Ob) × LR(LVH) × LR(Hs).

(Caveat = components, ie Ag etc must be statistically independent).

---

[155] B Robertson and GA Vignaux, *Interpreting Evidence: Evaluating Forensic Science in the Courtroom* (Chichester, John Wiley & Sons 1995) 17.

[156] http://www.cebm.net/?o=1043

[157] The relationship between odds and probability is:

$$\text{Odds} = \frac{\text{Probability}}{1 - \text{Probability}}$$

Thus the probability of 0.9 = odds of 9:1.

[158] *Merck Sharp & Dohme (Australia) Pty Ltd v Peterson* [2011] FCAFC 128.

[159] I am grateful to Professor Philip David for his explanation of this point.

[160] *Merck Sharp & Dohme (Australia) Pty Ltd v Peterson* [2011] FCAFC 128, [120].

The use of all these factors is dependent on the specific case information available. If all specific case information in respect of the factors is available, the posterior odds is calculated as follows:

$$\text{Posterior Odds} = \text{Prior Odds} \times \text{LR(Ag)} \times \text{LR(Gh)} \times \text{LR(Hypl)} \times \text{LR(Ob)}$$
$$\times \text{LR(LVH)} \times \text{LR(Hs)}.$$

Thus the posterior odds can be further refined by combining the prior odds, based on background information and the likelihood ratios, based on case-specific information, to produce as accurate a posterior probability as possible.[161] The nature of each risk factor likelihood ratio can represent a particularistic property of the individual claimant, providing they can be determined in the case in issue.[162] There is therefore a need to obtain statistics with a strong evidential foundation before such likelihood ratios can be calculated.[163]

This would seem to be a possible tool in improving probabilistic precision in the *Peterson* type of case and in other cases involving medicinal products, and in so doing, helping to overcome the difficulties of the statistical chance–personal chance dichotomy. It is clear that while Bayes' theorem could provide a normative approach to legal decision-making in the context of causation and medicinal products, implementation of it in practice is likely to be difficult.[164] We have seen that Bayes' theorem assumes the presence of conditionally independent new evidence to update the previous evidence, the absence of which in many cases involving alleged adverse drug reactions makes its application even more complex. The use of individual risk factor likelihood ratios in respect of individual items of evidence is potentially useful, but these may be difficult to calculate in practice.[165] It should also be conceded that if sample sizes are so small that one cannot disaggregate the data to provide information on individual risk factors then the statistical refining process will fail. Moreover, while more detailed individual ratios might improve the accuracy of the posterior odds, the introduction of too many additional quantities with imperfect estimation could degrade it.[166] However, the basic point here is not to suggest that Bayes' theorem is necessarily the answer to the problem of establishing specific causation in the context of epidemiological evidence. It is rather that logistic regression statistical techniques and other forms of statistical refining mechanisms using specific risk factors can and do help in

---

[161] B Donatini et al, 'Causality Assessment of Spontaneous Reporting: Correlation Between Bayesian and Other Approaches' (1993) 7 *Pharmaceutical Medicine* 255, 256.

[162] Personal Communication, Professor Philip David, Statistical Laboratory, Centre for Mathematical Sciences, Cambridge University, 12 July 2013. Robertson and Vignaux advocate that scientific evidence concerning an issue 'should be combined with other evidence relating to the same issue' and that the most effective way of doing so is to express the evidence in likelihood ratio form for it to be subsequently combined with other evidence: B Robertson and GA Vignaux, *Interpreting Evidence: Evaluating Forensic Science in the Courtroom* (Chichester, John Wiley & Sons, 1995) 220. In addition, Robertson and Vignaux have observed that the likelihood ratio's importance is that it combines relevance and probative value, the key determinants of admissibility of expert evidence: *ibid*, 22, 29. While Robertson and Vignaux have submitted that it is not essential to have precise numbers for each of the probabilities to assess the likelihood ratio (ibid, 22), this would seem, however, arguable in complex cases involving the establishment of causation with medicinal products: see R Goldberg, *Causation and Risk in the Law of Torts: Scientific Evidence and Medicinal Product Liability*, 43, n 242.

[163] K Grevling, Book Review, Robertson and Vignaux, 'Interpreting Scientific Evidence: Evaluating Forensic Science in the Courtroom' (1996) 112 *Law Quarterly Review* 509, 510.

[164] SE Fienberg and MJ Schervish, 'The Relevance of Bayesian Inference for the Presentation of Statistical Evidence and for Legal Decision Making' (1986) 66 *Boston University Law Review* 771, 772, 782, 794.

[165] Ibid 794.

[166] See, further, AP Dawid, 'The Role of Scientific and Statistical Evidence in Assessing Causality' in R Goldberg (ed), *Perspectives on Causation* (Oxford, Hart Publishing, 2011) 140–145.

the process of giving quantitative or quasi-quantitative expression to conclusions about the cause of disease in an individual claim that is based on epidemiological evidence.

Support for the refining and personalising of epidemiological evidence in cases of individual causation involving medicinal products is now gaining traction. A recognition that the doubling of risk standard is merely a *presumptive* threshold, so that a negative finding on causation could be rebutted utilising probative individualised evidence in a subsequent individual trial, has recently emerged with the decision of the Ontario Supreme Court of Justice in *Anderson v St Jude*,[167] a trial on the merits of a class claim concerning the safety of mechanical prosthetic heart valves and annuloplasty rings coated with Silzone that were designed and manufactured by the defendants and approved for sale in Canada in the late 1990s.[168] Silzone was a proprietary term for a coating comprising layers of titanium, pallodium and an outer layer of metallic silver, which was applied to a polyester sewing cuff that surgeons used to attach a prosthetic heart valve to heart tissue. Silver is known as an antimicrobial, and the Silzone coating was designed to inhibit the growth of bacteria that could cause endocarditis, an infection of the lining of the heart that is a serious complication of heart valve surgery. Other than the application of the coating to the sewing cuff, the Silzone valves were of the same design as conventional mechanical valves that the defendants had manufactured for many years.[169] Following a randomised clinical trial called AVERT, which had revealed a small but statistically significant increase in explants, due to a medical complication known as paravalvular leak (PVL) in patients who had received a Silzone implant, the defendants issued a worldwide recall of all Silzone-coated products in early 2000.[170] A proposed class action against St Jude Medical was commenced in 2001. At its core was a claim in negligence, which focused on breach of duty and questions of general causation.[171] The plaintiffs advanced the theory that Silzone was a toxic substance that interfered with the cells involved in tissue healing and impaired the body's ability to incorporate properly the Silzone device into the heart, thereby causing or contributing to a variety of serious medical complications for Silzone patients. Since medical complications can occur with all prosthetic valves, a key inquiry in the trial was whether Silzone '*materially increased* [the] *risk*' of experiencing one or more of these complications.[172] While the couching of this inquiry in terms of 'material increase in risk' may seem peculiar,[173] the issue being addressed was whether the plaintiffs could prove that the Silzone valve caused a true excess risk of the medical complications over that caused by the conventional valves. In essence, the Canadian court was adopting the same approach to the issue as the English High Court in *XYZ v Schering Health Care Ltd*.[174] Notwithstanding that Lax J found that the defendants did not breach any duty of care in the pre-market design, manufacture and

---

[167] *Anderson v St Jude Medical Inc* 2012 CarswellOnt 8061, 2012 ONSC 3660, 219 ACWS (3d) 725, [542], [544], [555], [558]–[559].

[168] Ibid [1].

[169] Ibid [2].

[170] Ibid [1].

[171] Ibid [4].

[172] Ibid [5].

[173] The reason for the use of the word 'material', which was formulated by Cullity J in his certification decision (ibid [5], [520]) was 'to ensure that findings with respect to whether Silzone increases the risk of complications would be sufficiently meaningful that they would be indicative of something more than a remote possibility of causation': ibid [528].

[174] *XYZ v Schering Health Care Ltd* [2002] EWHC 1420, (2002) 70 BMLR 88 (QB), [20]–[21].

testing or in the post-market surveillance, warning and recall of Silzone-coated products,[175] she proceeded to determine the common issues of causation had the court found differently on the breach issue. She explained that epidemiological evidence had been presented to assist her in determining whether or not Silzone valve patients experience a higher risk of medical complications than conventional valve patients, ie the purpose of this evidence was 'to determine the risk of medical complications posed by the Silzone valve *relative* to the risk posed by the conventional valve'.[176] This introduced the concept of relative risk, which was 'a numerical expression of the risk of medical complications for one class of patients relative to another'.[177] While recognising the limitations of epidemiological evidence, in that it ought not to be considered determinative of individual causation,[178] Lax J utilised simple arithmetic, the application of the 'but for' test and the balance of probabilities to conclude that for the purposes of issues of *general* causation in a class action trial, a doubling of risk standard should be adopted, so that a product (here the Silzone valve) creates a material risk of an adverse event where the risk is at least twice the risk of the adverse effect occurring in the absence of its use (ie when using the conventional valve).[179] However, in an important development which may help to constrain the overemphasis upon doubling of risk as some magic formula with which to restrict cases going forward to trial, Lax J explained that the determination of material risk and the application of the doubling of risk standard were not determinative of individual causation. Instead, for the purpose of individual class member claims, the application of the doubling of risk standard is merely a *presumptive* as opposed to a prescriptive threshold, so that a negative finding on causation (where the relative risk is below two) could be rebutted utilising probative individualised evidence in a subsequent individual trial.[180] The trial judge added that if she had found the defendants negligent, she would have applied the doubling of risk standard for materiality presumptively. Accordingly, patients who suffered complications for which the increase in risk was not material (ie where the relative risk was below two) or even not statistically significant would still be able to recover at the individual stage of those proceedings, provided they presented sufficient individualised evidence to rebut the presumption of a lack of causation flowing from a relative risk below two, and to persuade their trier of fact that Silzone was the 'but for' cause of their complications.[181] The benefit of adopting this approach is that 'it does not shut the door on individual class members solely on the basis of evidence regarding group risk'.[182] As Lax J explained, the adoption of a presumptive approach to materiality, allowing negative findings on causation to be rebutted by individualised evidence, allowed her to advance the litigation and to outline how the trier of fact at the individual stage of those proceedings could properly utilise relative risk as ascertained by epidemiological data.[183]

---

[175] 2012 ONSC 3660, [6], [182]–[183], [214].
[176] Ibid [384].
[177] Ibid.
[178] Ibid [395].
[179] Ibid [532]–[538]. The arithmetical explanation for adopting the 'doubling of risk' rule (ibid [532]–[534]) is almost identical to that provided in *XYZ v Schering Health Care Ltd* [2002] EWHC 1420, (2002) 70 BMLR 88 (QB), [21].
[180] Ibid [542], [544], [555], [558]–[559].
[181] Ibid [559].
[182] Ibid [560].
[183] Ibid [562].

III. CONCLUSIONS

We can make the following observations about recent cases involving the role of epidemiological evidence in assessing causation in medicinal product cases in the UK.

There remain considerable difficulties in reconciling the standards of proof in law and science. Despite the trenchant criticisms of the doubling of risk theory in the US, its support appears to be gaining ground in the UK. However, the majority of the Supreme Court in *Sienkiewicz* appears to be sceptical of introducing a threshold for the use of epidemiological evidence and remains of the view that epidemiological evidence can be useful but must be viewed with caution; without further non-statistical evidence there is reluctance for courts to proceed to find the existence of a causal relationship. A danger otherwise is that counsel, in assessing the chances of success of 'no win, no fee' multi-party product liability litigation, especially involving medicinal products, may regard this doubling of risk theory as the sole basis on which to allow or prevent cases from going forward to trial, even in cases where epidemiological evidence is lacking. This could potentially prejudice access to justice in future cases. If the doubling of risk approach is to be embraced by the UK courts, it is submitted that the doubling of risk standard should be treated as in the Canadian decision of *Anderson* as merely a *presumptive* as opposed to a prescriptive threshold, so that a negative finding on causation (where the relative risk is below two) could be rebutted utilising probative individualised evidence in a subsequent individual trial. In such cases where there is a dearth of epidemiological evidence, courts and, for that matter, funding bodies, should learn from the US experience and should avoid insisting on epidemiological studies which have a relative risk of greater than two, allowing all evidence which falls 'within a zone of reasonable scientific disagreement'[184] to be considered.

While it seems the UK is becoming more receptive to the need for epidemiologists to come to court to speak to their evidence and for it to be taught to the factfinder, there has recently developed an overly cautious approach to the use of epidemiological evidence, particularly in Scots law. We have seen two main reasons for judicial scepticism about epidemiologic evidence emerging from the case law, namely the propriety of drawing causal inferences from observed associations (a general causation issue) and the propriety of drawing causal inferences in individual cases from concededly causal associations observed in samples of populations (a 'specific causation' issue). It has been submitted that the concern with such a cautious approach to epidemiological evidence is that it may make it harder to even discern that there is any reconciliation of the legal standard of proof on a balance of probabilities with the scientific standard of statistical significance. Moreover, there is also concern that the mere placing of an obligation on the pursuer to teach the epidemiology to the court suggests that the court can act passively in this process. This is surely an unhelpful approach in cases such as *McTear*, where there is a clear societal function of a judge to resolve these matters to the satisfaction of both parties. Had the pursuer explained the epidemiologic evidence properly, and had Lord Nimmo Smith been more receptive to evidence of relative risk, taken a more active role in forcing the pursuers to

---

[184] C Cranor, *Toxic Torts: Science, Law, and the Possibility of Justice* (above, n 28) 366, 289–90, 335. Courts should not exclude causal opinions based on non-epidemiological evidence where a body of epidemiological data does not exist: DL Faigman, DH Kaye, MJ Saks, J Sanders, 'How Good is Good Enough?: Expert Evidence Under *Daubert* and *Kumho*' (2000) *Case Western Reserve Law Review* 645, 663.

present their evidence effectively, and given adequate weight to the generally accepted scientific evidence since 1950 that cigarette smoking can cause lung cancer, it would seem that general causation should have been established in this case.

There also remains a lack of clarity on the extent to which generalised epidemiological evidence can be useful in determining individual or specific causation. Accordingly, the chapter supports the use of logistic regression statistical techniques and other forms of statistical refining mechanisms using specific risk factors to give quantitative or quasi-quantitative expression to conclusions about the cause of disease in an individual drug product liability claim that is based on epidemiological evidence. Logistic regression is also closely linked to other forms of statistical refining such as Bayes' theorem. We have seen that while Bayes' theorem can modify evaluations of probability based on initial assumptions in the light of more data using specific factors embodied in the likelihood ratio, implementation of it in practice is likely to be difficult. It is important to stress that Bayes' theorem is not necessarily the answer to the problem of establishing specific causation in the context of epidemiological evidence. However, the crucial point is that statistical refining mechanisms using specific risk factors can assist courts in determining specific causation in drug product liability cases, when the dominating evidence is epidemiologic in nature. This is likely to be increasingly true, as the quality of scientific evidence increases with time.[185] It has been suggested that this approach could have been adopted with the specific case information available in Mr Peterson's case in the Vioxx representative action, instead of the personal circumstances being blindly treated as diminishing the strength of the epidemiological evidence as a strand in the cable of circumstantial proof.[186] Indeed, the Interdisciplinary Vaccine Safety Committee of the Institute of Medicine adopted such an 'informal Bayesian approach' to assessing case reports in its review of scientific and medical literature on specific risks to children associated with vaccines.[187] It is submitted that courts could utilise this information to refine these generalised statistics to produce as accurate a posterior probability as possible, especially in the pharmaceutical field. This, however, would need epidemiologists and physicians to assist the court in this exercise, and clearly without existing prior probabilities and the ability to quantify likelihood ratios, the process would be limited.

Nevertheless, in the absence of epidemiologic evidence, the Institute of Medicine in their report on Adverse Events Associated with Childhood Vaccines have supported the reliance upon individual case reports and case series, providing the nature and timing of the adverse event following vaccination and the absence of likely alternative aetiologic candidates were such that a reasonable certainty of causality could be inferred from one or more case reports.[188] And as Carl Cranor has astutely reported, while many US judges reject case reports in traditional tort cases as *inadmissible* on the *Daubert*[189] criteria,

---

[185] See, especially, support for a probabilistic model of specific causation in toxic torts, when the dominating evidence comprises population-based data of the toxic effect in SC Gold, 'When Certainty Dissolves Into Probability: A Legal Vision of Toxic Causation for the Post Genomic Era' (2013) 70 *Washington & Lee Law Review* 237, 281, 303–304, 338–339.

[186] Cf *Merck Sharp & Dohme (Australia) Pty Limited v Peterson* [2010] FCR 1, [113].

[187] KR Stratton, CJ Howe and RB Johnston, *Institute of Medicine, Adverse Events Associated with Childhood Vaccines: Evidence bearing on Causality* (National Academy Press, 1994) 3, 25.

[188] Ibid 31–33.

[189] The *Daubert* framework has been utilised in exercising the gatekeeping role to the admissibility of scientific evidence—in some cases in order to reduce the use of so-called 'junk science' by juries: see *Daubert v Merrill*

the Special Masters under the National Vaccine Injury Compensation Program, while following *Daubert* under their less formal procedures for introducing evidence, are much more receptive to the use of case reports supporting causation than most judges in traditional torts cases.[190]

Notwithstanding the scepticism of the majority of the Supreme Court in *Sienkiewicz*, there is little doubt that the utilisation of epidemiological evidence in medicinal product liability cases, especially where non-numerical solutions are elusive, has now come of age. Albeit with caution, courts are recognising the importance of such evidence. The challenge is now for lawyers and epidemiologists to come to some consensus as to what amounts to a suitable use of epidemiological evidence in such cases when establishing proof on a balance of probabilities. However, it is arguable that the so-called doubling of risk approach as mooted in *Sienkiewicz* is overly simplistic. In particular, doubling of risk takes no account of absolute risk (ie the risk of something occurring without any context)[191] and severity of outcome. Any attempt to reach a consensus in the future must address these difficult issues.

Dow Pharmaceuticals, Inc 509 US 579, 593–94 (1993). and, further, *General Electric Co v Joiner* 522 US 136, 139, 141, 143, 146 (1997); *Kumho Tire Co v Carmichael*, 526 US 137, 147–49, 152–53 (1999); *Weisgram v Marley Co* 528 US 440, 456–57 (2000); Fed R Evidence Rule 702, 28 USCA; Fed R Evidence 702 Advisory Committee's Note (2000 Amendment); see DG Owen, *Products Liability Law*, 2nd edn (St Paul, MN, Thomson West, 2008) § 6.3. For criticism that *Daubert* and its progeny have in some cases hindered the search for justice in product liability law, see, generally, C Cranor, *Toxic Torts: Science, Law, and the Possibility of Justice* (above, n 28) and, in particular, ibid 337, 340–41, 348, 353, 356, 368.

[190] C Cranor, *Toxic Torts: Science, Law, and the Possibility of Justice* (above, n 28) 256–59. But cf now the series of opinions from the special masters in the Vaccine Court concerning the role of thimerosal in allegedly causing autism, which seem to throw doubt about the role of case reports: see, eg, *Snyder v Sec'y HHS*, 2009 WL 332044 (Fed Cl Spec Mstr Feb 12, 2009). For discussion of these opinions, see below, chapter 6 of this volume. For further discussion of the National Childhood Vaccine Injury Compensation Program, see R Goldberg, *Causation and Risk in the Law of Torts: Scientific Evidence and Medicinal Product Liability* (above, n 4) 163–70.

[191] Feldschreiber, Mulcahy and Day provide a good illustration of the failure to take account of absolute risk: 'If there is an incidence of disease in an unexposed population of 1 in a million cases and in an exposed population of 2 in a million cases, the RR is 2 but the absolute risk is very low': see P Feldschreiber, L Mulcahy and S Day, 'Biostatistics and Causation in Medicinal Product Liability Suits' in R Goldberg (ed), *Perspectives on Causation* (Oxford, Hart Publishing, 2011) 188. The Federal Full Court of Australia observe in *Merck Sharp & Dohme (Australia) Pty Limited v Peterson* [2011] FCAFC 128, [119] that ('[d]oubling a very low absolute risk of an adverse result may produce an absolute risk which itself remains so low that a positive finding of causation on the balance of probabilities would itself be an affront to common sense'). However, it is respectfully submitted that as a matter of statistics, this observation is incorrect. If one accepts the premise of this chapter that population-based estimates are relevant to causal conclusions in individual cases, then doubling of risk is doubling of risk, irrespective of absolute risk. One can concede the intuitive appeal of the court's statement. Thus, if in a population of 100 million unexposed individuals, only one case of disease were expected, who could submit that finding 2 cases represented anything other than a fluke? However, that intuition is merely an illustration of the difficulty in obtaining statistically significant results in the epidemiological investigation of rare conditions. If there was a way of designing an epidemiologic study sufficiently capable of identifying an association that truly exists (ie one with sufficient power) and one with sufficient quality, it could be said with great confidence that the exposure (generally) causes the disease.

6

The Rise and Fall of the MMR Litigation: A Comparative Perspective[*]

I. INTRODUCTION

Autism is the term used to describe 'a complex and severe set of developmental disorders characterised by sustained impairments in social interaction, impairments in verbal and nonverbal communication, and stereotypically restricted or repetitive patterns of behaviours and interests'.[1] Over the last 15 years, stories surrounding the challenging condition of autism have never been far from the headlines. Many parents who have autistic children continue to search for a possible cause. When, in 1998, Andrew Wakefield and his colleagues hypothesised that there could be an association between the Measles, Mumps, Rubella (MMR) vaccine and autism, several though not all parents of autistic children became partially or totally convinced that this was the answer.[2] As a consequence, many parents in the UK took to seeking legal advice as to whether they could proceed in a legal action against the manufacturers of the vaccine. In the US, these proceedings were brought against the Secretary for Health and Human services under the National Childhood Vaccine Compensation Program.

This chapter seeks to assess the significance of the rise and fall of this litigation in the US and UK. The importance of the 1998 Wakefield study to the fuelling of such litigation is explained, as well as the reasons for its collapse pre-trial in the UK. It then examines the value of the relevant scientific evidence exposed in six test cases of the Omnibus Autism Proceeding (OAP) under the National Childhood Vaccine Injury Act of 1986 (NVIA), decided in February 2009 and March 2010. These cases essentially explored two causation theories, viz that MMR vaccines and thimerosal-containing vaccines could combine to cause autism, and that thimerosal vaccines alone can cause autism. The legal implications of these complex and lengthy judgments are explored. The position in the United States is contrasted with the much more liberal approach to causation established in France by the

[*] I am grateful to the General Medical Council for permission to use the Transcripts of the hearings of the Fitness to Practise Panel (Misconduct) in the case of Wakefield, Walker-Smith and Murch, 16 July 2007 to 24 May 2010 in the writing of this chapter.

[1] Institute of Medicine, *Immunization Safety Review: Vaccines and Autism* (Washington DC, The National Academies Press, 2004), Executive Summary, p 3.

[2] See especially, D Goldberg, 'MMR, autism, and Adam' (2000) 320 *British Medical Journal* 389. (In this Personal View for the *British Medical Journal*, Professor David Goldberg, a consultant clinical epidemiologist and Honorary Professor of Public Health at the University of Glasgow, wrote about his then 10-year-old son who is severely autistic, commenting that, by virtue of his NHS and public health affiliations, he was 'tarred with the establishment brush' by some parents of other autistic children for failing to join the 'Wakefield bandwagon').

Cour de Cassation for medicinal product liability cases in the context of injury allegedly caused by the Hepatitis B vaccine through the use of presumptions of causation.

Finally, a discussion of the outcome of the General Medical Council Hearing on Dr Wakefield and his two co-authors of the 1998 study is provided. The paper concludes with some lessons to be learned from this litigation, both in the UK and in France in the light of its liberal approach.

II. BACKGROUND: THE VACCINES AND AUTISM CONTROVERSY

The hypothesis that the receipt of the MMR vaccine was linked to the development of autism spectrum disorders and gastrointestinal problems in children principally emerged from the notorious (now retracted) paper by Andrew Wakefield, then of the Royal Free Hospital in London, John Walker-Smith and 11 other colleagues from the same institution.[3] This paper was published in *The Lancet* on 28 February 1998, and it reported on 12 children with chronic enterocolitis and regressive developmental disorder. Until its retraction on 6 February 2010,[4] it was this publication that provided the basis for litigation both in the UK and US and generated 'a decade long public health scare',[5] which has led to hundreds of thousands of children in the UK being unprotected.[6] The paper noted that the 'onset of behavioural symptoms was associated by the parents with measles, mumps, and rubella vaccination in eight of the 12 children', and that in eight children, 'the average interval from exposure to first behavioural symptoms was 6.3 days (range 1–14)'.[7] Over the ensuing decade, the epidemiological evidence has consistently shown no causal link between MMR vaccine and autism and inflammatory bowel disease.[8]

III. UK MMR LITIGATION

A. Legal Aid Funding and Establishment of Group Litigation

By far the majority of claims against the manufacturers of the MMR vaccine were initially funded by the Legal Aid Board in England and Wales (which became the Legal Services Commission).[9] This body was responsible for providing legal aid for Multi-Party Actions,

---

[3] AJ Wakefield, et al, 'Ileal-lymphoid-nodular hyperplasia, non-specific colitis, and pervasive developmental disorder in children' [retracted] (1998) 351 *Lancet* 637–41); The Editors of *The Lancet*, 'Retraction-Ileal-lymphoid-nodular hyperplasia, non-specific colitis, and pervasive developmental disorder in children' (2010) 375 *Lancet* 445.

[4] The Editors of *The Lancet*, 'Retraction-Illeal-lymphoid-nodular hyperplasia, non-specific colitis, and pervasive developmental disorder in children' (2010) 375 *Lancet* 445.

[5] B Deer, 'How the Case Against the MMR Vaccine Was Fixed' (2011) 342 *British Medical Journal* 77.

[6] F Godlee, J Smith and H Marcovitch, Editorial, 'Wakefield's article linking MMR vaccine and autism was fraudulent' (2011) 342 *British Medical Journal* 64, 65.

[7] AJ Wakefield, et al, 'Ileal-lymphoid-nodular hyperplasia, non-specific colitis, and pervasive developmental disorder in children' [retracted] (1998) 351 *Lancet* 637, 638.

[8] See below, n 53.

[9] Access to Justice Act 1999, s 1. Repealed by Legal Aid, Sentencing and Punishment of Offenders Act 2012, Sch 5(1) para 51(a) (1 April 2013 subject to saving and transitional provisions as specified in SI 2013/534, regs 6–13). The Legal Services Commission was abolished by the Legal Aid, Sentencing and Punishment of Offenders Act

providing that the individuals satisfied a financial means test and that the case met a legal merits test, which required cases to have a reasonable prospect of success, and for the costs of the action to be reasonable, compared to the potential damages.[10] Consequent upon representations in the form of a proposed protocol and costing proposals by Richard Barr (a solicitor in England, who had public funding in relation to the pursuit of litigation against manufacturers of the MMR vaccine, viz GlaxoSmithKline, Aventis Pasteur and Merck) the Legal Aid Board authorised funding of £50,000 in two instalments of £25,000, in late 1996 and 1999 respectively, for Wakefield to investigate a potential link between MMR and autism in respect of 10 named children.[11] This money was paid into a numbered hospital charity account which was held by the Special Trustees of the Royal Free Hampstead NHS Trust, and then paid out for research by Wakefield on the MMR vaccine in the medical school.[12] At least four of the eventual 12 children included in the *Lancet* Study were involved in the investigations which were covered by Legal Aid funding.

As a result of a confidential report to the Legal Aid Board in January 1999,[13] one month later the Legal Aid Board awarded £800,000 to Unigenetics, a company incorporated with Wakefield and a Dublin pathologist, John O'Leary as directors, to perform polymerase chain reaction tests on the bowel tissue and blood samples of children in order to provide evidence of the alleged vaccine-derived measles virus.[14] A Practice Direction of 8 July 1999, promulgated by the then Lord Chief Justice of England and Wales, resulted in all claims for damage alleged to have arisen out of the inoculation with the MMR/MR vaccines being given the status of, and being dealt with under the umbrella of, Group Litigation.[15]

B. Withdrawal of Funding and Dissolution of Group Litigation

However, in December 1999, in the light of increasing concerns about a potentially serious conflict of interest between Wakefield's academic employment by University College

---

2012, s 38. An Executive Agency within the Ministry of Justice (the Legal Aid Agency) has been created within the Ministry of Justice to administer legal aid.

[10] The Legal Services Commission (LSC) Funding Code set out the criteria according to which cases could be funded, in accordance with the Access to Justice Act 1999, s 8 (repealed by Legal Aid, Sentencing and Punishment of Offenders Act 2012, Sch 5(1) para 51(a)). The criteria were laid down in Part 1 of the Code. The criteria for Multi-Party Actions (MPAs) are described in the *Legal Services Commission Manual*, vol 3, Part C, ch 15. See also the *Legal Services Commission Manual*, vol 3, Part C, ch 4, Merits, Costs and Damages. From 1 April 2013, civil legal services provided in relation to personal injury or death are exempted from legal aid: Legal Aid, Sentencing and Punishment of Offenders Act 2012, Sch 1, Part 2. Personal injury claims against pharmaceutical companies will no longer be eligible for legal aid.

[11] General Medical Council, Fitness to Practise Panel (Misconduct), Day 11, 30 July 2007, Transcript, 11-4C–11-17H, 11-26B–E. For discussion of the history of the anti-MMR campaign, including Mr Barr's involvement, see M Fitzpatrick, *MMR and Autism: What Parents Need to Know* (London and New York, Routledge, 2004) 101–17.

[12] General Medical Council, Fitness to Practise Panel Hearing, 28 January 2010, p 6. It subsequently transpired that Wakefield had failed to inform either his colleagues at the Royal Free, or the editor of *The Lancet*, about his involvement in the MMR litigation and his personal interest in establishing the autism link: see below, V.A.

[13] AJ Wakefield, 'Developmental disorders in children and measles, mumps, rubella (MMR) vaccine, Interim Report to the Legal Aid Board', January 1999, cited in B Deer, 'How the Vaccine Crisis was Meant to Make Money' (2011) 342 *British Medical Journal* 136, 142, fn 24.

[14] B Deer, 'How the Vaccine Crisis was Meant to Make Money' (2011) 342 *British Medical Journal* 136, 140.

[15] Practice Direction: MMR/MR Vaccine Litigation, 8 July 1999.

London (UCL),[16] and his involvement in a company to develop products based on his MMR claims, the provost of UCL demanded that Wakefield confirm or refute the possible causal relationships between MMR and autism/autistic enterocolitis/inflammatory bowel disease.[17] The study never transpired, as the original study had been fraudulent and it would have been impossible to replicate it with greater numbers. Wakefield then left UCL.[18] Over the next few years a series of epidemiological studies were published which repeatedly found no evidence of a causal link between the MMR vaccine and autism or bowel disorder. Accordingly, following counsel for the claimants' submission of a report to the Legal Services Commission that they were unable to establish a case that MMR causes autism or bowel disease, on 29 September 2003 the Legal Services Commission decided to cease all funding for cases related to autism and bowel disease on the grounds that the litigation had no reasonable prospect of success. The decision was supported on 30 September 2003 by the Funding Review Committee (FRC), an independent appeal body chaired by a Queen's Counsel and three expert solicitors. The High Court rejected an application for a judicial review of the decision on 27 February 2004.[19] 37 individual appeals were then heard by the FRC, which upheld the LSC's decision to cease all funding for cases related to autism and bowel disease on 15 October 2004.[20] With only two claimants continuing with claims (those two having had their public funding restored, the rest having had their funding withdrawn by the Legal Services Commission), and there being no realistic prospect of any new claims being progressed in the light of the unavailability of public funding, the status of the litigation as group litigation was dissolved in June 2007.[21] It was stressed, however, that the claims were not being allowed to proceed not because the court believed that the claims had no merit (which had never been addressed by the court), but because it was not practicable for the claims to go ahead without public funding.[22]

IV. THE US OMNIBUS AUTISM PROCEEDING TEST CASES

A. The Omnibus Autism Proceeding (OAP)

Just as the UK MMR litigation was grinding to a halt in 2007, the United States were about to commence three test cases in the Omnibus Autism Proceeding (OAP) under the National Childhood Vaccine Injury Act of 1986 (NVIA). The OAP is a coordinated proceeding, established in July 2002 and devised as a means by which 5,000 cases filed with the National Childhood Vaccine Injury Compensation Program—in which it has been alleged

---

[16] The Royal Free and University College Medical Schools had now merged.
[17] B Deer, 'How the Vaccine Crisis was Meant to Make Money' (2011) 342 *British Medical Journal* 136, 142.
[18] Ibid.
[19] 'Parents refused aid to fight MMR', 27 February 2004, available at: news.bbc.co.uk/1/hi/health/3494360.stm.
[20] Press Release, MMR Appeals, 15 October 2004, available at: www.legalservices.gov.uk/press/press_release31.asp; C Dyer, 'Parents claiming a link between MMR vaccine and autism lose final appeal for legal aid' (2004) 329 *British Medical Journal* 939.
[21] See *Re MMR and MR Vaccine Litigation; Sayers and others v Smithkline Beecham plc and others* [2007] EWHC 1335, QB, [2007] All ER (D) 67 (Jun), [35], [37].
[22] Ibid [37], Keith J.

that autism or a similar disorder was caused by one or more vaccines—could be handled by the program in a timely and effective manner.[23] The Office of Special Masters of the US Court of Federal Claims did this by dividing the claims into several theories of causation, and allocating three test cases for each theory. Shortly before the first test case, *Cedillo*, was due to begin, the US Secretary of Health and Human Services was granted permission to obtain from the records of the English High Court, copies of expert witness reports filed by the defendants in the UK MMR/MR Vaccine Litigation, so as to use these documents in the Omnibus Autism Proceedings in the US.[24]

While the court cases in the UK were brought against the three manufacturers of the MMR vaccine, GlaxoSmithKline, Aventis Pasteur and Merck, cases under the National Childhood Vaccine Injury Compensation Program are brought against the Secretary for Health and Human Services. Unlike in the UK, where proceedings never reached the trial stage, in the US there has been an exhaustive analysis of the scientific and legal evidence by the Special Masters of the Court of Federal Claims. In the context of the US MMR Litigation, the assessment of the value of the scientific evidence came to prominence in the first three test cases of the OAP under the NVIA, which were decided in February 2009, as well as a further three test cases in March 2010. A group of counsel selected from attorneys representing petitioners in the autism cases, known as the Petitioners' Steering Committee (PSC)—which was established in 2002 to obtain and present evidence on the general issue of whether certain vaccines could cause autism and, if so, in what circumstances[25]—presented two different theories of 'general causation' in the OAP, designating three 'test cases' for each of the two theories. The long-awaited test cases in these proceedings are of considerable importance, since they have irrefutably rejected the petitioners' first and second general causation theories. The Special Masters in these proceedings, having considered all the available scientific evidence, concluded in the first three test cases that there was no merit in the petitioners' first general causation theory that MMR vaccines and thimerosal-containing vaccines could combine to cause autism, and concluded in the second three test cases that there was no merit in the petitioners' second causation theory that thimerosal vaccines alone can cause autism. The proceedings in these six test cases are concluded, and those petitioners remaining in the OAP must now decide whether to pursue their cases by submitting new evidence on causation, or take other action to exit the Program.[26] Other theories of causation are being advanced in individual cases, but there are no new test cases planned.[27]

---

[23] The OAP was established by the Chief Special Master of the US Court of Federal Claims: see Autism General Order # 1 2002 WL31696785, 2002 US Claims LEXIS 365 (Fed Cl Spec Mstr July 3, 2002).

[24] *Sayers v Smithkline Beecham Plc, Smith Kline & French Laboratories Ltd, Merck & Co Inc, Sanofi Pasteur MSD Ltd* [2007] EWHC 1346, QB.

[25] The PSC has now disbanded, and the remaining cases will be resolved on a firm-by-firm or individual basis, without PSC input or participation: *In Re: Claims for Vaccine Injuries Resulting in Autism Spectrum Disorder or a Similar Neurodevelopmental Disorder, Various Petitioners v Secretary of Health and Human Services*, Autism Update, January 12, 2011, 2.

[26] Ibid 3.

[27] Ibid 4.

B. The First Three Test Cases and the Petitioners' First Theory

(i) The First Three Test Cases

The United States Vaccine Court Omnibus Autism Proceeding under the NVIA gave three rulings in the three test cases where the petitioners claimed that measles-mumps-rubella vaccines combined with thimerosal-containing vaccines administered to three children had caused several conditions, including autism[28] and chronic gastrointestinal symptoms. The key question under the National Vaccine Injury Compensation Program is the establishment of a causal link between the vaccination and the injury. In some cases the petitioner may simply demonstrate the occurrence of a so-called Table Injury, ie that the vaccine recipient was administered a vaccine and suffered an injury covered by the NVIA, occurring within an applicable time period following the vaccination specified in the Vaccine Injury Table.[29] If so, the Table Injury is presumed to have been caused by the vaccination.[30] However, in the Omnibus Autism Proceeding, each of the petitioners' test cases was based on an exception to the Table. Here, the petitioners claimed that they suffered injuries not of the type covered in the Table, but that they could show by a preponderance of evidence that their injuries were 'caused-in-fact' by the vaccination in question.[31] This is known as an *off-Table injury* or *causation-in-fact claim*. In contrast to the relaxation of the burden of proving causation for injuries satisfying the Table, the burden of proof on the petitioner in a causation-in-fact claim is a heavy one.[32]

Essentially, the three test cases, *Cedillo*,[33] *Snyder*[34] and *Hazlehurst*,[35] were three of more than 5,000 cases filed with the National Vaccine Injury Compensation Program, in which it has been alleged that autism or a similar disorder was caused by one or more vaccines. The evidentiary record was described by the Special Master in *Cedillo* as 'massive',[36] and one which dwarfed, by far, any evidentiary record in any Program case. The amount of medical

---

[28] In the Omnibus Proceeding, it was noted that the terms 'autism', 'autistic' and 'autism spectrum disorder' would interchangeably be used to refer to the entire group of disorders within the category of 'pervasive developmental disorder' (PDD).

[29] 42 USC § 300aa-11(c)(1)(C)(i).

[30] 42 USC § 300aa-11(c)(1)(C)(i); § 300aa-13(a)(1)(A).

[31] 42 USC § 300aa-11(c)(1)(C)(ii)(I); § 300aa-13(a)(1)(A); *Moberly v Secretary of Health & Human Services* 592 F 3d 1315, 1322 (Fed Cir 2010); *Shyface v Secretary of Health & Human Services* 165 F 3d 1344, 1352–53 (Fed Cir 1999); *Hines v Secretary of Health & Human Services* 940 F 2d 1518, 1525 (Fed Cir 1991).

[32] *Grant v Secretary of Dept of Health & Human Services* 956 F 2d 1144, 1148 (Fed Cir 1992); *Hodges v Secretary of Dept of Health & Human Services* 9 F 3d 958, 961 (Fed Cir 1993). Nonetheless, it has been judicially observed that Congress 'clearly intended' that its goal of rendering expeditious, certain and generous determinations should apply equally to Table and off-Table claims: *Stevens v Secretary of HHS*, No 99-594 V, 2001 WL 387418 (Fed Cl Mar 30, 2001) at *7, Chief Special Master Golkiewicz (noting the difficulties associated with causation in fact cases under the National Childhood Vaccine Injury Compensation Program); HR Rep No 99-908, 13; see further, KE Strong, Note, 'Proving Causation Under the Vaccine Injury Act: A New Approach for a New Day' (2007) 75 *George Washington Law Review* 426, 442–46 (submitting that the medical and scientific uncertainties surrounding vaccine injuries, as well as the lack of a uniform standard for causation in fact cases, has meant that the goals of Congress have not been met for petitioners who require to prove off-Table claims).

[33] *Cedillo v Secretary of Health & Human Services*, 98-916V, 2009 WL 331968 (Fed Cl Feb 12, 2009), aff'd, 89 Fed Cl 158, 164, 184 (2009), aff'd, 617 F 3d 1328, 1334, 1349–50 (Fed Cir 2010).

[34] *Snyder v Secretary of Health & Human Services*, 01-162V, 2009 WL 332044 (Fed Cl Feb 12, 2009), aff'd, 88 Fed Cl 706, 708, 748 (2009).

[35] *Hazlehurst v Secretary of Health & Human Services*, 03-654V, 2009 WL 332306 (Fed Cl Feb 12, 2009), aff'd, 88 Fed Cl 473, 475, 490 (2009), aff'd, 604 F 3d 1343, 1345, 1354 (Fed Cir 2010).

[36] *Cedillo v Secretary of Health & Human Services*, 2009 WL 331968 (Fed Cl Feb 12, 2009) at *14.

literature filed in records of the three cases was noted as being 'staggering'.[37] During the evidentiary hearings, a total of 28 expert witnesses testified. A total of 939 different items of medical literature were filed in the three cases, the complexity of the material involving many different specialities of biology and medicine, including neurology, gastroenterology, virology, immunology, molecular biology, toxicology, genetics and epidemiology.[38]

(ii) The First General Causation Theory

The petitioners advanced a causation theory which had several parts, including three main contentions, viz: (1) that thimerosal-containing vaccines can cause immune dysfunction; (2) that the MMR vaccine can cause autism; and (3) that the MMR vaccine can cause gastrointestinal dysfunction.[39] It was agreed that the Petitioners' Steering Committee (PSC) would present its general causation evidence concerning the first theory, along with all the evidence specific to the *Cedillo* case.[40] As to each of the general causation theory elements, Special Master Hastings concluded that 'the evidence was overwhelmingly contrary to the petitioners' contentions'.[41] Considerable emphasis was placed on the respondent's expert witnesses, who were 'far better qualified, far more experienced and far more persuasive than the petitioners' experts concerning most of the key points'.[42] The numerous medical studies came down strongly against the petitioners' contentions. Having considered all the evidence, the Special Master found that the petitioners had failed to demonstrate that thimerosal-containing vaccines in general could contribute to causing immune dysfunction or that the MMR vaccine could contribute to causing either autism or gastrointestinal dysfunction.[43]

The petitioners' general causation theory concerning the causation of autism was contingent on a weakening of the immune system by thimerosal-containing vaccines which allowed the measles virus contained in the MMR vaccine to persist within the child's body.[44]

---

[37] Ibid at *14–15.

[38] Ibid. For a comprehensive discussion of the early stages of the Omnibus Autism Proceeding prior to the decisions in the test cases being decided, as well as discussion of potential problems in the aftermath of the Proceeding, see, G Shemin, 'Mercury Rising: The Omnibus Autism Proceeding and What Families Should Know Before Rushing Out of Vaccine Court' (2008) 58 *American University Law Review* 459.

[39] *Cedillo v Secretary of Health & Human Services*, 2009 WL 331968 (Fed Cl Feb 12, 2009) at *1.

[40] *Cedillo v Secretary of Health & Human Services*, 2009 WL 331968 (Fed Cl Feb 12, 2009) at *10. Then, over the following months, the PSC would present its case-specific evidence concerning the two additional test cases, viz, *Snyder v Secretary of Health & Human Services*, 01-162V, 2009 WL 332044 (Fed Cl Feb 12, 2009) and *Hazlehurst v Secretary of Health & Human Services*, 03-654V, 2009 WL 332306 (Fed Cl Feb 12, 2009): ibid.

[41] *Cedillo v Secretary of Health & Human Services*, 2009 WL 331968 (Fed Cl Feb 12, 2009) at *1. See, also, *Snyder v Secretary of Health & Human Services*, 01-162V, 2009 WL 332044 (Fed Cl Feb 12, 2009) at *1, Special Master Vowell.

[42] *Cedillo v Secretary of Health & Human Services*, 2009 WL 331968 (Fed Cl Feb 12, 2009) at *1. See also *Snyder v Secretary of Health & Human Services*, 01-162V, 2009 WL 332044 (Fed Cl Feb 12, 2009) at *1, Special Master Vowell (stating that 'it was abundantly clear that petitioners' theories of causation were speculative and unpersuasive'); and *Hazlehurst v Secretary of Health & Human Services*, 03-654V, 2009 WL 332306 (Fed Cl Feb 12, 2009) at *13.

[43] *Cedillo v Secretary of Health & Human Services*, 2009 WL 331968 (Fed Cl Feb 12, 2009) at *1. See also *Snyder v Secretary of Health & Human Services*, 01-162V, 2009 WL 332044 (Fed Cl Feb 12, 2009) at *1, *76, *104, *137; *Hazlehurst v Secretary of Health & Human Services*, 03-654V, 2009 WL 332306 (Fed Cl Feb 12, 2009) at *85, *150, *171.

[44] *Cedillo v Secretary of Health & Human Services*, 2009 WL 331968 (Fed Cl Feb 12, 2009) at *15; *Snyder v Secretary of Health & Human Services*, 01-162V, 2009 WL 332044 (Fed Cl Feb 12, 2009) at *28; *Hazlehurst v Secretary of Health & Human Services*, 03-654V, 2009 WL 332306 (Fed Cl Feb 12, 2009) at *86. The Special Master

However, the determination by the Special Masters in all three cases that the testing for the presence of the measles virus in the intestinal tissue of Cedillo, Snyder and Hazlehurst and other autistic children was *unreliable*[45] was fatal to all three decisions.

The petitioners' general theory concerning the causation of autism was rejected on the basis of nine grounds, viz:

(1) the general theory depended upon the existence of reliable laboratory test findings of persisting measles virus, but such a reliable test did not exist;[46]

(2) the available evidence did not demonstrate any substantial likelihood that measles virus persistence in the brain would cause autism;[47]

(3) the evidence indicated that the wild measles virus had never been shown to cause autism, which made it quite unlikely that the vaccine strain form of the measles virus could cause autism;[48]

(4) the petitioners' theory seemed unlikely in the light of several accepted understandings concerning the causation of autism, in particular that there was a very strong genetic component to the causation of autism;[49]

---

in *Hazlehurst* summarised the theory of causation as follows: 'Specifically, petitioners assert that the measles component of the MMR vaccine causes an immune dysfunction that impairs the vaccinee's ability to clear the measles virus. Unable to clear properly … the measles virus from the body, the vaccinee experiences measles virus persistence which leads to chronic inflammation in the gastrointestinal system and, in turn, chronic inflammation in the brain. Petitioners argue that the inflammation in the brain causes neurological damage that manifests as autism. It is also the position of petitioners that the viral persistence is facilitated by the vaccinee's receipt of thimerosal containing vaccines that suppress the immune system of the vaccinee and impair the immune system's ability to respond properly to the viral presence': ibid at *86.

[45] *Cedillo v Secretary of Health & Human Services*, 2009 WL 331968 (Fed Cl Feb 12, 2009) at *29–59, aff'd, 89 Fed Cl 158, 171–72 (2009), aff'd 617 F 3d 1328, 1345 (Fed Cir 2010); and, further, *Snyder v Secretary of Health & Human Services*, 01-162V, 2009 WL 332044 (Fed Cl Feb 12, 2009) at *116; *Hazlehurst v Secretary of Health & Human Services*, 03-654V, 2009 WL 332306 (Fed Cl Feb 12, 2009) at *150. The studies purported to find the presence of the measles virus in the biological material of autistic children and primarily derived from two sources: the work of Dr Andrew Wakefield of the Royal Free Hospital in London (see, in particular, his article, AJ Wakefield, et al, 'Ileal-lymphoid-nodular hyperplasia, non-specific colitis, and pervasive developmental disorder in children' [retracted] (1998) 351 *Lancet* 637–41), and his colleagues John O'Leary and Orla Sheils at the for profit, non-accredited Unigenetics laboratory in Dublin; and the research of Dr Stephen Walker of Wake Forest University School of Medicine, North Carolina. Dr Wakefield and his colleagues were 'the principle proponents of the hypothesis that the receipt of the MMR vaccine results in the development of autism spectrum disorders and gastrointestinal problems in certain children': *Hazlehurst v Secretary of Health & Human Services*, 03-654V, 2009 WL 332306 (Fed Cl Feb 12, 2009) at *87, *126. The Special Master found that the work of Dr Wakefield had been largely discredited and that none of the studies indicating the presence of the measles virus in autistic children had been successfully replicated independently of Wakefield or Unigenetics: ibid at *90, 124. The testimony of a government expert, Professor Stephen Bustin (who had also been an expert for the vaccine manufacturers in the UK MMR litigation) helped to discredit the reliability of the testing conducted at Unigenetics: ibid at *129–32. It was held on appeal that this testimony had been properly admitted: *Hazlehurst v Secretary of Health & Human Services* 88 Fed Cl 473, 480–83 (2009), aff'd, 604 F 3d 1343, 1349–50 (Fed Cir 2010). Shortly before the first test case, *Cedillo*, was due to begin, the Secretary of Health and Human Services was granted permission to obtain from the records of the High Court, copies of expert witness reports of Professors Bustin, Simmonds and Rima, filed by the defendants in the UK MMR/MR Vaccine Litigation, so as to use these documents in the Omnibus Autism Proceedings in the US: *Sayers v Smithkline Beecham Plc, Smith Kline & French Laboratories Ltd, Merck & Co Inc, Sanofi Pasteur MSD Ltd* [2007] EWHC 1346 (QB).

[46] Ibid at *67–68.

[47] Ibid at *67–69.

[48] Ibid at *67, *69–71.

[49] Ibid at *67, * 71–77.

(5)   there were contradictions and inconsistencies in the testimony concerning the
      appropriate time period between the MMR vaccination and the onset of autism
      symptoms;[50]

(6)   the testimony of three other experts failed to provide substantial support to the cau-
      sation theory of the petitioners' expert Dr Kinsbourne;[51]

(7)   the qualifications of the respondent's experts concerning this issue substantially
      exceeded the qualifications of the petitioners' expert witnesses;[52]

(8)   the epidemiologic evidence consisting of numerous studies by qualified medical
      researchers around the world[53] added another reason to reject the petitioners' theory
      that vaccines could contribute to the causation of autism;[54] and

(9)   Two reports of well-qualified experts published by the Institute of Medicine in 2001
      and 2004 studied the general MMR/autism causation issue and concluded that the
      evidence favoured rejection of the proposition that the MMR vaccine could cause
      autism.[55]

Taken together, all this evidence was irrefutable.

---

[50] Ibid at *67, *77–79.

[51] Ibid at *67, *79–83.

[52] Ibid at *67, *83–84.

[53] See B Taylor, et al, 'Autism and Measles, Mumps, and Rubella Vaccine: No Epidemiological Evidence for
a Causal Association' (1999) 353 *Lancet* 2026–29; F DeStefano, et al, 'Age at First Measles-Mumps-Rubella
Vaccination in Children With Autism and School-Matched Control Subjects: A Population-Based Study
in Metropolitan Atlanta' (2004) 113 *Pediatrics* 259–66; L Smeeth, et al, 'MMR Vaccination and Pervasive
Developmental Disorders: A Case-Control Study' (2004) 364 *Lancet* 963–69; B Taylor, et al, 'Measles, Mumps,
and Rubella Vaccination and Bowel Problems or Developmental Regression in Children with Autism: Population
Study' (2002) 324 *British Medical Journal* 393–96; CP Farrington, et al, 'MMR and Autism: Further Evidence
Against a Causal Association' (2001) 19 *Vaccine* 3632–35; E Fombonne and S Chakrabarti, 'No Evidence for a
New Variant of Measles-Mumps-Rubella-Induced Autism' (2001) 108 *Pediatrics* e58; S Dewilde, 'Do Children
Who Become Autistic Consult More Often After MMR Vaccination?', (2001) 51 *British Journal of General Practice*
226–27; A Mäkelä, et al, 'Neurologic Disorders After Measles-Mumps-rubella Vaccination' (2002) 110 *Pediatrics*
957–63; H Takahashi, et al, 'An Epidemiological Study on Japanese Autism Concerning Routine Childhood
Immunization History' (2003) 56 *Japanese Journal of Infectious Diseases* 114–17; W Chen, et al, 'No Evidence for
Links Between Autism, MMR and Measles Virus' (2004) 34 *Psychological Medicine* 543–53; H Honda, et al, 'No
Effect of MMR Withdrawal on the Incidence of Autism: A Total Population Study (2005) 46 *Journal of Child
Psychology and Psychiatry* 572–79.

[54] Ibid at *67, *92–93. Special Master Hastings effectively destroyed the sufficiency of the epidemiologic evidence proffered by the petitioners in the following two paragraphs: 'The numerous epidemiologic studies done
over the past ten years, when taken together, make it *very unlikely* that the MMR vaccination has played any significant role in the *overall causation* of autism. It is true, as the petitioners argue, that the available epidemiologic
studies do not *completely rule out* the possibility that the MMR vaccine might be associated with some small
subset of autism, such as regressive autism. However, there are three reasons why the epidemiologic evidence
still must be said to provide significant evidence *against* the petitioners' general causation theory set forth in
this case. First, none of the numerous competent studies *has yielded the slightest bit of evidence in the petitioners'
favor.* Second, the failure of so many studies to find any association between MMR vaccine and autism, while
not *completely ruling out* a possible causal role with respect to a *subset* of autism, at least *casts considerable doubt*
upon the proposition that the MMR vaccine *ever* plays a role in causing any kind of autism, including regressive
autism. And, third, five studies provide evidence that is *directly relevant* to the petitioners' "regressive autism only"
argument, supplying significant evidence *against* the theory that the MMR vaccine plays a causal role *even* in the
subset of autism known as regressive autism.
      Accordingly, my conclusion is that the epidemiologic evidence *does* provide yet another strong reason to
reject the petitioners' general causation theory presented in this case': ibid at* 92–93.

[55] Ibid at *68, *93–94; see Institute of Medicine, *Immunization Safety Review: Measles-Mumps-Rubella Vaccine
and Autism* (Washington DC, The National Academies Press, 2001), p 60; Institute of Medicine, *Immunization
Safety Review: Vaccines and Autism* (Washington DC, The National Academies Press, 2004) 7, 16, 126, 151–52.

C. The Second Three Test Cases and the Petitioners' Second Theory

(i) The Second Three Test Cases

The Petitioners Steering Committee's second causation theory was that thimerosal-containing vaccines alone can cause autism.[56] The same three Special Masters who had been tasked with hearing the first three test cases concerning the first theory of general causation were also tasked with hearing the second three test cases concerning the second theory of general causation advanced by the petitioners.[57] The evidentiary record was described as 'massive',[58] and one which exceeded any evidentiary record in any Program case, with the exception of the record in the first three test cases. During the evidentiary hearings, a total of 26 expert witnesses testified. The amount of medical literature filed into the records of the three cases was a 'staggering' figure of more than 1200 different items.[59] In March 2010, each of the three Special Masters issued a decision in the test case assigned to them, ie respectively in *Mead*,[60] *Dwyer*[61] and *King*.[62] All three Special Masters found that the parents had failed to prove that their children's autism was caused by the thimerosal-containing vaccines that they received.[63]

(ii) The Second General Causation Theory

The petitioners' medical theory contended that 'the thimerosal component of the received childhood vaccines dissociates into organomercurial ethylmercury once in the body'.[64] That ethylmercury 'then courses through the blood stream to diffuse across the blood-brain barrier to reach the brain'.[65] On reaching the brain, 'the ethylmercury is de-ethylated to become inorganic mercury—a form of mercury that is not quickly removed from the brain—and once deposited, provokes a series of detrimental responses that ultimately manifest as autism'.[66] It was found that the underpinnings for the opinions of the petitioners' experts concerning the second theory were 'scientifically flawed', and in the absence of a sound basis for the offered opinions of causation, these opinions '[could not] be credited'.[67]

---

[56] *Mead v Secretary of Health & Human Services*, 03-215V, 2010 WL 892248 (Fed Cl March 12, 2010) at *2.

[57] *Mead v Secretary of Health & Human Services*, 03-215V, 2010 WL 892248 (Fed Cl March 12, 2010) at *4.

[58] *King v Secretary of Health & Human Services*, 03-584V, 2010 WL 892296 (Fed Cl March 12, 2010) at *12.

[59] Ibid.

[60] *Mead v Secretary of Health & Human Services*, 03-215V, 2010 WL 892248 (Fed Cl March 12, 2010).

[61] *Dwyer v Secretary of Health & Human Services*, 03-1202V, 2010 WL 892250 (Fed Cl March 12, 2010).

[62] *King v Secretary of Health & Human Services*, 03-584V, 2010 WL 892296 (Fed Cl March 12, 2010).

[63] *Mead v Secretary of Health & Human Services*, 03-215V, 2010 WL 892248 (Fed Cl March 12, 2010) at *1, 13, 113; *Dwyer v Secretary of Health & Human Services*, 03-1202V, 2010 WL 892250 (Fed Cl March 12, 2010) at *1–2, 201; *King v Secretary of Health & Human Services*, 03-584V, 2010 WL 892296 (Fed Cl March 12, 2010) at *1, 90–91.

[64] *Mead v Secretary of Health & Human Services*, 03-215V, 2010 WL 892248 (Fed Cl March 12, 2010) at *106; and further, at *17.

[65] Ibid.

[66] Ibid.

[67] *Mead v Secretary of Health & Human Services*, 03-215V, 2010 WL 892248 (Fed Cl March 12, 2010) at *109, citing *Perreira v Secretary of Health & Human Services* 33 F 3d 1375, 1377 fn 6 (Fed Cir 1994) ('An expert opinion is no better than the soundness of the reasons supporting it').

The theory that the thimerosal content of the vaccines contributed to the development of autism was 'scientifically unsupportable'.[68]

Several epidemiological studies[69] were examined and it was found that they showed no association between thimerosal-containing vaccines and the development of autistic spectrum disorders.[70] Reference was made to the evidence given by the eminent paediatric psychiatrist, Professor Sir Michael Rutter who, having examined the limitations of the epidemiological studies, had concluded that 'taken as whole, the studies were all "unsupportive of a causal association"'.[71]

---

[68] *Mead v Secretary of Health & Human Services*, 03-215V, 2010 WL 892248 (Fed Cl March 12, 2010) at *113; see, further, *Dwyer v Secretary of Health & Human Services*, 03-1202V, 2010 WL 892250 (Fed Cl March 12, 2010) at *165, 198–99; *King v Secretary of Health & Human Services*, 03-584V, 2010 WL 892296 (Fed Cl March 12, 2010) at *34–35.

[69] See A Hviid, et al, 'Association Between Thimerosal-Containing Vaccine and Autism' (2003) 290 *Journal of American Medical Association* 1763–66; K Madsen, et al, Thimerosal and the Occurrence of Autism: Negative Ecological Evidence From Danish Population-Based Data (2003) 112 *Pediatrics* 604–6; T Verstraeten, et al, 'Safety of Thimersoal-Containing Vaccines: A Two Phased Study of Computerized Health Maintenance Organinzation Databases' (2003) 112 *Pediatrics* 1039–48; P Stehr-Green, et al, 'Autism and Thimerosal-Containing Vaccines' (2003) 25 *American Journal of Preventative Medicine* 101–6; N Andrews, et al, 'Thimerosal Exposure in Infants and Developmental Disorders: A Retrospective Cohort Study in the United Kingdom Does Not Support a Causal Association' (2004) 114 *Pediatrics* 584–91; H Jick and J Kaye, 'Autism and DPT Vaccination in the United Kingdom' (2004) 350 *New England Journal of Medicine* 2722–23; E Fombonne, et al, 'Pervasive Development Disorders in Montreal, Quebec, Canada: Prevalence and Links with Immunizations' (2006) 118 *Pediatrics* e139–50; R Schechter and J Grether, 'Continuing Increases in Autism Reported to California's Developmental Services System' (2008) 65 *Archives of General Psychiatry* 19–24. Two other studies did not directly address the question of an association between thiomersal and autism, but provided relevant information: (see J Heron and J Golding, 'Thimerosal Exposure in Infants and Developmental Disorders: A Prospective Cohort Study in the United Kingdom Does Not Support a Causal Association' (2004) 114 *Pediatrics* 577–83; and WW Thompson, et al, 'Early Thimerosal Exposure and Neuropsychological Outcomes at 7 to 10 Years' (2007) 357 *New England Journal of Medicine* 1281–92). In the light of the strength of the epidemiological evidence of no association, and given the absence of any direct evidence for a biological mechanism, the Institute of Medicine concluded that the evidence favoured rejection of a causal association between thimerosal-containing vaccines and autism: Institute of Medicine, *Immunization Safety Review: Vaccines and Autism* (Washington DC, The National Academies Press, 2004) 16, 151–52.

[70] *Mead v Secretary of Health & Human Services*, 03-215V, 2010 WL 892248 (Fed Cl March 12, 2010) at *39. See, further, *Dwyer v Secretary of Health & Human Services*, 03-1202V, 2010 WL 892250 (Fed Cl March 12, 2010) at *77 ('In this case, the epidemiological studies furnish powerful evidence refuting a causal association between TCVs [thimerosal-containing vaccines] and ASD'); and *King v Secretary of Health & Human Services*, 03-584V, 2010 WL 892296 (Fed Cl March 12, 2010) at * 66–67. While the petitioners conceded through their expert, Professor Sander Greenland, that the epidemiologic literature to date had not detected an association of mercury-containing vaccines and autism in general or autistic spectrum disorders, Dr Greenland claimed that the performed epidemiological studies lacked the requisite specificity to detect an association between the receipt of thimerosal-containing vaccines and regressive autism: *Mead v Secretary of Health & Human Services*, 03-215V, 2010 WL 892248 (Fed Cl March 12, 2010) at *41–45. This position presumed that regressive autism was a distinct phenotype of autism. However, the Special Master found that studies of the developmental patterns in children described as having early onset autism and in children described as having regressive autism, militated against a finding that regression in autism constituted a separate phenotype of autistic disorder: ibid at *45,112; and further, *Dwyer v Secretary of Health & Human Services*, 03-1202V, 2010 WL 892250 (Fed Cl March 12, 2010) at *62–63 (petitioners failed to demonstrate the existence of 'clearly regressive autism' as a separate phenotype; Dr Greenland's opinion that the existing epidemiologic studies could not rule out a substantial causal rule for thimerosal-containing vaccines in one form of autism was 'not relevant or persuasive'); and *King v Secretary of Health & Human Services*, 03-584V, 2010 WL 892296 (Fed Cl March 12, 2010) at *39 70–72. When the results of the epidemiological studies were viewed as a whole, they were found to reach the consistent conclusion that there was no association between thimerosal-containing vaccines and autism: *Mead v Secretary of Health & Human Services*, 03-215V, 2010 WL 892248 (Fed Cl March 12, 2010) at *45; *King v Secretary of Health & Human Services*, 03-584V, 2010 WL 892296 (Fed Cl March 12, 2010) at *75.

[71] Ibid at *40.

D. Implications of the Test Cases

(i) Epidemiological Evidence Should be Given Appropriate Weight

Some of the most significant evidence used to reject the general causation theory were the numerous epidemiologic studies performed over the previous 10 years which, when taken together, made it very unlikely that the MMR vaccination played a significant role in the overall causation of autism.[72] Both the *Cedillo* and *King* test cases, determined by Special Master Hastings, clarify the position surrounding the use of such epidemiological evidence supporting a causation-in-fact claim under the National Vaccine Injury Compensation Program (the Program). They reaffirm the settled legal position that while there is no requirement that epidemiological evidence supports a causation-in-fact claim under the Program,[73] in the relatively rare instance in which general causation *has* been the subject of published epidemiological studies, such evidence should be given appropriate weight, along with the other evidence of the record.[74]

(ii) Reliability of Expert Testimony

Crucial to the determination of these test cases are the factors that a Special Master is required to consider in evaluating the *reliability* of expert testimony and other scientific evidence relating to causation. Even though the Federal Rules of Evidence do not apply in Program cases,[75] the test cases reaffirm that it is appropriate to use the *Daubert*[76] factors as a tool or framework for conducting the inquiry into the reliability of causation in fact theories.[77] In particular, two of the important factors listed in *Daubert* and utilised by the

---

[72] *Cedillo v Secretary of Health & Human Services*, 2009 WL 331968 (Fed Cl Feb 12, 2009) at *123.

[73] *Capizzano v Secretary of Health & Human Services* 440 F 3d 1317, 1325–26 (Fed Cir 2006). Indeed, causation can be demonstrated under the Programme without any support from medical literature: *Althen v Secretary of Health & Human Services* 418 F 3d 1274, 1281 (Fed Cir 2005).

[74] *Cedillo v Secretary of Health & Human Services*, 2009 WL 331968 (Fed Cl Feb 12, 2009) at *92; *King v Secretary of Health & Human Services*, 03-584V, 2010 WL 892296 (Fed Cl March 12, 2010) at *74. See, further, *Hazlehurst v Secretary of Health & Human Services*, 03-654V, 2009 WL 332306 (Fed Cl Feb 12, 2009) at *39; *Terran v Secretary of Health & Human Services* 195 F 3d 1302, 1315–17 (Fed Cir 1999); *Grant v Secretary of Health & Human Services* 956 F 2d 1144, 1149 (Fed Cir 1992). Epidemiologic evidence should be considered in evaluating scientific theories: *Scott v Secretary of Health & Human Services*, 03-2211V, 2006 WL 2559776 at *21; *Garcia v Secretary of Health & Human Services*, 05-720V, 2008 WL 5068934, at *3, *10. The reliance of a Special Master on epidemiologic evidence has been subject to express approval: see, eg, *Moberly v Secretary of Health & Human Services* 85 Fed Cl 571, 596 (2009), aff'd, 592 F 3d 1315, 1325 (Fed Cir 2010); *Estep v Secretary of Health & Human Services* 28 Fed Cl 664, 668 (1993); *Sharpnack v Secretary of Health & Human Services* 27 Fed Cl 457, 459 (1993); *Sumrall v Secretary of Health & Human Services* 23 Cl Ct 1, 8 (1991); *Hennessey v Secretary of Health & Human Services*, 01-190V, 2010 WL 94560, at *6–7, *11–13.

[75] 42 USC §300aa-12(d)(2)(B): Vaccine Rules 'shall include flexible informal studies of admissibility of evidence'.

[76] *Daubert v Merrill Dow Pharmaceuticals, Inc* 509 US 579, 593–94 (1993); and, further, *General Electric Co v Joiner*, 522 US 136, 139, 141, 143, 146 (1997); *Kumho Tire Co v Carmichael*, 526 US 137, 147–49, 152–53 (1999); *Weisgram v Marley Co* 528 US 440, 456–57 (2000); Fed. R. Evidence Rule 702, 28 USCA; Fed. R. Evidence 702 Advisory Committee's Note (2000 Amendment); see DG Owen, *Products Liability Law*, 2nd edn (St Paul, MN Thomson/West, 2008) § 6.3. For criticism that *Daubert* and its progeny have in some cases hindered the search for justice in product liability law, see, generally, C Cranor, *Toxic Torts: Science, Law, and the Possibility of Justice* (Cambridge University Press, 2007) and, in particular, ibid 337, 340–41, 348, 353, 356, 368.

[77] *Cedillo v Secretary of Health & Human Services*, 2009 WL 331968 (Fed Cl Feb 12, 2009) at *3; aff'd, 89 Fed Cl 158, 182 (2009), aff'd 617 F 3d 1328, 1338–38 (Fed Cir 2010), (applying *Terran v Secretary of Health & Human*

Special Masters in evaluating these theories[78] were whether the scientific theory had been subject to peer review or publication and also whether the theory or technique enjoyed general acceptance.[79] Such epidemiological evidence, while not dispositive, should be considered in evaluating scientific theories, such as the general causation theory in issue in the test cases.[80]

(iii) The Causation-in-Fact Standard: General and Specific Causation and Temporal Proximity

One of the most interesting aspects of the test cases is their utilisation of the causation-in-fact standard. The cases emphasise the importance of establishing both general and specific causation in vaccine damage cases, as well as the need for temporal proximity between the vaccine and the damage in each case. This legal standard of proof for causation in fact under the Program was elaborated on in the leading case of *Althen v Secretary of Health & Human Services*.[81] There, the Federal Circuit established three factors which had to be satisfied to overcome the burden of proof, viz: (1) a medical theory causally connecting the vaccination and the injury; (2) a logical sequence of cause and effect showing that the vaccination was the reason for the injury; and (3) a showing of a proximate temporal relationship between the vaccination and the injury.[82] In all six test cases in the Omnibus Autism Proceeding, the Special Masters were able to explain how their analyses of the petitioners' contentions on the scientific evidence fitted within the three prongs of the test and how in each case none of the requirements of the three factors were satisfied.[83]

Services 195 F 3d 1302, 1316 (Fed Cir 1999)); *Snyder v Secretary of Health & Human Services*, 01-162V, 2009 WL 332044 (Fed Cl Feb 12, 2009) at *30, *138, *194, aff'd 88 Fed Cl 706, 736, 744–45 (2009); *Hazlehurst v Secretary of Health & Human Services*, 03-654V, 2009 WL 332306 (Fed Cl Feb 12, 2009) at *16–17; aff'd, 88 Fed Cl 473, 483 (2009), aff'd, 604 F 3d 1343, 1353 (Fed Cir 2010); *Mead v Secretary of Health & Human Services* 03-215V, 2010 WL 892248 (Fed Cl March 12, 2010) at *13–15; *Dwyer v Secretary of Health & Human Services*, 03-1202V, 2010 WL 892250 (Fed Cl March 12, 2010) at *7, 25–26 ; *King v Secretary of Health & Human Services*, 03-584V, 2010 WL 892296 (Fed Cl March 12, 2010) at *3, 73. For further approval of the utilisation of the *Daubert* factors in evaluating the reliability of scientific evidence in cases under the Program, see *Moberly v Secretary of Health & Human Services* 592 F 3d 1315, 1324 (Fed Cir 2010); *Andreu v Secretary of Health & Human Services* 569 F 3d 1367, 1379 (Fed Cir 2009); *Knudsen v Secretary of Health & Human Services* 35 F 3d 543, 548 (Fed Cir 1994); *Perreira v Secretary of Health & Human Services* 33 F 3d 1375, 1377 fn 6 (Fed Cir 1994).

[78] *Cedillo v Secretary of Health & Human Services*, 2009 WL 331968 (Fed Cl Feb 12, 2009) at *3.

[79] *Daubert v Merrill Dow Pharmaceuticals, Inc* 509 US 579, 593–94 (1993).

[80] *Terran v Secretary of Health & Human Services* 195 F 3d 1302, 1315–17 (Fed Cir 1999); *Grant v Secretary of Health & Human Services* 956 F 2d 1144, 1149 (Fed Cir 1992); *Scott v Secretary of Health & Human Services*, 03-2211V, 2006 WL 2559776 at *21; *Garcia v Secretary of Health & Human Services*, 05-720V, 2008 WL 5068934, at *3, *10; *King v Secretary of Health & Human Services*, 03-584V, 2010 WL 892296 (Fed Cl March 12, 2010) at *74.

[81] *Althen v Secretary of Health & Human Services* 418 F 3d 1274 (Fed Cir 2005).

[82] Ibid, 1278.

[83] *Cedillo v Secretary of Health & Human Services*, 2009 WL 331968 (Fed Cl Feb 12, 2009) at *132–33; aff'd, 89 Fed Cl 158, 182–83 (2009); For discussion of the application of the *Althen* test in the other two test cases of the first general causation theory, see *Snyder v Secretary of Health & Human Services*, 01-162V, 2009 WL 332044 (Fed Cl Feb 12, 2009) at *29, *192–98, aff'd 88 Fed Cl 706, 745–46 (2009) and *Hazlehurst v Secretary of Health & Human Services*, 03-654V, 2009 WL 332306 (Fed Cl Feb 12, 2009) at *15–19, *83–86. For discussion of the application of the *Althen* test in the three test cases of the second general causation theory, see *Mead v Secretary of Health & Human Services*, 03-215V, 2010 WL 892248 (Fed Cl March 12, 2010) at *15–16, 106–13; *Dwyer v Secretary of Health & Human Services*, 03-1202V, 2010 WL 892250 (Fed Cl March 12, 2010) at *23–24, 196–201; *King v Secretary of Health & Human Services*, 03-584V, 2010 WL 892296 (Fed Cl March 12, 2010) at *87–89.

The principal test case of the first general causation theory, *Cedillo*, provides an important explanation of the three prongs of the *Althen* test. The first prong, viz the requirement of a medical theory causally connecting the vaccination and the injury is explained as a *general* causation requirement, ie that the type of vaccination in question *can* cause the type of injury in question. The second prong, a logical sequence of cause and effect showing that the vaccination was the reason for the injury, is explained as a *specific* causation requirement, ie that the particular vaccination received by the specific vaccinee *did* cause the vaccinee's own injury. *Cedillo* affirms the '*can/did* cause' test, as being equivalent to the first two prongs of *Althen*.[84] Applying the available scientific evidence, the Special Master held that the petitioners' arguments fell far short of demonstrating that the MMR vaccination *could* contribute in general to the causation of either autism or chronic gastrointestinal dysfunction, or that the MMR vaccination *did* contribute to the causation of Cedillo's own autism and gastrointestinal symptoms.[85] Moreover, there was no doubt that the *Althen* test required that as an overall matter, a petitioner had to demonstrate that it was more probable than not that the particular vaccine was a substantial contributing factor in causing the particular injury in question.[86] This was clear from the 'preponderance of evidence' standard in the Vaccine Act.[87] Regardless of the precise meanings of *Althen*, the overall evidence fell far short of demonstrating that it was 'more probable than not' that the MMR vaccine contributed to the causation of either Cedillo's autism or gastrointestinal symptoms.[88] The petitioners also failed to satisfy the third element of *Althen*, viz the need to show a 'proximate temporal relationship between vaccination and injury'.[89] They were unable to establish that the first symptom of autism and/or the first symptoms of the chronic gastrointestinal problems occurred within a time-frame consistent with causation by the MMR vaccination in question.[90]

---

[84] *Cedillo v Secretary of Health & Human Services*, 2009 WL 331968 (Fed Cl Feb 12, 2009) at *131, affirming *Pafford v Secretary of Health & Human Services* 451 F 3d 1352, 1355–56 (Fed Cir 2006); and, further, in respect of the second general causation theory, *Dwyer v Secretary of Health & Human Services*, 03-1202V, 2010 WL 892250 (Fed Cl March 12, 2010) at *197; *King v Secretary of Health & Human Services*, 03-584V, 2010 WL 892296 (Fed Cl March 12, 2010) at *87.

[85] *Cedillo v Secretary of Health & Human Services*, 2009 WL 331968 (Fed Cl Feb 12, 2009) at *132; aff'd, 89 Fed Cl 158, 182–83 (2009); aff'd 617 F 3d 1328, 1338 (Fed Cir 2010).

[86] Ibid.

[87] Ibid, citing § 300aa-13(a)(I)(A).

[88] *Cedillo v Secretary of Health & Human Services*, 2009 WL 331968 (Fed Cl Feb 12, 2009) at *132; aff'd, 89 Fed Cl 158, 182–83 (2009); and, further, in respect of the second general causation theory, *King v Secretary of Health & Human Services*, 03-584V, 2010 WL 892296 (Fed Cl March 12, 2010) at *88.

[89] *Althen v Secretary of Health & Human Services* 418 F 3d 1274, 1278 (Fed Cir 2005).

[90] *Cedillo v Secretary of Health & Human Services*, 2009 WL 331968 (Fed Cl Feb 12, 2009) at *132–33, aff'd, 89 Fed Cl 158, 182–83 (2009); *Pafford v Secretary of Health & Human Services* 451 F 3d 1352, 1358 (Fed Cir 2006) (need for evidence demonstrating petitioner's injury within medically accepted time-frame). Cf the view that the OAP reveals the competing policy tensions between compensating injured petitioners and upholding the public confidence in vaccines and their use, and that these unresolved policy conflicts have revealed a tension that has fallen on the shoulders of the Special Masters presiding over the OAP, which is illustrated by *Cedillo*: LA Binski, 'Balancing Policy Tensions of the Vaccine Act In Light of the Omnibus Autism Proceeding: Are Petitioners Getting a Fair Shot at Compensation?' (2011) 39 *Hofstra Law Review* 683, 688, 705–10, 715, 720. Binski submits that more guidance needs to be given to Special Masters as to how to strike the balance between these competing concerns in causation-in-fact cases: ibid 716–20.

(iv) Looking Beyond the Epidemiology: The Overall Evidence

A strength of these Omnibus Autism Proceeding test cases is that in determining whether the petitioners have demonstrated causation by a preponderance of evidence, the Special Masters have looked *beyond* the epidemiologic evidence to determine whether the *overall evidence*—ie medical opinion and circumstantial evidence and other evidence considered as a whole—tipped the balance even slightly in favour of a causation showing.[91] Ultimately, in each case, the overall weight of the evidence was overwhelmingly contrary to the petitioners' causation theories. In respect of general causation, the evidence advanced by the petitioners had fallen far short of demonstrating a causal link.[92]

(v) On the Side of Science

Thus we can conclude that in these important test cases, the Special Masters have come down clearly on the side of science, and in doing so have considered the evidence overall. Indeed, one master, Special Master George Hastings in *Cedillo* severely criticised those physicians who are supporting a link between MMR and autism. He stated that: 'Unfortunately, the Cedillos have been misled by physicians who are guilty of gross medical misjudgment'.[93] All of the Special Masters concluded that the petitioners had failed to demonstrate that the vaccinations played any role in causing autism.

V. A FRENCH COMPARISON: THE LIBERAL FRENCH APPROACH TO HEPATITIS B VACCINE AND DEMYELINATING DISEASES USING PRESUMPTIONS OF CAUSATION

In contrast to the US, a much more liberal approach to causation appeared to be established in France by the Cour de cassation, principally in the context of claims for compensation for demyelinating diseases, allegedly caused or exacerbated by vaccinations against hepatitis B.

In 2003, the Cour de cassation held that causation between the hepatitis B vaccination and multiple sclerosis could not be established given the absence of scientific certainty on the possible link between the vaccine and the disease.[94] However, the Cour de cassation shifted its position on 22 May 2008, when it acknowledged in a series of five cases

---

[91] In determining if a petitioner is entitled to compensation, the Special Master is not bound by any diagnosis, conclusion, judgment, test result, report, or summary, and in evaluating the weight to be afforded to such matters, 'shall consider the *entire* record': 42 USC § 300aa-13(b)(1) (emphasis added).

[92] *Cedillo v Secretary of Health & Human Services*, 2009 WL 331968 (Fed Cl Feb 12, 2009) at *134–35; and, further, in respect of the second general causal theory, *King v Secretary of Health & Human Services*, 03-584V, 2010 WL 892296 (Fed Cl March 12, 2010) at *91.

[93] *Cedillo v Secretary of Health & Human Services*, 2009 WL 331968 (Fed Cl Feb 12, 2009) at *135; and, further, *Dwyer v Secretary of Health & Human Services*, 03-1202V, 2010 WL 892250 (Fed Cl March 12, 2010) at *201 ('Unfortunately the Dwyers (and uncounted other parents of children with ASD) have relied upon practitioners who peddled hope, not opinions grounded in science and medicine'). It has been predicted that the plaintiffs' experts, while singled out for their lack of expertise and personal integrity, will continue to testify in future trials, 'charging handsomely for their services': PA Offit, *Deadly Choices: How the Anti-Vaccine Movement Threatens Us All* (New York, Basic Books, 2011) 102.

[94] Cass civ 1, 23 September 2003, n° 01-13063, n° 01-13064. See, further, J-S Borghetti, 'Litigation on Hepatitis B Vaccination and Demyelinating Diseases in France: Breaking Through Scientific Uncertainty?' (2012) (on file with author). I am grateful to Professor Jean-Sébastien Borghetti, Professor à l'université Panthéon-Assas (Paris II) for a copy of this paper.

concerning hepatitis B in which it was alleged to have caused neurological disorders,[95] and one case concerning two medications that were alleged to have caused Lyell's syndrome,[96] that a causal link could be established by the presence of 'serious, precise and concurrent' presumptions of causation. Such presumptions had to be supported by specific causation-related data submitted by each specific claimant on a case-by-case basis relating to the claimant's medical history, but not through generalised statistical or probabilistic studies. As a result, despite the absence of any scientific and statistical data showing a causal link between hepatitis B vaccine and multiple sclerosis or other neurological illnesses, the Cour de cassation quashed two[97] out of five judgments concerning the hepatitis C vaccine which had previously dismissed claims for compensation. The decisions were quashed on the grounds that the appellate courts had followed 'a probabilistic approach based exclusively on the lack of scientific and statistical link between vaccination and the development of the disease'[98] without investigating the specific causation-related data submitted by each claimant and whether this constituted serious, precise and concurrent presumptions of causation. In one appellate judgment, the court had relied on general studies and statistics to determine that there was no causal link between hepatitis B and multiple sclerosis. Accordingly, a claim against a pharmaceutical producer could not be rejected on the sole basis of the absence of any scientific and statistical data showing a causal link between a medicinal product and an illness. This decision to allow the claimants to prove a causal link on the basis of serious, precise and concordant presumptions of causation was confirmed by the Cour de cassation in a judgment of 25 June 2009, where it observed that lower judges cannot require an 'unquestionable scientific proof'.[99]

This led to considerable concern from the pharmaceutical industry, since the existence of a causal link could no longer be excluded on the basis of an absence of general statistical evidence of a causal link between drug and damage. The industry became worried that this position had opened the door to compensation for the alleged side-effects of medicinal products generally, especially when the Cour de cassation's position conflicted with legal certainty and fairness in the absence of conclusive epidemiology. It also appeared unclear in what circumstances trial judges would be able to demonstrate the necessary presumption of causation, in cases where there was an absence of scientific evidence of general causation.[100]

The opportunity to confirm what type of facts could potentially give rise to serious, precise and concurrent presumptions quickly arose with the judgment of the Cour de cassation of 9 July 2009.[101] In an extremely controversial judgment, the court went beyond its previous decisions of 22 May 2008 and 25 June 2009, and upheld a judgment by the Court of Appeal of Lyon, granting a patient's claim against the manufacturer of the hepatitis B vaccine, by finding that causation had been proven even in the absence of general

---

[95] Cass Civ 1, 22 May 2008, 5 judgments, no 05-20.317, no 06-14.952, no 05-10.593, no 06-10.967, no 06-18.848, I am grateful to Cécile Derycke and Agnès Roman-Amat, Hogan Lovells, Paris, for the provision of copies of several of the French cases utilised in this paper.

[96] Cass Civ 1, 22 May 2008, no 07-17.200.

[97] Cass Civ 1, 22 May 2008, 2 judgments, no 06-10.967 and no 05-20.317.

[98] J-S Borghetti, 'Litigation on Hepatitis B Vaccination and Demyelinating Diseases in France: Breaking Through Scientific Uncertainty?' (lecture, University of Girona, 15 March 2012).

[99] Cass civ 1, 25 June 2009, no 08-12781.

[100] C Derycke and A Roman-Amat, 'Law against science: French Civil Supreme Court opens the door to compensation in product liability cases involving the hepatitis B vaccine' (June 2008) Lovells' *European Product Liability Review* 14, 17–18.

[101] Cass civ 1, 9 July 2009, no 08-11.073; P Brun and O Gout, *Recueil Dalloz* 2010, p 49, 2.

causation, but where such a causal link could not be excluded. The Court of Appeal of Lyon had utilised two factual criteria to establish a presumption of a causal link between the vaccination and the development of multiple sclerosis, viz (1), a temporal proximity between the vaccine injection and the development of the illness; and (2) the absence of other personal risk factors. The Cour de cassation held that while scientific evidence had failed to establish a statistically significant increase in relative risk of multiple sclerosis following vaccination against hepatitis B, nevertheless it could not exclude such a possible link, and there existed proximity between the injection and the development of the disease and an absence of other individual risk factors, such facts could constitute serious precise and concurrent presumptions. From this, a causal link would be inferred between the vaccine and the damage.[102] It is strongly suspected that the purpose of the Cour de cassation's judgment was to adopt the same position as the Conseil d'État in actions brought by individuals subject to compulsory vaccination to prevent hepatitis B against the state or other employers.[103]

However, certain French Courts of Appeal have resisted this controversial approach adopted by the Cour de cassation and have continued to refuse to hold manufacturers liable where there is an absence of scientific evidence of general causation.[104] In particular, the Paris Court of Appeal stressed the need to base the decisions on specific personal data of the claimant, whilst at the same time reaffirming the absence of any scientific consensus between hepatitis B vaccine and neurological disorders, the fact that that the aetiology is unknown and that multiple sclerosis can be caused by various genetic factors.[105] Moreover, in its judgment of 19 June 2009, the Paris Court of Appeal held that temporal proximity and the absence of personal risk factors did not constitute serious, precise and concurrent presumptions.[106] This position was upheld by the Cour de cassation in its decisions of 24 September 2009, and 25 November 2010.[107] Accordingly, the Cour de cassation appeared to be retreating somewhat from its position on 9 July 2009. Unfortunately, a recent decision of the Cour de cassation[108] suggests that it has performed yet another reversal in upholding

---

[102] Cass civ 1, 9 July 2009, n° 08-11.073.

[103] CE, n° 267635, 9 March 2007. See further, D Fairgrieve and F G'sell-Macrez, 'Causation in French Law: Pragmatism and Policy' in R Goldberg (ed), *Perspectives on Causation* (Oxford, Hart Publishing, 2011) 127; C Derycke and A Roman-Amat, 'The adverse side effects of the French Supreme Court's judgments in relation to the Hepatitis B vaccine' (September 2009) Lovells' *European Product Liability Review* 13, 14.

[104] Cour d'Appel de Paris, n° 04/19067, n° 04/19068, 9 January 2009, Cour d'Appel de Paris, n° 06/13741, 19 June 2009 (upheld by Cour de cassation: Civ 1, n° 09-16.556, 25 November 2010). See also, Cour d'Appel de Bourges, 22 January 2009, n° 07/01489.

[105] Cour d'Appel de Paris, 9 January 2009, RG n° 08/1407, 6; RG n° 04/19067, 8.

[106] Cour d'Appel de Paris, n° 06/13741, 19 June 2009 (upheld by Cour de cassation: Civ 1, n° 09-16.556, 25 November 2010).

[107] Cass civ 1, 24 September 2009, n° 08-16.097, (evidence of claimant (seven month period between vaccination and outbreak of multiple sclerosis, and fact that claimant presented no personal or family history in relation to multiple sclerosis), did not constitute serious, precise and concurrent presumptions of a causal link); Cass civ 1, 25 November 2010 n° 09-16.556 (refusal to establish causation in the absence of scientific consensus in favour of a causal link between the hepatitis B vaccine and multiple sclerosis, despite the existence of proximity between the vaccine injection and the disease (two weeks) and an absence of other individual risk factors. Such evidence, without a scientific consensus in favour of causation, was insufficient to constitute serious, precise and concurrent presumptions). See also the decision of the Cour de cassation prior to its judgment of 9 July 2009: Cass civ 1, 22 January 2009, n° 07-16.449, which confirmed that appellate courts could dismiss patient claims concerning the hepatitis B vaccine, provided that they assess with care not only general causation, but also specific causation, and are able to conclude that the factual evidence submitted to them does not amount to serious, precise and concurrent presumptions of causation; C Derycke and A Roman-Amat, 'The judge and science: a new episode in the hepatitis B vaccine saga' (March 2009) Lovells' *European Product Liability Review* Issue 34, 21, 22.

[108] Cass civ 1, 26 September 2012, n° 11-17.738.

the Court of Appeal of Versaille's decision[109] that temporal proximity between the hepatitis B vaccination and the appearance of the demyelinating disease, in the absence of any other known cause for the disease, allowed a presumption that the vaccine had caused the claimant's injury. However, it also ruled, in overturning the decision of the Court of Appeal, that it should have checked if the elements, on the basis of which causation had been presumed, did not also allow a presumption that the vaccine was defective. It therefore suggests that the elements that allow for a presumption of causation may also allow for a presumption of defectiveness. Professor Borghetti has noted that this form of 'intuitive' reasoning is unsupported by scientific evidence,[110] and as Fairgrieve and G'Sell-Macrez observe, the 'constant reference to "serious precise and concurrent presumptions" seems somehow to prevent French courts from adopting probabilistic reasoning regarding causation'.[111] It seems that lower French law courts are free to follow their own approaches to the potential link between hepatitis B vaccinations and demyelinating diseases. While a majority of lower courts, including the Paris Court of Appeal, consider that the current state of scientific uncertainty does not permit causation to be presumed on the facts of the case, irrespective of the temporal proximity between the hepatitis B vaccination and the appearance of the demyelinating disease, in a minority of cases the appellate courts are prepared to recognise such a presumption. Unfortunately, this recent decision of the Cour de cassation follows that minority view. However, in its most recent decision, the Cour de cassation, while upholding the approach of assessing all elements at hand when considering a product's defectiveness and the existence of a causal link, has now also held that demonstration of 'imputability' (i.e. general causation between a product and a disease) must be met as a prerequisite prior to the demonstration of damage, defect and causal link.[112] It appears that the aim of this approach is to prevent a complete disconnection between causation in science and law, but it will also result in an increase in the claimant's burden of proof.[113]

The inconsistency of these decisions has been unhelpful in generating uncertainty for both claimant and defendant. However, it is submitted that, without scientific evidence of general causation, there should be no question of overcoming the burden of proof of causation in such cases. The Cour de cassation would be wise to study the factors required to overcome that burden as established in the National Vaccine Injury Compensation Program.[114] While the current decisions of the French courts appear to accept prongs two and three of the *Althen*[115] test, viz (2) a logical sequence of cause and effect showing that the vaccination was the reason for the injury; and (3) a showing of a proximate temporal relationship between the vaccination and the injury, the uncertainty seems to stem from whether there should be an acceptance of prong (1), ie a medical theory causally connecting the vaccination and the injury, which is a general causation requirement that the type of vaccine can cause the type of injury in question.[116]

---

[109] Cour d'appel de Versailles, 10 February 2011.

[110] J-S Borghetti, 'Qu'est-ce qu'un vaccin défectueux?', *Recueil Dalloz* 2012 2853.

[111] D Fairgrieve and F G'sell-Macrez, 'Causation in French Law: Pragmatism and Policy' in R Goldberg (ed), *Perspectives on Causation* (Oxford, Hart Publishing, 2011) 127.

[112] Cass civ 1, 29 May 2013, n° 12-20.9033.

[113] I am grateful to Dr Duncan Fairgrieve of the British Institute of International Law for sight of an unpublished commentary on this case.

[114] See *Althen v Secretary of Health & Human Services* 418 F 3d 1274, 1278 (Fed Cir 2005), above, 3.(v)(c).

[115] Ibid.

[116] *Cedillo v Secretary of Health & Human Services*, 2009 WL 331968 (Fed Cl Feb 12, 2009) at 131, affirming *Pafford v Secretary of Health & Human Services* 451 F 3d 1352, 1355–56 (Fed Cir 2006); and, further, in respect of the second general causation theory, *Dwyer v Secretary of Health & Human Services*, 03-1202V, 2010 WL 892250

Were the French courts to adopt an *Althen* type approach, which gives primacy to the general causation issue, this would help create more consistency in its decisions, in line with the Cour de cassation's objective laid down in its Annual Report for 2008 to harmonise case law on the hepatitis B vaccine.[117]

VI. MMR AND THE GENERAL MEDICAL COUNCIL

A. The Professional Conduct Hearing

While the test cases have come to their conclusion, the position in the UK shifted to issues of professional misconduct on behalf of Dr Wakefield, and two other doctors who were co-authors on the *Lancet* paper, viz Professor Walker-Smith and Professor (formerly Dr) Murch. These three doctors were referred to the General Medical Council, the body in the UK which is charged with the role of protecting, promoting and maintaining the health and safety of the public by ensuring proper standards in the practice of medicine.[118]

After a hearing lasting 148 days which took over two and a half years to complete, the longest in the history of the GMC, Wakefield was found guilty of dishonesty and irresponsibility by the GMC. In particular, they found that: he had carried out research on the children in breach of Research and Ethics Committee approval;[119] he had subjected several children to intrusive procedures such as lumber-puncture and colonoscopy that were not clinically indicated;[120] he had intentionally misled the Legal Aid Board by failing to disclose that certain funding subsequently provided by them was not required; he had caused or permitted public funds supplied by the Legal Aid Board to be used for purposes other than those for which it was needed; in respect of conflict of interests, he had failed to disclose to the Editor of the *Lancet* his involvement in the MMR Litigation and that the study had received funding from the Legal Aid Board; and that he had filed a patent application for a new vaccine for the elimination of the MMR and measles virus and for the treatment of inflammatory bowel disease.[121] He also unethically caused blood to be taken from a group of children for research purposes at his son's birthday party.[122] In all these circumstances, and taking into account the standard that might be expected of a doctor practising in the same field of medicine in similar circumstances, the Panel concluded that Wakefield's misconduct not only collectively amounted to serious professional misconduct, but also, when considered individually, constituted multiple separate instances of serious professional misconduct.[123] The Panel concluded that Dr Wakefield's shortcomings and the

---

(Fed Cl March 12, 2010) at *197; *King v Secretary of Health & Human Services*, 03-584V, 2010 WL 892296 (Fed Cl March 12, 2010) at *87.

[117] See: www.courdecassation.fr/publications_cour_26/rapport_annuel_36/rapport_2008_2903/quatrieme_partie_jurisprudence_cour_2922/responsabilite_civile_assurances_2953/droit_responsabilite_2954/produits_defectueux_12240.html.

[118] Medical Act 1983, s 1. See, generally, M O'Rourke and J Holl-Allen, 'Regulating Health Care Professionals' in A Grubb, J McHale and J Lang (eds), *Principles of Medical Law*, 3rd edn (Oxford, University Press, 2010).

[119] General Medical Council, Fitness to Practise Panel Hearing, 28 January 2010, pp 7–11.

[120] Ibid 11–42.

[121] Ibid 49–50.

[122] Ibid 54–55.

[123] Dr Andrew Jeremy Wakefield, Determination on Serious Professional Misconduct (SPM) and sanction, 24 May 2010, p 7.

aggravating factors in this case[124] could not be addressed by any condition on his registration. Accordingly, it determined that his name should be erased from the medical register, concluding that this was

> the only sanction that [was] appropriate to protect patients and [was] in the wider public interest, including the maintenance of public trust and confidence in the profession and [was] proportionate to the serious and wide-ranging findings made against him.[125]

The Panel also concluded that the only appropriate sanction against Professor Walker-Smith was erasure from the medical register.[126] However, while the Panel concluded that Professor Murch had demonstrated errors of judgement, he had acted in good faith, and any professional misconduct on his part could not reach the threshold of serious professional misconduct.[127]

B. Consequences of the Professional Conduct Hearing

On 6 February 2010, about a week after the findings of fact made against Wakefield and his colleagues, and 12 years after its original publication, the Editors of the *Lancet* finally retracted the 1998 *Lancet* paper. It has been submitted that this should not have taken so long and that until the article's retraction, both Wakefield and claimants could continue to argue that their position was supported in a peer-reviewed journal, albeit an article which had not received general acceptance. Part of the problem here—as any respected epidemiologist will tell us—is that no study can entirely rule out the possibility of a link between MMR and autism. But under the burden of proof in law, it was the claimants who were required to show such a link; there was no burden on the defendants to shown that there was none. It is clear that they decisively failed in the United States, and that there was no prospect of them succeeding in the UK.

By the time of its retraction few could deny that Wakefield's *Lancet* paper was fatally flawed, both scientifically and ethically.[128] However, to compound matters, even more disturbing news was to emerge. In early 2011, a series of articles in the British Medical Journal claimed that the 1998 *Lancet* paper was fraudulent on the basis that in not one of the 12 cases could the medical records be fully reconciled with what was published in the descriptions, diagnoses or histories in the journal.[129]

---

[124] Including 'the wide-ranging transgressions relating to every aspect of his research; his disregard for the clinical interests of vulnerable patients; his failure to heed the warnings he received in relation to the potential conflicts of interest associated with the Legal Aid Board funding; his failure to disclose [his] patent; his dishonesty in relation to the drafting of the Lancet paper; and his subsequent representations about it, all played out against a background of research involving such major health implications': ibid 8.

[125] Ibid 9.

[126] Professor John Angus Walker-Smith, Determination on Serious Professional Misconduct (SPM) and sanction, 24 May 2010, p 9. This was due to Professor Walker-Smith's 'extensive failures in relation to the clinical care of potentially vulnerable children, his non-compliance with ethical research requirements, and the irresponsible and misleading reporting of research findings potentially having such major implications for public health': ibid.

[127] Professor (formerly Dr) Simon Harry Murch, Determination on Serious Professional Misconduct (SPM) and sanction, 24 May 2010, p 7.

[128] F Godlee, J Smith and H Marcovitch, Editorial, 'Wakefield's article linking MMR vaccine and autism was fraudulent' (2011) 342 *British Medical Journal* 64, 65.

[129] B Deer, 'How the Case Against the MMR Vaccine Was Fixed' (2011) 342 *British Medical Journal* 77; B Deer, 'How the Vaccine Crisis was Meant to Make Money (2011) 342 *British Medical Journal* 136; B Deer, 'The Lancet's

VII. CONCLUSION

The MMR litigation has shown the incalculable damage that can be caused by one peer reviewed article in a prestigious scientific journal. But for this article, the ensuing publicity in the UK and US would never have transpired. It was this article which fuelled the publicity, which in turn generated the law suits on both sides of the Atlantic. More importantly, it can be argued, it resulted in considerable damage to public health. While vaccination rates in the UK have recovered slightly, they remain below the 95 per cent level recommended by the World Health Organisation to ensure herd immunity.[130] The other damage in the UK was that since the MMR Litigation, the Legal Services Commission became reluctant to fund other multi-party actions in respect of medicinal products that claimants alleged had caused harm.[131]

While there was considerable justification for withdrawal of public funding in the UK, there are some positives that have emerged from the test cases in the US Omnibus Autism Proceeding. Indeed, it is arguable that the US experience in the test cases in autism is in many ways a paradigm of how to address such controversial issues. Unburdened by the emotions of a jury and the usual restrictions imposed by the Federal Rules of Evidence, a single trier of fact has been able to look at all the available evidence and come to a reasoned decision. In these autism test cases, issues of general and specific causation have been addressed and factors personal to the individual children have been taken into account. While the *Daubert* factors have been utilised, they have not prevented evidence being made admissible in these proceedings through an overly strenuous evidentiary threshold. They have been relevant to the assessment of weight at the *adjudication* stage, which has allowed the evidence as a whole to ventilate in the proceedings. It suggests that this more flexible approach to scientific evidence, albeit with high standards at the adjudication stage, is welcome and may counter some of the criticisms[132] of *Daubert* that it has in some cases hindered the search for justice in product liability law. No doubt the most radical approach would be to build on the template of the National Vaccine Injury Compensation Program, and extend it to one involving all prescription drugs generally. This is unlikely to take place in the short term. But what should be possible is a greater flexibility in the use the gatekeeping role for scientific evidence in these types of cases.

Two Days to Bury Bad News' (2011) 342 *British Medical Journal* 200; F. Godlee, J. Smith and H Marcovitch, Editorial, 'Wakefield's article linking MMR vaccine and autism was fraudulent' (2011) 342 *British Medical Journal* 64, 65.

[130] F Godlee, J Smith and H Marcovitch, Editorial, 'Wakefield's article linking MMR vaccine and autism was fraudulent' (2011) 342 *British Medical Journal* 64, 65; see, further, Editorial, 'Junk Science: The Welsh measles epidemic is the price of attacking medical evidence', *The Times*, 16 April 2013, www.thetimes.co.uk/tto/opinion/leaders/article3740134.ece, accessed 22 April 2013 (discussing a recent measles epidemic that broke out in Wales, and blaming the fall in MMR vaccinations on Wakefield's 1998 *Lancet* paper and on 'credulous commentators who elected to ventriloquise his sensationalist campaign').

[131] This has been seen with the recent withdrawal of funding for the multi-party action claim against the manufacturers of the anti-convulsant medicinal product Epilim, which 80 families had claimed had caused spina bifida, heart damage, learning difficulties, cleft palate and deformities of the hands and feet: see Legal Services Commission, Press Release, 'LSC statement on FACS-Epilim funding', 28 January 2011, available at: www.legalservices.gov.uk/aboutus/11556_12406.asp?page=1. Personal injury claims against pharmaceutical companies will no longer be eligible for legal aid in England and Wales, although they will continue to be eligible in Scotland. See chapter 1 of this volume.

[132] See, for instance, RL Cupp Jr, 'Believing in Products Liability: Reflections on *Daubert*, Doctrinal Evolution and David Owen's *Products Liability Law*' (2006) 40 *University of California, Davis, Law Review* 511, 528–30; and, generally, C Cranor, *Toxic Torts: Science, Law, and the Possibility of Justice* (CUP, 2007).

In France, a liberal approach to causation appeared to be established in France by the Cour de cassation, principally in the context of claims for compensation for demyelinating diseases, allegedly caused or exacerbated by vaccinations against hepatitis B. The Cour de cassation has acknowledged that causal link can be established by the presence of serious, precise and concurrent presumptions of causation. However, the inconsistency of the decisions has been unhelpful in generating uncertainty for both claimant and defendant. It is submitted that, without scientific evidence of general causation, there should be no question of overcoming the burden of proof of causation in such cases. The Cour de cassation would be wise to study the factors required to overcome that burden as established in the National Vaccine Injury Compensation Program, as adumbrated in the *Althen* case, and utilised by the OAP test cases, which, it is submitted, generate more clarity and consistency in approach.

There are also lessons to be learned from the outcome of the General Medical Council hearing. In particular, co-authors of scientific papers will require to verify the source data of studies in a more thorough manner than they have done previously.[133] Such researchers will need to remember that they have a duty to disclose not only actual conflicts of interest, but also perceived conflicts.[134] Research Ethics Committees will be required to establish mechanisms to determine that what was done in a study was actually permitted; they must also be required to work to an effective governance procedure that can impose sanctions when an eventual publication proves that unpermitted acts have taken place.[135]

Another important lesson lies with the role of the media in its reporting of the MMR vaccine scare. They repeatedly reported the concerns of Wakefield, without giving methodological details of the research, whilst ignoring the epidemiological evidence showing no link between MMR and autism.[136] It is important that in future the media recognise the importance of peer-reviewed scientific evidence in such cases, and report it impartially.

However, the principal lesson to be learned from the MMR litigation lies with the wider scientific community. In exercising its freedom to sanction, conduct and publish scientific research, the scientific community as a whole must always exercise eternal vigilance against scientific fraud and misconduct. It is only in these circumstances that good science will have the necessary confidence of the public and the legal system that engages with it.

---

[133] F Godlee, J Smith and H Marcovitch, Editorial, 'Wakefield's article linking MMR vaccine and autism was fraudulent' (2011) 342 *British Medical Journal* 64, 65.

[134] Professor Sir Michael Rutter, General Medical Council, Fitness to Practise Panel (Misconduct), Day 37, 1 October 2007, Transcript, 37–55D. This was the position in 1996 as well as now: ibid.

[135] Ibid.

[136] B Goldacre, 'Expert view: The media are equally guilty over the MMR vaccine scare', *The Guardian*, 28 January 2010, available at: www.guardian.co.uk/science/2010/jan/28/mmr-vaccine-ben-goldacre/print. Professor David Salisbury, Director of Immunisation at the Department of Health, has argued that unlike the US, which has three newspapers that cross the country, the UK has at least 15 national newspapers competing for coverage of a smaller population, which 'leads to more histrionic, more aggressive reporting to seize the audience': PA Offit, *Deadly Choices: How the Anti-Vaccine Movement Threatens Us All* (New York, Basic Books, 2011) 92.

7

Regulatory Compliance and Medicinal Product Liability

I. INTRODUCTION

This chapter seeks to address the question as to whether compliance with regulatory standards should protect pharmaceutical manufacturers from product liability suits. It examines the current position surrounding compliance with common practice, regulatory and statutory standards of the pharmaceutical industry from the perspectives of both negligence and strict liability, as well as the currently available defence to strict liability that a defect is attributable to mandatory statutory or community requirements. In the United States, by far the most significant attempt to eliminate product liability claims involving drugs has been through the doctrine of federal preemption, which is predicated on a similar basis to a defence of compliance with regulatory standards, namely that since the Food and Drug Administration determines the safety and efficacy of drugs and their labelling, and is equipped with the power to act if new information emerges over time, a lay jury should be prevented from second-guessing the expert decisions of the FDA by stating that a drug is defective or its warning inadequate.[1] In this context, the chapter examines recent developments in *Wyeth v Levine*, in which the Supreme Court has ruled that US FDA labelling approvals do not preempt State laws and shield companies from State product liability claims. In the light of the rationales behind this decision, particularly the Court's emphasis on the role of State law as a complement to the FDA's mission of consumer protection, and the increasing importance of pharmacovigilance and post-marketing surveillance in both Europe and the US respectively, the chapter concludes with a discussion of the advantages and disadvantages of introducing a regulatory compliance defence for medicinal products under the Product Liability Directive.

II. COMPLIANCE WITH COMMON PRACTICE, REGULATORY AND STATUTORY STANDARDS

A. Compliance with Common Practice of the Pharmaceutical Industry

(i) Negligence

Where liability is based on negligence, evidence of compliance or non-compliance with common practice is relevant and admissible to determining whether in all the

---

[1] M Hermann and DB Alden, *Drug and Device Litigation Strategy* (Oxford, Oxford University Press, 2012) 318.

circumstances of the case the defendant has exercised reasonable care, but it is not conclusive.[2] Guidelines as to what amounts to appropriate pre-marketing research for the purposes of accompanying an application for a marketing authorisation[3] are issued by the regulatory authorities (the licensing authority, and its advisory bodies)[4] and by the industry itself (through its Code of Practice for the Pharmaceutical Industry):[5] these reflect and explain standard practice, but mere compliance with such recommended testing procedures is not an automatic defence to a claim in negligence. For instance, a court may determine that the application of general pre-clinical animal testing guidelines may not be directly applicable to research into the product in question and that additional research should have been performed.[6]

(ii) Strict Liability

While the vast majority of requirements in respect of medicinal products are mandatory statutory ones, the Code of Practice for the Pharmaceutical Industry reflects the presence of voluntary standards. It has been suggested that persons generally may be entitled to expect that goods conform to voluntary standards, where they have been widely accepted as establishing an industry norm.[7] This is consistent with the position which would be adopted where the claim is based on negligence.[8] Also, the General Product Safety Directive provides that a product shall be presumed safe when it conforms to voluntary national standards transposing European standards, the references of which have been published in the Official Journal of the European Communities.[9] In addition, in respect of other circumstances, the conformity of a product to the general safety requirement is to be assessed by taking into account, in particular:

(a)   other voluntary national standards transposing relevant European Standards;
(b)   standards drawn up in the Member State in which the product is marketed;
(c)   [European] Commission recommendations setting guidelines on product safety assessment;
(d)   product safety codes of practice in force in the sector concerned;
(e)   the state of the art and technology; and
(f)   reasonable consumer expectations concerning safety.[10]

---

[2] *Morris v West Hartlepool Navigation Co* [1956] AC 552; *Brown v Rolls Royce Ltd* [1960] 1 All ER 577, [1960] 1 WLR 210, HL; *Cavanagh v Ulster Weaving Co Ltd* [1960] AC 145, [1959] 2 All ER 745, HL; *General Cleaning Contractors Ltd v Christmas* [1953] AC 180, [1953] 2 All ER 1110; *Thompson v Smiths Shiprepairers (North Shields) Ltd* [1984] QB 405, [1984] 1 All ER 881; CJ Miller and RS Goldberg, *Product Liability*, 2nd edn (Oxford, Oxford University Press, 2004) para 14.146.

[3] See, generally, Human Medicines Regulations 2012, SI 2012/1916, regs 49–57, Sch 8.

[4] Ibid regs 6, 9–16.

[5] See, generally, *Code of Practice for the Pharmaceutical Industry: Second 2012 Edition* (London, Association of the British Pharmaceutical Industry, 2012), available at: www.pmcpa.org.uk/thecode/Documents/Code%20of%20Practice%202012.pdf.

[6] I Dodds-Smith, M Spencer and J Bore, 'Product Liability for Medicinal Products' in MJ Powers, NH Harris and A Barton (eds), *Clinical Negligence*, 4th edn (London, Tottel Publishing, 2008) para 24.35.

[7] G Howells in Howells (ed), *The Law of Product Liability*, 2nd edn (London, LexisNexis Butterworths, 2007) para 4172.

[8] See Miller and Goldberg (above, n 2) para 14.146.

[9] Dir 2001/95/EC [2002] OJ L1/4, Art 3(2).

[10] Art 3(3).

Notwithstanding that such provisions do not apply directly to the Product Liability Directive, it is arguable that they are relevant by analogy, not least because of the explicit reference to reasonable consumer expectations concerning safety.[11] However, it should not be assumed that there is necessarily a complete symmetry between the definition of a 'safe' or non-dangerous product under Directive 2001/95/EC[12] and that of a defective product under the Product Liability Directive.[13] This lack of complete symmetry is illustrated by the approach taken by the Court of Appeal in *Pollard v Tesco Stores*[14] to the role of voluntary safety standards in determining the level of safety persons are entitled to expect. In that case, Laws LJ rejected arguments that a child-resistant closure 'CRC' cap on a dishwasher bottle should comply with a British Standard torque measure, since that standard was not referred to on the product and members of the public could not be supposed to have appreciated that any public authority would have pronounced on the matter.[15]

B. Compliance with Statutory Requirements

(i) Negligence

Compliance with standards and regulations prescribed by official agencies and by statute is no doubt evidence that due care has been exercised and reasonable safety measures or devices adopted.[16] Manufacturers of medicinal products must comply with the statutory requirements of the Medicines Act 1968 and the Human Medicines Regulations 2012.[17] If an independent body, such as the Commission on Human Medicines (CHM) or the Committee on Medicinal Products for Human Use (CHMP) has come to the same conclusion as the manufacturer on the safety or adequacy of warnings of a medicinal product,

---

[11] Art 3(3)(f).

[12] Art 2(b) and (c).

[13] Miller and Goldberg (above, n 2) para 10.81.

[14] *Pollard v Tesco Stores* [2006] EWCA Civ 1393, [2006] All ER (D) 86.

[15] Ibid [16]. For criticism of this as a 'relatively weak interpretation of consumer expectations', focusing on actual expectations of consumers rather than the legal test that requires consideration of what persons generally are *entitled* to expect, see G Howells in Howells (ed), *The Law of Product Liability*, 2nd edn, para 4.151 and, further, M Mildred, [2006] *Journal of Personal Injury Law* C130–133; cf the argument that the court in *Pollard* should have reasoned that the public were not entitled to expect compliance with British Standards because the CRC was not a regulatory requirement, and therefore failure to comply with the British Standard was not a breach of the regulatory regime: C Webber, 'The Role of Voluntary Safety Standards in Determining the Level of Safety a Person is Entitled to Expect Under the Product Liability Directive' (2006) 23 *European Product Liability Review* 21, 22. Cf violation of mandatory safety standards, which can constitute conclusive evidence of a product's defectiveness under the Product Liability Directive: District Court of Dusseldorf Landgericht Dusseldorf, 30 November 2005, 100 144/04, NJW-RR 2006, 1033 ff, noted in S Lenze, 'Product Safety Regulations and Defect' (2006) 24 *European Product Liability Review* 20, 21 (who observes that there was nothing in the Dusseldorf Court's decision to suggest that the case would have been decided differently in the context of *voluntary* standards, and that in German and Austrian courts violation of voluntary standards is proper, though not conclusive evidence of a product's defectiveness). Accordingly, Lenze submits that there is a seeming divergence between the national courts of Member States on the role of safety standards under the Product Liability Directive: ibid.

[16] See *Qualcast (Wolverhampton) Ltd v Haynes* [1959] AC 743, 756, [1959] 2 All ER 38, 43, Lord Keith (employers' duty to provide safe system of work). See also *Miller v Lee Apparel Co Inc* 881 P 2d 576, 583–85 (Kan 1994) (clothing which ignited); *Kaufman v Meditec Inc* 353 NW 2d 297, 301 (ND 1984) (prosthetic hip pin). A presumption of non-defectiveness is applied.

[17] See generally, The Human Medicines Regulations 2012, SI 2012/1916.

this will be a significant factor[18] to be taken account of by the court in its determination of whether there has been negligence, assuming that the same information has been disclosed to the CHM or CHMP by the manufacturer and in the absence of the CHM's negligence.[19] However, compliance cannot be regarded as conclusive. English cases have mainly involved employers and factory occupiers,[20] but there is little doubt that the same view would be adopted in the case of a manufacturer, especially in the context of heavily regulated industries.[21] In *Best v Wellcome Foundation*,[22] a manufacturer of pertussis vaccine was held negligent in releasing a batch of the vaccine which had exceeded the recommended levels of potency, when it was known that potency could be linked with high levels of toxicity, despite the fact that British regulations had laid down minimum but not a maximum potency figure.[23] In addition, the batch in question had failed a 'mouse weight gain test', which was widely used as an optional but not mandatory toxicity test.[24] In such circumstances, the Irish Supreme Court held that compliance with mandatory or minimum requirements was insufficient to discharge the manufacturer's duty of care.[25] A fortiori,

---

[18] See *Thompson v Johnson and Johnson Pty Ltd* [1992] 3 Med LR 148; [1991] 2 VR 449, SC of Victoria, App Div, the court stated that the attitude, advice and response of the Australian Department of Health, the Public Health Advisory Committee and the National Health and Medical Research Council (NHMRC) to a reported case of toxic shock syndrome caused by tampons, while not dispositive, 'was a significant factor to have regard to' when determining whether the manufacturers had been negligent in failing to provide warnings of the risk of toxic shock syndrome to the public: ibid 493. As the court put it: 'Whether or not the NHMRC recommended that a warning be given was not determinative of the question of reasonable care, for to accept that proposition would permit the respondents to abrogate the duty of reasonable care owed by them. It is not the response of such a body which determines whether a person in the position of the respondents is or is not negligent. That is for the courts to decide. However, it is a relevant fact to be taken into account when determining whether reasonable care had been exercised': ibid 494.

[19] M Jones, *Medical Negligence*, 4th edn (London, Sweet & Maxwell, 2008) para 10-055; I Dodds-Smith, M Spencer and J Bore, 'Product Liability for Medicinal Products' in MJ Powers, NH Harris and A Barton (eds), *Clinical Negligence*, 4th edn (London, Tottel Publishing, 2008) para 24.37. In *Buchan v Ortho Pharmaceuticals (Canada) Ltd* (1986) 25 DLR (4th) 658, the issue of whether compliance by the manufacturer with the requirements set by the advisory committee of the Canadian Food and Drug Directorate as to warnings to be provided directly to users of oral contraceptives absolved manufacturers of liability was left undecided, since the court assumed that the learned intermediary doctrine was applicable: ibid 671–73.

[20] See eg *Bux v Slough Metals Ltd* [1974] 1 All ER 262, 267–68, CA (compliance with Non-Ferrous Metals Regulations, but not with duty to provide safe system of work); *Franklin v Gramophone Co Ltd* [1948] 1 KB 542, [1948] 1 All ER 353, CA. See also *Wintle v Bristol Tramways and Carriage Co* (1917) 86 LJKB 240 (light locomotive).

[21] See *Lambson Aviation v Embraer-Empresa Brasileira De Aeronautica SA* [2001] All ER (D) 152 (Oct); (QBD, 10, 11 October 2001) (noted in R Freeman, 'Assessing Manufacturers' Liability in Highly Regulated Industries' (December 2001) Lovells' *European Product Liability Review* , Issue 5, 25). In *Lambson Aviation*, an aircraft manufacturer and supplier of on-board navigation equipment were held not liable in negligence for a fatal aeroplane crash occurring after progressive failure of the navigation equipment, in circumstances where the design of the aircraft, including the navigation equipment, had been certified by the regulatory authorities: [2001] All ER (D) 152, paras 40, 45, 50. The Court stressed that while compliance with regulatory requirements should not necessarily absolve a defendant from liability in negligence, in heavily regulated industries, such as the aircraft industry, compliance with such requirements 'should ... carry considerable but not decisive weight in the evaluation of what reasonably is required of those engaged in the industry': ibid para 17, Tomlinson J.

[22] *Best (an Infant) v Wellcome Foundation Ltd* [1992] ILRM 609; [1994] 5 Med LR 81, Supreme Court of Ireland.

[23] [1992] ILRM 609, 626–27; [1994] 5 Med LR 81, 98, Finlay CJ.

[24] [1992] ILRM 609, 622–24; [1994] 5 Med LR 81, 96–97, Finlay CJ.

[25] [1992] ILRM 609, 626–27; [1994] 5 Med LR 81, 98, Finlay CJ. As Finlay CJ put it: 'Merely to comply, in my view with mandatory or minimum requirements imposed by national health authorities in the area in which the vaccine was manufactured, or merely to rely on one particular point of view in a debated question concerning the risks involved, would not necessarily, in any given case, constitute a sufficient degree of care to discharge the legal duty of a manufacturer of vaccine in these circumstances'. While failure to comply with the statutory requirements

in the context of the licensing of medicinal products, Article 25 of Directive 2001/83/EC provides a marketing authorisation 'shall not affect the civil and criminal liability of the manufacturer and, where applicable, of the marketing authorisation holder'.[26] However, a court in such cases would be reluctant to impose standards higher than (and thus inconsistent with) statutorily prescribed standards. This was the position in *Albery-Speyer & Budden v BP Oil Ltd and Shell Oil Ltd*,[27] where the Court of Appeal dismissed the claims of children in negligence who had allegedly suffered physical injury as a result of ingestion of quantities of lead from exposure to the defendant's petrol, on the grounds that BP had complied with regulations limiting the maximum amount of lead per litre of petrol, prescribed by the Secretary of State and approved by Parliament. To hold them negligent would mean that the courts would necessarily be, in effect, laying down limits different from and inconsistent with those prescribed by Parliament, which would result in an unacceptable constitutional anomaly. Although a decision reached in the context of a claim in negligence, it has been submitted that the same principles would be applicable under a strict liability regime.[28] Accordingly, mere compliance with licensing regulations under the Medicines Act 1968 'will often be strong evidence that the "consumer expectation" test of safety has been met'.[29] Unlike petrol, medicinal product licenses do not lay down statutory standards with which all manufacturers must comply since each licence is confined to the particular medicinal product in issue. However, manufacturers of medicinal products are arguably entitled to believe that where they have disclosed to the licensing authority all the relevant facts pertaining to a drug's safety,[30] the decision to grant a UK marketing authorisation would be representative of the public interest. The licensing authority is ideally equipped to determine the safety of drugs in the public interest and performs this role conscientiously.[31] In such circumstances, a court may be prepared to treat the licensing authority decision to grant a UK marketing authorisation as a finding of fact which it would be 'reluctant to criticise'.[32]

Nonetheless, as well as reiterating the position that compliance with the regulatory regime does not conclusively preclude liability in negligence, recent Australian case law has emphasised that the regulatory regime for medicines lays down minimum and not

---

of the Medicines Act 1968 may be evidence of negligence, breach of the Act or regulations made under it does not constitute negligence per se: Medicines Act 1968, s 133(2).

[26] Directive 2001/83/EC of the European Parliament and of the Council of 6 November 2001 on the Community Code Relating to Medicinal Products for Human Use [2001] OJ L311/67, Art 25; Medicines Act 1968, s 133(2).

[27] *Albery-Speyer & Budden v BP Oil Ltd and Shell Oil Ltd* (1980) 124 *Solicitors' Journal* 376, CA.

[28] Miller and Goldberg (above, n 2) para 10.77.

[29] H Teff, 'Products Liability' in A Grubb, J Lang and J McHale (eds), *Principles of Medical Law*, 3rd edn (Oxford, Oxford University Press, 2010) para 18.63.

[30] Human Medicines Regulations 2012, reg 75.

[31] C Newdick, 'The Impact of Licensing Authority Approval on Pharmaceutical Product Liability: A Survey of American and UK Law' (1992) 47 *Food & Drug Law Journal* 41, 52–53.

[32] *R v Licensing Authority Established Under Medicines Act 1968, ex parte Smith, Kline & French Laboratories Ltd* [1990] 1 AC 64, 108, Lord Templeman. See also the High Court's discussion of the Code of Practice Committee of the Association of the British Pharmaceutical Industry, where Popplewell J observed: 'Where there is a committee dealing with a matter which is not immediately familiar to the court and laying down standards which are peculiar to that organization or profession, a court should not be too ready to criticise that body for reaching a decision which the court itself might not have reached': *R v Code of Practice Committee of the Association of the British Pharmaceutical Industry, ex parte Professional Counselling Aids Ltd* (1990) 10 BMLR 21, Popplewell J; *The Independent*, 1 November 1990, at 32.

optimum standards. In *Merck Sharp & Dohme (Australia) Pty Limited v Peterson*,[33] the Full Federal Court of Australia held that mere compliance with the requirements of the regulatory regime of the Therapeutic Goods Act 1989 (Cth) (TGA) was insufficient to discharge Merck's duty of care in negligence. The court stressed that the legislation established minimum safety standards for the availability and use of regulated medicines and that it did not reveal an intention to abrogate common law consumer rights. While such compliance with a regulatory regime might be relevant under the common law, it was not dispositive.[34] As the trial judge put it:

> By placing on the market a product to be consumed by end users, the manufacturer of a prescription medicine, no less than the manufacturer of any other product intended for human consumption, establishes the setting for the creation of the relationship of proximity from which the common law duty of care arises. I would be slow to hold that a law which did not in terms deal with that very subject implicitly qualified the manufacturer's obligation—as it would otherwise be defined by the common law—so as to permit it, in effect, to act less than reasonably in the discharge of the duty, and to act in a way that produced loss or damage, yet to be shielded from claims by injured parties. There is, in my view, nothing unworkable or anomalous about such a manufacturer remaining under an obligation to take reasonable steps to avoid loss or injury to the end user at the same time as being required to comply with the regulatory system for which the TGA provided. The manufacturer's obligation is not, in my view, exhausted upon compliance with the statute—no more so than the motorist's obligation to take care in the driving of his or her vehicle is exhausted upon compliance with road traffic regulations'.[35]

(ii) Compliance with Mandatory Standards as an Element in Determining Whether a Medicinal Product is Defective

It is clear that conformity with mandatory standards in matters touching on the safety of a medicinal product will provide *evidence* that, in respect of pure design or composition matters, the requisite level of safety has been satisfied and that the product is not defective[36] Conversely, failure to conform to such standards will be evidence of defectiveness, since persons generally are entitled to expect conformity of products with such standards.[37]

---

[33] *Merck Sharp & Dohme (Australia) Pty Limited v Peterson* [2011] FCAFC 128, leave to appeal refused, [2012] HCATrans 105.

[34] Ibid [161]–[163], upholding (2010) 184 FCR 1, [792]–[795], Jessup J.

[35] (2010) 184 FCR 1, [794], Jessup J. See, further, the decision of the Ontario Superior Court of Justice in *Anderson v St Jude Medical Inc* 2012 CarswellOnt 8061, 2012 ONSC 3660. While holding that compliance with regulatory and industry standards can provide useful evidence of reasonable conduct, it was held that this was not necessarily extensive with the standard of care: ibid [101], citing *Ryan v Victoria (City)* (1999) 168 DLR (4th) 513, [29]. The trial judge relied on regulatory approval of the Silzone valve by Health Canada and the FDA as corroborating evidence of the defendants' experts' opinions that the testing of the valve met industry and regulatory standards: ibid [181]. Thus the trial judge was not using regulatory approval to displace the common law standard of care, but was using it as corroborative evidence of expert opinions of the defendants.

[36] In the US, compliance with a relevant government standard is generally regarded as probative of non-defectiveness: *Miller v Lee Apparel Co* 881 P 2d 576, 583–85 (Kan App 1994) (product complying with Federal flammability standards is presumed non-defective unless plaintiff rebuts presumption by proving reasonably prudent manufacturer could and would have taken additional safety standards); *Kaufman v Meditec, Inc* 353 NW 2d 297, 301 (ND 1984) (statutory rebuttable presumption that a product is non-defective where the alleged defect or designs were in conformity with government standards established for that industry).

[37] In the US, breach of such standards may be effectively equated with defectiveness: *Elsworth v Beech Aircraft* 691 P 2d 630, 636–37 (Cal 1984) (FAA standards). The *Restatement, Third, Torts: Products Liability* § 4(a) provides that the non-compliance of a product 'with an applicable product safety statute or administrative regulation

In *Richardson v LRC Products Ltd*,[38] in holding that it had not been proved that a particular condom was defective, Ian Kennedy J placed reliance on evidence which had demonstrated that in a large-scale trial in the United States, condoms had failed inexplicably under American standards, and also on evidence that the defendants' condoms were manufactured to a standard in excess of the relevant British standard.[39]

In particular, however, whereas evidence of conformity with standards supports a finding that a product has achieved an acceptable level of safety it does not follow that the same is true of evidence of industry standards laying down failure rates within quality control systems which result in the production of a predictable number of defective products.[40] However, this is not to say that such general statistics point to there being a defect in any *given* product (whether a condom or a bottle or whatever) since the claimant must establish that this is so. It seems that in *Richardson* the likelihood was that the ozone cracking in the condom had occurred after the fracture and was not the cause of it.

Whilst compliance with mandatory standards is relevant, it does not provide an automatic defence; this is in part due to regulations and standards being seen as minimum and not optimum standards.[41] It is submitted that the Full Federal Court of Australia's emphasis in *Merck Sharp & Dohme (Australia) Pty Limited v Peterson*[42] on medicines legislation as establishing minimal and not optimal standards is highly instructive, in that as well as emphasising that compliance with such standards does not foreclose the issues of reasonable safety and reasonable care in negligence, it suggests that when one examines the question of whether compliance with medicines regulations or standards should preclude a medicinal product from being found defective under the strict liability provisions of the Consumer Protection Act 1987, such standards would not *necessarily* reflect the optimum standard that persons generally would be entitled to expect.[43] Nevertheless, as has been previously noted, while mere compliance with the Human Medicines Regulations 2012 is not a defence to liability under the Consumer Protection Act 1987, it will often be strong evidence that the consumer expectation test is satisfied. There thus remains some support for the view that once the licensing authority has given approval to the drug, based on its safety, quality and efficacy, and providing a manufacturer has disclosed all information that reasonably bears on the drug's safety, such a drug could probably not be 'defective' under the 1987 Act.[44] This position is consistent with decisions from German courts which hold that while compliance with regulations and standards does not of itself preclude the

---

renders the product defective [in design or by virtue of inadequate instructions or warnings] with respect to the risks sought to be reduced by the statute or regulation'. This rule is based on the policy that designs and warnings which fail to comply with applicable safety standards established by statute or regulation are defective. Since design and marketing decisions are made before distribution to users and consumers, the manufacturer can defer sale until statutory or regulatory compliance is achieved: see comment *d*.

[38] *Richardson v LRC Products Ltd* [2000] Lloyd's Rep Med 280.
[39] Ibid 285.
[40] Miller, *Product Liability and Safety Encyclopaedia*, Div III, para 255.
[41] G Howells in Howells (ed), *The Law of Product Liability*, 2nd edn, para 4.172, citing the view of an Austrian Court, KG Ried im Innkreis, 17 March 1992, R 51/92.
[42] [2011] FCAFC 128, [161]–[163] leave to appeal refused, [2012] HCATrans 105, upholding [2010] 184 FCR 1, [792]–[795], Jessup J.
[43] G Howells in Howells (ed), *The Law of Product Liability*, 2nd edn, para 4.172, citing the view of an Austrian Court, KG Ried im Innkreis, 17 March 1992, R 51/92.
[44] C Newdick, 'The Impact of Licensing Authority Approval on Pharmaceutical Product Liability: A Survey of American and UK Law' (1992) 47 *Food & Drug Law Journal* 41, 53–54.

finding of a design defect, such compliance is *indicative* of the fact that a product is as safe as could be legitimately expected.[45] That said, if the claim concerned a known danger that the licensing authority had not been notified of, or which had been misrepresented, a presumption might arise that the medicinal product was defective. This presumption could also apply to risks that became known at a post-marketing authorisation stage, but which were not communicated to the licensing authority: such an approach could help incentivise prompt and full disclosure on the part of the pharmaceutical manufacturer.[46]

This is also consistent with the position in the United States, where the *Restatement, Third, Torts: Products Liability* § 4(b), provides that compliance of a product with an applicable product safety statute or administrative regulation 'is properly considered in determining whether the product is defective with respect to the risks sought to be reduced by the statute or regulation, but compliance does not preclude as a matter of law a finding of product defect'. Subsection (b) reflects the view that the majority of product safety statutes or regulations set only *minimum* standards, establishing a floor of safety below which product sellers fall only at their peril. They leave open, however, the question of whether a higher standard of public safety should be applied.[47] Thus mere compliance with warning standards or regulations as to warnings, such as those issued by the United States Food and Drug Administration (FDA), may not be sufficient to protect the manufacturer from a claim based on an inadequate warning, if a finder of fact concludes that a more effective warning was necessary. As the Californian Supreme Court stated in *Stevens v Parke, Davis & Co*, '[t]he warnings required by such agencies may only be minimal in nature and when the manufacturer or supplier knows of, or has reason to know of, greater dangers not included in the warning, its duty to warn may not be fulfilled'.[48] Virtually all State legislatures and courts that have addressed compliance with FDA standards have assigned conformity with no or minimal significance,[49] on the grounds that the FDA sets minimum standards for drug manufacturers.[50] However, a small but increasing number of legislatures and courts have afforded compliance greater relevance. Such considerations have restricted exposure of manufacturers to liability for allegedly defective products.[51]

---

[45] Decision of Cologne Court of Appeal, noted by S Lenze and D Vierheilig, 'Life tastes good: the German Coca-Cola and liquorice litigation' (2005) 21 *European Product Liability Review* 34, 35–36; Hamm Court of Appeal, 27 January 2002, 311 116/00 ('Log Flame'); Dusseldorf Court of Appeal, 20 December 2002, 14 u/99/02 ('Mars Bar') (reported on the British Institute of International and Comparative Law Product Liability Forum Database). Cf the decision of the Swiss Supreme Court that the owner of a building was liable for injuries caused by a malfunctioning elevator, despite compliance with the product's technical and safety standards: Case 4C 386/2005, noted in L Wyss, 'The Role of Product Safety Standards as a Defence to Product Liability Claims' (2006) 22 *European Product Liability Review* 39.

[46] C Newdick, 'The Impact of Licensing Authority Approval on Pharmaceutical Product Liability: A Survey of American and UK Law' (1992) 47 *Food & Drug Law Journal* 41, 57.

[47] Comment *e*.

[48] 507 P 2d 653, 661 (Cal 1973).

[49] C Tobias, 'FDA Regulatory Compliance Reconsidered' (2008) 93 *Cornell Law Review* 1003, 1015–17.

[50] See *Edwards v Basel* 933 P 2d 298, 302 (Okla 1997) ('[T]he FDA sets minimum standards for drug manufacturers as to design and warnings ... We conclude that compliance with these minimum standards does not necessarily complete the manufacturer's duty'); *Hill v Searl Laboratories* 884 F 2d 1064, 1068 (8th Cir 1989) ('FDA approval is not a shield to liability ... FDA regulations are generally minimal standards of conduct'); *Cartwright v Pfizer, Inc* 369 F Supp 2d 876, 882 (ED Tex 2005) ('The Food, Drug, and Cosmetics Act and the FDA's regulations 'merely set minimum standards with which manufacturers must comply').

[51] C Tobias, 'FDA Regulatory Compliance Reconsidered' (2008) 93 *Cornell Law Review* 1003, 1025–27, 1031; *Sims v Washex Machinery Corp* 932 SW 2d 559, 565 (Tex App 1995); *Lorenz v Celotex Corp* 896 F 2d 148, 150–51 (5th Cir 1990) (compliance with government safety standards is strong and substantial evidence, although not

III. DEFECT ATTRIBUTABLE TO MANDATORY STATUTORY
OR COMMUNITY REQUIREMENTS

By section 4(1)(a) of the 1987 Act the person proceeded against has a defence on proving 'that the defect is attributable to compliance with any requirement imposed by or under any enactment or with any Community obligation'. The equivalent provision in Article 7(d) of the Directive provides a defence on proving 'that the defect is due to compliance of the product with mandatory regulations issued by the public authorities'. While at one stage in the development of the draft Directive, it appeared that the fact of complying with regulations or a recognised standard might provide a defence to the manufacturer,[52] after amendment of the wording the section 4(1)(a) defence is narrower in scope. The defect must be 'attributable to' compliance with the relevant requirement 'imposed by or under any enactment or with any Community obligation'.[53] The position was explained by Lord Lucas when the Consumer Protection Bill was in its Committee stage in the House of Lords. According to his Lordship:[54]

> The purpose of the subsection we are discussing is to allow the producer of a defective product a defence if the defect in the product was solely due to compliance by the producer with either a United Kingdom enactment or with a Community obligation. This is a very strict defence and is intended to cover the situation, which I believe would be against the law of possibility, where the producer of a product has made a defective product because of the inevitable result of compliance with a national or Community law. It does not mean that compliance with a safety regulation would be a complete defence.[55]

The defence will therefore not operate unless the defect was the *inevitable* result of compliance with a statutory requirement.[56] It is difficult to imagine realistic circumstances in which such a tight test might be met, but one possible hypothetical example would be where the licensing authority refuses to permit the marketing authorisation holder to incorporate a warning in his prescribing information or where the precise form of warning is mandated by the authorities pursuant to a statutory power, leaving the producer with no discretion

---

conclusive, that a product is not defective). In the area of direct-to-consumer advertising of pharmaceuticals, and 'absent deliberate concealment or nondisclosure of after-acquired knowledge' of adverse effects, compliance with FDA standards should be 'virtually dispositive' and compelling evidence that a manufacturer has satisfied its duty to warn a consumer about potentially harmful side effects of its products: *Perez v Wyeth Laboratories Inc* 734 A 2d 1245, 1259 (NJ 1999).

[52] I Dodds-Smith, M Spencer and J Bore, 'Product Liability for Medicinal Products' in MJ Powers, NH Harris and A Barton (eds), *Clinical Negligence*, 4th edn (London, Tottel Publishing, 2008) para 24.61.

[53] This form of words clearly covers secondary legislation made under the authority of statute and mandatory requirements imposed by public authorities acting under statutory authority. Where the defendant has complied with a Community 'obligation' which has not been transposed timeously into national law (and is not directly applicable) s 4(1)(a) is, it seems, unavailable as a defence.

[54] *Hansard*, HL Deb (series 5) vol 483, col 804 (19 January 1987).

[55] Cf the additional language used in the implementing provisions in French law (Art 1386-10 of the French Civil Code) to emphasise the limited nature of the Art 7(d) defence, stressing that a defect may be found notwithstanding that the relevant product has been manufactured in accordance with existing trade standards or 'was the subject of an administrative authorisation': noted in D Fairgrieve and G Howells, 'Rethinking Product Liability: A Missing Element in the European Commission's Third Review of the European Product Liability Directive' (2007) 70 *Modern Law Review* 962, 972.

[56] I Dodds-Smith, M Spencer and J Bore, 'Product Liability for Medicinal Products' in MJ Powers, NH Harris and A Barton (eds), *Clinical Negligence*, 4th edn (London, Tottel Publishing, 2008) para 24.60.

as to whether the warning is effective.[57] No case has as yet been litigated to judgment on the proper interpretation of Article 7(d). However, in December 1993 and January 1994, two batches of immunoglobulin manufactured by Baxter Healthcare and imported into England by its UK subsidiary were contaminated with hepatitis C. Several persons suffering primary immunodeficiency were infected by the virus, and pursued claims. It was asserted by the defendants' insurers that the presence of the hepatitis C virus was attributable to a manufacturing requirement of the FDA. They were persuaded that this was inadequate to attract the protection of Article 7(d), and the cases were settled without proceedings.[58]

IV. FEDERAL PREEMPTION AND PRESCRIPTION DRUGS

A. Nature and Importance of the Doctrine

In the United States, by far the most significant attempt to eliminate product liability claims involving drugs has been through the doctrine of federal preemption. Under the Supremacy Clause of the United States Constitution,[59] federal law preempts State law when the two conflict. Its importance lies in the fact that it 'is an extraordinarily powerful defence'[60] which may eliminate all product liability claims involving a particular drug or even claims involving entire categories of drugs.[61] The doctrine is predicated on a similar basis to a defence of compliance with regulatory standards, namely that since the FDA determines the safety and efficacy of drugs and their labelling, and is equipped with the power to act if new information emerges over time, a lay jury should be prevented from second-guessing the expert decisions of the FDA by stating that a drug is defective or its accompanying warning inadequate.[62] However, while the doctrine of preemption is powerful it is in many ways inscrutable. As Professor Owen eloquently explains:

> [I]t is a formless and elusive creature, based on ephemeral notions of federalism and the oft-obscure intent of Congress, that vacillates according to shifting political sentiments of the courts—views on federal versus states' rights, on Congress versus the courts, and on regulatory versus product liability law.[63]

B. The Preemption Taxonomy

Different forms of preemption are contingent on the nature of the conflict between State and federal law. The first type of preemption, *express* preemption, applies when Congress

---

[57] Ibid para 24.61.

[58] M Mildred, 'Pharmaceutical Products: The Relationship Between Regulatory Approval and the Existence of a Defect' [2007] *European Business Law Review* 1267, 1271–72.

[59] US Constitution art VI, cl 2.

[60] See, M Hermann and DB Alden, *Drug and Device Litigation Strategy* (Oxford, Oxford University Press, 2012) 317.

[61] Ibid 317–18.

[62] Ibid 318.

[63] DG Owen, *Products Liability Law*, 2nd edn (St Paul, MN, Thomson/West, 2008) § 14.4, 939.

declares through a statutory provision that particular State law claims are to be preempted.[64] The second type of preemption, *implied* preemption invalidates State laws which conflict with a regulatory regime. Such conflict transpires when compliance with both federal and State law is either 'impossible' or 'stands as an obstacle' to the full purposes and objectives of federal law.[65] The third type of preemption, *field* preemption occurs when Congress has taken exclusive control over an entire regulatory subject which is so complete and 'so pervasive as to make reasonable the inference that Congress left no room for the States to supplement it'.[66] In the context of pharmaceutical product liability litigation, express preemption provisions govern vaccines[67] and over-the-counter drugs,[68] but not prescription drugs, since with the latter there is no express provision in the Federal Food, Drug, and Cosmetic Act.[69] Accordingly, in the context of prescription drugs, other than the scenario of a regulation having preemptive effect, only implied preemption is potentially available.

C. Presumption Against Preemption

Prior to 2002, preemption was rarely accepted in personal injury claims involving prescription drugs.[70] The view of the FDA was that its regulatory efforts could coexist with State law damage claims by consumers injured by drugs, since State damages litigation acted as

---

[64] See, eg *Jones v Rath Packing Co* 430 US 519, 525 (1977); *Shaw v Delta Air Lines, Inc* 463 US 85, 95–98 (1983). State law is expressly preempted '[w]hen Congress has considered the issue of preemption and has included in the enacted legislation a provision explicitly addressing that issue, and when that provision provides a "reliable indicium of congressional intent with respect to state authority"[.]': *Cipollone v Liggett Group, Inc* 505 US 504, 517 (1992).

[65] See *Buckman Co v Plaintiffs' Legal Committee* 531 US 341, 358 (2001) (Supreme Court held State law claims conflicted with federal law since 'the federal statutory scheme amply empowers the FDA to punish and deter fraud against the Administration, and that this authority is used by the administration to achieve a somewhat delicate balance of statutory objectives'); *Geier v American Honda Motor Co, Inc* 529 US 861 (2000) (Supreme Court held State tort claims based on Honda's failure to install airbags conflicted with a federal regulation that did not require airbags for all cases. Since the plaintiff's claim was that car manufacturers had a duty to install airbags, it presented an obstacle to achieving 'the variety and mix of devices that the federal regulation sought': ibid 881.

[66] *Rice v Santa Fe Elevator Corp* 331 US 218, 230 (1947).

[67] See the National Childhood Vaccine Injury Compensation Act of 1986 42 USC §§ 300aa-22(b)(1), which preempts all State law design defect claims against manufacturers for injury or death caused by vaccine side effects: *Bruesewitz v Wyeth LLC* 131 S Ct 1068, 1082 (2011). For criticism of this decision as the finding of preemption in a 'hyper-textual analysis', assessing Congressional intent solely through the text of express preemption, see Mary J Davis, 'The Case Against Preemption: Vaccines and Uncertainty' (2011) 8 *Indiana Health Law Review* 293, 307, 313.

[68] Food and Drug Administration Modernization Act of 1997, Pub L No 105-115, § 751, 111 Stat 2296, 2374 (1997), codified as amended at 21 USC §379r; see, further, M Hermann and DB Alden, *Drug and Device Litigation Strategy* (Oxford, Oxford University Press, 2012) 346–48.

[69] In contrast to the Food, Drug and Cosmetic Act, which provides no express preemption provision, the Medical Device Amendments Act of 1976 (MDA) expressly preempts inconsistent State law by providing that a State shall not establish or continue in effect any requirement for a medical device 'which is different from, or in addition to', any federal law requirement 'applicable ... to the device': 21 USC § 360k(a). The Supreme Court has ruled that the use of such provisions in a preemption clause, expressly preempting State 'requirements' can preempt products liability claims that would, if allowed, establish a form of common law safety standard different from that imposed under federal law: *Riegel v Medtronic, Inc* 522 US 312, 128 S Ct 999, 1007–08 (2008); *Cipollone v Liggett Group, Inc* 505 US 504, 521 (1992); and, further, DG Owen, *Products Liability Law*, 2nd edn (St Paul, MN, Thomson/West, 2008) § 14.4.

[70] See *Ohler v Purdue Pharma, LP*, 2002 WL 88945, at *13 fn 34 (ED La 2002); *Caraker v Sandoz Pharms Corp* 172 F Supp 2d 1018, 1036 (SD Ill 2001).

a 'feedback loop' by helping uncover and assess risks that were not apparent to the agency during the drug's approval process.[71]

D. Emergence of an FDA Preemption Policy

A shift in FDA policy began in 2002, when the FDA argued that a determination in civil litigation that an FDA-approved label failed adequately to warn of risks could force manufacturers to add warnings not approved by the FDA, thus rendering the product misbranded. Adverse State rulings could force manufactures to add warnings that had been rejected by the FDA, and consequently placing manufacturers in an untenable position of violating federal law to avoid State damages judgments.[72] The FDA thus submitted that the Federal Food Drug and Cosmetic Act (FDCA) impliedly preempted failure to warn claims based on product labelling. In the context of prescription drugs, a formalisation of this approach emerged when the FDA issued its final rule entitled 'Requirements on Content and Format of Labeling for Human Prescription Drug and Biological Products (the Rule).[73] In the Preamble to the Rule, the FDA addressed the issue of federal conflict preemption. Noting that the discussion represented 'the government's long standing views on preemption',[74] it stated that the 'FDA believes that under existing preemption principles, FDA approval of labeling under the act, whether it be in the old or new format, preempts conflicting or contrary state law'.[75] The FDA interpreted the FDCA as 'both a "floor" and a "ceiling"' for labelling content, and declared that 'the determination whether labeling revisions are necessary is, in the end, squarely and solely FDA's under the Act'.[76] It cautioned that State law actions, such as failure to warn claims, 'also threaten FDA's statutorily prescribed role as the expert Federal agency responsible for evaluating and regulating drugs'.[77] Stressing that it had the upper hand on expertise in this field, it observed that State law actions 'are not characterized by centralized expert evaluation of drug regulation issues', but instead 'encourage, and ... require lay judges and juries to second guess the assessment of benefits versus risks of a specific drug to the general public—the central role of FDA'.[78] While recognising that the FDA's position on the preemption of State law had 'not been the model of consistency'[79] some courts reasoned that its interpretation of the preemptive effect of the Food Drugs and Cosmetics Act and its corresponding federal regulations could change over time and was entitled to deference,[80] holding that FDA approval of a manufacturer's labelling impliedly

---

[71] DA Kessler and DC Vladeck, 'A Critical Examination of the FDA's Efforts to Preempt Failure-to-Warn Claims' (2008) 96 *Georgetown Law Journal* 461, 463.

[72] Ibid.

[73] 71 Fed Reg 3922 (Jan 24, 2006).

[74] Ibid 3934.

[75] Ibid.

[76] Ibid 3934–35.

[77] Ibid 3935.

[78] Ibid.

[79] *Sykes v Glaxo-SmithKline* 484 F Supp 2d 289, 315 (ED Pa 2007); and, further, *Colacicco v Apotex, Inc* 432 F Supp 2d 514, 531(ED Pa, 2006), aff'd 521 F 3d 253 (3d Cir 2008); *In re Bextra & Celebrex Mktg Sales Practices & Products Liability Litigation*, 2006 WL 2374742 at *8(ND Cal 2006).

[80] See *Chevron USA, Inc v National Resources Defence Counsel, Inc*, 467 US 837, 844 (1984).

preempted State failure to warn claims.[81] Other courts rejected this position,[82] pointing to the existing FDA regulatory framework as permitting and indeed encouraging the addition of strengthened warnings.[83]

E. Rejection of the FDA Preemption Policy: *Wyeth v Levine*

(i) Introduction

These issues were addressed in a landmark decision of the Supreme Court, *Wyeth v Levine*,[84] where the FDA Preemption Policy was rejected in the context of State law product liability failure to warn claims.[85] In so doing, the Court stressed the role of State product liability law as a complementary, retrospective form of drug regulation, and 'an additional and important layer of consumer protection' serving a compensatory function distinct from federal regulation.[86]

The primary issue to be determined by the Supreme Court was whether the FDA's drug labelling judgements preempted 'state law product liability claims premised on the theory that different labeling judgments were necessary to make drugs reasonably safe for use'.[87] Wyeth manufactured the anti-nausea medicine, Phenergan (the brand name for promethazine hydrochloride), the injectable form of which could be administered intramuscularly or intravenously. Intravenous administration could be by either of two methods, viz the 'IV-push' method, whereby the drug was injected directly into a patient's vein, or the 'IV-drip' method, whereby the drug was introduced into a saline solution in a hanging intravenous bag and it slowly descended through a catheter inserted in a patient's vein. Phenergan is corrosive and intra-*arterial* blood exposure during administration causes irreversible gangrene.[88] A physician's assistant injected Diana Levine, a professional musician, with Phenergan by the riskier IV-push method and it entered her artery, causing her to develop gangrene and ultimately to lose her entire forearm.[89]

Having settled claims against the health care providers, Ms Levine brought a State tort law action for damages relying on both common law and strict liability theories. She alleged that Wyeth had failed to provide an adequate warning of the significant risks of

---

[81] *Sykes v Glaxo-SmithKline*, 484 F Supp 2d 289, 318 (ED Pa 2007); *Colacicco v Apotex, Inc* 432 F Supp 2d 514, 528–29, 537–38 (ED Pa 2006), aff'd 521 F 3d 253 (3d Cir 2008); *In re Bextra & Celebrex Mktg Sales Practices & Products Liability Litigation*, 2006 WL 2374742 at *12 (ND Cal 2006); *Ehlis v Shire Richwood, Inc* 233 F Supp 2d 1189, 1198 (DND 2002), aff'd on other grounds, 367 F 3d 1013 (8th Cir 2004).

[82] *In re Vioxx Products Liability Litigation* 501 F Supp 2d 776, 788–89 (ED La 2007); *In re Zyprexa Products Liability Litigation* 489 F Supp 2d 230, 273, 275 (EDNY 2007); *Levine v Wyeth* 944 A 2d 179, 193 (Vt 2006); *Coutu v Tracy*, 2006 WL 1314261 at *3–4 (RI Super Ct 2006); *Caraker v Sandoz Pharms Corp*, 172 F Supp 2d 1018, 1038–39 (SD Ill 2001); *Jackson v Pfizer, Inc* 432 F Supp 2d 964, 967, 2006 WL 1506886, at *4.

[83] *Levine v Wyeth* 944 A 2d 179, 185–86 (Vt 2006) (discussing use of 21 CFR §§ 314.70(c)(6)(iii)(A), (C)) (see below).

[84] *Wyeth v Levine* 129 S Ct 1187 (2009).

[85] Ibid 1204.

[86] Ibid 1193, 1202–3.

[87] Ibid 1193.

[88] Ibid 1191.

[89] Ibid. It entered into Levine's artery either because the needle penetrated an artery directly (inadvertent intra-arterial injection) or because the drug escaped from the vein into surrounding tissue (so-called 'pervascular extravasation') where it came into contact with arterial blood: ibid.

using the IV-push method of intravenous administration of Phenergan. Levine also offered evidence that the IV-push method should be contraindicated and that Phenergan should never be administered intravenously, even by the drip method.[90] The Vermont jury found Phenergan was a defective product as a result of inadequate warnings and instructions and that no intervening cause had broken the causal connection between the defective product and the plaintiff's injury, awarding damages for her pain and suffering, substantial medical expenses and the loss of her livelihood as a professional musician. The trial court entered judgment on the jury's verdict in Levine's favour, rejecting Wyeth's argument that the claims were preempted due to the FDA approval of the label.[91] The Vermont Supreme Court affirmed this ruling.[92] Wyeth made two separate preemption arguments before the United States Supreme Court. First, it argued that it would have been impossible for it to comply with the State law duty to modify Phenergan's labelling without violating federal law and, secondly, that recognition of Ms Levine's State tort action would create an 'obstacle to the accomplishment and execution of the full purposes and objectives of Congress', since 'it substitutes a lay jury's decision about labeling for the judgment of the FDA'.[93]

The United States Supreme Court also affirmed the jury's decision, finding that the FDA's approval of a warning label for Phenergan did not preempt Ms Levine's failure to warn claims, by rejecting on the basis that compliance with both federal and State requirements was not impossible,[94] and that such compliance would not obstruct the purposes and objectives of federal drug labelling regulation.[95] Preparatory to evaluating these two arguments, the Supreme Court stressed[96] that the two principles that guided its analysis were, first, that the purpose of Congress was 'the ultimate touchstone in every preemption case',[97] and secondly, the so-called presumption against preemption, viz that 'the historic police powers of the States were not to be superseded by a Federal Act unless that was the clear and manifest purpose of Congress',[98] which 'rest[ed] on the precept that the Constitution constrains the federal government from trampling on the reserved power of the state'.[99]

(ii) Impossibility Preemption

In rejecting Wyeth's claim that it was impossible for it to comply with both the State law duties underlying those claims and its federal labelling duties, the Court relied on the 'changes being effected' (CBE) regulation.[100] While generally a manufacturer may only change a drug label after the FDA approves a supplemental application, in certain circumstances the CBE regulation permits manufacturers to make certain labelling changes prior to receiving the FDA's approval. In particular, the CBE regulation permits manufacturers

---

[90] Ibid 1191–92.
[91] Ibid, 1191, 1193.
[92] *Levine v Wyeth* 944 A 2d 179, 184 (Vt 2006).
[93] 129 S Ct 1187, 1194 (2009).
[94] Ibid 1199, 1204.
[95] Ibid 1191, 1199, 1204–5. Stevens J delivered the opinion of the Court, which was joined by Kennedy, Souter, Ginsburg and Breyer, JJ. Thomas J filed an opinion concurring in the judgment and Alito J filed a dissenting opinion, which was joined by Roberts CJ and Scalia J.
[96] Ibid 1194–95.
[97] *Medtronic, Inc v Lohr* 518 US 470, 485 (1996).
[98] Ibid, citing *Rice v Santa Fe Elevator Corp* 331 US 218, 230 (1947).
[99] DG Owen, *Products Liability Law*, 2nd edn (St Paul, MN, Thomson/West, 2008) § 14.4, 943.
[100] 21 CFR §§ 314.70(c)(6)(iii)(A), (C).

to change a label without prior FDA approval if such changes reflect '*newly acquired information*', to 'add or strengthen a contraindication, warning, precaution, or adverse reaction' or to 'add or strengthen an instruction about dosage and administration ... intended to increase the safe use of the drug product'.[101] In holding that it was not impossible for Wyeth to comply with both federal and State requirements, the Court interpreted the 2008 version of the CBE regulation—which had made express the 'newly acquired information' limitation—as encompassing 'new analyses of previously submitted data'.[102] The Court explained that this 'newly acquired information' limitation accounted for the fact that 'risk information accumulates over time and that the same data may take on a different meaning in light of subsequent developments'.[103] While the record was limited concerning what newly acquired information Wyeth had or should have had concerning the risks of IV-push administration of Phenergan,[104] Ms Levine had presented 'evidence of at least 20 incidents prior to her injury in which a Phenergan injection resulted in gangrene and an amputation'.[105] After the first incident came to its attention in 1967, Wyeth had notified the FDA and had worked with the agency to change the Phenergan label. However, the Court concluded that Wyeth 'could have analyzed the accumulating data and added a stronger warning about IV-push administration of the drug'.[106] It also found that Wyeth could have unilaterally added a stronger warning about the IV-push administration of the drug via the CBE regulation, and that there was no evidence that the FDA would have rejected such a label change.[107] Contrary to the submissions of Wyeth, it remained 'a central premise of federal drug regulation that the manufacturer bore the ultimate responsibility for the content and adequacy of its label at all times'.[108] Observing that '[i]impossibility preemption is a demanding defense',[109] and that it would not find impossibility preemption 'absent clear evidence that the FDA would not have approved a change to [the drug's] label',[110] the Court found Wyeth had failed to demonstrate it was impossible to comply with both federal and State requirements.[111]

(iii) Obstacle to Purposes and Objectives

In rejecting Wyeth's second argument that compliance with State tort law duties to provide a stronger warning about IV-push administration would obstruct the purposes and

---

[101] 73 Fed Reg 49609.
[102] 129 S Ct 1187, 1197 (2009), citing 73 Fed Reg 49604.
[103] Ibid 1197.
[104] Ibid. This was the case since 'Wyeth did not argue before the trial court that such information was required for a CBE labelling change': ibid.
[105] Ibid.
[106] Ibid. Cf the contention that these facts per se 'do little to establish that there was "newly acquired information" after the FDA's 1981 approval of the Phenergan labelling': M Hermann, and DB Alden, *Drug and Device Litigation Strategy* (Oxford, Oxford University Press, 2012) 341, fn154.
[107] Ibid 1197–99. Wyeth would not have violated federal law governing unauthorised distribution (Phenergan was not a 'new drug' lacking an effective application) and misbranding (the mere alteration of an FDA-approved label was not a misbranding since misbranding focuses on the 'substance of the label'): ibid 1197.
[108] Ibid 1197–98.
[109] Ibid 1199.
[110] Ibid 1198. Cf where 'clear evidence' that FDA would have rejected a change to a drug's label: see *Dobbs v Wyeth Pharmaceuticals* 797 F Supp 2d 1264, 1277 (WD Okla 2011) (State law warnings preempted since the record reflected 'clear evidence that the FDA would have rejected a 2002 warning of suicidality for 53 year old Effexor patients').
[111] Ibid 1199.

objectives of federal drug labelling regulation,[112] the Court gave no deference to the FDA's view in the preamble to a 2006 FDA regulation governing the content and format of prescription drug labels that the FDCA was 'both a "floor" and a "ceiling"', so that 'FDA approval of labeling ... preempts conflicting or contrary State law'.[113] The Court assessed the objectives and purposes of the FDCA in respect of prescription drugs, concluding that the 2006 preamble was 'inherently suspect',[114] did not have the force of law[115] and did not merit deference[116] in view of: (1) the FDA's procedural failure to offer States or other interested parties notice or opportunity to comment on the preamble; (2) the fact that the preamble was at odds with the available evidence of Congressional intent; and (3) the fact that the preamble was inconsistent with the long-standing FDA position that State law offered 'an additional, and important, layer of consumer protection that complement[ed] FDA regulation'.[117]

By far the most significant of the three elements to the Court's analysis of the objectives and purposes of the FDCA is the third one, since it categorically defines the role of State product liability law as a complementary form of drug regulation. As the Court explained:

> The FDA has limited resources to monitor the 11,000 drugs on the market, and manufacturers have superior access to information about their drugs, especially in the postmarketing phase as new risks emerge. State tort suits uncover unknown drug hazards and provide incentives for drug manufacturers to disclose safety risks promptly. They also serve a distinct compensatory function that may motivate injured persons to come forward with information. Failure-to-warn actions, in particular, lend force to the FDCA's premise that manufacturers, not the FDA, bear primary responsibility for their drug labeling at all times. Thus, the FDA long maintained that state law offers an additional and important, layer of consumer protection that complements FDA regulation.[118]

The Court cited significant evidence of such 'limited resources' in the context of post-marketing drug safety,[119] and in emphasising the role of State law as a complement to the

---

[112] Ibid 1199, 1204–5.

[113] Ibid 1200, citing 71 Fed Reg 3934–35 (2006).

[114] Ibid 1201.

[115] Ibid 1203. Cf *Geier v American Honda Motor Co* 529 US 861, 881, 883 (2000).

[116] Ibid 1201, 1203.

[117] Ibid 1201–3; MJ Porter, 'The *Lohr* Decision: FDA Perspective and Position' (1997) 52 *Food & Drug Law Journal* 7, 10.

[118] Ibid 1202 (footnotes omitted). Cf *Riegel v Medtronic, Inc* 522 US 312, 128 S Ct 999, 1008 (2008) (criticising tort law as being 'less deserving of preservation' than other State regulations, and describing juries as incapable of balancing costs and benefits adequately since they 'see ... only the costs of a more dangerous design and [are] not concerned with [the] benefits' consumers reap by the manufacturer's design choices), and, in turn, the dissent in *Levine* of Alito J (joined by Roberts CJ and Scalia J), stating that juries are 'ill-equipped to perform the FDA's cost-benefit balancing function': 129 S Ct 1187, 1229 (2009).

[119] Ibid 1202, fn 11. See FDA Science Board, *Report of the Subcommittee on Science and Technology: FDA Science and Mission at Risk* 2, 6 (FDA Science Board, 2007); Alina Baciu, Kathleen Stratton and Sheila P Burke (eds), Institute of Medicine, *The Future of Drug Safety: Promoting and Protecting the Health of the Public* (The National Academies Press, 2007) 193–94 ('The [FDA] lacks the resources needed to accomplish its large and complex mission ... There is widespread agreement that resources for postmarketing drug safety work are especially inadequate and that resource limitations have hobbled the agency's ability to improve and expand this essential component of its mission'); United States Government Accountability Office (GAO), *Report to Congressional Requesters, Drug Safety: Improvement Needed in FDA's Postmarket Decision-making and Oversight Process* (GAO-06-402, 2006) 5. Most resources have been devoted to expediting the new drug review process at the premarketing stage: DA Kessler and DC Vladeck, 'A Critical Examination of the FDA's Efforts to Preempt Failure-to-Warn

FDA's mission of consumer protection it followed the position convincingly argued by previous commentators that this role was especially important, given the inability of the FDA to detect at the post-marketing stage unforeseen adverse effects of drugs and to take prompt and effective remedial action.[120] It supported the role of tort law in enhancing public safety by acting as a 'catalyst' in the generation of information about products, and hence an aid in the exposure of new dangers associated with them.[121]

The emphasis on tort law operating as a complementary form of drug regulation is highly significant in that it rejects the need for additional limits to contain its alleged excesses. It also recognises the inherent limitations of post-marketing surveillance of pre-scription drugs by allowing tort to return to its recognised pre-1992 role as a 'feedback loop',[122] enabling the uncovering and assessment of risks that were not apparent at the pre-marketing stage. It has been praised as demonstrating 'a welcome return to greater balance between the role of state tort law and the need to give federal regulation the breathing room that Congress intended, but not more'.[123] *Levine* also appears consistent with the important functions of tort law in the product liability arena, viz that of regulating product safety, compensation, enhancing the availability of risk information, corrective justice, and that of oversight of the regulatory process, a role particularly crucial in the context of drug regulation.[124] Notwithstanding the apparent logic of such a balanced approach, *Levine* has been subject to the trenchant criticism to the effect that the majority opinion of the Court delivered by Stevens J demonstrated a 'profound misunderstanding' of the 'historical arc' of the law of torts—in particular the huge expansion of State products liability law subsequent to the Second Restatement of Torts in 1965—and its relationship with preemption. This expansion, it is argued, has placed tort law and FDA policy on a 'collision course' in cases such as *Levine* and thus the majority opinion should be rejected.[125] However, it is submitted that Epstein's argument is flawed since in reality the judicial approach in respect

Claims' (2008) 96 *Georgetown Law Journal* 461, 486. But cf RA Epstein, 'What Tort Theory Tells Us About Federal Preemption: The Tragic Saga of *Wyeth v Levine*' (2010) 65 *NYU Annual Survey of American Law* 485, 490 (criticising Kessler and Vladeck for 'oversimplification of the basic situation', in that they fail to discuss the role of tort liability compounding the problem of the FDA in keeping drugs off the market for too long).

[120] See, especially, DA Kessler and DC Vladeck, 'A Critical Examination of the FDA's Efforts to Preempt Failure-to-Warn Claims' (2008) 96 *Georgetown Law Journal* 461, 463, 465–69, 471, 483–95.

[121] 129 S Ct 1187, 1203 (2009), citing *Bates v Dow Agrosciences LLC* (2005) 544 US 431, 451.

[122] DA Kessler and DC Vladeck, 'A Critical Examination of the FDA's Efforts to Preempt Failure-to-Warn Claims' (2008) 96 *Georgetown Law Journal* 461, 463.

[123] Mary J Davis, 'On Restating Products Liability Preemption' (2009) 74 *Brooklyn Law Review* 759, 776; MJ Davis, 'The Case Against Preemption: Vaccines and Uncertainty' (2011) 8 *Indiana Health Law Review* 293, 303 (referring to *Levine* as 'an important contribution to the continuing debate over the value of state tort law in the regulatory framework for pharmaceuticals').

[124] Ibid 777–79; and, further, Mary J Davis, 'The Battle Over Implied Preemption: Products Liability and the FDA' (2007) 48 *British Columbia Law Review* 1089, 1148–51, 1153–54 (the tort litigation system operates concurrently with the regulatory system as a means of providing oversight of the drug regulatory process; the products liability system 'is a critical component to create incentives for greater access to risk information to ensure the public's health').

[125] Richard A Epstein, 'What Tort Theory Tells Us About Federal Preemption: The Tragic Saga of *Wyeth v Levine*' (2010) 65 *NYU Annual Survey of American Law* 485, 490, 492, 521. In following the rationale of Alito J's dissent (see especially 129 S Ct 1187 at 1217–20, 1225–26, 1228–30) Epstein argues that since the case was one where responsibility to monitor the downstream risk of arterial injection lay exclusively with the physician's assistant, a claim for negligent supervision might lie exclusively with the physician, thus exculpating Wyeth in terms of liability and that the FDA is better than juries at the task of ensuring '[s]tability of expectations' in marketing drugs: (2010) 65 *NYU Annual Survey of American Law* 485, 516, 522.

of prescription drugs, in particular design defects, has been increasingly one of *limiting* products liability, and it has been convincingly argued that preemption in fact reflects this judicial outlook.[126] Despite Epstein's criticism, and his view that the argument that tort law must act as a supplement to FDA regulation is an 'oversimplification',[127] the majority in *Levine* had laid down a convincing marker to the FDA that its position on preemption was not legally justified. This position was reaffirmed by President Obama's Presidential Memorandum Regarding Preemption, which provided that 'preemption of State Law by executive departments and agencies should be undertaken only with full consideration of the legitimate prerogatives of the States and with a sufficient legal basis for preemption'.[128] After conducting a review of its existing regulations issued over a 10-year period that contained statements in regulatory preambles or codified provisions intended to preempt State law, the FDA appeared to have taken the heed of both the Memorandum and *Levine* in concluding that three regulatory preambles contained statements that were 'not legally justified'.[129]

F. Emergence of a Two-Tier Drug Liability System: *PLIVA v Mensing*

However, the view that tort law should continue to operate as a supplement to the federal regulation of prescription drugs has been seriously challenged in the context of generic drugs, which has established itself as an area where the preemption of State law tort claims will operate after *Levine*. In *PLIVA, Inc v Mensing*,[130] a case virtually identical to *Levine*, except that the drug in question (metoclopramide) was generic, the Supreme Court

---

[126] See Richard L Cupp Jr, 'Preemption's Rise (and Bit of a Fall) as Products Liability Reform: Wyeth, Riegel, Altria and the Restatement Third's Prescription Product Design Defect Standard' (2009) 74 *Brooklyn Law Review* 727, 728–34, 740–44, 756–58 (noting the 'restrictive tone' of § 6(c) *Restatement (Third) of Torts: Products Liability*, with its deference to federal regulation, the rationales for which overlap with the rationales used by the Supreme Court in the 1990s and most of 2000s to support its increasingly aggressive use of preemption analysis in prescription product decisions).

[127] Richard A Epstein, 'What Tort Theory Tells Us About Federal Preemption: The Tragic Saga of *Wyeth v Levine*' (2010) 65 *NYU Annual Survey American Law* 485, 490. For the argument that the product liability system in the US has become excessive in the context of pharmaceuticals, see RE Epstein, *Overdose: How Excessive Government Regulation Stifles Pharmaceutical Innovation* (New Haven CT, Yale University Press, 2006) 189–236 (describing the current system as 'a complex and faulty system of adjudication that chews up resources without providing any sensible way to reduce the number of adverse events in the first place': ibid 232, and supporting federal preemption on the basis that 'one system of regulation is the most that should be tolerated': ibid 201). See also the view that the effect of product liability in the US on the safety of pharmaceutical products is insignificant, and that market forces and the FDA work relatively well to discipline producers of unsafe drugs: AM Polinsky and S Shavell, 'The Uneasy Case for Product Liability' (2010) 123 *Harvard Law Review* 1438, 1475.

[128] Memorandum for the Heads of Executive Departments and Agencies, 74 Fed Reg 24693 (2009).

[129] 76 Fed Reg 61565 (2011). The preambles were to the 2006 rule entitled 'Requirements on Content and Format of Labeling for Human Prescription Drug and Biological Products', 71 Fed Reg 3922 (Jan 24, 2006) (already rendered nugatory by *Levine*: 129 S Ct 1187, 1200–1203 (2009)), and to two other rules, viz 'Exceptions or Alternatives to Labeling Requirements for Products Held by the Strategic National Stockpile' 72 FR 73589, 73595, Dec 28, 2007 and 'Supplemental Applications Proposing Labeling Changes for Approved Drugs, Biologics and Medical Devices' 73 FR 49603, 49605–49606, Aug 22, 2008 (the latter already addressed in *Levine*, where the Supreme Court had confirmed that the 2008 change did not affect its position on preemption: 129 S Ct 1187, 1196–97).

[130] *PLIVA, Inc v Mensing* 131 S Ct 2567 (2011) (the opinion of the Court was authored by Thomas J, and was joined in full by Roberts CJ, and Scalia and Alito JJ; Kennedy J joined Thomas J's opinion except for one part. Sotomayor J filed a dissenting opinion in which Ginsburg, Breyer and Kagan joined).

held that in respect of generic drugs, federal drug regulations directly conflict with and hence preclude State failure to warn claims.[131] The court found that the Hatch-Waxman Amendments,[132] which permitted a generic drug manufacturer to gain FDA approval by showing that its drug was equivalent to an already approved brand-name drug,[133] required generic drug manufacturers to have what the FDA called 'an ongoing federal duty of "sameness"' to make the warning labels of generic drugs conform with the FDA-approved labels of brand-name drugs.[134] In a classically skilled application of deference,[135] the Court determined that the FDA's views were 'controlling unless plainly erroneous or inconsistent with the regulation[s]'.[136] Accordingly, the Court rejected the plaintiffs' arguments that the generic manufacturers could have changed their labels through the 'changes-being-effected' (CBE) process, deferring to the FDA's interpretation of the CBE regulation as allowing 'changes to generic drug labels only when a generic drug manufacturer changes its label to match an updated brand-name label or to follow the FDA instructions'.[137] Since unilateral CBE changes to strengthen a generic drug's warning label would violate the statutes and regulations requiring 'sameness', the CBE process was not open to generic drug manufacturers for the sort of change required by State law.[138] The Court also rejected the plaintiffs' argument that the manufacturers could have used 'Dear Doctor' letters to provide additional warnings to prescribing physicians, deferring to the FDA's interpretation of such letters as labelling, and thus finding that any such letters had to be consistent with the brand-name drug's labelling.[139]

Addressing the question of preemption, the Court concluded that State and federal law conflicted since it would have been impossible for the generic manufacturers to comply with both State and federal requirements and thus the State tort claims were preempted.[140] The manufacturers could not satisfy their State law duty by unilaterally changing their labels without violating federal law. While the generic manufacturers could have complied with federal law by requesting FDA assistance in strengthening the corresponding brand-name label, such a request would not have satisfied their State law duty to provide adequate labelling.[141] As the Court put it:

> State law demanded a safer label; it did not instruct the manufacturers to communicate with the FDA about the possibility of a safer label.[142]

The Supreme Court rejected the plaintiffs' contention that generic drug manufacturers were required to ask the FDA for assistance in changing their labels to satisfy their federal affirmative defence of preemption by declaring that '[t]he question for "impossibility" is

---

[131]   Ibid 2572, 2577–78.

[132]   Drug Price Competition and Patent Term Restoration Act, 98 Stat 1585.

[133]   21 USC § 355(j)(2)(A)(v).

[134]   Ibid 2574.

[135]   Stacey B Lee, 'PLIVA v Mensing: Generic Consumers' Unfortunate Hand' (2012) XXII.2 *Yale Journal of Health Policy Law & Ethics* 208, 235.

[136]   131 S Ct 2567, 2575.

[137]   Ibid.

[138]   Ibid 2575–76.

[139]   Ibid 2576. The FDA asserted that the generic manufacturers could have proposed, and indeed were required to propose, stronger warning labels to the agency if they believed such warnings were necessary. Nonetheless, since the Court established preemption even assuming such a duty, it left this issue unresolved: ibid.

[140]   Ibid 2577–78, 2581.

[141]   Ibid 2577–78.

[142]   Ibid 2578.

whether the private party could independently do under federal law what state law required of it.[143] In rejecting the plaintiffs' argument, the Court held that when a party could not satisfy its State duties without the Federal Government's special permission and assistance, which was contingent on the exercise of judgement by a federal agency, that party could not independently satisfy those State duties for preemption purposes. Since State law imposed a duty on the manufacturers to take an action barred by federal law, viz altering the label, the plaintiffs' tort claims were preempted.[144] The Court distinguished *Levine* on the basis that the CBE regulation permitted a brand-name manufacturer like Wyeth to strengthen unilaterally its warning without prior FDA approval, in compliance with its State tort duty, while a generic drug manufacturer could not.[145] The direct conflict between federal and State law for generic drug labelling in *Mensing* was not present for brand-name manufacturers under *Levine*. The Court conceded that, from the plaintiffs' perspective, a finding of preemption in *Mensing* but not in *Levine* 'ma[de] little sense', since if the pharmacist had dispensed Reglan (the brand-name drug as opposed to the generic), their lawsuits would not have been preempted under *Levine*.[146] While the Court acknowledged 'the unfortunate hand that federal drug regulation ha[d] dealt' the patients and others who were similarly situated, it was not the Court's role 'to decide whether the statutory scheme established by Congress [was] unusual or even bizarre'.[147] The federal statutes and regulations applicable to brand-name manufacturers were 'meaningfully different'[148] from those applicable to generic drug manufacturers. It was the different regulation of generic drugs that allowed them to be brought more quickly and cheaply to the public. The Court refused to 'distort the Supremacy Clause in order to create similar pre-emption across a dissimilar statutory scheme', stressing that both Congress and the FDA retained the authority to change the law and regulations if they so desired.[149]

Of greatest concern in the Court's opinion in *Mensing* is that failure to hold generic drug manufacturers liable in tort for non-disclosure of known risks 'creates a gap in the parallel federal-state regulatory scheme'[150] which 'harbours the risk of a two tier drug liability system'.[151] This could result in insured patients insisting on the prescription by

---

[143] Ibid 2579.

[144] Ibid 2581. Thus, if the FDA required the defendants to seek approval to send a 'Dear Doctor' letter that provided updated label information, then the plaintiff's State law claim would be preempted. However, generic drug manufacturers need not seek out the FDA's approval when sending a 'Dear Doctor' letter that simply reiterates warnings already contained in the approved label. Claims that a defendant failed to send a letter that was 'consistent with and not contrary to' the brand-name labelling are not preempted by *Mensing*: *Brasley-Thrash v Teva Pharmaceuticals USA, Inc*, 2011 WL 4025734, at *2–*3 (SD Ala).

[145] Ibid. But cf the dissent of Sotomayor J, which argued that *Levine* did not stand for the proposition that it is impossible to comply with both federal and State law whenever federal agency approval is required. It noted that Wyeth's label change was contingent on FDA acceptance as the FDA retained 'authority to reject labeling changes made pursuant to the CBE regulation': ibid 2588, citing *Levine*, 129 S Ct 1187, 1199 (2009). Label changes to brand-name manufacturers such as Wyeth are subject to FDA review and acceptance. Moreover, even if *Levine* turned on the fact that the brand-named manufacturer could change its label unilaterally, Wyeth did *not* hold unilateral action to be a necessary condition in every case: 131 S Ct 2567, 2589–90.

[146] 131 S Ct 2567, 2581.

[147] Ibid 2581–82.

[148] Ibid 2582.

[149] Ibid.

[150] See 131 S Ct 2567, 2592 (2011) Sotomayor J (dissenting); Stacey B Lee, 'PLIVA v Mensing: Generic Consumers' Unfortunate Hand' (2012) XXII.2 *Yale Journal of Health Policy Law & Ethics* 208, 212, 241–42.

[151] Ina Brock, Lauren S Colton, Lindsay S Goldberg and Matthias Schweiger, 'Applicability of the pre-emption doctrine in US drug law based on the decision of the US Supreme Court in *PLIVA Inc v Mensing*' (2012) 46 *International Product Liability Review* 33, 36.

their doctors of brand-name drugs,[152] and a 'diminishing consumer confidence in the safety and effectiveness of generic drugs'.[153] As Sotomayor J convincingly argued in his dissenting opinion, the divergent treatment of brand-name and generic drugs results in both a compensation gap for injured plaintiffs as well as a deterrence gap, since legal incentives for generic drug manufacturers to strive for safety are eliminated.[154] *Mensing* has created an incentive for plaintiffs injured by the use of generic drugs with inadequate warnings to attempt to impose liability on the manufacturer of the counterpart brand-name drug.[155] It has also resulted in sophisticated attempts by plaintiffs to restrict the parameters of the exception.[156] However, these attempts to restrict the scope of the exception have recently been severely constrained by the Supreme Court. In *Mutual Pharmaceutical Co Inc v Bartlett*,[157] the Court, by a majority of 5:4, held that state law design defect claims that turn on the adequacy of a generic drug's warnings are preempted by federal law under *Mensing*.[158] The Court concluded that it was impossible for Mutual (a manufacturer of generic drugs) to comply with both its federal-law duty prohibiting it from unilaterally altering the label of the generic non-steroidal anti-inflammatory drug sulindac, and its

---

[152] Stacey B Lee, 'PLIVA v Mensing: Generic Consumers' Unfortunate Hand' (2012) XXII.2 *Yale Journal of Health Policy Law & Ethics* 208, 212, 241–42.

[153] Ibid 212, 240.

[154] See 131 S Ct 2567, 2592 (2011) Sotomayor J (dissenting); (2012) XXII.2 *Yale Journal of Health Policy Law & Ethics* 208, 212, 241–42.

[155] See the development of so-called 'innovator liability' in *Conte v Wyeth, Inc* 85 Cal Rptr 3d 299, 311–13 (Cal Ct App 2009) (brand-name drug manufacturer's duty to use due care when providing warnings extends to consumers whose doctors foreseeably rely on the brand-name product's labelling, when prescribing the generic equivalent), discussed in M Sean Laane and Kevin A Cline, 'Developments in Federal Pre-emption after PLIVA v Mensing', 30 August 2012, accessed at: www.internationallawoffice.com/newsletters/detail.aspx?g=b2f33321-99-db-44bb-b13b-464a85362395. This controversial new theory of innovator liability, rendering a brand-name drug manufacturer responsible for damages caused by generic drugs, has been applied by the Alabama Supreme Court: see *Wyeth, Inc v Weeks*, No 11011397, 2013 Ala LEXIS 2 (Ala Jan 11, 2013) at [*58]–[*60] (manufacturer of brand-name prescription drug may be held liable for fraud or misrepresentation based on statements it made in connection with the manufacture of the brand-name drug, by a plaintiff claiming physical injury caused by a generic drug manufactured by a different company). A Washington Legal Foundation Legal Opinion Letter authored by Victor Schwartz, Phil Goldberg and Gary Silverman has subjected *Weeks* to trenchant criticism (see 'Warning: Alabama Court's Blame-Shifting Pharma Decision Will Have Serious Side Effects', 8 February 2013 (describing the Court as allowing 'the "genie" of blaming one company for products made by a competitor out of a tightly sealed tort bottle')). See, further, VE Schwartz, P Goldberg & C Silverman, 'Warning: Shifting Liability to Manufacturers of Brand-Name Medicines When the Harm Was Allegedly Caused by Generic Drugs Has Severe Side Effects' (2013) 81 *Fordham Law Review* 1835; Editorial, 'The Threat of 'Innovator Liability'', *The Wall Street Journal*, 14 March 2013, A16.

[156] Cf *Demahy v SchwarzPharma, Inc* 702 F3d 177, 186–87 (5th Cir 2012) (design defect claims preempted); *Gross v Pfizer, Inc* 825 F Supp 2d 654, 659 (D Md 2011) (failure to warn claims preempted; rejection of plaintiff's argument that PLIVA could have simply stopped manufacturing metoclopramide and thus avoided violating either federal or State law); *Bowdrie v Sun Pharm Indus*, No 12-CV-853, 2012 US Dist LEXIS 161239 at **14–18 (EDNY Nov 9, 2012) (failure to warn claims preempted); *In re Darvocet, Darvon and Propoxyphene Products Liability Litigation*, 2012 WL718614 at *4 fn 8 (ED Ky March 5, 2012) (failure to update claims preempted), with *Bartlett v Mutual Pharma Co* 678 F 3d 30, 37–38 (1st Cir), cert granted, 133 S Ct 694 (2012) (design defect claims not preempted, as defendant could comply with both State and federal law by choosing not to make the drug), rv'd 133 SCt 2466 (2013); *Fisher v Pelstring* 817 F Supp 2d 791, 805 (DSC 2011) (failure to update claims not preempted; *Mensing* will not preempt claims where there is a potential deviation between generic and brand-name labelling consequent upon new FDA-approved warnings being added to the brand-name labelling but not being updated in a timely manner on the generic equivalent) and *Fulgenzi v PLIVA, Inc*, Case No 12-3504 (6th Cir March 13, 2013) 9 (failure to update claims not preempted).

[157] *Mutual Pharmaceutical Co Inc v Bartlett* 133 SCt 2466 (2013) (the opinion of the Court was authored by Alito J and was joined in full by Roberts CJ, Scalia, Kennedy and Thomas, JJ. Breyer J filed a dissenting opinion in which Kagan J joined. Sotomayor J filed a dissenting opinion in which Ginsburg J joined).

[158] Ibid 2470, 2473, 2477.

state law duty to render the drug safer by strengthening the warnings on the drug's label.[159] The Court rejected the reasoning of the First Circuit[160] that Mutual could escape the impossibility of complying with both its federal and state law duties by choosing to stop selling sulindac as being incompatible with the Court's preemption cases. These decisions had presumed that an actor seeking to satisfy both federal- and state-law obligations was not required to cease acting altogether.[161] If an option of ceasing to act defeated a claim of impossibility, it would render impossibility pre-emption '"all but meaningless"'.[162] In her dissenting judgment, Sotomayor J concluded that the majority's approach 'could have serious consequences for product safety'. In her view:[163]

> If manufacturers of products that require preapproval are given de facto immunity from design-defect liability, the public will have to rely exclusively on imperfect federal agencies with limited resources and sometimes limited legal authority to recall approved products. And consumers injured by those products will have no recourse.

The decision has already been subject to considerable criticism, with an Editorial in The New York Times describing it as one 'leav[ing] the regulation of generic drugs in a perilous state'.[164] Congressional response to the *Bartlett* ruling was swift, with a letter written by 7 US senators and representatives to FDA Commissioner Margaret Hamburg, urging it 'to expedite its consideration of revisions to the FDA's drug labeling regulations to enable manufacturers of generic drugs to update patient safety labeling in appropriate circumstances.'[165] Such changes were necessary to ensure that the public was 'adequately informed of the risks and benefits of prescription drugs, and that those who are injured by prescription drugs have the same legal rights as those who are injured by the brand-name versions of the same drugs'.[166]

There is much to be said for Mary Davis's argument in favour of a narrow application of the scope of the preemption doctrine in the case of pharmaceuticals, in order to preserve the role of the tort system as a complement to more formal regulatory action for

---

[159] Ibid 2473–2477.

[160] *Bartlett v Mutual Pharma Co* 678 F 3d 30, 37–38 (1st Cir 2012).

[161] *Mutual Pharmaceutical Co Inc v Bartlett* 133 SCt 2466, 2477–2478 (2013).

[162] Ibid 2477. In his dissenting opinion, Breyer J opined that it was 'not literally impossible for a company like petitioner to comply with conflicting state and federal law. A company can comply with both either by not doing business in the relevant State or by paying the state penalty, say damages, for failing to comply with, as here, a state-law tort standard': ibid, 2480–81. In her vigorous dissent, Sotomayor J described the extension of *Mensing* to preempt New Hampshire's law governing design defects with respect to generic drugs as unnecessary and unwise: ibid 2482. The majority's insistence that Mutual was required by New Hampshire's design defect law to strengthen its warning label was 'effectively recharacteris[ing] Barlett's design defect claim as a *de facto* failure to warn claim': ibid, 2486.This was notwithstanding the fact that a duty to redesign sulindac's label was not an element of New Hampshire design defect law: ibid 2488–91.

[163] Ibid 2495.

[164] Editorial, 'A Damaging Decision on Generic Drugs', *The New York Times*, 29 June 2013, A18.

[165] Letter from P Leahy, C Van Hollen, T Harkin, A Franken, B Braley, HA Waxman, and M Cartwright, to Doctor Margaret Hamburg, Commissioner, FDA, 24 June 2013, accessed at: http://vanhollen.house.gov/news/documentsingle.aspx?DocumentID=340315. See also the report of the consumer advocacy organization Public Citizen, which in the period January 2008 to March 2013 identified 53 drugs for which a black-box warning calling attention to serious or life-threatening risks was added after generic market entry. This Report describes generic drug manufacturers' 'inability under current regulations to update the labeling of their products' as 'a threat to the safety of prescription drugs, creating unnecessary risks to patients': 'Generic Drug Labeling: A report on serious warnings added to approved drugs and on generic drugs marketed without a brand-name equivalent', (Washington, DC, Public Citizen 2013) 1, 10, 25.

[166] Ibid.

responding to uncertainty surrounding risk information.[167] With the retirement of Justice Stevens, who had given the majority opinion in *Levine*, a different majority may well be emerging on the scope of preemption of state tort laws in the light of *Mensing*. This is certainly suggested by the extension of the *Mensing* exception to design defect claims in *Bartlett*. However, as Sotomayor J's dissent in *Bartlett* and the Congressional response to the decision makes clear, such a divergent treatment of brand-name and generic drugs does little to inspire consumer confidence in the safety of generics. Since the precise genesis of the preemption doctrine lies in the Supremacy Clause of the United States Constitution, it would seem to have little relevance to the EU. While it has been mooted that preemption might be adaptable to the European context, were the EMEA as a supranational body given powers to mandate product information in all Member States in all languages, and Article 7(a) amended to establish a defence where a producer could prove that its product had only been marketed with mandated information, it would arguably raise the same difficulties presented by a regulatory compliance defence.[168] In the light of the current emphasis on the reforms to pharmacovigilance legislation, and with preemption seen as a threat to pharmacovigilance incentives, there ought to be little appetite for such arguments. However, the pharmaceutical industry has been increasingly supportive of the introduction of a regulatory compliance defence into the Product Liability Directive, the arguments in favour of and against which we shall now explore.

V. A REGULATORY COMPLIANCE DEFENCE FOR MEDICINAL PRODUCTS

A. Introduction

The issue as to whether compliance with regulatory standards should provide a defence to liability for defective medicinal products under the Product Liability Directive has continued to command strong support from the pharmaceutical industry. This support has been documented in the 2003 Lovells study on product liability systems in the Member States of the EU,[169] and the two most recent five-yearly reports of the European Commission on the application of the Directive.[170] The Third Commission Report noted that a defence of regulatory compliance 'would apply to a product whose safety was closely regulated, provided that the product complied fully with the applicable regulations'.[171] However, no

---

[167] Mary J Davis, 'The Case Against Preemption: Vaccines and Uncertainty' (2011) 8 *Indiana Health Law Review* 293, 296, 315–16.

[168] Mark Mildred, 'Pharmaceutical Products: The Relationship between Regulatory Approval and the Existence of a Defect' [2007] *European Business Law Review* 1267, 1279–80.

[169] J Meltzer, R Freeman and S Thomson, *Product liability in the European Union: A Report for the European Commission*, MARKT/2001/11/D (Lovells, February 2003) vii, 51 (representatives of the pharmaceutical industry arguing strongly for the introduction of a defence of regulatory compliance, 'which would apply to a product whose safety was closely regulated, provided that the product complied fully with the applicable regulations', on the basis that 'it is not for the national civil courts to second guess or undermine regulations that deal comprehensively with the safety of particular products').

[170] Third Commission Report of 14 September 2006 on the Application of Dir 85/374 on liability for defective products, COM(2006) 496 final, p 11; Fourth Commission Report of 8 September 2011 on liability for defective products, COM(2011) 547 final, p 8.

[171] Third Commission Report of 14 September 2006 on the Application of Dir 85/374 on liability for defective products, COM(2006) 496 final, p 11.

view was expressed on the merits of such arguments or the legislative means by which such change to the Directive might be implemented.[172] In the Fourth Report, there was implied reiteration of support for a regulatory compliance defence from representatives of the pharmaceutical industry in Europe, who opined that the Directive 'does not sufficiently take into consideration that the medical products sector is very strictly regulated'.[173] In the light of this support from the pharmaceutical industry, it is necessary to weigh up the respective arguments in favour of and against a regulatory compliance defence for medicinal products.

B. Arguments in Favour of a Defence

(i) Risk of Overdeterrence

The principle argument in favour of a regulatory compliance defence,[174] which has emanated from the US experience, is that the overlap of regulation and tort law results in overdeterrence, which manifests itself in several undesirable ways; in particular, excessive liability and litigation costs. This, in turn, results in deterrence from research and development and restricts the availability of new and effective drugs, causes their withdrawal from the market and a loss of benefits to society, in addition to duplicated administrative costs through the overlap of dual systems.[175] Yet this argument appears somewhat outdated, since the experience of the last 20 years is that US courts have become increasingly conservative towards products liability in general and specifically liability for prescription products.[176] There is also no evidence in Europe that product liability claims have resulted in excessive

---

[172] M Mildred, 'Pharmaceutical Products: The Relationship between Regulatory Approval and the Existence of a Defect' [2007] *European Business Law Review* 1267. Since the Directive is one of maximum harmonisation, amendment of it would be required: ibid; see Case C-183/00 *Gonzalez Sanchez v Medicinia Asturiana SA* [2002] ECR I-3901, para 24; Case C-52/00 *Commission v France* [2002] ECR I-3827, para 24 and Case C-154/00 *Commission v Greece* [2002] ECR I-3879, para 20; Case C-402/03 *Skov v Bilka* [2006] ECR I-199, paras 22, 23, 44.

[173] Fourth Commission Report of 8 September 2011 on liability for defective products, COM(2011) 547 final, p 8. The Fourth Report betrays a misunderstanding of Article 7(d) of the Directive, which provides a defence on proving 'that the defect is due to compliance of the product with mandatory regulations issued by the public authorities' (see above, pp 144–45), by classifying Art 7(d) in a heading as a 'defence of regulatory compliance': ibid. The Fourth Report also noted the pharmaceutical industry's view that the fact that use of a medicinal product is generally subject to external examination by health professionals (including doctors, nurses or pharmacists) and that the producer does not have any control over the way in which medicines are prescribed or administered, 'should be taken into account when analysing the defect of the product and the producer's liability': ibid. While these comments may relate to the question of whether the learned intermediary rule is applicable under the Directive, they seem to bear little relation to the question of a regulatory compliance defence.

[174] The regulatory compliance defence has been described as 'the flip-side of preemption' since the courts use their own authority, rather than that of the Federal Government, to establish common law deference to the FDA's prescription drug regulatory scheme: Victor E Schwartz and Phil Goldberg, 'A Prescription For Drug Liability and Regulation' (2005) 50 *Oklahoma Law Review* 135, 174–75.

[175] American Law Institute Reporters' Study, *Enterprise Responsibility for Personal Injury Vol II: Approaches to Legal and Institutional Change* (American Law Institute, 1991) 86–89, 103; Michael D Green, 'Statutory Compliance and Tort Liability: Examining the Strongest Case' (1997) 30 *University of Michigan Journal of Law Reform* 461, 466–67.

[176] Richard L Cupp Jr, 'Preemption's Rise (and Bit of a Fall) as Products Liability Reform: Wyeth, Riegel, Altria and the Restatement Third's Prescription Product Design Defect Standard' (2009) 74 *Brooklyn Law Review* 727, 755–56. Cf the observation that 'the major empirical gap is the lack of systematic study of compensation patterns for medical product injuries': Steven Garber, 'Should We Give Up on Medical Product liability?', RAND Review, Summer 2004, accessed at: www.rand.org/publications/randreview/issues/summer2004/38.html.

costs to or the inhibition of research and development by pharmaceutical companies, or that there has been a shortfall in insurance capacity or increased premiums, since the overall volume of claims has been very modest in comparison with the US.[177]

(ii) Expertise of Regulatory Agencies with an Optimum Standard of Safety

Another justification for the regulatory compliance defence that emerges from the US is the 'superior institutional competence'[178] of the FDA in determining the appropriate level of safety accorded to pharmaceuticals,[179] together with its close regulation of the industry.[180] This is premised on the standard of safety being provided as optimum, rather than minimum standards[181]—a premise which has been subsequently rejected by the Supreme Court in *Levine*.[182]

(iii) Economic Efficiency

The RAND Corporation, in its report *Product Liability and the Economics of Pharmaceuticals and Medical Devices* supported the conclusion that a regulatory compliance defence would promote economic efficiency for drugs, provided four conditions were met, viz that FDA standards were efficient; that liability costs due to non-compliance were sufficient to induce compliance; that company decision-makers understood the standards; and that decision-makers were confident that the doctrine would be applied accurately.[183] In its view, a liability system approximating to these conditions would appear preferable to the current system by providing companies with substantial incentives for compliance with FDA regulations and providing plaintiffs and their attorneys with substantial incentives for discovering instances of non-compliance with FDA regulations that cause injuries.[184]

---

[177] M Mildred, 'Pharmaceutical Products: The Relationship between Regulatory Approval and the Existence of a Defect' [2007] *European Business Law Review* 1267, 1276–77. Drawing on more than 30 years' interest in the field, Professor Mildred submits the thesis that 'the costs inherent in the present system are tolerable', but explains that the evidence to support this argument is not publically available. He challenges the industry to produce detailed figures for damages paid and costs incurred (and cases where the prospect of liability has had a deterrent effect on the development of new medicinal products) to refute his thesis: ibid 1277, fn 48.

[178] C Tobias, 'FDA Regulatory Compliance Reconsidered' (2008) 93 *Cornell Law Review* 1003, 1027.

[179] Michael D Green, 'Statutory Compliance and Tort Liability: Examining the Strongest Case' (1997) 30 *University of Michigan Journal Law Reform* 461, 466–67; see, eg, *Ramirez v Plough, Inc* 863 P 2d 167, 174–75 (Cal 1993) (noting that 'legislative and administrative bodies are particularly well suited' for the task of determining the appropriateness of second language warnings).

[180] *Brown v Superior Court* 751 P 2d 470, 483, fn 12 (Cal 1988). It was observed over two decades ago by the American Law Institute Reporters' Study that prescription pharmaceuticals present the 'special combination of circumstances justifying' a regulatory compliance defence, since: (1) they have public health benefits that depend heavily on innovation; (2) the pharmaceutical regulatory regime 'carefully balances therapeutic risk and benefit' in approving each medical product; (3) there are some residual harms that inevitably cannot be prevented through liability or regulation; (4) there are 'pervasive reporting requirements', a 'detailed regime of regulatory controls', together with 'strong market incentives to generate safer products'; and (5) the activity is 'the manufacture and sale of uniform, nationally marketed products'. With a closely regulated product such as pharmaceuticals with important safety implications, 'the advantages of consistent regulation over case by case litigation are likely to be greatest': American Law Institute Reporters' Study, *Enterprise Responsibility for Personal Injury Vol II: Approaches to Legal and Institutional Change* (American Law Institute, 1991) 103–4.

[181] Ibid 467.

[182] 129 S Ct 1187, 1201, 1203 (2009).

[183] Steven Garber, *Product Liability and the Economics of Pharmaceuticals and Medical Devices* (Santa Monica, RAND, 1993) 193.

[184] Ibid. However, the RAND report conceded that incentives might be substantially weakened by protective orders which maintain the confidentiality of evidence of non-compliance discovered by plaintiffs: ibid fn 26.

C. Arguments Against a Defence

(i) Erosion of Existing Tort Incentives to Disclose Post-marketing Risks

The key concerns about the viability of a regulatory compliance defence are: the major role of the post-approval period in identifying new risks concerning drugs; the incorporation of that information into the drug's labelling; and the regulator's ability to monitor both manufacturer compliance and information provided by the adverse drug reaction process.[185] A regulatory compliance defence undercuts the goal of deterrence[186] by 'wip[ing] out' existing tort incentives, since the presence of the defence would mean manufacturers no longer have the incentive to seek labelling changes that would disclose additional post-marketing risks.[187] The existence of such a defence would also undercut the goal of compensation, resulting in the presence of a 'compensation void': this would arguably increase pressure on regulators to minimise injuries from products passing through the pre-marketing regulatory scheme, thus increasing regulatory lag and social costs.[188]

(ii) Deficiencies in Post-marketing Surveillance Systems

In addition, the FDA's 'limited ability' to enforce its post-approval marketing process has raised serious issues about a regulatory compliance defence.[189] The FDA's post-marketing surveillance programme has been subject to criticism over the last decade. Much of this criticism developed with the voluntary withdrawal in 2004 by Merck of Vioxx (rofecoxib), a non-steroidal anti-inflammatory drug (NSAID), after evidence emerged from placebo-controlled clinical trials suggesting that the drug caused fatal heart attacks and strokes, and that the FDA had failed to make the appropriate evaluation of risk–benefit.[190] This led to a loss of public confidence in the agency,[191] and at its request, the Institute of Medicine (IOM) of the National Academy of Sciences assessed the FDA's regulatory system and issued a report in 2007[192] on the future of drug safety, recommending a transformed safety system which had at its core a lifecycle approach to drug risk and benefit. This lifecycle

---

[185] Michael D Green, 'Statutory Compliance and Tort Liability: Examining the Strongest Case' (1997) 30 University of Michigan Journal Law Reform 461, 495–96, 499.

[186] C Tobias, 'FDA Regulatory Compliance Reconsidered' (2008) 93 Cornell Law Review 1003, 1021.

[187] Michael D Green, 'Statutory Compliance and Tort Liability: Examining the Strongest Case' (1997) 30 University of Michigan Journal of Law Reform 461, 502. Cf the view that the effect of product liability in the US on the safety of pharmaceutical products is insignificant, and that market forces and the FDA work relatively well to discipline producers of unsafe drugs: AM Polinsky and S Shavell, 'The Uneasy Case for Product Liability' (2010) 123 Harvard Law Review 1438, 1475.

[188] RL Rabin, 'Reassessing Regulatory Compliance' (2000) 88 Georgetown Law Journal 2049, 2076; M Mildred, 'Pharmaceutical Products: The Relationship Between Regulatory Approval and the Existence of a Defect' [2007] European Business Law Review 1267, 1278.

[189] Ibid 503.

[190] EJ Topol, 'Failing the public health-Rofecoxib, Merck, and the FDA' (2004) 351 New England Journal of Medicine 170–79; see, further, M Gilhooley, 'Vioxx's History and the Need for Better Procedures and Better Testing' (2007) 37 Seton Hall Law Review 941 and P Feldschreiber, L Mulcahy and S Day, 'Biostatistics and Causation in Medicinal Product Liability Suits' in R Goldberg (ed), Perspectives on Causation (Oxford, Hart Publishing, 2011) 185–86.

[191] M Gilhooley (above, n 179) (2007) 37 Seton Hall Law Review 941.

[192] A Baciu, K Stratton and SP Burke (eds), Institute of Medicine, The Future of Drug Safety: Promoting and Protecting the Health of the Public (National Academy Press, 2007) 4.

approach required the FDA to have continuous availability of new data and ongoing, active reassessment of risk and benefit, as well as regulatory authority that was strong both pre- and post-approval.[193] In this highly critical report, the IOM found that the drug safety system of the FDA was impaired by several factors,[194] viz: serious resource constraints that weakened the quality and quantity of science bearing on drug safety, resulting in unclear and unidentifiable risk–benefit analysis standards;[195] a suboptimal and dysfunctional organisational culture in the Center for Drug Evaluation and Research (CDER) at the FDA;[196] a lack of adequate statutory authority to compel product safety by pharmaceutical manufacturers;[197] financial dependence on the pharmaceutical industry;[198] and a lack of accountability and transparency to the public through a failure to communicate safety concerns in a timely and effective fashion.[199]

As similar level of criticism was levelled at the Medicines and Health Care Products Regulatory Agency (MHRA) in the UK, when in 2005 the House of Commons Health Select Committee report highlighted the inadequacy of the post-marketing surveillance system.[200] The report considered that the MHRA had insufficient resources for effective post-marketing surveillance and that the process appeared 'extremely passive'.[201] It recommended that the MHRA employ sufficient staff numbers to monitor recently licensed drugs and that they should 'investigate options for the development of more effective post-marketing surveillance systems'.[202]

Like its American counterpart, the MHRA also failed to make an appropriate evaluation of risk–benefit with the anti-depressant Seroxat (paroxetine). During post-marketing surveillance, several spontaneous anecdotal reports emerged of akisthesia (extreme agitation) and suicidal behaviour in children and adolescents prescribed the drug. Since it was difficult to distinguish between underlying depressive illness and drug-induced injury, both the manufacturer (at the time SmithKlineBeecham) and the regulators concluded that the epidemiological data were insufficient to demonstrate a safety signal strong enough to result in the drug's withdrawal. However, eventually sufficient evidence accrued to justify contraindication in children and adolescents, in addition to warnings on withdrawal

---

[193] Ibid 4.

[194] Ibid.

[195] Ibid 108, 193–94.

[196] Ibid 81–90.

[197] Ibid 155–57.

[198] Ibid 73–74, 155, 195–97.

[199] Ibid 178–79, 184–87. It has been noted that there has been a long history of complaints about the post-market surveillance system and that these go back to the 1960s at the latest: D Carpenter, *Reputation and Power: Organizational Image and Pharmaceutical Regulation at the FDA* (Princeton, NJ, Princeton University Press, 2010) 588–89, 634. Many of their conclusions 'have often revisited the perceived conflict between pre-market and post-market processes': ibid 589 and, further, 621–34.

[200] HC Health Select Committee, *The Influence of the Pharmaceutical Industry*, Fourth Report of Sessions 2004–05 (Stationary Office, 2005) paras 296–302, 312, 349. The inadequacy of the post-marketing surveillance system was attributed to the 'the lack of effective post-marketing investigation of drug benefits and harms in real life situations, and institutional indifference to the experience and reports of medicine users'. The emphasis on drug licensing and on the safety profiles of individual drugs had 'contributed to a dearth of information about the overall impact of drug induced illness in the community': ibid para 312.

[201] Ibid para 367.

[202] Ibid. See, further, Royal College of Physicians, *Innovating for Health: Patients, Physicians, the Pharmaceutical Industry and the NHS* (Working Party Report) (Royal College of Physicians, 2009) para 2.41 (recommending post-marketing surveillance to be integrated into routine clinical practice throughout the NHS).

effects, suicidal feelings and akisthesia.[203] The MHRA conducted an investigation into whether GlaxoSmithKline (the corporate successor to SmithKlineBeecham) had failed to notify the MHRA (licensing authority) of evidence of the increased risk of suicidal behaviour in children and adolescents under the age of 18 years, and whether a prosecution should be pursued for alleged breaches of medicinal product safety regulations. While it was conclusively established that the manufacturer had failed to disclose studies of the drug's effects in children, and that there were gaps in medicinal product safety regulations, it was ultimately decided by government lawyers that the case should not proceed to criminal prosecution.[204] This was followed by some trenchant academic criticism of the MHRA's failure to scrutinise licensing data as well as its post-marketing surveillance system.[205]

While in 2007 there was a significant increase in the FDA's power to require drug and biological product application holders unilaterally to make safety-related labelling changes on the basis of post-approval safety data,[206] continuing controversy emerged with the FDA's decision in September 2010 to restrict significantly the use of the diabetes drug Avandia (rosiglitazone)[207] in response to data suggesting an elevated risk of cardiovascular events, such as heart attack and stroke.[208] The US Senate Committee on Finance had earlier in the year expressed concern about the FDA's role in protecting patients in an ongoing Avandia clinical trial, when the Committee released a report on Avandia showing that its manufacturer, GlaxoSmithKline, had been aware of possible cardiac risks associated with the drug years before such evidence became public.[209] The FDA had already itself estimated that the drug caused approximately 83,000 excess heart attacks between 1999 and 2007, and in 2008 FDA officials had called the clinical trial 'unethical and exploitative of patients'.[210] While noting that the legislation in 2007 had given the FDA new tools to better protect patients from harm caused by drugs brought to market without sufficient safety oversight or consumer warnings, the Committee opined that the legislation had failed to fix a fundamental problem at the FDA, viz 'the imbalance between the office responsible for monitoring the safety of drugs after approval and the office that puts drugs on the market in the first

---

[203] P Feldschreiber, L Mulcahy and S Day, 'Biostatistics and Causation in Medicinal Product Liability Suits' in R Goldberg (ed), *Perspectives on Causation* (Oxford, Hart Publishing, 2011) 186.

[204] MHRA Investigation into Glaxosmithkline/Seroxat, 6 March 2008, accessed at: www.mhra.gov.uk/home/groups/es-policy/documents/websiteresources/con014155.pdf. For discussion of the investigation, and the decision not to prosecute, see L McGoey and E Jackson, 'Seroxat and the Suppression of Clinical Trial Data: Regulatory failure and the Uses of Legal Ambiguity' (2009) 35 *Journal of Medical Ethics* 107, 107–9; and further, E Jackson, *Law and the Regulation of Medicines* (Oxford/Portland, Hart Publishing, 2012) 108–11. The Regulations were subsequently amended: Medicines for Human Use (Marketing Authorisations) Regulations 1994, SI 1994/3144, Sch 3, para 6AA. See now, Human Medicines Regulations 2012, SI 2012/1916, reg 75(2),(4),(5).

[205] L McGoey and E Jackson, (2009) 35 *Journal of Medical Ethics* 107, 110–11.

[206] Section 505(o)(4) of the Federal Food, Drug, and Cosmetic Act (21 USC §§ 355(o)(4)), added by s 901 of the Food and Drug Administration Amendments Act of 2007. See further, CM Dickenson, 'Issues and Trends in Drug Product Labelling' in *Recent Developments in Food and Drug Law: 2012 Edition* (Thomson Reuters/Aspatore, 2011) 62–72.

[207] J Woodcock, Memorandum, Decision on continued marketing of rosiglitazone (Avandia, Avandamet, Avandaryl) ID: 2839558, 23 September 2010, available at: www.fda.gov/drugs/DrugSafety/PostmarketDrugSafetyInformationforPatientsandProviders/ucm226956.htm.

[208] SE Nissen and K Wolski, 'Effect of Rosiglitazone on the Risk of Myocardial Infarction and Death from Cardiovascular Causes' (2007) 356 *New England Journal of Medicine* 2457–71.

[209] Staff Report on GlaxoSmithKline and the Diabetes Drug Avandia. Prepared by the Staff of the Committee on Finance, United States Senate, January 2010, 11th Congress, 2d Session, Committee Print, S Prt 111-41.

[210] The United States Senate Committee on Finance, Press Release, 20 February 2010.

place'.[211] It was of little surprise that in 2012 the IOM continued to find the FDA's current approach to post-marketing surveillance insufficiently systematic and one which failed to ensure consistent assessment of benefits and risks of drugs over its lifecycle.[212] These concerns have been reiterated in the September 2012 Report to the President on Propelling Innovation in Drug Discovery, Development and Innovation,[213] which recommended the need to strengthen post-marketing surveillance and risk–benefit assessment by Congress providing an initial US$40 million per year to the FDA to expand post-marketing surveillance capability.[214]

Prompted by the increased burden of adverse drug reactions in the EU,[215] changes to pharmacovigilance legislation[216] have come into effect across the EU in 2012, as a consequence of changes set out in an EU Regulation[217] and a Directive.[218] The aim of this legislation is to improve the health of EU citizens by strengthening and rationalising pharmacovigilance, thereby reducing the burden of ADRs and optimising the use of medicinal products.[219] While the scope of changes is considerable, and includes the new extension of Risk Management Plans (RMPs) to all new medicinal product applications,[220] the centralisation of the recording and reporting of suspected ADRs in the EudraVigilance database,[221] and the creation of a new scientific committee, the Pharmacovigilance Risk Assessment

---

[211] Ibid.

[212] Institute of Medicine, *Ethical and Scientific Issues in Studying the Safety of Approved Drugs* (National Academies Press, 2012) 10, 90. In order to implement this lifecycle approach, the IOM recommended that the FDA require and maintain a comprehensive publically available and understandable Benefit and Risk Assessment Management Plan (BRAMP) to track the medicine's benefits and harms during its entire lifecycle: ibid 6, 110. The IOM suggested that in order to determine when post-marketing surveillance is required, the FDA should prospectively determine and publicly identify the risk factors associated with greater uncertainty about a drug's benefit–risk profile in the post-marketing setting; ibid 17, 112–13. Both recommendations reflect the influence of recent changes to EU pharmacovigilance (see below).

[213] *Report to the President on Propelling Innovation in Drug Discovery, Development and Innovation* (President's Council of Advisors on Science and Technology, 2012) 30–31

[214] Ibid xi, 40, 70. The objective is for this post-market surveillance 'to cover the US population in a rigorous active surveillance and evaluation program to identify and evaluate the potential benefits and risks of medical products and the populations at highest risk for adverse events': ibid 70.

[215] The public health burden of adverse drug reactions (ADRs) amounts to the death in hospital of 100,800– 197,000 annually in the EU. A reasonable estimate of the total societal cost of ADRs in the EU is 79 Billion Euros: Commission Staff Working Document, Accompanying document to the Proposal for a Regulation of the European Parliament and of the Council amending, as regards pharmacovigilance of medicinal products for human use, Regulation (EC) No 726/2004 laying down Community procedures for the authorisation and supervision of medicinal products for human and veterinary use and establishing a European Medicines Agency, and the Proposal for a Directive of the European Parliament and of the Council amending, as regards pharmacovigilance, Directive 2001/83/EC on the Community code relating to medicinal products for human use, IMPACT ASSESSMENT, Brussels, 10 December 2008SEC(2008) 2670, vol I, 12.

[216] See generally: www.mhra.gov.uk/Howweregulate/Medicines/Pharmacovigilancelegislation/index.htm. The legislation has been transposed into UK law in the Human Medicines Regulations 2012, SI 2012/1916, Part II.

[217] Regulation (EU) No 1235/2010 of the European Parliament and of the Council of 15 December 2010 amending, as regards pharmacovigilance of medicinal products for human use, Regulation (EC) No 726/2004 laying down Community procedures for the authorisation and supervision of medicinal products for human and veterinary use and establishing a European Medicines Agency, and Regulation (EC) No 1394/2007 on advanced therapy medicinal products [2010] OJ L348/1.

[218] Directive 2010/184/EU of the European Parliament and of the Council of 15 December 2010 amending, as regards pharmacovigilance, Directive 2001/83/EC on the Community code relating to medicinal products for human use [2010] OJ L348/74.

[219] IMPACT ASSESSMENT, Brussels, 10 December 2008 SEC(2008) 2670, vol I, 20.

[220] Directive 2001/83, Art 104(3)(d), 104a(2).

[221] Ibid Art 107. It will be a legal obligation for all reports of suspected adverse reactions to come centrally to the EudraVigilance database only: ibid.

Committee (PRAC),[222] such reforms have been subject to criticism.[223] It has also been argued that there is a need to separate drug approval from pharmacovigilance, since having both functions under a single body 'implies a sort of conflict of interest, quite apart from the enormous workload', and that what is required is a new drug safety evaluation agency for pharmacovigilance.[224] In any event, since the new pharmacovigilance scheme in Europe will be supported by no increase in resources, it is doubtful, given the existing lack of funding for pharmacovigilance,[225] that existing resources would be sufficient to monitor and ensure universal compliance.[226] Moreover, it would seem that the recent track record of failing to report suspected ADRs has not tailed off since 2007, and that the recent Avandia scandal suggests that pharmaceutical companies continue to be undeterred from unlawful behaviour.[227] The existence of a regulatory compliance defence would shift the inquiry to these issues of non-compliance, proof of which would add to the complexity and expense of the process.[228] In short, the regulatory compliance defence fails to address the implications of post-marketing surveillance.[229] Far from eliminating the role of the litigation system, it is submitted that Struve is correct in arguing for greater structural links to be made between it and the regulatory processes of the FDA and the EMEA.[230] The regulators should use each opportunity of litigation as an opportunity to reassess its determinations on drug safety.[231]

---

[222] Regulation (EC) No 726/2004, Art 56(1)(aa).

[223] B Goldacre, *Bad Pharma* (Fourth Estate, 2012) 161 (describing the legislation as 'a very mixed bag'); S Garattini and V Bertele, 'Anything new in EU pharmacovigilance?' (2011) 67 *European Journal of Clinical Pharmacology* 1199–1200 (criticising the failure to render the EudoVigilance database accessible to health professionals, scientists and the public; criticising the fact that the PRAC is not a completely independent body, since the final responsibility for issuing an opinion on a risk–benefit assessment remains with the Committee for Medicinal Products for Human Use (CHMP); and noting the lack of funding for pharmacovigilance, including the problem that raising the money for pharmacovigilance by empowering the agency to charge fees to marketing authorisation holders fails to guarantee sufficiently the EMA's independence); A Herxheimer, 'Looking at EU Pharmacovigilance' (2011) 67 *European Journal of Clinical Pharmacology* 1201–2; S Frau, M Font Pous and MR Luppino, 'Risk Management Plans: are they a tool for improving drug safety?'(2010) 66 *European Journal of Clinical Pharmacology* 785–90 (criticising poor communication of changes in risk identified from RMPs to practitioners and to the public, and 'the lack of publically available data regarding the most significant aspects of the RMPs', particularly in the area of additional pharmacovigilance activities).

[224] S Garattini and V Bertele, 'Rosiglitazone and the need for a new drug safety agency' (2010) 341 *British Medical Journal* c5506. There has been a criticism that the division of the FDA which approves new drugs (the Office of New Drugs) is also the office with legal authority over post-marketing and that this has created a conflict of interest in US drug regulation: D Carpenter, *Reputation and Power: Organizational Image and Pharmaceutical Regulation at the FDA* (Princeton, NJ, Princeton University Press, 2010) 630.

[225] A Herxheimer, 'Looking at EU Pharmacovigilance' (2011) 67 *European Journal of Clinical Pharmacology* 1201–2.

[226] Cf Michael D Green, 'Statutory Compliance and Tort Liability: Examining the Strongest Case'(1997) 30 *University of Michigan Journal of Law Reform* 461, 502.

[227] K Thomas and MS Schmidt, 'Glaxo Agrees to Pay $3 Billion in Fraud Settlement', *The New York Times*, 2 July 2012 (detailing GlaxoSmithKline's agreement to plead guilty to criminal charges and pay US$3 billion in fines for promoting two anti-depressant drugs (Paxil and Wellbutrin) for unapproved uses, and failing to report safety data about Avandia).

[228] M Mildred, 'Pharmaceutical Products: The Relationship between Regulatory Approval and the Existence of a Defect' [2007] *European Business Law Review* 1267, 1278. The point about non-compliance would need to be determined by the regulator on investigation or as a very complex issue at trial to which the regulator would not be a party: ibid.

[229] RL Rabin, 'Reassessing Regulatory Compliance' (2000) 88 *Georgetown Law Journal* 2049, 2077.

[230] CT Struve, 'The FDA and the Tort System: Postmarketing Surveillance, Compensation, and the Role of Litigation' (2005) 5 *Yale Journal of Health Policy & Ethics* 587, 592–93, 616, 618.

[231] Ibid 593, 662–66, 658–59. Note that in the EU, both health professionals and patients are now able to report suspected ADRs: Directive 2001/83, Art 107(h).

VI. CONCLUSION

This chapter has examined the question as to whether compliance with regulatory standards should protect pharmaceutical manufacturers from product liability suits.

It is submitted that the Full Federal Court of Australia's emphasis in *Merck Sharp & Dohme (Australia) Pty Limited v Peterson*[232] on medicines legislation as establishing minimal and not optimal standards is highly instructive. As well as emphasising that compliance with such standards does not foreclose the issues of reasonable safety and reasonable care in negligence, it suggests that when one examines the issue of whether compliance with medicines regulations or standards should preclude a medicinal product from being found as defective under the strict liability provisions of the Consumer Protection Act 1987, such standards would not *necessarily* reflect the optimum standard that persons generally would be entitled to expect.[233] Nevertheless, while mere compliance with the Human Medicines Regulations 2012 is not a defence to liability under the Consumer Protection Act 1987, it will often be strong evidence that the consumer expectation test is satisfied. There thus remains some support for the view that once the licensing authority has given approval to the drug, based on its safety, quality and efficacy, and providing a manufacturer has disclosed all information that reasonably bears on the drug's safety, such a drug could probably not be 'defective' under the 1987 Act. It has been noted that this position is consistent with decisions from German courts which hold that while compliance with regulations and standards does not of itself preclude the finding of a design defect, such compliance is *indicative* of the fact that a product is as safe as could be legitimately expected.[234] That said, if the claim concerned a known danger that the licensing authority had not been notified of, or which had been misrepresented, a presumption could arise that the medicinal product was defective. This presumption could also apply to risks that became known at a post-marketing authorisation stage, but which were not communicated to the licensing authority: such an approach could help incentivise prompt and full disclosure on the part of the pharmaceutical manufacturer.[235]

The issue of incentivisation of prompt and full disclosure of adverse effects through the availability of tort litigation remains an increasingly important issue. In the US, we have seen that the FDA Preemption Policy was rejected by the Supreme Court in *Levine* in the context of State law product liability failure to warn claims.[236] In so doing, the Court stressed the role of State product liability law as a complementary, retrospective form of drug regulation, and 'an additional and important layer of consumer protection' serving a compensatory function distinct from federal regulation. The emphasis on tort law

---

[232] [2011] FCAFC 128, [161]–[163], leave to appeal refused, [2012] HCATrans 105, upholding (2010) 184 FCR 1, [792]–[795], Jessup J.

[233] G Howells in Howells (ed), *The Law of Product Liability*, 2nd edn, para 4.172, citing the view of an Austrian Court, KG Ried im Innkreis, 17 March 1992, R 51/92.

[234] Decision of Cologne Court of Appeal, 7 September 2005, noted by S Lenze and D Vierheilig, 'Life tastes good: the German Coca-Cola and liquorice litigation' (2005) 21 *European Product Liability Review* 34, 35–36; Hamm Court of Appeal, 27 January 2002, 311 116/00 ('Log Flame'); Dusseldorf Court of Appeal, 20 December 2002, 14 u/99/02 ('Mars Bar') (reported on the British Institute of International and Comparative Law Product Liability Forum Database).

[235] C Newdick, 'The Impact of Licensing Authority Approval on Pharmaceutical Product Liability: A Survey of American and UK Law' (1992) 47 *Food & Drug Law Journal* 41, 57.

[236] Ibid 1204.

operating as a complementary form of drug regulation is highly significant in that it rejects the need for additional limits to reject its alleged excesses. It also recognises the inherent limitations of post-marketing surveillance of prescription drugs by allowing tort to return to its recognised pre-1992 role as a 'feedback loop',[237] enabling the uncovering and assessment of risks that were not apparent at the pre-marketing stage. However, the view that tort law should continue to operate as a supplement to the federal regulation of prescription drugs has been seriously challenged in the context of generic drugs in both *Mensing* and *Bartlett*, which have both permitted the establishment of an area where the preemption of State law tort claims will operate after *Levine*. The greatest concern with the Court's opinions in *Mensing* and *Bartlett* is that failure to hold generic drug manufacturers liable in tort for non-disclosure of known risks 'creates a gap in the parallel federal–state regulatory scheme'[238] which 'harbours the risk of a two tier drug liability system'.[239] In the light of the current emphasis on the reforms to pharmacovigilance legislation, and with preemption seen as a threat to pharmacovigilance incentives, there ought to be little appetite for such arguments in the UK and EU.

Nonetheless, the issue as to whether a compliance with regulatory standards should provide a defence to liability for defective medicinal products under the under the Product Liability Directive has continued to command strong support from the pharmaceutical industry. However, the key concerns about the viability of a regulatory compliance defence continue to be the major role of the post-approval period in identifying new risks concerning drugs, the incorporation of that information into the drug's labelling and the regulator's ability to monitor both manufacturer compliance and information provided by the adverse drug reaction process.[240] It is submitted that the recent track record of pharmaceutical companies failing to report suspected ADRs has not tailed off since 2007, and that the recent Avandia scandal suggests that pharmaceutical companies continue to be undeterred from unlawful behaviour. The existence of a regulatory compliance defence under the Directive would shift the inquiry to these issues of non-compliance, proof of which would add to the complexity and expense of the process. In short, the regulatory compliance defence fails to address the implications of post-marketing surveillance and should be rejected.

However, there is one controversial defence particularly associated with medicinal products which already exists in the Directive, the inclusion of which played a deciding part in the negotiation of the final text in 1985, namely the so-called development risk defence. It is to this defence that we now turn.

---

[237] DA Kessler and DC Vladeck, 'A Critical Examination of the FDA's Efforts to Preempt Failure-to-Warn Claims' (2008) 96 *Georgetown Law Journal* 461, 463.

[238] See 131 S Ct 2567, 2592 (2011) Sotomayor J (dissenting); Stacey B Lee, 'PLIVA v Mensing: Generic Consumers' Unfortunate Hand' (2012) vol XXII.2 *Yale Journal of Health Policy Law & Ethics* 208, 212, 241–42

[239] Ina Brock, Lauren S Colton, Lindsay S Goldberg and Matthias Schweiger, 'Applicability of the pre-emption doctrine in US drug law based on the decision of the US Supreme Court in *PLIVA Inc v Mensing*' (2012) 46 *International Product Liability Review* 33, 36.

[240] Michael D Green, 'Statutory Compliance and Tort Liability: Examining the Strongest Case' (1997) 30 *University of Michigan Journal of Law Reform* 461, 495–96, 499.

8

The Development Risk Defence and Medicinal Products

I. NATURE AND SCOPE OF THE DEFENCE

A. Introduction

The development risk defence has been one of the most controversial elements of the Product Liability Directive and the Consumer Protection Act 1987. The controversies surrounding it arise from the inability to foresee with certainty the long-term effects of technologically innovative products and the belief that producers should not be liable where dangers were genuinely unforeseeable.[1] Medicinal products, more than any other type of product, continue to exemplify this uncertainty,[2] since as new technologies such as genomics become more significant in drug discovery, fresh drug safety problems arise.[3] As a result of the concerns of several EU Member States about the impact of the Directive on innovative industries, the European Commission was forced to concede the inclusion of the defence.[4] The United Kingdom's identification with this position was clear from the outset. Indeed, during the last period of negotiation of the final text of the Directive in 1985, the then Conservative Government under Margaret Thatcher demanded that producers' interests be properly represented by its inclusion and it was only when it was included that the United Kingdom was willing to agree to the text of the Directive, which required unanimity under Article 100 EEC Treaty (now Article 115, TFEU) for its adoption.[5] This chapter examines the interpretation, scope and the impact of the defence in the context of medicinal products, including the meaning and implications of discoverability of defects, scientific and technical knowledge and the problem of known but undetectable defects.

---

[1] Commission Green Paper: *Liability for Defective Products*, Brussels, COM(1999) 396 final (28 July 1999), para 3.2, pp 22–25.

[2] R Goldberg, 'The Development Risk Defence and the European Court of Justice; Increased Injury Costs and the Supplementary Protection Certificate' in R Goldberg and J Lonbay (eds), *Pharmaceutical Medicine, Biotechnology and European Law* (Cambridge, Cambridge University Press, 2000) 194.

[3] M Emanuel, M Rawlins, G Duff and A Breckenridge, 'Thalidomide and its sequelae' (2012) 380 *Lancet* 781.

[4] G Howells and M Mildred, 'Is European Products Liability More Protective than the Restatement (Third) of Torts: Products Liability?' (1998) 65 *Tennessee Law Review* 985, 998.

[5] J Stapleton, 'Products Liability in the United Kingdom: The Myths of Reform' (1999) 34 *Texas International Law Journal* 45, 56–57.

B. Background and Definition

The European Commission and European Parliament were divided on the issue of the development risk defence. The European Commission supported liability for development risks, whereas the Parliament supported the existence of the defence. The first version of the proposed EEC Product Liability Directive established liability for development risks, by providing in Article 1 that: 'The producer of an article shall be liable for damage caused by a defect in the article, whether or not he knew or could have known of the defect'.[6] It continued: 'The producer shall be liable even if the article could not have been regarded as defective in the light of the scientific and technological development at the time when he put the article into circulation'.[7]

The Commission reaffirmed this 'steadfast refusal to exclude development risks'[8] in the Second Draft Directive[9] and in its Explanatory Memorandum to that Draft of September 1979,[10] in the face of opposition from the European Parliament in the form of a Resolution.[11] However, this position did not prevail, since in February 1982, at the final legislative stage of approval by the Council of Ministers, the Council's Permanent Representatives Committee (COREPER) worked out the basis for a compromise. In addition to declining explicitly to endorse blanket liability for development risks, COREPER allowed each Member State an option to introduce or maintain liability for such risks in particular product sectors.[12] The final revision of Article 1 omitted the words 'whether or

---

[6] First Proposal for a Council Directive relating to the Approximation of the Laws, Regulations and Administrative Provisions of the Member States Concerning Liability for Defective Products [1976] OJ C241/9, Art 1.

[7] Ibid. See also the Sixth Recital: 'Whereas liability cannot be excluded for those products which at the time when the producer put them into circulation could not have been regarded as defective according to the state of science and technology (development risks), since otherwise the consumer would be subjected without protection to the risk that the defectiveness of a product is discovered only during use': ibid.

[8] KM Nilles, 'Defining the Limits of Liability: A Legal and Political Analysis of the European Community Products Liability Directive' (1985) 25 *Virginia Journal of International Law* 729, 753.

[9] Amendment of the Proposal for a Council Directive Relating to the Approximation of the Laws, Regulations, and Administrative Provisions Concerning Liability for Defective Products COM(79) 415 final, Art 1 (p 11) and Sixth Recital (pp 3–4).

[10] Explanatory Memorandum to the Second Draft Directive COM(79) final, pp 1–2. The Commission stated in its Explanatory Memorandum of 26 September 1979 that it felt unable to accept the exclusion of liability for development risks since 'the effect would be to require the consumer to bear the risk of the unknown', which would be inequitable: Explanatory Memorandum to the Second Draft Directive COM(79) final, p 1.

[11] [1979] OJ C127/61, 62. The European Parliament and the Council had consistently taken a line against liability for development risks, and indeed had exercised concerns about the uncertainty which surrounded undiscoverability of scientific and technical knowledge: Economic and Social Committee (ECOSOC) Report on Proposal for a Council Directive on Liability for Defective Products COM(76) 372 final, pp 41–45, cited in J Stapleton, 'Bugs in Anglo-American Products Liability' (2002) 53 *South Carolina Law Review* 1225, 1231. The Legal Affairs Committee of the European Parliament had also favoured exclusion of liability for development risks on the grounds of equity and economics, although a large minority had felt that the inclusion of liability was 'essential for consumer protection and was not likely to constitute a bar on innovation': Eur Parl Doc (COM 246) pp 26–7 (1978); Eur Parl Doc (COM 71) pp 16–17 (1979).

[12] Dir 85/374/EEC, Art 15(3). See CJ Miller and RS Goldberg, *Product Liability*, 2nd edn (Oxford, Oxford University Press, 2004) paras 13.39–13.41. Eur Parl Doc (COM 71) pp 16–17 (1979); KM Nilles, 'Defining the Limits of Liability: A Legal and Political Analysis of the European Community Products Liability Directive' (1985) 25 *Virginia Journal International Law* 729, 754.

not he knew or could have known of the defect'. In addition, by Article 7(e), the development risk defence was inserted into the Directive, which provides that:

> The producer shall not be liable as a result of this Directive if he proves ... that the state of scientific and technical knowledge at the time when he put the product into circulation was not such as to enable the existence of the defect to be discovered.[13]

The United Kingdom did not avail itself of the option to derogate from Article 7(e),[14] declining to follow the position of the Pearson Commission and the Law Commission,[15] and despite similar concerns having been raised before the defence's introduction into English law.[16] Nevertheless, it should be noted that there has long been considerable support both for excluding and including liability for development risks under strict liability.[17]

In transposing Article 7(1)(e) of the Directive, section 4(1)(e) of the Act provides a defence where the defendant proves:

> that the state of scientific and technical knowledge at the relevant time was not such that a producer of products of the same description as the product in question might be expected to have discovered the defect if it had existed in his products while they were under his control.

---

[13] It has thus been convincingly argued that the Commission documents 'do not in any way capture the true compromise finally adopted in the text of the Directive': J Stapleton, 'Bugs in Anglo-American Products Liability' (2002) 53 *South Carolina Law Review* 1225, 1248.

[14] The Department of Trade and Industry Consultative Note of November 1985 considered that grounds existed for the inclusion of the defence, and was influenced by the fear that its absence would raise insurance costs and inhibit innovation, particularly in high-risk areas. However, it considered that it would not be easy for a producer to raise the defence: *Implementation of EC Directive on Product Liability: An Explanatory and Consultative Note* (DTI, 1985) paras 21–22. The Council of Ministers permitted individual Member State delegations to append Unilateral Declarations or Unilateral Statements to the Directive 'to expound their local interpretations of its provisions': J Stapleton, 'Bugs in Anglo-American Products Liability' (2002) 53 *South Carolina Law Review* 1225, 1232. One such Unilateral Statement, by the UK Delegation, on Art 7(e), declared: 'This provision should be interpreted in the sense that the producer shall not be liable if he proves that, given the state of scientific knowledge at the time the product was put into circulation, no producer of a product of that kind could have been expected to have perceived that it was defective in design': 'Note Point "A" au Conseil (8205/85): Statements To Be Entered in the Council Minutes', para 7 (23 July 1985), cited in Stapleton, ibid 1247. Professor Stapleton suggests that, unless the ECJ is willing to imply that the other Member States had acted in bad faith in acquiescing to the UK's Unilateral Statement, the Directive should be read, at least by UK courts, in the light of that Unilateral Statement and its 'clear demands ... for a substantial defence for industry': ibid 1248.

[15] The Pearson Commission recommended that, in introducing a system of strict liability for defective products, the 'producer should not be allowed a defence of development risk' despite arguments that the cost of insurance might affect new product development (Royal Commission on Civil Liability and Compensation for Personal Injury) (Cmnd 7054-1, 1978) para 1259). The dismissal of the defence was based on the premise that to include it 'would be to leave a gap in the compensation cover, through which, for example, the victims of another thalidomide disaster might easily slip' (ibid). The Law Commission had similarly rejected the defence: Law Com Rep, para 105.

[16] A Forte, 'Medical Products Liability' in SAM McLean (ed), *Legal Issues in Medicine* (Aldershot, Gower, 1981) 76; P Cane, *Atiyah's Accidents Compensation and the Law*, 4th edn (New York, Weidenfeld & Nicolson, 1987) 145. See also the view expressed in Miller, *Product Liability and Safety Encyclopaedia*, Div III, para 131, that those who support the existence of the defence 'are saying in effect that liability for design or composition defects should continue to be based on negligence or fault' and that although '[t]his is a perfectly tenable point of view', it is inconsistent with purporting to introduce strict liability along the lines of the Pearson Commission's or the Law Commission's proposals.

[17] See J Fleming, 'Drug Injury Compensation Plans' (1982) 30 *American Journal of Comparative Law* 297, 308–9. Compensation for development risks may be desirable for reason of compensating the injured from a 'deeper pocket'. However, it is unjustifiable on the ground of inefficient resource allocation since development risks 'are unavoidable and preventable only by incurring socially undesirable costs' (eg longer testing): ibid 312–13.

The decision to include the defence has continued to receive considerable support from manufacturing organisations, which still regard it as an important element of the strict liability regime, as well as criticism from consumer organisations, which regard it as an area ripe for reform.[18]

While the defence is capable of benefiting all industrial sectors, it is likely that its greatest impact will be in the context of medicinal products, and in other industries operating at the forefront of scientific and technical knowledge. It may also be of more general benefit to industry in the out-of-court bargaining and settlement process.[19] It should also be noted that no equivalent defence exists where the claim is in contract under the Sale of Goods Act 1979,[20] or, subject to the usual choice of law rules, when goods are exported to and cause damage in a European Union country which has not adopted the defence in its implementing legislation.

C. Some Criticisms of the Statutory Wording

It has long been argued that whereas the Directive focuses upon a state of knowledge enabling discovery of a defect, the Act stresses the conduct of producers.[21] However, it has been convincingly reasoned that HM Government's interpretation, which manifested itself in the form of section 4(1)(e) of the Act, is correct.[22] First, when an assessment of the relevant state of scientific and technical knowledge takes place, it will not require the defendant to prove 'a worldwide absence of knowledge of the defect'. In practice, the defence will operate when the defendant shows that there is no prior knowledge of the defect in the field with which he is expected to be familiar. Secondly, the claimant could expose information which revealed the defect but which could not reasonably be expected to be known to the producer. If such unrelated knowledge denied the defence's operation, the search for evidence would be 'haphazard and wasteful'.[23]

The section 4(1)(e) definition has been favoured by the Association of the British Pharmaceutical Industry (ABPI) in their capacity of representing the interests of the pharmaceutical industry.[24] Nevertheless, it is submitted that the words 'a producer of products of the same description as the product in question' cloud the definition with inherent

---

[18] J Meltzer, R Freeman and S Thomson, *Product Liability in the European Union: A Report for the European Commission*, MARKT/2001/11/D (Lovells, February 2003) 2.2(c), p 50.

[19] Miller, *Product Liability and Safety Encyclopaedia* (above, n 16) Div III, para 256.

[20] See Miller and Goldberg (above n 12) para 4.107.

[21] AM Clark, *Product Liability* (London, Sweet & Maxwell, 1989) 153.

[22] C Newdick, 'The Development Risk Defence of the Consumer Protection Act 1987' (1988) 47 *Cambridge Law Journal* 455, 459–60.

[23] Ibid 465. See, further, C Newdick, 'Special Problems of Compensating Those Damaged by Medicinal Products' in SAM McLean (ed), *Compensation for Damage: An International Perspective* (Aldershot, Dartmouth, 1993) 18. Indeed, it has been suggested that any narrower reading of the defence would fail to achieve the Seventh Recital of the Directive's goal of 'a fair apportionment of risk between the injured person and the producer [which] implies that the producer should be able to free himself from liability if he furnishes proof as to the existence of certain exonerating circumstances': Dir 85/374/EEC, Seventh Recital; J Stapleton, 'Products Liability in the United Kingdom: The Myths of Reform' (1999) 34 *Texas International Law Journal* 45, 60. See below for Professor Stapleton's criticism of the little weight given to Recital 7 of the Directive in *A v National Blood Authority* [2001] 3 All ER 289, paras 74–76, the emphasis being placed on the prevention of injury and the facilitation of compensation for injury: ibid para 75.

[24] See ABPI Briefing on the Consumer Protection Bill (6 March 1987).

complications. For example, does 'a producer of products of the same description as the product in question' refer to all producers of, say, medicinal products or drugs of the same therapeutic class, or does the definition embrace a more comprehensive group of drugs?[25] In certain respects, the words have a limiting effect on the scope of the defence. In particular, they make it clear that one is not concerned with the technical expertise and research facilities of the individual producer who is being sued.[26]

However, it has been suggested that the words represent a 'considerable softening' of the defence when compared to the literal meaning of Article 7(e) of the Directive since they suggest that a producer of finished products cannot be expected to be technically expert with respect to all the components or raw materials which are incorporated in it. This suggests that, apart from the reversal of the burden of proof, the scope of liability is unlikely to differ from that under the law of negligence.[27] It also remains unclear how the test would apply where there is but one or a limited number of producers who dominate the market for the product in question, since such a producer would effectively determine the state of scientific and technical knowledge with respect to that product.[28]

It is likely that courts will return to the Directive, in accordance with section 1(1) of the Act, and to case law for an answer to these and other problems, albeit that the Directive is singularly un-illuminating. Indeed, in *A v National Blood Authority*,[29] both parties focused almost exclusively on the Directive, Burton J proceeding on the basis that, in so far as the Act's wording differed from the Directive's equivalent articles, 'it should not be construed differently from the directive, and consequently the practical course was to go straight to the fount, the directive itself'.[30] Burton J went as far as to add, in relation to section 4(1)(e), that although the United Kingdom had not amended section 4(1)(e) of the Act so as to bring it in line with the wording of Article 7(e), the decision in *Commission v United Kingdom*[31] amounted to 'binding authority'[32] of the European Court that it was to be so construed.[33]

D. Development Risk and the State of the Art Defence

Section 4(1)(e) of the Act has become known as the 'development risk defence'. It is a term preferable to 'state of the art defence', since 'development risk' refers to undiscoverable

---

[25] For support for the former position, see R Goldberg, *Causation and Risk in the Law of Torts: Scientific Evidence and Medicinal Product Liability* (Oxford, Hart Publishing, 1999) 229.

[26] Miller, *Product Liability and Safety Encyclopaedia* (above, n 16) Div III, para 256. As Lord Lucas explained at the Committee Stage in the House of Lords: 'It will be of no help to the producer to plead how difficult or how expensive it had or it might have been for him to have found the answers to that defect. If other producers of products of that type had the knowledge available to them, then the defence is of no use to the producer of the product': *Hansard*, HL Deb (series 5) vol 483, col 841 (20 January 1987).

[27] Miller, *Product Liability and Safety Encyclopaedia* (above, n 16) Div III, para 256.

[28] Ibid.

[29] *A v National Blood Authority* [2001] 3 All ER 289.

[30] Ibid para 2.

[31] C-300/95 *Commission v United Kingdom* [1997] ECR I-2649.

[32] *A v National Blood Authority* [2001] 3 All ER 289, para 21.

[33] Cf the views of one commentator, who has regarded this as 'put[ting] the position too strongly': see A Arnull, Editorial, 'Product Liability and the Effect of Directives' (2001) 26 *European Law Review* 213, 213–14, and, further, G Howells, 'Defect in English Law—Lessons for the Harmonisation of European Product Liability Law' in D Fairgrieve (ed), *Product Liability in Comparative Perspective* (Cambridge, Cambridge University Press, 2005) 139 (suggesting Burton J was 'arguably too willing to acknowledge the supremacy of the Directive').

defects[34] whereas 'state of the art' is associated with the most up-to-date technology and safety standards in a particular industry against which a product is to be judged, the latter term (state of the art) being relevant to ascertaining whether a product is defective.[35]

In the United States, state of the art problems usually concern one of two issues, namely the potential liability of a manufacturer for failure to warn consumers of an unknown and (it is alleged) unknowable risk; and the potential liability of a manufacturer for failing to adopt a design feature, undeveloped or unavailable at the time of sale, which could have eliminated a known risk.[36] The first issue concerns the discoverability and foreseeability of risk and seems closest to the development risk defence of the Directive. Thus, in *A v National Blood Authority*,[37] Burton J held that as soon as the risk of the hepatitis C infection became known, the defendants could no longer use the defence, even although the virus was undiscoverable in a particular bag of blood. However, it has been noted that Article 7(e) of the Directive in fact refers to discoverability of the defect, and not of the risk.[38] The second issue concerns the feasibility of implementing a safe design and is closest to the UK and European approaches to state of the art.

By virtue of the diffuse nature of the state of the art concept in the United States, both American courts and legislatures have failed to agree a definition.[39] Some cases have interpreted state of the art as industry practice and custom,[40] whereas others interpret it as the best technological capability, irrespective of source.[41] The fairest and most pragmatic definition lies between these two extremes,[42] with state of the art being referred to by American courts as, for example, 'dangers ... which [manufacturers] know or should have known on the basis of reasonably obtainable or available knowledge';[43] 'evidence that the particular risk was neither known nor knowable by the application of scientific knowledge available at the time of manufacture and/or distribution';[44] 'the best technology reasonably

---

[34] 'Development risks' have been defined as 'risks present in production sectors in which an advance in technological and scientific knowledge may make a product appear defective *ex post*, whereas it was not regarded as such at the time when it was manufactured': Case C-300/95 *Commission v United Kingdom* [1997] ECR I-2649, I-2658, AG Tesauro, para 18. Cf Professor Stapleton's view that the term 'development risk defence' is misleading since s 4(1)(e) of the Act not only covers those risks present in newly developed innovative products but also risks in established goods which have been on the market for a considerable amount of time: 'Products Liability in the United Kingdom: The Myths of Reform' (1999) 34 *Texas International Law Journal* 45, 51, fn 50, 56, fn 83. It is clear that the defence is indeed potentially available in the latter type of case, no less than with innovative products.

[35] Clark, *Product Liability* (above, n 21) 151; C Newdick, 'The Development Risk Defence of the Consumer Protection Act 1987' (1988) 47 *Cambridge Law Journal* 455. Indeed, AG Tesauro seemed aware of this distinction when he said that since Art 7(e) referred 'solely to the scientific and technical knowledge at the time when the product was marketed, it [was] not concerned with the practices and safety standards in use in the industrial sector in which the producer [was] operating': Case C-300/95 [1997] ECR I-2649, I-2658, AG Tesauro, para 20. This position was affirmed by the ECJ's judgment in Case C-300/95 [1997] ECR I-2670, para 26.

[36] *Madden & Owen on Products Liability*, 3rd edn (Thomson/West, 2000) § 10:4.

[37] [2001] 3 All ER 289, para 75.

[38] J Stapleton, *Product Liability* (London, Butterworths, 1994) 237.

[39] '[T]he term "state of the art" has been the source of substantial confusion': *Potter v Chicago Pneumatic Tool Co* 694 A 2d 1319, 1345 (Conn 1997).

[40] See eg *Lane v Amsted Industries Inc* 779 SW 2d 754, 758 (Mo App 1989); *Smith v Minster Machine Co* 669 F 2d 628, 633 (10th Cir 1992); *Sturm, Ruger & Co v Day* 594 P 2d 38, 44 (Alaska 1979), modified on other grounds, 615 P 2d 621 (Alaska 1980), on rehearing, 627 P 2d 204 (Alaska 1981), and overruled on other grounds, *Dura Corp v Harned* 703 P 2d 396 (Alaska 1985).

[41] *Owens-Illinois Inc v Zenobia* 601 A 2d 633, 644–45 (Md 1992).

[42] *Madden & Owen on Products Liability* (above, n 36) § 10:5.

[43] *Feldman v Lederle Laboratories* 479 A 2d 374, 376 (NJ 1984).

[44] *Anderson v Owens-Corning Fiberglas Corp* 810 P 2d 549, 559 (Cal 1991).

feasible at the time when the product was manufactured';[45] whether 'safety features ... were unknown or unavailable at the time the product in question was manufactured and distributed';[46] and 'the level of relevant scientific, technological and safety knowledge existing and reasonably feasible at the time of design'.[47] Indeed, it has been argued that it is hard to better the State of Nebraska's straightforward and balanced definition of the state of the art as 'the best technology reasonably available at the time'.[48] Several American States have provided manufacturers with an explicit statutory state of the art defence for products liability claims.[49]

E. Optional Nature of the Defence

The development risk defence is not mandatory, since by Article 15(1)(b) of the Directive a Member State may, by way of derogation from Article 7(e), provide that a producer shall be liable, 'even if he proves that the state of scientific and technical knowledge at the time when he put the product into circulation was not such as to enable the existence of a defect to be discovered'. Thus Member States are at liberty to choose whether to adopt or to derogate from the defence. Article 15(3) provides that the matter shall be reviewed by a European Commission report after 10 years. The Commission has, however, yet to produce this report.

F. Member States Which have Derogated from the Defence

All Member States, including now France,[50] have adopted national legislation implementing the Directive. All, except Luxembourg and Finland, have adopted the development risk defence and Germany has adopted the defence[51] except with regard to pharmaceuticals.[52] Spain has adopted the defence[53] except in respect of medicines, food or food products intended for human consumption,[54] and France in its adoption of the defence,[55] has excluded products derived from the human body.[56]

---

[45] *Indianapolis Athletic Club Inc v Alco Stand Corp* 709 NE 2d 1070 (Ind App 1999).

[46] *Owens-Corning Fiberglas Corp v Golightly* 976 SW 2d 409, 411 (Ky 1998).

[47] *Potter v Chicago Pneumatic Tool Co* 694 A 2d 1319, 1346 (Conn 1997).

[48] Neb Rev Stat § 25–21, 182, cited in *Madden & Owen on Products Liability* (above, n 36) § 10:5.

[49] See *Madden & Owen on Products Liability* (above, n 36) §§ 10:5–10:7, referring to statutes in the States of Arizona, Iowa, Louisiana, Mississippi, Missouri, Nebraska, New Hampshire, and New Jersey.

[50] France had been censured by the ECJ in 1993 for failing to transpose the Directive within the time limit of three years from the date of its notification (see Art 19 of the Directive): Case C-293/91 *Commission v France* [1993] ECR I-1. In the absence of any transposition, the Commission decided in March 1998 to refer the daily fine of 158, 250 ECU to be imposed in accordance with Art 171 (now 228) EC. As a consequence of the Commission's decision, France adopted Law No 98-389 on 19 May 1998, to comply with its obligations.

[51] ProdHaftG, § 1(2)5.

[52] ProdHaftG, § 15.

[53] LRPD, art 6.1.e.

[54] LRPD, art 6.3.

[55] Code Civil, art 1386-11(4).

[56] Code Civil, art 1386-12. In the first appellate judgment on the Directive in France, the development risk defence was held inapplicable in a case concerning the contraction of trichinellosis after eating horsemeat. The

The reason for Germany not adopting the defence in respect of pharmaceuticals is that it has its own separate strict liability regime for drugs under the German Pharmaceuticals Act 1976. Section 84 of the Act imposes strict liability on manufacturers or producers of pharmaceuticals in respect of the harmful side-effects of their products, and there is no provision for a development risk defence under the Act. Thus a manufacturer or producer of a medicinal product is legally responsible for adverse effects of the drug which were not apparent at the time when the medicinal product was first marketed.[57] Spain's reasons for excluding the defence in respect of pharmaceuticals are not precisely known, particularly where medicinal products and food products are those for which the defence would be most likely to be utilised.[58] However, Spain's exclusion of drugs, food, or food products can be explained by a toxic syndrome in the early 1980s, which was caused by poor-quality cooking oil, and several drug disaster cases, all of which had their effect in Spain, viz MER 29 (a cholesterol-reducing drug which caused serious damage to the eyesight of at least 5,000 people), Aralen (an arthritis drug which caused blindness), quadrigen (a child vaccine which caused serious brain inflammation) and earlier, of course, thalidomide. The cooking oil disaster resulted in the Spanish Consumer Protection Act 1984, which introduced strict liability for high-risk products.[59] It is conceivable that Spain's position may have been prejudiced by its having a predominantly generic drug industry.[60] The reason why France excluded the defence in respect of products derived from the human body, was confirmation of the decision of the Cour de Cassation in the 'contaminated blood' affair.[61]

G. The Relevant Time at Which to Apply the Test

Under Article 7(e) of the Directive the time for making an assessment of the state of scientific and technical knowledge is when the producer 'put the product into circulation'.[62] The equivalent expression in section 4(1)(e) of the 1987 Act is 'the relevant time' and this is in turn defined by section 4(2). In the case of persons who are potentially liable under section

---

Toulouse Court of Appeal held that the defendant was unable to rely on the defence since at the time the product was put on the market the defect (viz the existence of trichins in horsemeat) was well-known: Decision of 22 February 2000 (Toulouse Court of Appeal), noted by C Larroumet, (March 2001) Lovells' *European Product Liability Review* 22. France's requirement in Code Civil, art 1386-12 that the producer had to prove that he had taken appropriate measures to avert the harmful consequences of a defective product in order to rely on the grounds of exemption from liability in art 1386-11(4) has been held contrary to the wording of Art 7(e) and accordingly a failure to fulfil its obligation of complete harmonisation in this area: Case C-52/00 *Commission v France* [2002] ECR I-3827, paras 10, 49.

[57] See J Finch and P Ranson, *Product Liability in Europe: What the New EEC Directive Will Mean for Pharmaceutical Companies?* (Richmond, PJB Publications, 1986) 95–96.

[58] G Howells and M Mildred, 'Is European Products Liability More Protective than the Restatement (Third) of Torts: Products Liability?' (1998) 65 *Tennessee Law Review* 985, 1016.

[59] MIA Vega, 'The Defence of Development Risks in Spanish Law' [1997] *Consumer Law Journal* 144, 148–49.

[60] R Goldberg, 'The Development Risk Defence and the European Court of Justice; Increased Injury Costs and the Supplementary Protection Certificate' in R Goldberg and J Lonbay (eds), *Pharmaceutical Medicine, Biotechnology and European Law* (Cambridge, Cambridge University Press, 2000) 194.

[61] Cass 1iere civ, 9 July 1996, *X v GAN incendie accidents et autres*, D 1996 Jur 610 translation reproduced in Van Gerven, J Lever and P Larouche, *Ius Commune Casebooks for the Common Law of Europe Casebooks: Tort Law* (Oxford, Hart Pubishing, 2000) 629–30.

[62] For discussion of the meaning of this expression, see Miller and Goldberg, *Product Liability*, 2nd edn (Oxford, Oxford University Press, 2004) paras 8.54–8.59.

2(2) of the Act,[63] the relevant time is when they 'supplied[64] the product to another' and in the case of others (those potentially liable as mere suppliers under section 2(3)),[65] the time when the product was last supplied by a person to whom section 2(2) does apply. The pinpointing of the relevant moment in time may be particularly significant in the context of medicinal products, where the state of knowledge is advancing rapidly.

II. INFRINGEMENT PROCEEDINGS IN THE EUROPEAN COURT OF JUSTICE: *COMMISSION v UNITED KINGDOM*

A. Initial Stages

As has been noted, Article 7(e) of the Directive states that the defence will arise if 'the state of scientific and technical knowledge at the time when [the producer] put the product into circulation was not such as to enable the existence of the defect to be discovered'. Section 4(1)(e) of the Act provides that there will be a defence for the person proceeded against on proving that

> the state of scientific and technical knowledge at the relevant time was not such that a producer of products of the same description as the product in question might be expected to have discovered the defect if it had existed in his products while they were under his control.

Prima facie, it would seem that the wording of these two versions of the defence is different and that the United Kingdom version is broader in its scope and more amenable to the interests of innovative producers, particularly of pharmaceuticals.[66]

The alleged distinction between the two versions of the defence led to infringement proceedings being brought by the Commission against the United Kingdom under Article 169 (now 226) EC for failure to fulfil the obligation of implementing the Directive correctly in this respect. The United Kingdom made a formal reply to the Commission's formal notice regarding incorrect implementation of the Directive, saying that it was considered that it had been implemented in the only way possible in the United Kingdom. A reasoned opinion for failure to implement the Directive was sent by the European Commission to the United Kingdom,[67] to which the United Kingdom replied. The Commission considered that the complaint relating to section 4(1)(e) of the Consumer Protection Act was justified and brought an action for a declaration that the United Kingdom did not implement Article 7(e) correctly.[68] An oral hearing took place on 7 November 1996.[69] The Commission argued that the United Kingdom had broadened the defence under Article 7(e) of the Directive and converted strict liability imposed by Article 1 of the Directive into

---

[63] Ibid paras 8.05–8.31 and 13.16.

[64] The word 'supply' is defined in s 46 of the Act; see generally, ibid paras 8.60–8.63.

[65] See generally, ibid paras 8.32–8.51; also para 13.16.

[66] R Goldberg, 'The Development Risk Defence and the European Court of Justice; Increased Injury Costs and the Supplementary Protection Certificate' in R Goldberg and J Lonbay (eds), *Pharmaceutical Medicine, Biotechnology and European Law* (Cambridge, Cambridge University Press, 2000) 187.

[67] J Searles and U Scott-Larson, 'European Update' [October 1990] *Product Liability International* 155.

[68] Case C-300/95 *Commission v United Kingdom* [1997] ECR I-2649, I-2664, para 1.

[69] M Mildred, 'Group Litigation' in Miller, *Product Liability and Safety Encyclopaedia* (above, n 16) Div III A, para 136.

mere negligence liability,[70] and submitted that the Article 7(e) test was objective, referring 'to a state of knowledge, and not to the capacity of the producer of the product in question ... to discover the defect', whereas section 4(1)(e) of the Act presupposed 'a subjective assessment based on the behaviour of a reasonable producer'.[71]

The United Kingdom Government, on the other hand, argued that both the test in the Act and that in the Directive were objective.[72] Article 7(e) laid down an objective test in the sense that the

> state of scientific and technical knowledge [did] not refer to what the producer in question actually [knew] or [did] not know, but to the state of knowledge which producers of the class of the producer in question, understood in a generic sense, may objectively be expected to have.[73]

It added that, in any event, courts in the United Kingdom were required to interpret section 4(1)(e) consistently with Article 7(e) of the Directive, in accordance with section 1(1) of the Act.[74] It was the United Kingdom's view that the Commission could succeed in arguing that section 4(1)(e) had failed to implement Article 7(e) of the Directive only if section 4(1)(e) was 'completely incapable of bearing the same legal meaning as Article 7(e)'.[75] In view of section 1(1) of the Act, and the absence of any national decision on the meaning of section 4(1)(e), the United Kingdom submitted that the Commission was not in a position to state that section 4(1)(e) was incompatible with Article 7(e).[76]

B. Advocate General's Opinion

Advocate General Tesauro delivered his opinion on 23 January 1997 and proposed that the Court should dismiss the application and order the Commission to pay the costs.[77] In seeking to describe the concept of the state of scientific knowledge he observed: '[T]he state of scientific knowledge cannot be identified with the views expressed by the majority of learned opinion, but with the most advanced level of research which has been carried out at a given time'.[78]

Prima facie, this appears to give clear guidance to researchers in the major innovative industries at the forefront of scientific and technical knowledge, especially the pharmaceutical industry.[79] At this point, however, his observations became less clear. He observed that 'one isolated opinion' which might eventually become the generally accepted view as to the potentially defective and/or hazardous nature of a product was outside the scope of the rules imposed by the Directive, since 'the manufacturer is no longer faced with an

---

[70] Case C-300/95 [1997] ECR I-2649, I-2667, para 16.
[71] Ibid I-2668, para 17.
[72] Ibid I-2668, para 19.
[73] Case C-300/95 [1997] ECR I-2649, I-2668–2669, paras 20–21.
[74] Ibid I-2669, para 21.
[75] Ibid I-2669, para 22.
[76] Ibid.
[77] Ibid I-2662, AG Tesauro, para 31.
[78] Ibid I-2659, AG Tesauro, para 21.
[79] R Goldberg, 'The Development Risk Defence and the European Court of Justice; Increased Injury Costs and the Supplementary Protection Certificate' in R Goldberg and J Lonbay (eds), *Pharmaceutical Medicine, Biotechnology and European Law* (Cambridge, Cambridge University Press, 2000) 188–9.

unforeseeable risk'.[80] It would seem, however, that the word 'isolated' could have two possible connotations, namely isolated in terms of the accessibility of such scientific and technical knowledge or isolated in terms of the general acceptance of such knowledge.[81] Although Advocate General Tesauro linked isolation closely with availability and accessibility of such knowledge,[82] his choice of the word 'isolated' created an uncertainty as to whether there was a link between an isolated opinion and one which might be regarded as a maverick opinion and lacking general acceptance.

The Advocate General defined the state of knowledge as including 'all data in the information circuit of the scientific community as a whole, bearing in mind, however, on the basis of a reasonableness test, the actual opportunities for the information to circulate'.[83] There is obviously a need to take into account the instantaneous nature of modern scientific knowledge on CD-ROM, the Internet, and other data retrieval systems for scientific and medical research.[84] It is thus regrettable that the opinion lacks discussion of the impact of the information superhighway on scientific and technical knowledge.[85]

The Advocate General considered that there was no 'irremediable conflict' between Article 7(e) and section 4(1)(e) of the Act, although he conceded the potential ambiguity of section 4(1)(e).[86] Three reasons were given for this conclusion. First, the producer was central not only to the rules of the Directive as a whole, but also to Article 7(e), which is aimed at the producer. Thus section 4(1)(e) of the Act was merely expressing in a clear way a concept which was implied in the Directive.[87] Secondly, the reference to the producer's ability to discover the defect was insufficient to make the test which it laid down a subjective one. To exclude the producer's liability, it had to be proved 'in the light of the most advanced scientific and technical knowledge objectively and reasonably obtainable', that the product was defective.[88] Thirdly, the system of liability was not one based on negligence, since under section 4(1)(e) the burden of proof of the defence was on the manufacturer.[89] However, it has been rightly pointed out that there is a distinction between substantive rules of liability, eg rules of negligence or strict liability, and those relating to the burden of proof.[90]

The Advocate General reaffirmed the settled legal position of the European Court of Justice that the scope of national laws, regulations, or administrative provisions had to

---

[80]   Case C-300/95 [1997] ECR I-2649, I-2660, AG Tesauro, para 22.

[81]   Ibid.

[82]   Ibid I-2660, para 23.

[83]   Ibid para 24.

[84]   It has been argued that powerful computerised databases are available without regard to the industrial sector within which a producer works and that there is therefore no reason to confine discoverability by accessibility to a particular sector: M Mildred and G Howells, 'Comment on "Development Risks: Unanswered Questions"' (1998) 61 *Modern Law Review* 570, 572. However, since the knowledge content of databases is great, it might be argued that it is impossible and unjust for a producer to be aware of all knowledge in respect of a defect in *every* sector.

[85]   R Goldberg, 'The Development Risk Defence and the European Court of Justice; Increased Injury Costs and the Supplementary Protection Certificate' in R Goldberg and J Lonbay (eds), *Pharmaceutical Medicine, Biotechnology and European Law* (Cambridge, Cambridge University Press, 2000) 189.

[86]   Case C-300/95 [1997] ECR I-2649, I-2660, AG Tesauro, para 25.

[87]   Ibid I-2661, para 26. cf the criticism by Howells and Mildred that this is tantamount to arguing that since the producer is the defendant, he should be judged by the standard of the producer, despite Art 7(e)'s language and purpose: G Howells and M Mildred, 'Is European Products Liability More Protective than the Restatement (Third) of Torts: Products Liability?' (1998) 65 *Tennessee Law Review* 985, 1008.

[88]   Case C-300/95 [1997] ECR I-2649, I-2661, AG Tesauro, para 26.

[89]   Ibid para 27.

[90]   G Howells and M Mildred, 'Is European Products Liability More Protective than the Restatement (Third) of Torts: Products Liability?' (1998) 65 *Tennessee Law Review* 985, 1008.

be assessed in the light of their interpretation by national courts,[91] and that the failure of the Commission to wait until the Act was applied by the national courts before bringing an action against the United Kingdom for incorrectly implementing the Directive was 'over hasty'.[92] In the light of these observations, the Advocate General concluded that the Commission had failed to show that section 4(1)(e) of the Consumer Protection Act had not implemented Article 7(e) of the Directive correctly.[93]

C. The Judgment of the European Court of Justice

The European Court of Justice followed the Opinion of the Advocate General as outlined above,[94] and dismissed the application and ordered the Commission to pay the costs on five grounds.[95]

First, the Court explained that section 4(1)(e) placed the burden of proof on the producer, as required by Article 7. Nevertheless, it might be argued that the defence itself has been drafted in a manner that reflects the requirements of negligence in that it stresses the conduct of producers and whether they might be expected to discover the defect. Thus, there is a marked failure on the part of the Court, as there was with Advocate General Tesauro,[96] to recognise or at least articulate the distinction between rules relating to substantive liability and those which concern the burden of proof.

Secondly, the Court noted that section 4(1)(e) 'placed no restriction on the state and degree of scientific and technical knowledge at the material time which was to be taken into account'. Following the Advocate General, it agreed that Article 7(e) was unreservedly directed at 'the most advanced level of such knowledge, at the time when the product in question was put into circulation'.[97] As Professor Mildred has observed, the notion that the state of scientific and technical knowledge is set by the standard of the most advanced idea would appear 'puzzling', since it is arguable that a state of knowledge implies a degree of consensus or settled basis.[98] However, the judgment as a whole suggests that the discoverability and accessibility of such knowledge is an important element in determining the scope of the defence, although, as the Advocate General had earlier observed, the appropriate yardstick was that of the knowledge of an expert in the sector.[99] Thus the Court stressed that it was implicit in Article 7(e)'s wording 'that the relevant scientific and technical knowledge must have been *accessible* at the time when the product in question was

---

[91] Case C-382/91 *Commission v United Kingdom* [1994] ECR I-2435, para 36; Joined Cases C-132/91, C-138/91 and C-139/91 *Katsikas and Others* [1992] ECR I-6577, para 39.

[92] Case C-300/95 [1997] ECR I-2649, I-2662, AG Tesauro, para 29.

[93] Case C-300/95 [1997] ECR I-2649, I-2662, AG Tesauro, para 29.

[94] See Miller and Goldberg (above, n 62) paras 13.47–13.51.

[95] Case C-300/95 [1997] ECR I-2649, I-2671–I-2673, paras 34–40.

[96] Cf G Howells and M Mildred, 'Is European Products Liability More Protective than the Restatement (Third) of Torts: Products Liability?' (1998) 65 *Tennessee Law Review* 985, 1008.

[97] Case C-300/95 [1997] ECR I-2649, I-2670, para 26.

[98] M Mildred, 'The Development Risks Defence' in D Fairgrieve (ed), *Product Liability in Comparative Perspective* (Cambridge, Cambridge University Press, 2005) 169, 184.

[99] Ibid I-2659, AG Tesauro, para 20.

put into circulation' (emphasis added)[100] and the Advocate General observed that the state of knowledge 'included all data in the information circuit of the scientific community as a whole, *bearing in mind, however, on the basis of a reasonableness test the actual opportunities for the information to circulate*' (emphasis added).[101] He illustrated the point by the much discussed example of a study based on research carried out by an academic in Manchuria and published in a local scientific journal in Chinese which does not go outside the boundaries of the region. As to this he advised that:

> I do not consider that in such a case a producer could be held liable on the ground that at the time at which he put the product into circulation the brilliant Asian researcher had discovered the defect in it.[102]

Therefore, there is clearly a limit to what counts as relevant scientific and technical knowledge which is to be taken into account. As Professor Stapleton has noted, the distinction appears to be that although the Court did not consider that accessibility was relevant to the issue of whether information was part of the state of scientific and technical knowledge, it did rule 'that accessibility was relevant to the discoverability of information within that state of knowledge'.[103] This emphasis on reasonableness in the context of accessibility appears to strengthen the view that the defence should be given the wide interpretation of 'undiscoverability by reasonable means', in contradistinction to the narrow interpretation of 'absolute undiscoverability'.[104]

Thirdly, the Court held that the wording of section 4(1)(e) did not suggest that the defence's availability depended on the subjective knowledge of a producer taking reasonable care in the light of the standard precautions of the relevant industrial sector. The producer's ability to discover the defect was formulated as an objective test by Advocate General Tesauro on the basis that reference to the producer's ability is an 'objectively verifiable and assessable parameter, which is in no way influenced by consideration of the actual subjective knowledge of the producer or by his organisational and economic requirements'.[105] But even if one were to concede that the test is objective, there remains an element of subjectivity in the sense that individual judges may differ in assessing whether, in the circumstances of the particular case, a reasonable producer might have been expected

---

[100] Ibid para 28. See also ibid para 29, where the Court emphasised that 'for the relevant scientific and technical knowledge to be successfully pleaded against the producer, that knowledge must have been accessible at the time when the product in question was put into circulation'.

[101] Ibid I-2660, para 24.

[102] Case C-300/95 *Commission v United Kingdom* [1997] ECR I-2649, I-2660, para 24.

[103] J Stapleton, 'Products Liability in the United Kingdom: The Myths of Reform' (1999) 34 *Texas International Law Journal* 45, 59–60. Cf C Hodges, Note, 'Development Risks: Unanswered Questions' (1998) 61 *Modern Law Review* 560, 565, 567, who considers that the European Court's approach based on the most advanced level of scientific and technical knowledge does not accord with the *reality* of scientific and technical knowledge, and is so high a standard that it could arguably never succeed in practice. However, an alternative view is that the reality of such knowledge is reflected in the ECJ's judgment in that the scope of such knowledge is delimited by the requirements of discoverability and accessibility: R Goldberg, 'The Development Risk Defence and the European Court of Justice; Increased Injury Costs and the Supplementary Protection Certificate' in R Goldberg and J Lonbay (eds), *Pharmaceutical Medicine, Biotechnology and European Law* (Cambridge, Cambridge University Press, 2000) 191, fn 38.

[104] M Mildred, 'The Development Risks Defence' in D Fairgrieve (ed), *Product Liability in Comparative Perspective* (Cambridge, Cambridge University Press, 2005) 170, 179.

[105] Case C-300/95 *Commission v United Kingdom* [1997] ECR I-2649, I-2661, AG Tesauro, para 26. However, the pharmaceutical industry has consistently argued that discoverability should be linked to economic feasibility. See below, text to nn 144–45.

to discover the defect. As Lord MacMillan observed in *Glasgow Corporation v Muir*[106] when describing the standard of foresight of the reasonable man in the context of the law of negligence:[107]

> The standard of foresight of the reasonable man is, in one sense, an impersonal test. It eliminates the personal equation and is independent of the idiosyncrasies of the particular person whose conduct is in question ... The reasonable man is presumed to be free both from over-apprehension and from over-confidence, but there is a sense in which the standard of care of the reasonable man involves in its application a *subjective* element. It is still left to the judge to decide what, in the circumstances of the particular case, the reasonable man would have had in contemplation and what, accordingly, the party sought to be made liable ought to have foreseen ... What to one judge may seem far-fetched may seem to another both natural and probable (emphasis added).

Fourthly, having reaffirmed the rule that national laws, regulations, or administrative provisions must be assessed in the light of the interpretation given to them by national courts,[108] the European Court held that the Commission had failed to refer to any national judicial decision which interpreted section 4(1)(e) (the national law) as inconsistent with Article 7(e) (the Directive provision). However, there was always a fear that this issue would be triable only in the context of a case involving the discoverability of allegedly unforeseeable or undiscoverable defects, often in medicinal products, which would take several years to come to trial in the United Kingdom. If such a case fell to be decided on this issue, the development risk defence in its section 4(1)(e) form might have operated to deny liability in circumstances where the Article 7(e) definition might have accepted liability.[109]

Fifthly, the European Court held that nothing in the material submitted to the Court suggested that the United Kingdom courts, if called upon to interpret section 4(1)(e), would not do so in the light of the wording and purpose of the Directive, as required by Article 189 (now 249) EC. Moreover, section 1(1) of the Consumer Protection Act 1987 imposed such an obligation on the national courts.[110]

In a critique of the decision, Professor Stapleton has argued that the ambiguous nature of Article 7(e) allowed the possibility that the United Kingdom implementation had 'captured the, as yet, undetermined meaning of the article'.[111] She develops the argument by claiming that since the article was ambiguous, specifically in relation to the degree of accessibility of knowledge needed before a defect was held to be discoverable and thus ousting the defence, it could not be said that the 'covert, paraphrased "reasonableness" standard of the Act had clearly not achieved the result intended by the Directive'.[112] However, it might

---

[106] [1943] AC 448, HL.

[107] Ibid 457. Indeed, as Professor Whittaker has noted, while the ECJ decision confirms that liability under the Directive is objective and that it rests on a standard independent of the defendant's activities, and what he knew, so, in English law, does liability in negligence. The ECJ decision illustrates the potential for confusion that may ensue from equating civilian ideas of 'liability for fault' and 'objective liability' with the common law's 'liability for negligence' and 'strict liability': S Whittaker, *Liability for Products: English Law, French Law, and European Harmonisation* (Oxford, Oxford University Press, 2005) 496, 498.

[108] See Case C-382/92 *Commission v United Kingdom* [1994] ECR I-2435, I-2672, para 37.

[109] Cf *A v National Blood Authority* [2001] 3 All ER 289.

[110] Case C-300/95 *Commission v United Kingdom* [1997] ECR I-2649, I-2671–I-2673, paras 34–40.

[111] J Stapleton, 'Products Liability in the United Kingdom: The Myths of Reform' (1999) 34 *Texas International Law Journal* 45, 60.

[112] Ibid.

similarly be claimed that section 4(1)(e) is itself unclear as to its precise scope,[113] thus permitting resort to be made to the Directive to assist in resolving the lack of clarity.[114] The United Kingdom then remains protected from an allegation of failure to implement under Article 226 EC since the Directive will assist in the interpretation of section 4(1)(e). To put it another way, only if section 4(1)(e) had been *unambiguous* would there have been a strong argument that the legislation had not implemented the Directive correctly. The United Kingdom thus seems to have benefited from the ambiguous way in which section 4(1)(e) has been drafted.[115]

III. EUROPEAN COMMISSION REFORM PROPOSALS

A. Green Paper

Following the European Court of Justice's decision, the European Commission's Green Paper on Liability for Defective Products reopened a discussion of the possible abolition of the development risk defence. The Green Paper suggested the need to discover whether the removal of the exemption would discourage producers from innovation, particularly in the pharmaceuticals sector, and whether it would be feasible to insure this kind of risk in the insurance market.[116]

B. Second Commission Report and Fondazione Rosselli Study

However, the Second Commission Report on the Application of the Directive was hampered by the lack of available data on the development risk defence. It noted that no detailed research existed on national court rulings in respect of the defence. The known few cases indicated that it is not so easy for a producer to prove that the defect could not be discovered on the basis of knowledge that was available when the product was marketed.[117] The Report concluded that the occurrence of damages due to a development risk would most likely be in the pharmaceutical products, chemical substances, genetically modified organism, and foodstuffs sectors. In discussing the issue whether damage caused by development

---

[113] Cf the view of Professor Stapleton that it is the *Directive* which is ambiguous, and that the producer-friendly construction of the Act is unambiguous: 'Products Liability in the United Kingdom: The Myths of Reform' (1999) 34 *Texas International Law Journal* 45, 57–58.

[114] See s 1(1) of the 1987 Act.

[115] R Goldberg, 'The Development Risk Defence and the European Court of Justice; Increased Injury Costs and the Supplementary Protection Certificate' in R Goldberg and J Lonbay (eds), *Pharmaceutical Medicine, Biotechnology and European Law* (Cambridge, Cambridge University Press, 2000) 193. cf the view of AG Tesauro that the ambiguity of s 4(1)(e) was irrelevant. What was at issue was the 'irremediable inconsistency with the Community provision which it purports to implement': Case C-300/95 [1997] ECR I-2649, I-2656, AG Tesauro, para 14. However, it is submitted that the ambiguous nature of s 4(1)(e) reduced the possibility of any such 'irremediable inconsistency' with Art 7(e) of the Directive.

[116] Commission Green Paper, *Liability for Defective Products*, Brussels, COM(99) 396 final (28 July 1999) para 3.2, 24–25.

[117] Second Commission Report of 31 January 2001 on the Application of Directive 85/374 on liability for defective products, COM(2000) 893 final, p 18, para 3.2.2.

risks should be borne by society as a whole, by means of a compensation fund using government revenue, and/or by the relevant manufacturing sector by means of a fund to which those in the sector contribute, the Report considered[118] that public compensation funds might be seen as the exception and that establishing a fund by companies of the manufacturing sector concerned should be preferred.

The most significant contribution of the Second Commission Report was its commissioning of a study on the economic impact for industry, insurance, consumers and society as a whole of the removal of the development risk defence,[119] which was undertaken and reported on by the Fondazione Rosselli in 2004.[120] While acknowledging the difficulties in obtaining empirical evidence about the economic impact of the clause, due to the relatively limited number of cases and unsatisfactory response rates to questionnaires, and the difficulty in identifying appropriately competent persons,[121] the authors of the Rosselli study were nonetheless able to uphold the argument that the defence was 'a significant factor in achieving the Directive's balance between the need to preserve incentives to innovation and consumers' interests'.[122] The defence was regarded as necessary to protect innovation and was probably a 'key factor in determining the relative stability of product liability insurance costs in European industry and keeping litigation at a reasonable level'.[123] There was an indication that, in a strict liability regime, companies in high-tech/high risk sectors would find it difficult to obtain reasonable insurance cover for developmental risks.[124] The report considered that steps should be taken to harmonise the approach to the application of the defence in Member States, and envisaged the creation of a mixed public-private compensation fund at EU level to guarantee EU citizens adequate protection from product development risks. It was suggested that the option of having different industry-specific schemes should be evaluated.[125] The study made reference to several national compensation schemes, including special compensation schemes for the damage caused by infected blood, medicinal products and vaccines, as well as foodstuffs and chemicals.[126] However, the suggestion of a mixed public-private compensation fund at EU-level appears unworkable for several reasons. First, the existing special schemes have been established in respect of either specific products or specific injuries and would appear to be at odds with a general compensation scheme funded by compulsory contributions by industry.[127] Secondly, the establishment of centralised compensation funds would appear to have major economic disadvantages.[128] In particular, it has been argued that two basic obstacles or preconditions would need to be overcome to make a compensation scheme within other Member States or across the Community viable, viz the presence of other sources of compensation

---

[118] Ibid.

[119] Ibid p 29, para 4.1.1.

[120] Analysis of the Economic Impact of the Development Risk Clause as provided by Directive 85/374/EEC on Liability for Defective Products (Fondazione Rosselli, 2004).

[121] Ibid 17.

[122] Ibid 4, 135.

[123] Ibid.

[124] Ibid.

[125] Ibid.

[126] Ibid 85–86, 91–100.

[127] R Freeman, 'The Future of the Development Risk Defence in EU Strict Liability Laws Hits the Spotlight' (2004) 15 *European Product Liability Review* 31, 32–33.

[128] C Hodges, 'Nordic Compensation Schemes for Drug Injuries' (2006) *Journal of Consumer Policy* 143, 173.

to cover a significant proportion of the payments, and the absence of a right of recourse between the sources of compensation.[129]

C. Report on Product Liability in the European Union for the European Commission (February 2003)

A study on product liability systems in the Member States of the EU, carried out by the City law firm Lovells on behalf of the European Commission, examined the potential reform of the development risk defence.[130] The study writes of a 'growing view, particularly amongst lawyers and academics, that the defence is read so narrowly as to be of little practical value to producers in its present formulation'.[131] Notwithstanding the limited practical significance of the development risk defence (thus far), it reported that producers and insurers still regard it as an important element of the strict liability regime.[132] In the light of the 'evidently limited practical scope' of the defence, the study concluded that there would seem to be little need for reconsideration of it at this time, since it has 'historically been regarded as a significant factor in achieving the Directive's balance between the interests of consumers and producers'.[133]

D. Third and Fourth Commission Reports

The Third Commission Report on the Application of the Directive recognised that the precise scope of the development risk defence remained uncertain, and noted that the defence remained one of the matters that the Commission wished to monitor.[134] However, case law subsequent to the report appears to have done little to help resolve the lack of clarity. In a decision of the Paris Court of Appeal,[135] the producer (Ferring SAS) of the medicinal product Pentasa raised the development risk defence in response to a claim that the drug had caused interstitial nephritis (a disease of the kidneys). The Court held that the state of scientific and technical knowledge at the time the medicine was put into circulation was not such as to enable the existence of the defect to be discovered. While there had been a few

---

[129] Ibid. The other significant point about the Rosselli study is that given that the situations in which the development risk defence might operate are very rare (since the risk of unforeseeable injury is very low), there would appear to be problems in justifying the cost of a pan-Community compensation scheme with its large administrative costs: ibid. However, as Professor Owen has postulated, the context of a 'brave new world' of rapid scientific and technological advancement makes it ever harder to predict consequences: DG Owen, 'Bending Nature, Bending Law' (2010) 62 *Florida Law Review* 569, 573 (supporting a continued use of a robust and flexible principle of foreseeability at the heart of private law to define the proper boundaries of responsibility for harm in the context of rapid advances in science and technology). Accordingly, such a complex context, particularly in the field of medicinal products, may increase the likelihood of operation of the development risk defence.

[130] J Meltzer, R Freeman and S Thomson, *Product liability in the European Union: A Report for the European Commission*, MARKT/2001/11/D (Lovells, February 2003) 2.2(c), p 50.

[131] Ibid.

[132] Ibid.

[133] Ibid.

[134] Third Commission Report of 31 January 2001 on the Application of Directive 85/374 on liability for defective products, COM(2006) 496 final, 10–12.

[135] CA Paris 23 September 2004, *Société Ferring v Mauduit* N° 02/16713, *Dalloz* 2005 p 1012.

publications on a potential risk of the disease, the state of knowledge of the adverse effects of Pentasa had been limited and 'there did not exist an international consensus to alert the medical practitioners of the immune-allergic risk when taking Mesalazine (Pentasa's active molecule)'. The decision appeared to adopt a more liberal interpretation of the notion of the state of scientific knowledge than had the ECJ.[136] However, in a ruling that the defence was not available to the defendant (since the product had been put into circulation before the implementation of the Product Liability Directive in France in 1998), the Cour de cassation was not required to determine whether the Paris Court of Appeal had correctly understood and applied the development risk defence on the facts.[137] Accordingly, in the absence of specific case law in the Court de cassation, there remains continuing uncertainty over the development risk defence.[138]

The Fourth Commission Report on the Application of the Directive reiterated the doubt as to the way the defence should be interpreted. It noted criticism from representatives of pharmaceutical companies of the French case law holding that the defence should not be invoked for identical products put into circulation between 1988 and 1998 (the date of the transposition legislation), the representatives reasoning that the ground for invocation of the defence cannot be contingent on the date of the putting into circulation of products that are identical.[139]

IV. DEFECTS WHICH MIGHT BE EXPECTED TO BE DISCOVERED

A. General Observations

Section 4(1)(e) of the Act addresses the situation where the defendant claims a lack of knowledge of dangers associated with the product. As has been noted, the test to be applied

---

[136] Arguably, this generous interpretation of the defence is inconsistent with *A v National Blood Authority* [2001] 3 All ER 289 (on which see below): I Dodds-Smith, M Spencer and J Bore, 'Product Liability for Medicinal Products' in MJ Powers, NH Harris and A Barton (eds), *Clinical Negligence*, 4th edn (London, Tottel Publishing, 2008) para 24.86. See, further, T Rouhette and T d'Honincthun, 'The expanding obligation to provide information on the undersirable effects of medication' (2005) 19 *European Product Liability Review* 29 (criticising the Paris Court of Appeal for stating that, had it not applied the defence, the manufacturer would have been liable for failing to warn the user or prescribing physician about potential, even very unusual side effects. In the absence of a specific warning, a drug would be considered defective each time an adverse reaction occurred in relation to a known risk, regardless of whether the adverse reaction was serious or extremely rare).

[137] Cass Civ 1, 15 May 2007, *Société Ferring v Mauduit* N° 05-10234. The Cour de cassation confirmed previous case law (Cass Civ 1, 19 July 1996, Bull Civ 1 n° 303 p 210, n° 304 p 211 and n° 306 p 214) that since the development risk defence was an optional feature of the Directive, the Community law principle of harmonious interpretation was inapplicable and thus the defence could not be available to the defendant.

[138] See J-S Borghetti, 'Application du Régime special de responsabilité du fait des produits défectueux', *Revue des contrats* (1 October 2007) 1147 (explaining the need to wait a bit longer to determine how the Cour de cassation will interpret the defence) (I am grateful to Professor Borghetti for providing me with a copy of this case note).

[139] Fourth Commission Report of 8 September 2011 on the Application of Directive 85/374 on liability for defective products, COM(2011) 547 final 8–9. However, this appears inconsistent with European law which suggests that in the context of optional features of a Directive (in this case Art 15(1)(b) of Directive 85/374), the Community law principle of harmonious interpretation is inapplicable: Case 14/83 *Von Colson and Kamann v Land Nordrhein-Westfalen* [1984] ECR 1891, para 26 and Case C-106/89 *Marleasing SA v La Comercial Internacional de Alimentacion SA* [1990] ECR I-4135, para 8. See, further, Miller and Goldberg (above, n 62) paras 7.33–7.36.

represents a considerable softening of a literal reading of the uncompromising words of Article 7(e) of the Directive, viz 'not such as to enable the existence of the defect to be discovered', particularly if 'reasonably' is mentally inserted between 'might' and 'be'.[140]

The probability of such an approach occurring is apparent from Lord Lucas's explanation of the test during the Committee stage of the Consumer Protection Bill in the House of Lords, where he stated:[141]

> Only if the producer can prove to the court that he took all the steps that a producer of products of that kind might reasonably have been expected to take, and that the state of scientific and technical knowledge would have allowed him to take, will this defence be of any value.

The test would therefore appear to be very similar to that applied in an action based on negligence, the only material difference being the reversal of the burden of proof.

B. Discoverability and Economic Feasibility

The Directive makes no reference to the practicability of measures to enable a defect to be discovered.[142] However, in the field of medicinal products a distinction can be made between defects that are economically feasible to detect at the pre-clinical and clinical trial stages and those that are not.[143] Given that 'any narrow interpretation would remove the utility of the defence for the innovative medicinal product manufacturer', it has been suggested that there is a strong case for saying discoverability should incorporate a consideration of economic feasibility.[144] Because of economic considerations, some American pharmaceutical companies moved out of high-risk areas such as vaccines and contraception.[145] Moreover, HM Government stated in a minute of the Council of Ministers that it interpreted the defence as incorporating some consideration of what is reasonable to expect a manufacturer to discover. By way of contrast, the French minute was to the effect that economics have no relevance to the scientific issue of whether a defect is discoverable.[146] However, in the Commission's application against the United Kingdom for failing to implement the Directive correctly in respect of Article 7(e), Advocate General Tesauro stated that in his opinion 'the practicability and expense of measures suitable for eliminating the defect from the product' are outside the scope of Article 7(e).[147] It is submitted that the Advocate General's view is, arguably, unrealistic given the inevitable bearing of economics on the design, manufacture and marketing of products.

---

[140] Miller, *Product Liability and Safety Encyclopaedia* (above, n 16) Div III, para 256.

[141] *Hansard*, HL Deb (series 5) vol 483, col 841 (20 January 1987).

[142] I Dodds-Smith, M Spencer and J Bore, 'Product Liability for Medicinal Products' in MJ Powers, NH Harris and A Barton (eds), *Clinical Negligence*, 4th edn (London, Tottel Publishing, 2008) para 24.88.

[143] I Dodds-Smith, 'The Implications of Strict Liability for Medicinal Products Under the Consumer Protection Act 1987' in R Mann (ed), *Risk and Consent to Risk in Medicine* (Carnforth, Parthenon, 1989) 124.

[144] I Dodds-Smith, M Spencer and J Bore, 'Product Liability for Medicinal Products' in MJ Powers, NH Harris and A Barton (eds), *Clinical Negligence*, 4th edn (London, Tottel Publishing, 2008) para 24.93; M Griffiths, 'Defectiveness in EEC Product Liability' [1987] *Journal of Business Law* 222, 225–26.

[145] I Dodds-Smith, M Spencer and J Bore, 'Product Liability for Medicinal Products' in MJ Powers, NH Harris and A Barton (eds), *Clinical Negligence*, 4th edn (London, Tottel Publishing, 2008) para 24.93.

[146] Ibid.

[147] Case C-300/95 *Commission v United Kingdom* [1997] ECR I-2649, I-2659, para 20.

C. Discoverability of Unknown and Unknowable Defects

As has been discussed in a previous chapter,[148] if we accept Professor Stapleton's submission that since a failure to warn claim is assessed according to the reasonableness of including a warning at the time of supply, there will therefore be no role for the Article 7(e) defence in failure to warn claims, then Article 7(e)'s role will be restricted to the context of design defect claims[149] and possibly manufacturing defect claims.[150] In cases where the defect alleged is one of design, the position under the Directive and the 1987 Act will, it seems, be broadly the same as the law as it has developed in at least most jurisdictions in the United States. In other words, strict liability will not be incurred where the characteristic is unknown and, in the state of scientific and technical knowledge at that time, unknowable in the sense that it could not have been expected to have been discovered. The test is an objective one and the defendant will be held to the standard of an expert in the relevant field. In relation to medicinal products, in particular, it is appropriate that the standard should be high. The area is one where there is often rapid innovative development which may outstrip existing safety research, thus placing a heavy burden on manufacturers to discover what aspects of their products may be harmful. For example, the traditional technique for obtaining insulin is by extraction from bovine or porcine pancreatic glands,[151] whereas it can now be manufactured with the use of organisms by a process of genetic engineering, a multi-stage technique which is more complicated and involves additional stages and potential hazards. In 2006, a humanised monoclonal antibody (TGN 1412) was introduced into early volunteer studies in the UK and produced life-threatening effects (the release of cytokines) that were unpredicted from pre-clinical research. The response to TGN 1412 differed considerably across mammalian species, and even responses in primates were unable to predict the effect of the antibody in humans.[152]

D. Defects Hidden from View by Limited Scientific and Technical Knowledge

It is clear that products may be introduced into the market of which at the relevant time 'complete understanding is impossible'.[153] For example, at the time of the thalidomide tragedy, drug companies were generally aware that a drug (the anti-cancer agent aminopterin),[154] or maternal rubella (German measles), might cause teratogenesis.

---

[148]   See chapter 4 of this volume.

[149]   J Stapleton, 'Liability for Drugs in the US and EU: Rhetoric and Reality' (2007) 26 *Review of Litigation* 991, 1018.

[150]   The Fourth Commission Report of 8 September 2011 on the Application of Directive 85/374 on liability for defective products, COM(2011) 547 final observes that national courts differ as to whether the defence applies to all types of defect, and there remains uncertainty as to whether the defence applies to manufacturing defects: ibid 8; M Mildred, 'The Development Risks Defence' in D Fairgrieve (ed), *Product Liability in Comparative Perspective* (Cambridge, Cambridge University Press, 2005) 188.

[151]   PN Bennett and MJ Brown, *Clinical Pharmacology*, 9th edn (Edinburgh, Churchill Livingstone, 2003) 680.

[152]   M Emanuel, M Rawlins, G Duff and A Breckenridge, 'Thalidomide and its sequelae' (2012) 380 *Lancet* 781, 782.

[153]   C Newdick, 'The Development Risk Defence of the Consumer Protection Act 1987' (1988) 47 *Cambridge Law Journal* 455, 461.

[154]   DM Davies (ed), *Textbook of Adverse Drug Reactions*, 3rd edn (Oxford, Oxford University Press, 1985) 79.

However, pharmaceutical science had not yet accepted the necessity for a routine screening process in experiments with animals to predict whether thalidomide could have such an effect.[155] Diethylstilbestrol (DES) taken in pregnancy took up to 20 years before cancer of the vagina became detectable in the female offspring.[156] Practolol (Eraldin)[157] caused damage to the eyes, skin, peritoneum, and lungs which was detectable only after four years; the drug was the only one of a number of beta blockers to do so.[158] If similar examples were to occur when the 1987 Act was in force the development risk defence could, it might be argued, have been applicable to negate liability.

V. THE MEANING AND IMPLICATIONS OF SCIENTIFIC
AND TECHNICAL KNOWLEDGE

A. General Observations

Both Article 7(e) of the Directive and section 4(1)(e) of the 1987 Act refer to the 'state of scientific and technical knowledge'. This raises two preliminary issues, namely (i) what constitutes 'knowledge' and (ii) when knowledge can be said to be of a scientific and technical nature.

The first issue is discussed further below, but, as is well known, most advances in knowledge accrue incrementally through hunches, hypotheses, and testing until they become accepted by the generality of informed opinion, with the exception of those who are not impartial or who are simply eccentric. The association between cigarette smoking and lung cancer is a well-known example.[159] The implication is that hunches and fears do not amount to 'knowledge', not least because they may ultimately prove to be entirely groundless. Contemporary examples of such fears are said to include the alleged dangers of prolonged use of mobile telephones and proximity to their masts and genetically modified food.

The question of what constitutes 'scientific and technical' knowledge may also be problematic. It has been doubted whether a record of accidents associated with a product would qualify.[160] In the event of doubt, the decision can usually be reached on some alternative ground. Take, for example, the case of child-proof medicine bottles in the days before they were widely used. On one approach it might be said that such bottles are hardly inventions

---

[155] W Sneader, *Drug Discovery: The Evolution of Modern Medicines* (Chichester, John Wiley & Sons, 1985) 32; H Teff and C Munro, *Thalidomide: The Legal Aftermath* (Farnborough, Saxon House, 1976) 32.

[156] AL Herbst, H Ulfelder and DC Poskanzer, 'Adenocarcinoma of the Vagina: Association of Maternal Stilboestrol Therapy with Tumour Appearance in Young Women' (1971) *New England Journal of Medicine* 284, 878.

[157] PN Bennett and MJ Brown, *Clinical Pharmacology*, 9th edn (Edinburgh, Churchill Livingstone, 2003) 478–79.

[158] A Goldberg, 'Development of Drug Regulation—A Global View' (1986) 5 BIRA journal 2–5.

[159] See the seminal articles of the (then Dr) Richard Doll and Professor Sir Austin Bradford Hill: R Doll and A Bradford Hill, 'Lung Cancer and Other Causes of Death in Relation to Smoking' (1956) *British Medical Journal* 1071–81; R Doll and A Bradford Hill, 'Mortality in Relation to Smoking: Ten Years Observations of British Doctors' (1964) *British Medical Journal* 399–410, 1460–67.

[160] See *Abouzaid v Mothercare (UK) Ltd* [2000] All ER (D) 2436, Pill LJ, para 29, *The Times*, 20 February 2001.

based on 'scientific and technical knowledge' and so a section 4(1)(e) type of defence would not apply.[161] Alternatively, it might be said that they are the product of 'technical' knowledge, but, having regard to the then prevailing standards, the earlier versions were not defective when they were supplied.[162] It would be surprising if a court were to rule that all the other requirements of section 4(1)(e) were satisfied, except that the relevant gap in knowledge was not scientific and technical in nature.

While the European Court of Justice agreed with the Advocate General that Article 7(e) was unreservedly directed at 'the most advanced level of such knowledge, at the time when the product in question was put into circulation,[163] Professor Stapleton has convincingly argued that there must be seen implicit in the notion of scientific and technical knowledge some limits, based on consideration of four relevant factors, viz whose ideas were relevant, the weight to be afforded them, the accessibility of the 'knowledge', and that such knowledge 'must include creative leaps of application and methodology'.[164] Though this has been criticised by Pugh and Pilgerstorfer as implying other elements into the defence and seemingly utilising common law principles relevant to the tort of negligence,[165] their emphasis on rendering the defence nugatory by the performance of a known test, provided such performance is merely 'possible', irrespective of whether it is usual or novel to do so,[166] is unrealistic and impracticable in the context of medicinal products. Such an approach seems hardly consistent with the concept of a 'state' of knowledge, which 'seems to imply some consensus or settled basis'.[167]

B. The Constituents of Knowledge

It has been submitted,[168] and clearly correctly, that the state of scientific and technical knowledge should include both *present* and *constructive* knowledge. 'Present knowledge' would be relevant when a product could not be tested for a specific effect as there was no basis to believe that it could have such an effect—for example, HIV-contaminated blood before the virus was isolated. But the 'state of knowledge', it is suggested, can in some ways be best described as ignorance.[169] This proposition is derived from *IBA v EMI Electronics*

---

[161] See *Atiyah's, Sale of Goods*, 12th edn (Pearson, 2010) 280.

[162] See the Human Medicines Regulations 2012, SI 2012/1916 (requiring medicinal products consisting of or containing aspirin, paracetamol or more than 24 mg of elemental iron (reg 272)) to be packaged in containers that are child resistant, which is defined with reference to British Standards Institution Standards or any equivalent or 'higher technical specification' for child-resistant packaging recognised for use in the EEA (reg 273(1), (2), (3)).

[163] Case C-300/95 [1997] ECR I-2649, I-2670, para 26.

[164] J Stapleton, 'Products Liability in the United Kingdom: The Myths of Reform' (1999) 34 *Texas International Law Journal* 45, 59.

[165] C Pugh and M Pilgerstorfer, 'The Development Risks Defence-Knowledge, Discoverability and Creative Leaps' (2004) *Journal of Personal Injury Law* 258, 266.

[166] Ibid 268. They suggest such a known test would apply in the context of drugs, irrespective of whether it is unusual or novel to perform the test during clinical trials: ibid.

[167] M Mildred, 'The Development Risks Defence' in D Fairgrieve (ed), *Product Liability in Comparative Perspective* (Cambridge, Cambridge University Press, 2005) 184.

[168] S Whittaker, 'The EEC Directive on Product Liability' (1995) 5 *Yearbook of European Law* 233, 257–58.

[169] Ibid 258.

and BICC Construction,[170] where the House of Lords held that a television transmission mast designer (BICC) negligently failed to consider the possible, yet un-researched, effects of asymmetric ice loading on the stays of a cylindrical mast in conjunction with the effects of vortex shedding. So, to avoid the scenario where the law of negligence would be stricter than under the Act, 'state of knowledge' should include 'constructive knowledge'—'what the producer ought to have known at the relevant time'.[171] Professor Powles[172] has emphasised that the knowledge that a manufacturer of innovative products would be expected to have should not be reduced to a standard of 'all known measures to ensure the safety of the product', since his innovative research may require unique approaches.[173]

There are several relevant decisions in the law of negligence which indicate that the courts have been prepared to impose a high standard of care concerning the accuracy of product information of risks associated with normal use and possible foreseeable misuse, and to find companies negligent where they have failed to exercise care in their research, design, manufacture, labelling or warnings. Certainly this was true of the decision in *Vacwell Engineering Co Ltd v BDH Chemicals Ltd*,[174] where the context was a failure to warn of the explosive qualities of boron tribromide on contact with water. Similarly, in *Wright v Dunlop Rubber Co*,[175] ICI were held liable for the plaintiffs' contraction of cancer through being exposed to Nonox X from the commencement of their employment with Dunlop in 1946 and 1947 respectively, since, it was held, ICI knew or ought to have realised by 1943 that the product was carcinogenic and should have taken appropriate steps to warn users. Again, in *Buchan v Ortho Pharmaceutical (Canada) Ltd*,[176] in an action against the manufacturer of oral contraceptives for failing adequately to warn of the danger of a stroke inherent in the use of the product, the Ontario Court of Appeal held the manufacturer liable, Robins JA saying:[177]

> A manufacturer of prescription drugs occupies the position of an expert in the field; this requires that it be under a continuing duty to keep abreast of scientific developments pertaining to its product through research, adverse reaction reports, scientific literature and other available methods. When additional dangerous or potentially dangerous side-effects from the drug's use are discovered, the manufacturer must make all reasonable efforts to communicate the information to prescribing physicians.

The decision of the Supreme Court of Victoria in *Thompson v Johnson and Johnson Pty Ltd*[178] fell on the other side of the line. The plaintiff sued the defendants who were manufacturers and distributors of a particular brand of tampon manufactured in New Zealand and purchased by her in November or December 1980 in Australia and used by her soon

---

[170] *Independent Broadcasting Authority v EMI Electronics and BICC Construction* (1980) 14 Build LR 1, 20–21, Viscount Dilhorne, 28, 31, Lord Edmund-Davies, 36–37, Lord Frazer.

[171] S Whittaker, 'The EEC Directive on Product Liability' (1995) 5 *Yearbook of European Law* 233, 257–58.

[172] D Powles, 'Product Liability—A Novel Dimension in Scots Law' in A Gamble (ed), *Obligations in Context: Essays in Honour of Professor DM Walker* (Edinburgh, W Green & Son, 1990) 58.

[173] As noted above (see text to n 78), the state of scientific knowledge is to be identified with 'the most advanced level of research which has been carried out at a given time': AG Tesauro in Case C-300/95 *Commission v United Kingdom* [1997] ECR I-2649, I-2659, para 21, as affirmed by the judgment: para 26.

[174] *Vacwell Engineering Co Ltd v BDH Chemicals Ltd* [1969] 3 All ER 1681; see also [1971] 1 QB 88 (reduction of damages by 20% on appeal to reflect possible contributory negligence).

[175] *Wright v Dunlop Rubber Co Ltd; Cassidy v Dunlop Rubber Co Ltd* (1972) 13 KIR 255.

[176] *Buchan v Ortho Pharmaceutical (Canada) Ltd* (1986) 25 DLR (4th) 658.

[177] Ibid 678.

[178] *Thompson v Johnson and Johnson Pty Ltd* [1991] 2 VR 449.

thereafter. She alleged negligence in failing to warn her of the risks and symptoms of toxic shock syndrome. This potentially fatal condition had come to light over the previous year and a link with these tampons had been suggested. Prior to 5 October 1980 all reported cases had been confined to North America and a different type of tampon was involved, but on 5 October 1980 a case of toxic shock syndrome was reported in New Zealand and confirmed on 14 October 1980. The Court was satisfied that the plaintiff had suffered from the condition and that it was causally related to her use of the tampons. However, her claim failed as she had not established that in the relevant period the defendants should have warned users of tampons of the risk of toxic shock syndrome, nor that they were in breach of their duty to her as a user of the product in failing to advise the medical profession.[179]

C. Knowledge in the Context of an Adverse Drug Reaction

When addressing the development risk defence in the context of medicinal products it is clearly instructive to take the example of the acquisition of knowledge in the context of an adverse drug reaction or ADR. It has been stated[180] that:

> there are three main stages in the defining of an adverse drug reaction. First, the alerting message; second, the validation that such a suspicion truly associates a disease, syndrome, or symptom with a particular drug; and third, some evidence which provides a measure of the incidence of a particular ADR so that a proper judgment on the benefit-risk ratio may be taken.

Scientific and technical knowledge would arise at stage two, a point in time when a definite association between a medicinal product and an adverse effect could be established either at the clinical trial stage or at the post-marketing stage. The scientific knowledge in question may for a time be restricted to the producer and the Medicines and Healthcare Products Regulatory Agency (MHRA) and would then not be regarded as being in the public domain.[181] Traces of this approach may be found in the decision of the Full Federal Court of Australia in *Merck Sharp & Dohme (Australia) Pty Limited v Peterson*,[182] where it upheld the decision of the trial judge[183] as to section 75 AK(1)(c) of the Australian Trade Practices Act 1974 (in effect, an equivalent to Article 7(e) of the Directive),[184] that the objective state of knowledge at the time of the supply of Vioxx was not such as to enable the defect to have been discovered.[185] It was not until February 2004, at which time Vioxx

---

[179] Ibid 494.

[180] A Goldberg, 'Foreword to the Third Edition' in DM Davies (ed), *Textbook of Adverse Drug Reactions* (Oxford, Oxford University Press, 1985) xi.

[181] Exceptionally the MHRA may communicate this information to all medical practitioners, thus placing it effectively in the public domain.

[182] *Merck Sharp & Dohme (Australia) Pty Ltd v Peterson* [2011] FCAFC 128, leave to appeal refused, [2012] HCATrans 105.

[183] *Merck Sharp & Dohme (Australia) Pty Ltd v Peterson* (2010) 184 FCR 1, [927].

[184] Section 75AD of the Trade Practices Act 1974 (now s 138 of Sch 2 of the Competition and Consumer Act 2010) establishes liability on the part of a corporation which supplies defective goods manufactured by it where a person suffers injury as a consequence of the defect. However, s 75AK(1)(c) (now s 142 of Sch 2 of the Competition and Consumer Act 2010) provides a defence to such a claim if it is established that 'the state of scientific or technical knowledge at the time when they were supplied by their actual manufacturer was not such as to enable that defect to be discovered'.

[185] *Merck Sharp & Dohme (Australia) Pty Limited v Peterson* [2011] FCAFC 128, [208].

had been withdrawn from the market, that the state of scientific knowledge was such as to enable discovery of the fact that consuming the drug increased the risk of myocardial infarction, since prior to that the increase in risk could not be '"discovered" in the sense of established at the scientific level'.[186]

D. Knowledge and Accessibility

As previously noted,[187] the European Court of Justice in *Commission v United Kingdom* observed that before scientific and technical knowledge became relevant for the purposes of the defence such 'knowledge must have been accessible at the time when the product in question was put into circulation'.[188] Inevitably, there will be difficulties in establishing what accessibility entails. For example, this might depend on information having been published in a form that would come to the notice of a diligent producer, whether in a national or international journal, or allowance might be made for a 'conception period' for implementing a safer design or issuing a warning.[189] The latter seems unlikely since the producer will have the option of desisting from further supply.

An approach which was relatively generous to producers was adopted by Advocate General Tesauro in *Commission v United Kingdom* when he stated, in the context of the Manchuria example, that the circulation of information was contingent on objective factors, including its 'place of origin', 'the language in which it was given', and 'the circulation of journals in which it was published'.[190] He regarded it as 'unrealistic' and indeed 'unreasonable' to expect a European product manufacturer to know of a study published in a local scientific journal in Chinese, and rejected the view that a producer would be liable on the ground of one such person's discovery of a defect, irrespective of the country and language of the study.[191] In *A v National Blood Authority*,[192] Burton J did not find the so-called 'Manchuria exception' entirely clear, and stated that in his opinion the correct approach was to focus on 'accessibility' and to treat as inaccessible only scientific and technical knowledge in the form of an 'unpublished document or unpublished research not available to the general public, retained within the laboratory or research department of a particular company'.[193]

A significant decision of the Italian courts[194] has reaffirmed the importance of accessibility to the objective state of scientific and technical knowledge as laid down by the European Court of Justice in the context of medicinal products and the defence. The case concerned a patient who, after undergoing quadrantectomy (ie partial mastectomy) surgery due to a right mammary carcinoma, was treated with chemotherapy cycles between

---

[186] Ibid [206].
[187] See above, text to n 100.
[188] Case C-300/95 [1997] ECR I-2649, I-2670, para 29.
[189] M Griffiths, 'Defectiveness in EEC Product Liability' [1987] *Journal of Business Law* 222, 225.
[190] Case C-300/95 [1997] ECR I-2649, I-2670, para 23. For the 'Manchuria' example, see also Miller and Goldberg (above, n 62) para 13.54.
[191] Case C-300/95 [1997] ECR I-2649, I-2670, para 24.
[192] [2001] 3 All ER 289.
[193] Ibid para 49.
[194] Court of Sassari, Judgment of 12 July 2012, noted in J Bartolomeo, 'Pharmaceutical company's liability for injuries caused by a defective drug: the new trend in Italy' (2012) 49 *International Product Liability Review* 13.

May 2000 and May 2004, for which she was prescribed certain drugs. During the period she was undergoing chemotherapy treatment, she also underwent odontological treatments. Subsequent to discontinuation of these treatments, she developed osteonecrosis of the jaw (ONJ), which she alleged was due to the side-effects induced by the drug for chemotherapy treatment. While holding that the drug was intrinsically defective in 25 per cent of cases and, together with dental surgery, was defective in 75 per cent of cases, and resulted in ONJ, the Court held that the manufacturer's conduct had to be assessed, taking into account the objective knowledge of the defect based on the scientific and technical state-of-the-art, combined with the accessibility of that knowledge. In so doing, the Court upheld the conclusions of the court-appointed expert who had found that while the first, entirely isolated and atypical description of ONJ dated back to 2002, it had never reached a wide-ranging and shared level of knowledge within the international scientific community before early summer 2004, when that community became aware of a clinically relevant association between biophosphates and ONJ. This emphasis on accessibility again appears to strengthen the view that the defence should be given the wide interpretation of 'undiscoverability by reasonable means', in contradistinction to the narrow interpretation of 'absolute undiscoverability'.[195]

E. The Example of Thalidomide

In view of its importance in generating the impetus for the movement towards strict liability, it is appropriate to ask whether the manufacturer of thalidomide would have been able to benefit from the development risk defence had it been available at that time. This is a matter on which opinions differ.

In his important contribution to the debate Christopher Newdick has written in the context of assessing the importance of the reversed burden of proof that: 'In the early 1950s tests for teratogenicity were not routinely carried on in the pharmaceutical industry. On the other hand, there were a number of companies that were beginning to do so. The manufacturers of Thalidomide did not'.[196] He adds that whereas in negligence this might have been sufficient to negate liability (as being consistent with industry standards) the position would be different under the Act, since:

> In regard to Thalidomide it could be said, on the balance of probabilities, that another producer could have conducted tests for teratogenicity and have discovered the defect in the drug. The defence would not therefore succeed … [T]he standard … under the development risk defence may be that of the highest common factor of opinion in the industry.[197]

However, although it is certainly true to say that the standard is that of the highest common factor representative of informed opinion, the overall conclusion is at best problematic. At the relevant time there was no evidence to suggest that 'a producer of products of the same description as the product in question' (sedatives/hypnotics) was in fact using routine tests on pregnant animals of a relevant species such as would have enabled the danger of

[195] M Mildred, 'The Development Risks Defence' in D Fairgrieve (ed), *Product Liability in Comparative Perspective* (Cambridge, Cambridge University Press, 2005) 170, 179.

[196] C Newdick, 'The Development Risk Defence of the Consumer Protection Act 1987' (1988) 47 *Cambridge Law Journal* 455, 474.

[197] Ibid 474, 475.

birth defects to be discovered. As Professor Stapleton has observed, in respect of testing for teratogenicity at the time of the thalidomide disaster, the 'testing of pharmaceuticals on animals was known and the relevant species did in fact exist. All that was lacking was the idea of applying them to the task of screening Thalidomide for safety'.[198] However, it is doubtful whether this is sufficient to overcome the defence. Rather, it is strongly arguable that one would have to point to some standard or general acceptance within the advanced sectors of the relevant scientific community that there was a need for such testing on pregnant animals and that it would, in all probability, have been effective to detect any danger of teratogenicity. If this is so, the answer to the hypothetical question appears to be that, in the absence of any such agreed standard, a section 4(1)(e) defence may well have succeeded.[199]

VI. DEFECTS WHICH ARE KNOWN OF, BUT UNDETECTABLE IN ANY PARTICULAR CASE

A. Introduction

Most commentators would accept that the development risk defence of section 4(1)(e) has, and should have, no application to what may be termed a typical failure of a quality control system.[200] Indeed, if it did so, the scope of liability would be no greater, and might even be less, than under the law of negligence where the cases suggest that a very high standard of care is applicable.[201] Accordingly, if, for the sake of argument, the most developed quality control system available in the current state of scientific and technical

---

[198] J Stapleton, *Product Liability* (London, Butterworths, 1994) 240.

[199] For the background and more general discussion, see eg W Sneader, *Drug Discovery: The Evolution of Modern Medicines* (Chichester, John Wiley & Sons, 1985) 32 and M Emanuel, M Rawlins, G Duff and A Breckenridge, 'Thalidomide and its sequelae' (2012) 380 *Lancet* 781. Teratogenicity tests did not form part of a standard screening procedure in 1958: H Teff and C Munro, *Thalidomide: the Legal Aftermath* (Farnborough, Saxon House, 1976) 32; and, further, H Tuchmann-Duplessis, 'Design and Interpretation of Teratogenic Tests' in JM Robson, F Sullivan and RL Smith (eds), *Embryopathic Activity of Drugs* (London, J & A Churchill Ltd, 1965) (noting after the thalidomide tragedy, that tests performed in animals for predicting drug effects on the human embryo were 'still too recent to allow an objective opinion of their practical value' (at 56) but then recognising that 'drug screening in animals is at the present time the most appropriate approach to the problem of teratogenicity' (at 81)). For the arguments both for and against liability in negligence in the thalidomide disaster, see H Teff and C Munro, *Thalidomide: the Legal Aftermath* (Farnborough, Saxon House, 1976) 32–35. The majority of commentators have taken the view that Art 7(e)/s 4(1)(e) would operate in favour of the defendant in the thalidomide-type case: AL Diamond, 'Product Liability and Pharmaceuticals in the United Kingdom' in GF Woodroffe (ed), *Consumer Law in the EEC* (London, Sweet & Maxwell, 1984) 129, 134–35, citing the Pearson Commission Report, para 1259; M Griffiths, 'Defectiveness in EEC Product Liability' [1987] *Journal of Business Law* 222, 227. Lord Mackay (the Lord Advocate, as he then was) conceded that 'some of the thalidomide victims might have been deprived of a remedy by a state of the art defence': *Hansard*, HL Deb (series 5) vol 414, col 1455 (12 November 1980). Cf the view of Professor Taschner, one of the principal architects of the Directive (HC Taschner, 'European Initiatives: The European Communities' in CJ Miller (ed), *Comparative Product Liability* (London, BIICL, 1986) 1), who considered that Art 7(e) would operate only where 'the existing defect could not be discovered by anyone' (ibid 11) and where side-effects were 'absolutely unforeseeable' (ibid 6), and that thalidomide was 'wrongly considered by the two British Law Commissions' (ibid) to have satisfied the requirements of the defence. See also Clark, *Product Liability* (above, n 21) 155.

[200] See eg Clark, *Product Liability* (above, n 21) 166–68; C Newdick, 'The Development Risk Defence of the Consumer Protection Act 1987' (1988) 47 *Cambridge Law Journal* 455, 472–73.

[201] See eg *Grant v Australian Knitting Mills* [1936] AC 85, PC.

knowledge in a given sector will lead on average to a failure rate of 0.00003 per cent, then the producer will remain liable in respect of the three specific units in question. The failure rate is no more than an average and the flaws could equally have been in other items in the same batch.[202]

The Austrian Supreme Court appears to have supported the view that the development risk defence should not be extended to cover problems of quality control.[203] The case concerned a coffee machine which had caught fire and had burned down the claimant's house, and the defendant manufacturers had argued that they had produced 60,000 coffee machines of the type in question so far and not a single one had caused a fire. They further argued that this showed that if the defect had been present it could not have been discovered or avoided within the meaning of Article 7(e) of the Directive. The Austrian Supreme Court rejected the argument and held that the rationale of Article 7(e) was to exclude liability for development risks only. Whether the producer could discover or avoid a defect that was known about, but not identifiable, was irrelevant, and the defence would have applied only in a case where, given the state of scientific and technical knowledge, the manufacturer could not know that coffee machines had, in effect, the capacity to catch fire. This was plainly not the position on the facts of the case.

B. Defects Which are Undetectable

The question remains whether, in spite of a general acceptance of the position as outlined above, there is room for admitting an exceptional category of cases where the defence *might* apply. These might be defined as cases where the incidence of the risk is known of by manufacturers and relevant professional bodies but is literally undetectable in any given item within products of that type.

The above issue was addressed by Burton J in his important decision in *A v National Blood Authority*.[204] The facts of this case, which involved claims by persons who had received transfusions of hepatitis C-infected blood, have been outlined in an earlier chapter when considering Sir Michael Burton's conclusion that the blood was defective[205] and his distinction between 'standard' and 'non-standard' products.[206] It has been submitted that the former conclusion is open to criticism, mainly on the ground that it too readily dismissed the relevance of the fact that the risk was known to the medical profession, although not, it seems, to the generality of the public. The suggested distinction between 'standard' and 'non-standard' products is also seen as having no obvious advantages over the usual distinction between manufacturing and design defects. In this chapter the issue is Burton J's approach to the development risk defence.

---

[202] The decision of Ian Kennedy J in *Richardson v LRC Products Ltd* [2000] Lloyd's Rep Med 280 appears to be based on the view that the condom was not 'defective' by virtue of the accepted statistical probability of occasional failures rather than on any application of s 4(1)(e), which was held to be inapplicable where the defect was of a known characteristic, albeit that no test was able to reveal its existence in every case: ibid 285.

[203] 10 Ob 98/02 p (22 October 2002), noted by S Lenze, (June 2003) Lovells' *European Product Liability Review*, Issue 11 37, 38.

[204] [2001] 3 All ER 289.

[205] See above, chapter 2 of this volume, pp 26–30.

[206] See above, chapter 2 of this volume pp 32–37.

The background was that the virus was not identified until Spring 1988 when it was christened hepatitis C.[207] A screening test for the presence of the antibody to the hepatitis C virus was not developed until April 1989. This test, the hepatitis C assay, was introduced throughout England and Wales on 1 September 1991, and although commercially available in a first-generation from 1990, it was considered in the United Kingdom to be lacking in specificity and sensitivity.[208] The relevant date for the purposes of the proceedings was taken to be 1 April 1991, which was well after the 1987 Act came into force. Against this background, the submissions in relation to the development risk defence ran briefly as follows. The defendants submitted that the defence could be used, although the existence of the defect was known, where such knowledge could not enable a producer to discover the existence of the defect in the particular product. Their case was that the defect had to be discoverable in the particular blood product (ie the individual bag of blood) before the defence became inapplicable. The claimants responded that the defence could be used only when there was no accessible knowledge which could identify the defect. Once the defect was known about, it was a *known* risk, and they argued that a known but unavoidable risk did not fall within Article 7.[209]

Having obtained guidance from the judgment of the European Court of Justice in *Commission v United Kingdom*,[210] Burton J accepted the substance of the claimant's submissions in concluding:[211]

> If there is a known risk, i.e. the existence of the defect is known or should have been known in the light of non-Manchurianly accessible information,[212] then the producer continues to produce and supply at his own risk. It would, in my judgment, be inconsistent with the purpose of the directive if a producer, in the case of a known risk, continues to supply products simply because, and despite the fact that, he is unable to identify in which if any of his products that defect will occur or recur, or, more relevantly in a case such as this, where the producer is obliged to supply, continues to supply without accepting the responsibility for any injuries resulting, by insurance or otherwise ... the *existence of the defect* is in my judgment clearly generic. Once the *existence of the defect* is known, then there is then the *risk* of that defect materialising in any particular product.[213]

Consequently, he held that the producer could not rely on Article 7(e), since the existence of hepatitis C in blood was known at the relevant time.[214]

More generally, he did not rule out the possibility of what he describes as non-standard products falling within Article 7(e), saying:[215]

---

[207] [2001] 3 All ER 289, para 8, quoting a release which stated that scientists had 'identified, cloned and expressed proteins from a long-sought blood borne hepatitis non-A, non-B virus and have developed a prototype immunoassay that may lead to a screening test for hepatitis non-A, non-B antibodies'.

[208] Ibid para 11.

[209] Ibid para 50.

[210] Case C-300/95 [1997] ECR I-2649.

[211] [2001] 3 All ER 289, para 74.

[212] For the so-called Manchurian example, see above, text to n 102.

[213] It has been suggested that this gives little, if any, weight to Recital 7 of the Directive, which provides that: 'Whereas a fair apportionment of risk between the injured person and the producer implies that the producer should be able to free himself from liability if he furnishes proof as to the existence of certain exonerating circumstances'. Burton J merely referred to the purpose of Art 7(e) as being 'plainly not to discourage innovation', and as protecting 'the producer in respect of the unknown (*inconnu*)': ibid para 76. For criticism, see J Stapleton, 'Bugs in Anglo-American Products Liability' (2002) 53 *South Carolina Law Review* 1225, 1249.

[214] [2001] 3 All ER 289, paras 74–75, 78, 82.

[215] Ibid para 77.

Non-standard products may qualify *once*—i.e. if the problem which leads to an occasional defective product is (unlike the present case) not known: this may perhaps be more unusual than in relation to a problem with a standard product, but does not seem to me to be an impossible scenario. However, once the problem is *known* by virtue of accessible information, then the non-standard product can no longer qualify for protection under art 7(e).

In relation to the first passage cited above, it may be questioned whether the reference in Article 7(e) to the 'existence of the defect' is clearly to be understood in a generic sense, so that the word 'defect' is, in effect, treated as synonymous with 'risk'.[216] The point is of obvious importance in the context of risks like hepatitis C whose general existence was known but which were undetectable in practice. With respect, Burton J's interpretation of Article 7(e) is far from clear in view of the general lack of precision in the wording of Directive. Moreover, it has been argued that Burton J. proceeds to engage in over-subtlety with Stapleton's comments on the defence in order to buttress his position, despite the fact that there is nothing in Article 7(e) which supports his view. In a curious analysis, he suggests that since Professor Stapleton accepts[217] that the words 'to enable the existence of the defect to be discovered' were unlikely to be intended to imply 'to be discovered by him [ie, the producer]', and that since Article 7(e) only requires the defect 'to be discovered by someone', she appears be negating the suggestion that the test is whether the defect could have been discovered in the particular product produced by the producer.[218] This is arguably an illogical interpretation, in that discovery by 'someone else' is a completely different issue from discovery of a defect in a particular product, a problem germane to Burton J's so-called non-standard product, where the harmful characteristic is not present in all products.[219]

Burton J's view that a risk is not a 'development risk' once it is known to the scientific community as a whole is controversial, and would seem to present grave concerns to the producers of innovative products with foreseeable adverse effects that remain undiscoverable, particularly in the pharmaceutical and health care sectors.[220] Indeed, Professor Whittaker clearly articulates the illogicality and impracticality of this approach, in stating that:[221]

[W]here a risk is known to the scientific community but its manifestation (the 'defect') is incapable of being detected in individual products and therefore prevented at any cost and in any way given the contemporary state of scientific knowledge, why should this not be thought to be a 'development risk' in that the imposition of liability would inhibit the production of innovative products?

---

[216] It has been noted that the defence 'refers to the discoverability of the *defect* not of a product risk': see Stapleton, *Product Liability* (London, Butterworths, 1994) 237; also J Stapleton, 'Restatement (Third) of Torts: Products Liability: an Anglo-Australian Perspective' (2000) 39 *Washburn Law Journal* 363, 383; R Goldberg, 'Paying for Bad Blood: Strict Product Liability After the Hepatitis C Litigation' (2002) 10 *Medical Law Review* 165, 191.

[217] Stapleton, *Product Liability* (London, Butterworths, 1994) 238.

[218] *A v National Blood Authority* [2001] 3 All ER 289, para 54.

[219] R Goldberg, 'Paying for Bad Blood: Strict Product Liability After the Hepatitis C Litigation' (2002) 10 *Medical Law Review* 165, 191.

[220] Ibid 200.

[221] S Whittaker, *Liability for Products: English Law, French Law, and European Harmonisation* (Oxford, Oxford University Press, 2005) 500.

Moreover, Whittaker notes (and surely correctly) that the same arguments apply equally in the context of medicinal products. Like blood, these medicines 'should sometimes be produced and supplied despite their known risks and before the continuing research as to their avoidance is successful. Here too, further research will not avoid the risk in the products supplied in the meantime'.[222]

C. Comparative Jurisprudence

In view of the uncertainty which still surrounds the issue it is instructive to turn to the comparative jurisprudence to which Burton J referred. The starting point must be *Commission v United Kingdom*,[223] which was cited as authority for the proposition that 'very considerable restrictions' were to be placed on the scope of the defence.[224] However, the decision is of no direct relevance in the present context since it does not address the position where a risk is known, but is undiscoverable in practice. For what it is worth, the earlier Unilateral Statement by the United Kingdom delegation appears to assume that Article 7(e) is concerned only with products which are defective in design,[225] which might be seen as supporting Burton J's conclusion.

Other than *Commission v United Kingdom*,[226] the principal case on which Burton J relied was the *German Bottle Case*.[227] The case involved the explosion of a recycled mineral water bottle as a result of what the German Federal Supreme Court categorised as an undiscoverable crack attributable to 'a rare and inevitable production defect'. The potential danger of re-usable bottles filled with carbonated drinks had clearly been known for a long time and the fact that one such bottle had an undiscoverable microscopic fracture was not seen as being within the Article 7(e) defence. Obviously, this interpretation assisted the claimants' case.

By way of contrast, Professor Stapleton has pointed to Australian decisions which support the proposition that it is 'not unusual' for common law courts dealing with strict liabilities to support the norm of reasonable discoverability.[228] In favour of the defendants'

---

[222] Ibid 500–501. Cf Professor Howells point that for the purposes of determining defectiveness, Burton J treated the contaminated blood as a separate category of non-standard products, but for the development risk defence to be inapplicable it was sufficient that the presence of the risk in the generic blood product was known. Nonetheless, he opines that these stances are not 'logically inconsistent': G Howells, 'Defect in English Law-Lessons for the Harmonisation of European Product Liability Law' in D Fairgrieve (ed), *Product Liability in Comparative Perspective* (Cambridge, Cambridge University Press, 2005) 151.

[223] Case C-300/95 [1997] ECR I-2649.

[224] [2001] 3 All ER 289, para 76.

[225] Cf the reference to 'no producer of a product of that kind could have been expected to have perceived that it was defective in design': see 'Note Point "A" au Conseil (8205/85): Statements To Be Entered in the Council Minutes', para 7 (23 July 1985), cited in J Stapleton, 'Bugs in Anglo-American Products Liability' (2002) 53 *South Carolina Law Review* 1225, 1247. Prof Stapleton submits that, unless the ECJ is willing to imply that the other Member States had acted in bad faith in acquiescing to the UK's Unilateral Statement, the Directive should be read, at least by UK courts, in the light of that Unilateral Statement and its 'clear demands ... for a substantial defence for industry': ibid 1248.

[226] C-300/95 [1997] ECR I-2649.

[227] BGHZ 129, 153 (9 May 1995) NJW 1995, 2162, cited in the Commission Green Paper, *Liability for Defective Products*, COM(1999) 396 final, p 23.

[228] J Stapleton, 'Bugs in Anglo-American Products Liability' (2002) 53 *South Carolina Law Review* 1225, 1252, fn 160, (citing the example of the notion of reasonable discoverability being applied by the Federal Court of

case in *A v National Blood Authority*, is the Australian Federal Court's decision in *Graham Barclay Oysters Pty Ltd v Ryan*,[229] albeit that it was decided on the basis of section 75 AK(1)(c) of the Australian Trade Practices Act 1974 (as has been noted, in effect, an equivalent to Article 7(e) of the Directive).[230] The background was that oysters had been supplied carrying the hepatitis A virus (HAV), this being attributable to faecal contamination of a lake in which they were grown. The plaintiff brought a representative action, and an action on his own account, against several parties, including the largest oyster grower at the lake from whom he claimed damages under the Trade Practices Act 1974. As in the *National Blood Authority* case, not all the relevant products were affected, although some clearly were. The defendants argued, on the basis of section 75AK (1)(c),[231] that the state of scientific and technical knowledge could not enable discovery of the defect in individual oysters before supply since the only test available would involve their destruction. The Australian Federal Court used a literal interpretation of the Act and allowed the development risk defence to operate in the defendant's favour, holding that the defence was available if the defect was not capable of discovery before the date of supply of the oysters, namely December 1996.[232] The judgment rested on the basis that 'goods' referred to individual oysters: if an individual oyster were tested, it would be destroyed in the process. Thus supply to an individual would have become an impossibility. On appeal,[233] three judges, Lee,[234] Lidgren,[235] and Kiefel JJ[236] upheld the single judge on the grounds that the defendants had discharged the onus of establishing at the date of supply that the state of scientific and technical knowledge was not such as to enable the presence of HAV in the oysters to be discovered. The statement that discovery of the defect and supply were mutually exclusive and that the only test that would reveal the defect would destroy the goods, assumed two findings of fact for which there was ample evidence. First, it was legitimate to extrapolate from a sample test result only where there was relevant homogeneity between the total population and from which the sample was taken. This could not be so in respect of the HAV and oysters. Secondly, the only sophisticated testing available at that time was a type of testing which gave false negatives, and therefore could not be relied on, even in 1998.[237]

Australia in the context of the strict liability provision against misleading or deceptive conduct in s 52 Trade Practices Act 1974 in *Johnson Tiles Pty v Esso Australia Ltd* (2000) 104 FCR 564, 592, para 67), where the Court stated: 'Where the question involves disclosure of risks associated with the supply of a product or service, it cannot reasonably be expected that the supplier is to inform the public of every possible risk. That can be explained simply by the proposition that in the ordinary course of human affairs things go wrong in connection with the supply of products and services and that nobody could reasonably assume, absent disclosure, that such supply will be risk free'.

[229]   *Graham Barclay Oysters Pty Ltd v Ryan* (2000) 102 FCR 307.

[230]   See above, n 185. See also J Stapleton, 'Restatement (Third) of Torts: Products Liability, an Anglo-Australian Perspective' (2000) 39 *Washburn Law Journal* 363, 384.

[231]   For the wording of s 75AK (1)(c), see above, n 184.

[232]   *Ryan v Great Lakes Council* [1999] FCA 177, para 377.

[233]   *Graham Barclay Oysters Pty Ltd v Ryan* (2000) 102 FCR 307 (Austral Fed Ct).

[234]   Ibid para 70.

[235]   Ibid paras 542–43.

[236]   Ibid para 614.

[237]   Ibid paras 545–46. It should be noted that, while the Full Federal Court, Lee and Kiefel JJ upheld the first instance judgment that the Barclay companies were liable in negligence for failing to provide a reasonable surveillance of the water quality ((2000) 102 FCR 307, 330, para 68; ibid 461, para 608), the finding of negligence was reversed on appeal by the High Court of Australia: see (2002) 211 CLR 540.

On the face of it, both elements in the *Graham Barclay Oysters* case have points in common with the situation in the *National Blood Authority* case. In particular, blood could not allow one to extrapolate from a sample to every blood bag and, as the defendants argued, 'the virus only became discoverable as from the date at which it became reasonably practicable to introduce a routine screening test in the UK'.[238] Both the surrogate tests available, viz the ALT test and anti-HBC test were found by Burton J to be non-specific.[239] However, he avoided a straightforward disagreement with the approach of the Australian courts to the scope of the defence on two grounds, noting (i) that the wording of section 75AK(1)(c) was somewhat different from that of Article 7(e),[240] and (ii) that the argument had concentrated on whether physical verification of each and every oyster with their consequent destruction would have been necessary to discover the defect.[241]

The *Graham Barclay Oysters* approach finds some support from the decision in *Scholten v Foundation Sanquin of Blood Supply*.[242] In *Scholten*, the Foundation argued that the development risk defence was applicable, since it was 'impossible to detect the infection of the [donated] blood with HIV in the window phase',[243] (ie the period before antibodies to the HIV virus were formed, and before delivery to the recipient). The HIV-1/2 screening test and the HIV P24 antigen test did not detect HIV at the time, nor subsequently, and the HIV-1 RNA test, although carried out, gave a doubtful result and was insufficiently developed to recommend implementation. The County Court of Amsterdam held that the defence was successful. It stated that:

> Given the state of scientific and technical knowledge at the time of the blood donation and the transfusion to Scholten, this leads to the conclusion that it was, practically speaking, not possible to use the HIV-1 RNA test as a screening test in order to detect HIV contamination in blood products. This could therefore not have been expected of the Foundation.[244]

This approach has also been adopted by the Italian Court of Brescia.[245] In that case, the claimants were heirs of a haemophiliac who contracted HIV as a result of treatment with blood derivatives and subsequently died. The claimants sued the Italian distributor of the blood derivatives. Applying the criteria of the Supreme Court in a decision of 2005,[246] the Court of Brescia upheld the equivalent of the development risk defence (albeit in the context of negligence) and ruled that no liability could be ascribed to the distributor of blood derivatives, since the HIV infection was contracted in 1978, the HIV virus was only

---

[238] [2001] 3 All ER 289, para 184.

[239] Ibid para 9.

[240] In particular, s 75AK(1)(c) referred to the state of knowledge not being 'such as to enable *that* defect to be discovered' (emphasis added).

[241] [2001] 3 All ER 289, para 53.

[242] *Scholten v Foundation Sanquin of Blood Supply* H 98.0896 (3 February 1999, County Court of Amsterdam). For further discussion, see CC Van Dam, 'Dutch Case Law on the EU Product Liability Directive' in D Fairgrieve (ed), *Product Liability in Comparative Perspective* (Cambridge, Cambridge University Press, 2005) 128–30. See also above, chapter 2 of this volume for discussion in the context of whether the blood was defective.

[243] Ibid p 7 of translation.

[244] Ibid p 8 of translation, cited by Burton J in *A v National Blood Authority* [2001] 3 All ER 289, para 53.

[245] Decision of the Italian Court of Brescia No 1586 of 21 April 2006, noted in F Rolla and C di Mauro, 'Post-transfusion and Infected Blood Derivatives Damage: Italian Case Law Upholds the Development Risks Defence' (2006) 20 *European Product Liability Review* 22.

[246] Supreme Court, Division III, decision no 11609 of 31 May 2005 (liability only established in relation to transfusions or administration of blood derivatives carried out subsequent to the dates that HIV, HCV and HBV were discovered as pathogen agents of AIDS and hepatitis).

identified as a pathogen agent of AIDS in 1984, and tests to detect the presence in blood were only made available in 1985. Accordingly, the Court concluded that the risk of HIV was undiscoverable and unpreventable at the relevant time.

A similar philosophy appears to lie behind the decision of the Canadian Supreme Court in *Kobe ter Neuzen v Korn*.[247] The claim was in contract, rather than tort, and it alleged a breach of the implied warranty of merchantability in respect of biological material (semen) in a case concerning contraction of the human immunodeficiency virus (HIV) through participation in an artificial insemination programme. The donor had claimed to be heterosexual, but later admitted he was bisexual. The Supreme Court held that the relevant contract was not one for the sale of semen,[248] but was for medical services and that in the circumstances a common law warranty would have been no more demanding than an obligation to exercise reasonable care. The court also stated that:[249]

It must be recognized that biological products such as blood and semen, unlike manufactured products, carry certain inherent risks. In some ways, these substances are inherently dangerous, although they are essential to medical procedures ... As long as the entire procedure does not amount to an unreasonable risk such that it ought not to be offered at all, the patient is entitled to weigh those risks and elect to proceed.

D. Conclusions

It is clear that there are no straightforward answers to the question whether the development risks defence should apply in cases of defects or risks which are known in general terms, but entirely unpredictable and undetectable in their incidence. Although this was one of the central issues in the hepatitis C litigation, the case is by no means unique. For example, it appears that in the context of whole blood and blood products, a theoretical risk of contracting variant CJD from blood transfusions has been recognised.[250] Indeed, this risk has now advanced to one which may be described as potential.[251] On the basis

---

[247] *Kobe ter Neuzen v Korn* [1995] 3 SCR 674, (1995) 127 DLR (4th) 577.

[248] As such it would have attracted a liability which is strict and without even the limiting effect of a development risk type of defence: see Miller and Goldberg (above, n 62) paras 4.107–4.111 and 13.30.

[249] [1995] 3 SCR 674, (1995) 127 DLR (4th) 577, para 108.

[250] See 'Avoid UK Blood Transfusion', news.bbc.co.uk/hi/english/health/newsidn (22 August 2001); H Rumbelow, 'Americans Fear British Blood has CJD Taint', *The Times*, 23 August 2001; D Payne, 'Ireland Fears Blood Shortage with New Ban on Donors' (2001) 323 *British Medical Journal* 469.

[251] In a House of Commons Statement on 17 December 2003, Dr John Reid, the Secretary of State for Health, gave details of the first reported case in the world of the possible transmission of vCJD from person to person via blood transfusion. He explained that in 1996 a donor, who was at the time free of signs of vCJD, donated blood to a recipient. The donor developed the disease three years later in 1999 and died from it. The recipient died in the autumn of 2003 and was diagnosed with vCJD in December 2003. In the light of the facts, the Secretary of State said that it was thus possible that the disease was transmitted from donor to recipient by an infected blood transfusion, three years before the donor developed vCJD, and in circumstances where the recipient developed vCJD after a 6½ year incubation period. The Secretary of State stated that this was 'a possibility', not a proven causal connection', since it was possible that both individuals acquired vCJD by eating BSE infected meat or meat products. He confirmed that there is currently no blood test for vCJD or for BSE and that there remains no way of screening blood donations for the presence of the CJD group of diseases: *Hansard*, HC Deb cols 1571–73, 1581, 1584 (17 December 2003); N Hawkes, 'Thousands at risk of vCJD from blood transfusions', *The Times*, 18 December 2003, p 4; see further 'Variant CJD and blood', www.hpa.org.uk/Topics/InfectiousDiseases/InfectionsAZ/CreutzfeldtJakobDisease/VariantCJDAndBlood/, accessed 22 April 2013 (detailing four cases of

of the judgment in the *National Blood Authority* case,[252] even though the risk of infection in a particular bag of blood could not be discovered, the National Blood Authority might again be liable if it were shown that the whole blood was defective and that variant CJD was transferred to the recipient. As the Australian, Italian and Canadian experience shows, similar issues can arise.

It would be possible to interpret the development risk defence in a way which allowed it to apply in the above cases. However, it has been argued that this would be a very blunt instrument and would not lend itself to any principled distinction between (say) blood and medicinal products, on the one hand, and exploding carbonated bottles and car tyres on the other.[253] The principal alternative is, logically to rule out the defence in such cases and to draw the line by reference to the question whether the product is to be adjudged defective. This approach perhaps lends itself to reaching conclusions which would be more generally acceptable. The test would then be whether the generality of the public was entitled to expect that all units of the relevant medicinal or blood product would not contain the flaw that led to the damage in issue. It would be applied, irrespective of whether the flaw was actively created or took the form of a failure to eliminate something which was 'naturally' there, and, on the approach adopted in this work, the balance between the product's utility and risks associated with it would be a relevant circumstance to be taken into account. On that basis it might be surmised that undetectable infections in individual bags of blood should not lead to a conclusion that the blood was defective, since the product is indispensable to saving life and there is no available alternative. Bottles which explode because of microscopic flaws and car tyres which disintegrate might be readily placed at the opposite end of the spectrum.[254] Nonetheless, as Professor Whittaker has observed, there remains a strong argument that while balancing risks and utility and taking into consideration avoidability are all properly relevant to the assessment of a product's defect, such matters 'will not *conclude* it'.[255] In such circumstances, the development risk defence may operate as a means to avoid the judicial balancing of factors under Article 6 by the producer proving that he was unable to discover the alleged defect 'in products of the type in question, whether as regards particular examples of that type of product or more generally'.

VII. CONCLUSION

The development risk defence is arguably one of the main obstacles to the achievement of strict liability under the Consumer Protection Act 1987, since discoverability by the manufacturer of unknowable defects of medicinal products will be decided in a manner likely to be identical to the requirements of negligence. Nevertheless, it can be argued that the

---

variant CJD infection associated with blood transfusion). Certain plasma products, manufactured using plasma from donors who later developed vCJD, may have exposed those who received them to infection and a risk of developing vCJD: see 'Variant CJD and plasma products', www.hpa.org.uk/Topics/InfectiousDiseases/InfectionsAZ/CreutzfeldtJakobDisease/VariantCJDAndBlood/cjd10VariantCJDandplasmaproducts/, accessed 22 April 2013.

[252] *A v National Blood Authority* [2001] 3 All ER 289.
[253] Miller and Goldberg (above, n 62) para 13.105.
[254] Ibid.
[255] S Whittaker, *Liability for Products: English Law, French Law, and European Harmonisation* (Oxford, Oxford University Press, 2005) 501.

defence is of conceivable assistance to therapeutic innovation and development within the pharmaceutical industry. This argument has been strengthened by the conclusions of the authors of the Rosselli study, who upheld the argument that the defence was 'a significant factor in achieving the Directive's balance between the need to preserve incentives to innovation and consumers' interests'. The decision to include the defence has continued to receive considerable support from manufacturing organisations, which still regard it as an important element of the strict liability regime, as well as criticism from consumer organisations, which regard it as an area ripe for reform.[256]

While the European Court of Justice decision in *Commission v United Kingdom* generated some certainty over the issue as to whether section 4(1)(e) properly implemented Article 7(e) of the EC Product Liability Directive, there continues to be doubt about its interpretation. Indeed, the paucity of case law that has emerged has done little to help resolve the lack of clarity. Much, it seems, will depend on 'the rigour with which the courts chose to apply it, and its precise wording in national legislation'.[257] Nonetheless, the emphasis on reasonableness in the context of accessibility appears to strengthen the view that the defence should be given the wide interpretation of 'undiscoverability by reasonable means', in contradistinction to the narrow interpretation of 'absolute undiscoverability',[258] and a slight trend of cases supporting this approach in the context of medicinal and blood products seems to be emerging in Australia in the Vioxx litigation[259] and most recently in Italy.[260] In the absence of specific case law in the Court de cassation, there remains continuing uncertainty in French law over the interpretation of the development risk defence.

However, Burton J's interpretation of the *Commission v UK*[261] decision remains questionable in its determination that once the risk of a defect in a product is known, but yet remains undiscoverable in practice, the defence may no longer be used. The problem of undiscoverable defects has never been addressed by the ECJ, and a preliminary reference could have been made to the ECJ in both *A*[262] and the *German Bottle Case*. His decision on Art 7(e) would seem to present grave concerns to the producers of innovative products with foreseeable adverse effects that remain undiscoverable, particularly in the pharmaceutical and health care sectors.

Those judges who are in future given the rare opportunity to try a case utilising the development risk defence in the context of medicinal products would be wise to heed the

---

[256] J Meltzer, R Freeman and S Thomson, *Product Liability in the European Union: A Report for the European Commission*, MARKT/2001/11/D (Lovells, 2003), 2.2(c), 50; This position has been reaffirmed in the Fourth Commission Report of 8 September 2011 on the Application of Directive 85/374 on liability for defective products, COM(2011) 547 final, p 9. Professor Taschner considers that any possibility of abolishing the defence is doomed to failure, since '[e]ven if the Commission were to dare to submit a proposal in this respect, the necessary Council majority would not be obtainable': HC Taschner, 'Product Liability: Basic Problems in a Comparative Law Perspective' in D Fairgrieve (ed), *Product Liability in Comparative Perspective* (Cambridge, Cambridge University Press, 2005) 165.

[257] Miller, *Product Liability and Safety Encyclopaedia* (above, n 16) Div III, para 131.

[258] M Mildred, 'The Development Risks Defence' in D Fairgrieve (ed), *Product Liability in Comparative Perspective* (Cambridge, Cambridge University Press, 2005) 170, 179.

[259] *Merck Sharp & Dohme (Australia) Pty Limited v Peterson* [2011] FCAFC 128, [206], [208].

[260] Court of Sassari, Judgment of 12 July 2012.

[261] C-300/95 *Commission v United Kingdom* [1997] ECR I-2649.

[262] Burton J had previously refused to make a preliminary reference on the ground that its timing was premature: *A and Others v National Blood Authority* (28 October 1999, unreported), as cited in J Stapleton, 'Restatement (Third) of Torts: Products Liability, an Anglo-Australian Perspective' (2000) 39 *Washburn Law Journal* 363, 384.

advice of Professor Owen, who supports the continued use of a robust and flexible principle of foreseeability at the heart of private law to define the proper boundaries of responsibility for harm in the context of rapid advances in science and technology.[263] In so doing, it is submitted that they should adopt the wide interpretation of 'undiscoverability by reasonable means' in the context of the development risk defence and medicinal products.

[263] DG Owen, 'Bending Nature, Bending Law' (2010) 62 *Florida Law Review* 569, 573.

9

Conclusion

This book has attempted to address the problems that typify claims for drug-induced injury, as well as highlighting the complex interrelationship between liability exposure and drug regulation.

Chapter one examined medicinal product liability in its medical, legal and social contexts. Three propositions have emerged from that chapter. First, there is a need to appreciate the reasons why drugs are different in examining whether EU countries should move from treating liability for medicinal products in the same way as for any other product to the US approach of establishing special liability rules for prescription drugs, or to specific pharmaceutical liability regimes such as those present in Germany and in certain Nordic countries. Secondly, now that personal injury claims against pharmaceutical companies will no longer be eligible for legal aid in England and Wales, it seems unlikely that solicitors will be keen to enter into 'no win, no fee' arrangements in the near future, unless the probability of success is high. Thirdly, although there are considerable difficulties in applying strict liability to medicinal products, and the failure rates under the UK Vaccine Damage Payment Scheme are high, politically it would be singularly difficult to create an exception for pharmaceuticals, unless it were in the form of a centrally-funded or insurance-based 'no fault' scheme such as exists in Germany or Sweden. Moreover, it is uncertain how such a system would operate throughout the European Union without a generous social security system such as exists in Sweden. In the current political climate, there would appear to be little impetus for a no fault scheme for drug-induced injury. Accordingly, the remaining chapters of this book have presupposed that medicinal products continue to exist within the strict product liability regime, but that they merit distinct treatment within that regime, as occurs in the United States.

Chapter two provided an overview of the problem of defective medicinal products in the US and UK. Two propositions can be demonstrated by this chapter. First, the definition of defect in Article 6 of the Product Liability Directive and section 3 of the Consumer Protection Act 1987 is greatly challenged by the complexity of medicinal products, and the paucity of case law on the topic has done little to help matters. Indeed, when some cases have been decided on defective products and blood or medicinal products, they have failed to understand the special problems created by such products. Secondly, Burton J's standard/non-standard product dichotomy in *A v National Blood Authority* fails to add any clarity in establishing a taxonomy of defects in medicinal products.

Chapter three attempted to comprehend the true nature of a medicinal product design defect under the Product Liability Directive and to devise a coherent and workable approach for determining whether a medicinal product's design is defective. Five propositions have emerged from this study. First, there is arguably doctrinal incoherence in Member States' laws in respect of establishing that medicinal products are defective in design within the definition in Article 6 of the Product Liability Directive. Secondly, it is submitted that some form of analysis of the benefits and disadvantages associated with a medicinal product (or risk–utility) cannot realistically be avoided. Nonetheless, it has been noted that a risk–utility approach does not work well in the majority of cases involving drugs in the US. Thirdly, in the light of the problems with consumer expectations and risk–utility, there is much to be said for the view that reformers should be looking towards the US approach in § 6(c) of the *Restatement, Third, Torts: Products Liability*, which does not require proof of an alternative feasible design but permits a finding based on 'categorical liability', viz a determination of defectiveness based on the inherent risks that a product poses without proof of an alternative design. Medicinal products would therefore have their own test for design defects, utilising a net-benefit approach in line with § 6(c). Essentially, this would require a removal of the determination of design defectiveness from Article 6(1)/section 3(2), and a radical change to the Directive. Fourthly, it is arguable that de facto there is little difference between the combined effect of Article 6 and Article 7(e) in the context of design defects and that of § 6(c). Fifthly, even if a net-benefit approach to drug design defects is unlikely to be seen as reflecting a careful balance between the interests of the consumer and manufacturers of goods, as has been noted some form of assessment of the benefits and disadvantages associated with a medicinal product (or risk–utility) is still inescapable. At the very least, in view of the US experience of dealing with design defects for many years and the views of commentators, it seems entirely appropriate for the Directive and the 1987 Act to be construed as being based, in complex cases concerning medicinal products, on a *combined* consumer expectation-risk–utility analysis.

Chapter four examined the thorny issue of warning and instruction defects in the context of medicinal products, with particular emphasis on the position of warnings under the Product Liability Directive. Six propositions have emerged from this chapter. First, notwithstanding the fact that the category of warnings about risks and instructions for use is the most significant factor relevant to determining the expectation of safety with medicinal products, the position of warnings under the Product Liability Directive remains uncertain. Secondly, Newdick's objectification of the foreseeability of risk approach provides clearer guidance as to when an allegation of a 'failure to warn' defect becomes viable than Stapleton's reasonableness standard of feasibility of warning. It is perhaps easier to see these issues as matters of *foreseeability* of risk. Thirdly, notwithstanding Stapleton's persuasiveness in suggesting that there is no role for Article 7(e) in failure to warn claims, her elision of state of the art and state of scientific and technical knowledge in so doing is controversial. A better way to think of these issues is in terms of foreseeability of risk. If the injury or risk is *unforeseeable*, then it might be concluded that the claim for a defect on the grounds of failure to warn will fail. The product is simply not defective and the development risk defence would be rendered otiose. Fourthly, in the light of the uncertainties as to the position on warnings under the Directive, there is arguably a need to define expressly when a medicinal product is defective through failure to warn. The approach of the *Restatement, Third, Torts: Products Liability*, § 6(d) is to define prescription drugs as 'not reasonably safe as to inadequate instructions or warnings' where there has been a failure on behalf of a manufacturer to provide 'reasonable instructions or warnings regarding foreseeable risks of harm'. Fifthly, it has been submitted that the Directive should recognise the status of the 'learned intermediary' rule as a defence to a strict liability action in the same way that § 6(d)(1) does. The principal reason why the doctrine should be retained in the UK, and arguably in the other Member States too, is the fact that prescription drugs continue to require the intervention of a medical practitioner. In the UK, almost all of the prescribing of drugs in the community is carried out by general practitioners. In such circumstances, the focus of the law should continue to be on the duty of such practitioners to engage in the informed consent process by discussing the risks and benefits of prescription drugs with their patients when selecting the appropriate medication. Sixthly, in the context of drug defects through an alleged failure to warn, it is arguable that the amenable approach to causation suggested by *Chester v Afshar* could be applied to failure to warn in the context of medicinal products.

Chapter five examined the role of epidemiological evidence in proving causation in alleged cases of adverse drug reactions, in the light of recent cases involving product liability and causation in the UK, Australia and Canada. Eight propositions have emerged from this chapter. First, despite the trenchant criticisms of the doubling of risk theory in the US, its support appears to be gaining ground in the UK. Secondly, however, the majority of the Supreme Court in *Sienkiewicz v Greif* appears to be sceptical of introducing a threshold for the use of epidemiological evidence and remains of the view that epidemiological evidence can be useful but must be viewed with caution; without further non-statistical evidence there is reluctance for courts to proceed to find the existence of a causal relationship. Thirdly, a danger otherwise is that counsel, in assessing the chances of success of 'no win, no fee' multi-party product liability litigation, especially involving medicinal products, may regard this doubling of risk theory as the sole basis on which to determine whether litigation should go forward to trial, even in cases where epidemiological evidence is lacking. This could potentially prejudice access to justice in future cases. Fourthly, if the doubling of risk approach is to be embraced by the UK courts, it is submitted that the doubling of risk standard should be treated, as in the Canadian decision of *Anderson v St Jude Medical Inc*, as merely a *presumptive* as opposed to a prescriptive threshold, so that a negative finding on causation (where the relative risk is below two) could be rebutted, utilising probative individualised evidence in a subsequent individual trial. Fifthly, in such cases where there is a dearth of epidemiological evidence, courts and, for that matter, funding bodies, should learn from the US experience and should avoid insisting on epidemiological studies which have a relative risk of greater than two, allowing all evidence which falls 'within a zone of reasonable scientific disagreement' to be considered. Sixthly, there remains a lack of clarity on the extent to which generalised epidemiological evidence can be useful in determining individual causation. Seventhly, it is arguable that epidemiological evidence can be refined to draw conclusions about the cause of disease in an individual case using specific risk factors. Chapter five supports the use of logistic regression statistical techniques and other forms of statistical refining mechanisms using specific risk factors to give quantitative or quasi-quantitative expression to conclusions about the cause of disease in an individual drug product liability claim that is based on epidemiological evidence. It has been suggested that this approach could have been adopted with the specific case information available in the Vioxx representative action, instead of the personal circumstances being blindly treated as diminishing the strength of the epidemiological evidence as a strand in the cable of circumstantial proof. Eighthly, notwithstanding the scepticism of the majority of the Supreme Court in *Sienkiewicz*, there is little doubt that the utilisation of epidemiological evidence in medicinal product liability cases, especially where non-numerical solutions are elusive, has now come of age. The challenge is now for lawyers and epidemiologists to come to some consensus as to what amounts to a suitable use of epidemiological evidence in such cases when establishing proof on a balance of probabilities. However, it is arguable that the so-called doubling of risk approach as mooted in *Sienkiewicz* is overly simplistic. In particular, doubling of risk takes no account of absolute risk (ie the risk of something occurring without any context) and severity of outcome. Any attempt to reach a consensus in the future must address these difficult issues.

Chapter six examined the significance of the rise and fall of the MMR litigation in the US and the UK. Four propositions have emerged from this chapter. First, the MMR litigation has shown the incalculable damage that can be caused by one peer-reviewed article in a prestigious scientific journal. It was this article which fuelled the publicity, which in turn generated the lawsuits on both sides of the Atlantic. More importantly, it can be argued, it resulted in considerable damage to public health. While vaccination rates in the UK have recovered slightly, they remain below the 95 per cent level recommended by the World Health Organization to ensure herd immunity. The other damage in the UK was that after the MMR Litigation, the Legal Services Commission became reluctant to fund other multi-party actions in respect of medicinal products that claimants alleged had caused harm. Secondly, while there was considerable justification for withdrawal of public funding in the UK, there are some positives that have emerged from the test cases in the US Omnibus Autism Proceeding. Unburdened by the emotions of a jury and the usual restrictions imposed by the Federal Rules of Evidence, a single trier of fact has been able to look at all the available evidence and come to a reasoned decision. In these autism test cases, issues of general and specific causation have been addressed and factors personal to the individual children have been taken into account. While the factors listed in *Daubert v Merrill Dow Pharmaceuticals, Inc* have been utilised, they have not prevented evidence being made admissible in these proceedings through an overly strenuous evidentiary threshold. They have been relevant to the assessment of weight at the *adjudication* stage, which has allowed the evidence as a whole to be aired in the proceedings. It suggests that this more flexible approach to scientific evidence, albeit with high standards at the adjudication stage, is welcome and may counter some of the criticisms of *Daubert* that it has in some cases hindered the search for justice in product liability law. Thirdly, while there has been a liberal approach to causation established by the French Cour de cassation (principally in the context of claims for compensation for demyelinating diseases, allegedly caused by vaccinations against hepatitis B, where causal link can be established by the presence of serious, precise and concurrent presumptions of causation), the inconsistency of the decisions has generated uncertainty for both claimant and defendant. It is submitted that, without scientific evidence of general causation, there should be no question of overcoming the burden of proof of causation in such cases. The Cour de cassation would be wise to study the factors required to overcome that burden as established in the National Vaccine Injury Compensation Program, as adumbrated in the *Althen v Secretary of Health & Human Services* case, and utilised by the OAP test cases, which, it is submitted, generate more clarity and consistency in approach. Fourthly, in exercising its freedom to sanction, conduct and publish scientific research, the scientific community as a whole must always exercise eternal vigilance against scientific fraud and misconduct. It is only in these circumstances that good science will have the necessary confidence of the public and the legal system that engages with it.

Chapter seven examined the question as to whether compliance with regulatory standards should protect pharmaceutical manufacturers from product liability suits. Five propositions have emerged from this chapter. First, while mere compliance with the Human Medicines Regulations 2012 is not a defence to liability under the Consumer Protection

Act 1987, it will often be strong evidence that the consumer expectation test is satisfied. Accordingly, there remains some support for the view that once the licensing authority has given approval to the drug, based on its safety, quality and efficacy, and provided a manufacturer has disclosed all information that reasonably bears on the drug's safety, such a drug could probably not be 'defective' under the 1987 Act. Secondly, however, if the claim concerned a known danger that the licensing authority had not been notified of, or which had been misrepresented, a presumption could arise that the medicinal product was defective. As Newdick has argued, this presumption could also apply to risks that became known at a post-marketing authorisation stage, but which were not communicated to the licensing authority: such an approach could help incentivise prompt and full disclosure on the part of the pharmaceutical manufacturer. Thirdly, pharmaceutical product liability litigation should continue to operate as a complementary form of drug regulation, both in the US and in Europe. This recognises the inherent limitations of post-marketing surveillance of prescription drugs by allowing tort to enable the uncovering and assessment of risks that were not apparent at the pre-marketing stage. Fourthly, however, the view that tort law should continue to operate as a supplement to the federal regulation of prescription drugs has been seriously challenged in the context of generic drugs in the US Supreme Court cases of *PLIVA, Inc v Mensing* and *Mutual Pharmaceutical Co Inc v Bartlett*, which have permitted the establishment of an area where the preemption of State law tort claims will operate after *Wyeth v Levine*. The greatest concern with the Court's opinions in *Mensing* and *Bartlett* is that failure to hold generic drug manufacturers liable in tort for non-disclosure of known risks and failure to hold them liable for design defect claims that turn on the adequacy of a generic drug's warnings gives sanctuary to the risk of a two-tier drug liability system. Fifthly, in the light of the current emphasis on the reforms to pharmacovigilance legislation, and with preemption seen as a threat to pharmacovigilance incentives, there ought to be little appetite for such arguments in the UK and EU. Sixthly, the provision of a regulatory compliance defence under the Directive fails to address the implications of post-marketing surveillance and should be rejected.

Chapter eight examined the interpretation, scope and the impact of the development risk defence in the context of medicinal products, including the meaning and implications of discoverability of defects, scientific and technical knowledge and the problem of known but undetectable defects. Five propositions have emerged from this chapter. First, while the defence is arguably one of the main obstacles to the achievement of strict liability under the Consumer Protection Act 1987, it can be argued that the defence is of conceivable assistance to therapeutic innovation and development within the pharmaceutical industry. This argument has been strengthened by the conclusions of the authors of the Rosselli study, who upheld the argument that the defence was 'a significant factor in achieving the Directive's balance between the need to preserve incentives to innovation and consumers' interests'. Secondly, although the European Court of Justice decision in *Commission v United Kingdom* generated some certainty over the issue as to whether section 4(1)(e) properly implemented Article 7(e) of the EC Product Liability Directive, there continues to be doubt about its interpretation. Indeed, the paucity of case law that has emerged has done little to help resolve the lack of clarity. Thirdly, however, the emphasis on reasonableness in the context of accessibility appears to strengthen the view that the defence should be given what Mildred has described as the wide interpretation of 'undiscoverability by reasonable means', in contradistinction to the narrow interpretation of 'absolute undiscoverability', and a slight trend of cases supporting this approach in the context of medicinal and blood products seems to be emerging in Australia in the Vioxx litigation and most recently in Italy. Fourthly, in the absence of specific case law in the Cour de cassation, there remains continuing uncertainty in French law over the interpretation of the development risk defence. Fifthly, Burton J's decision on Article 7(e) in *A v National Blood Authority* would seem to present grave concerns to the producers of innovative products with foreseeable adverse effects that remain undiscoverable, particularly in the pharmaceutical and health care sectors. It is submitted that those judges who are in future given the rare opportunity to try a case utilising the development risk defence in the context of medicinal products should adopt the wide interpretation of 'undiscoverability by reasonable means'.

It is therefore submitted, in the light of the book's discussion and the propositions which have emerged from it, that the distinct treatment of medicinal products within the strict liability regime in Europe, as occurs in the United States in the context of prescription drugs, is a necessary development in addressing the special problems of medicinal product liability and regulation. These problems can be most usefully addressed by a *via media*, which supports greater clarity in the meaning of defective medicinal products, a consensus as to what amounts to a suitable use of epidemiological evidence in the context of establishing proof of causation on a balance of probabilities, the retention of the development risk defence, a rejection of the introduction of a regulatory compliance defence, and an increasingly effective role played by pharmacovigilance. It is this combination of initiatives that will help the victims of drug-induced injury to receive justice, while at the same time encouraging greater drug safety and innovation in drug development.

Index